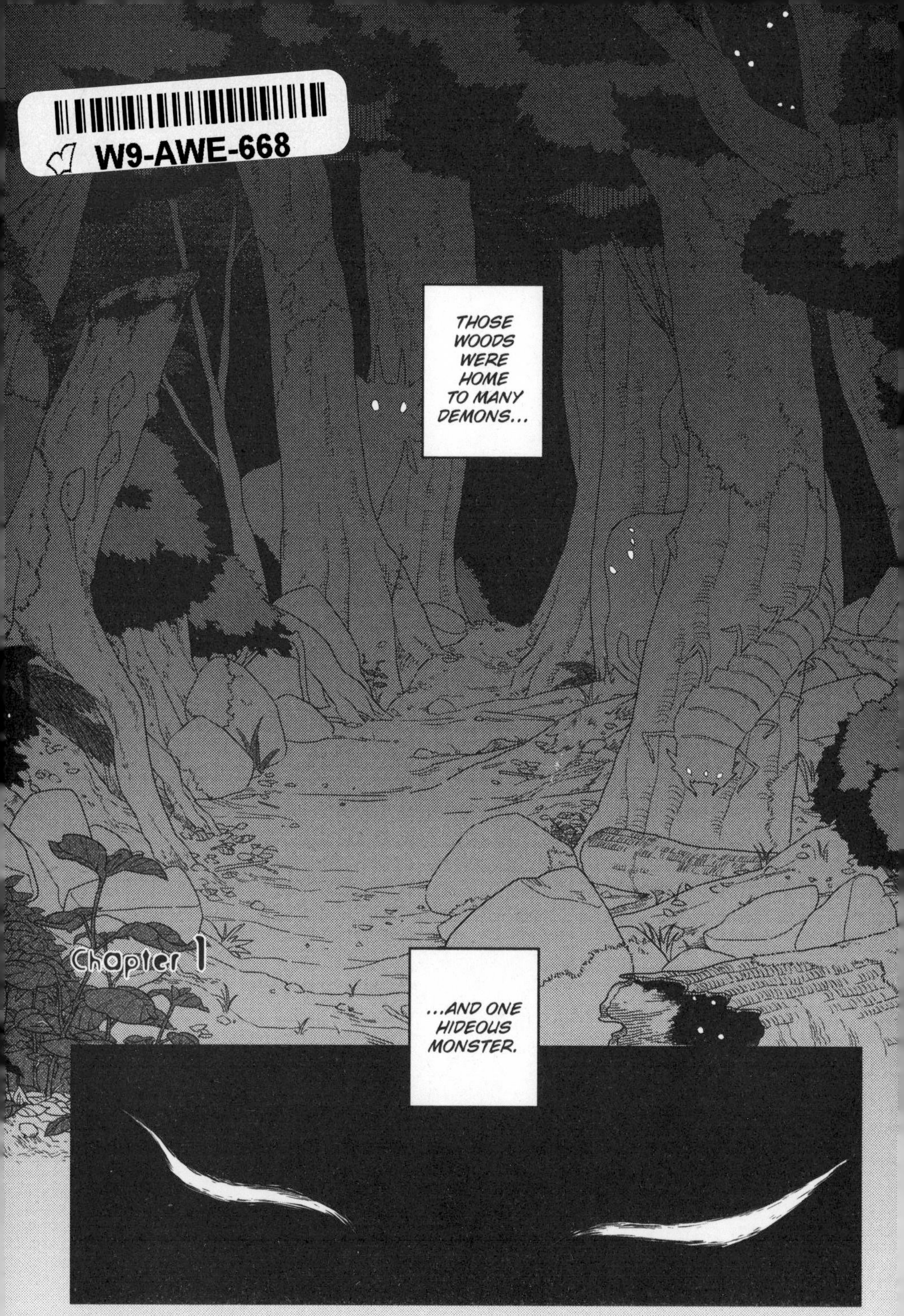
THOSE WOODS WERE HOME TO MANY DEMONS...
Chapter 1
...AND ONE HIDEOUS MONSTER.

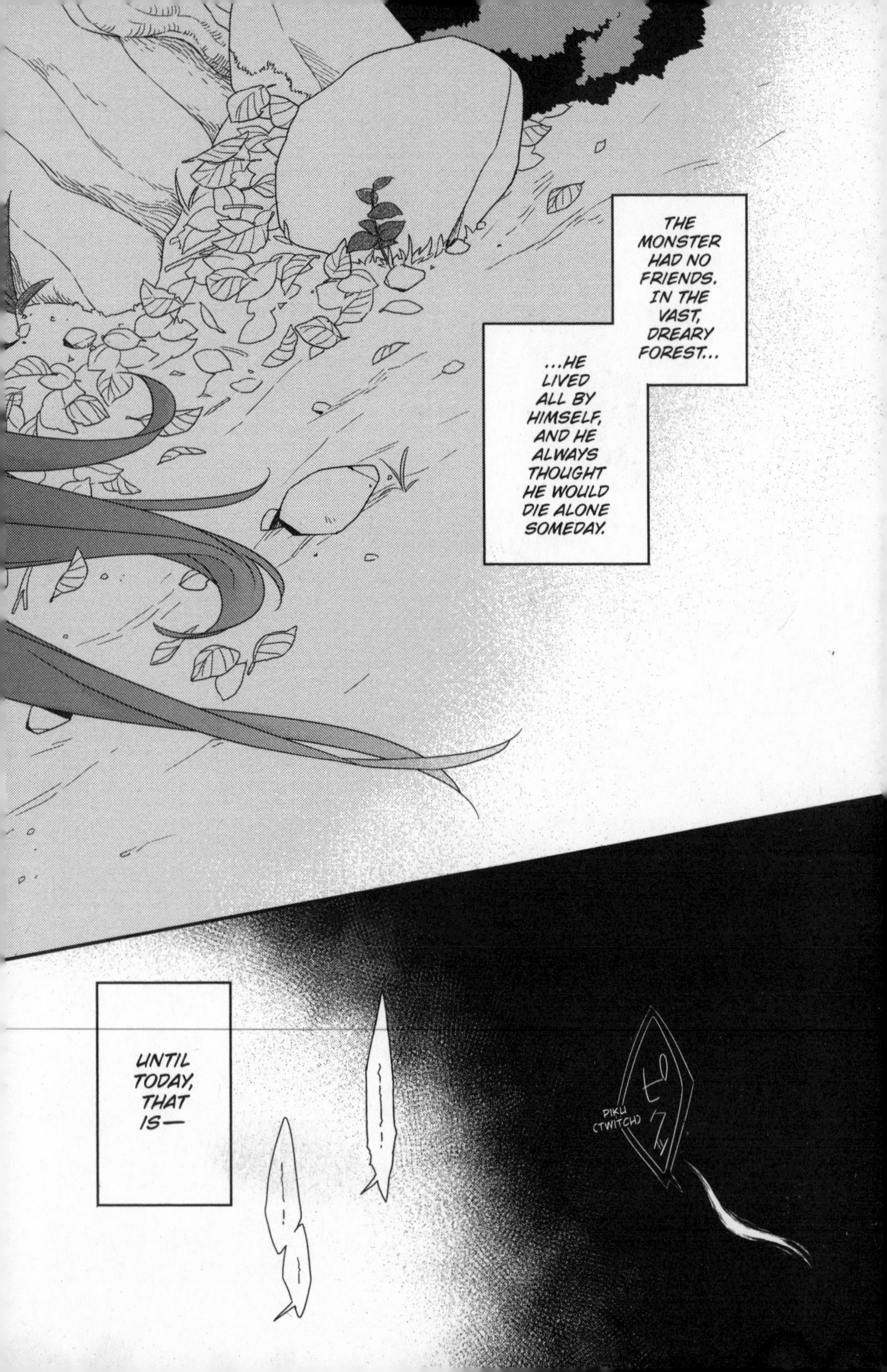
THE MONSTER HAD NO FRIENDS. IN THE VAST, DREARY FOREST...
...HE LIVED ALL BY HIMSELF, AND HE ALWAYS THOUGHT HE WOULD DIE ALONE SOMEDAY.
UNTIL TODAY, THAT IS—
PIKU (TWITCH)

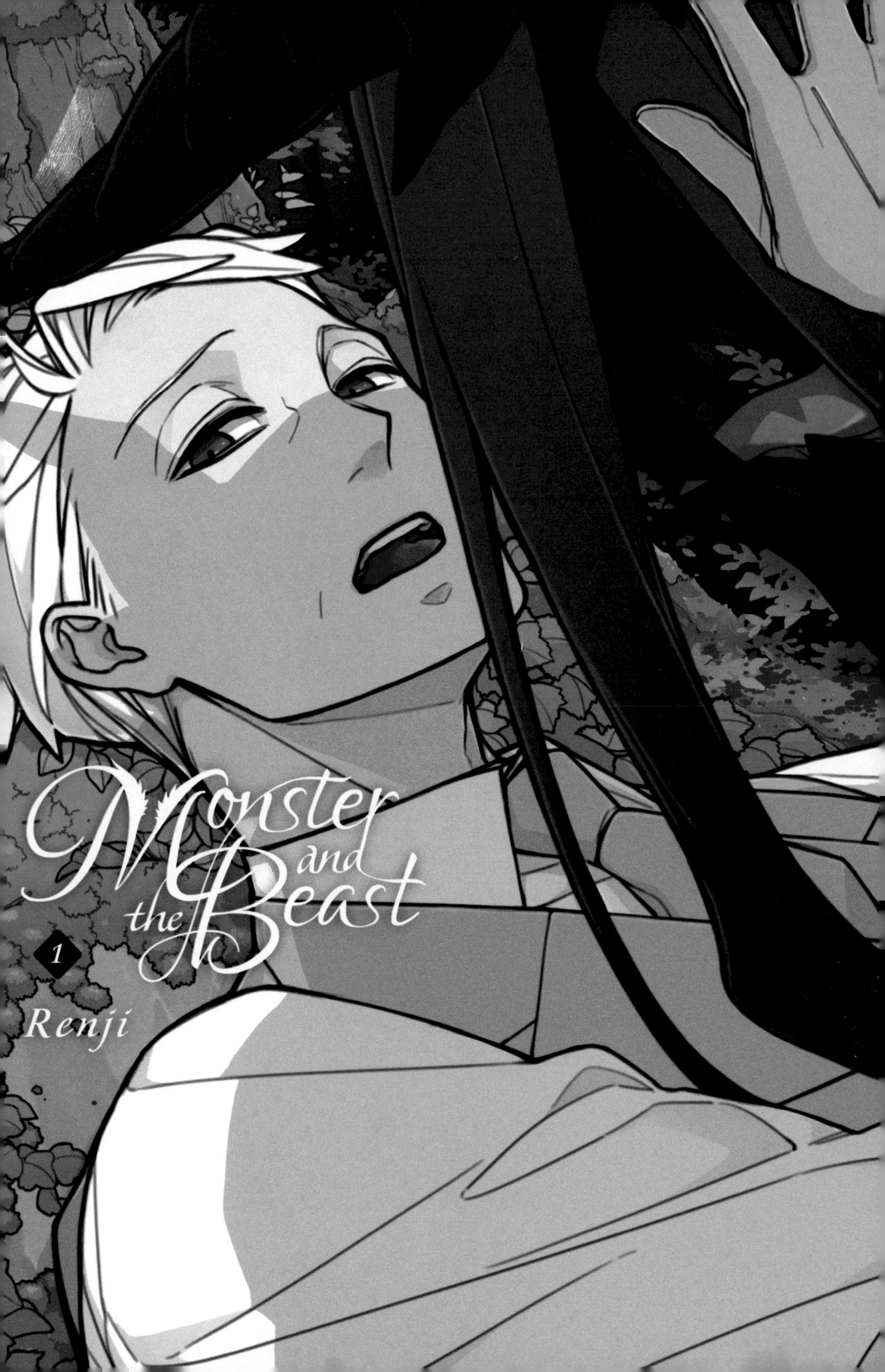
Monster and the Beast
1
Renji

Monster and the Beast
Renji

Contents

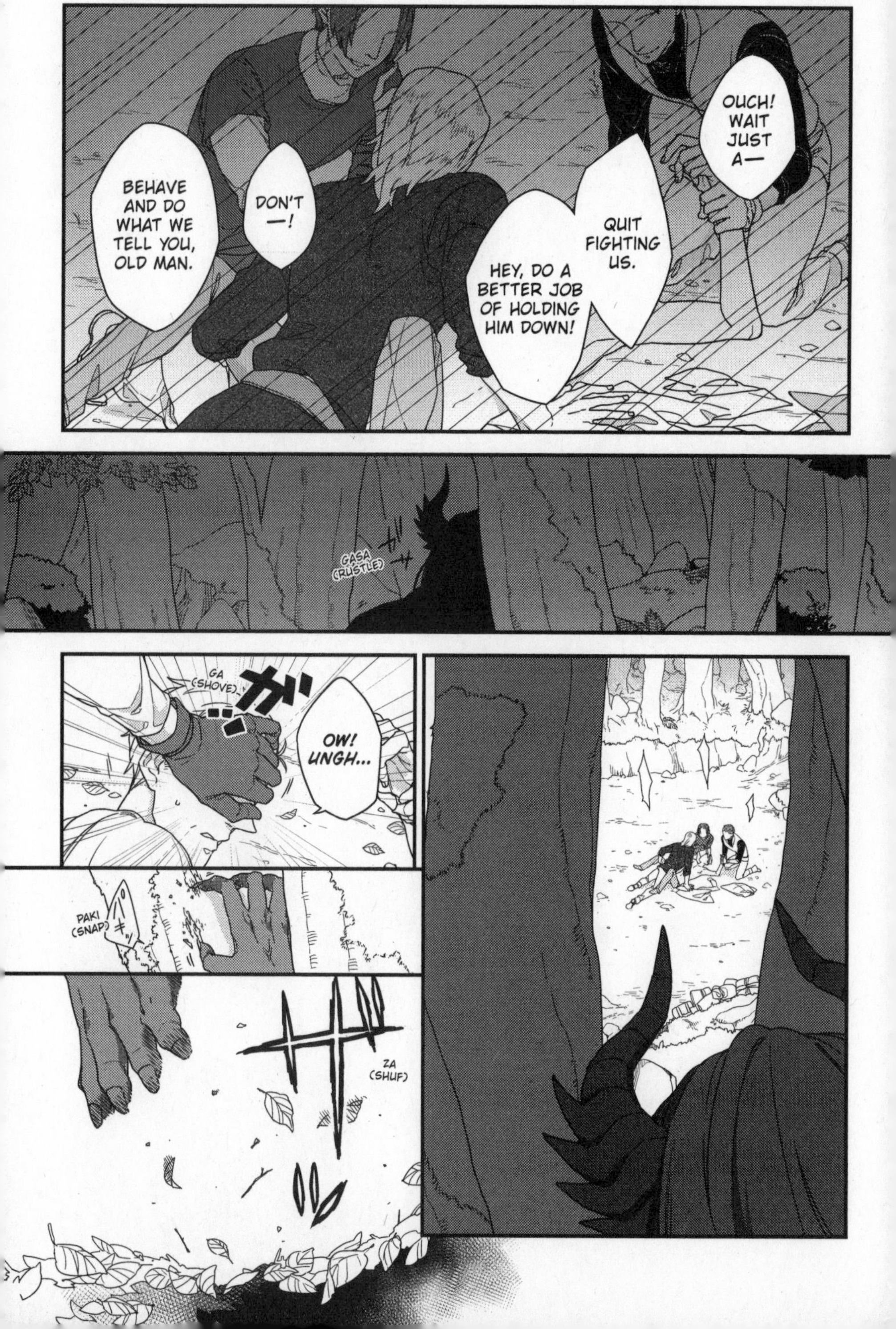
OUCH! WAIT JUST A—
QUIT FIGHTING US.
HEY, DO A BETTER JOB OF HOLDING HIM DOWN!
DON'T—!
BEHAVE AND DO WHAT WE TELL YOU, OLD MAN.
GASA (RUSTLE)
OW! UNGH...
GA (SHOVE)
PAKI (SNAP)
ZA (SHUF)

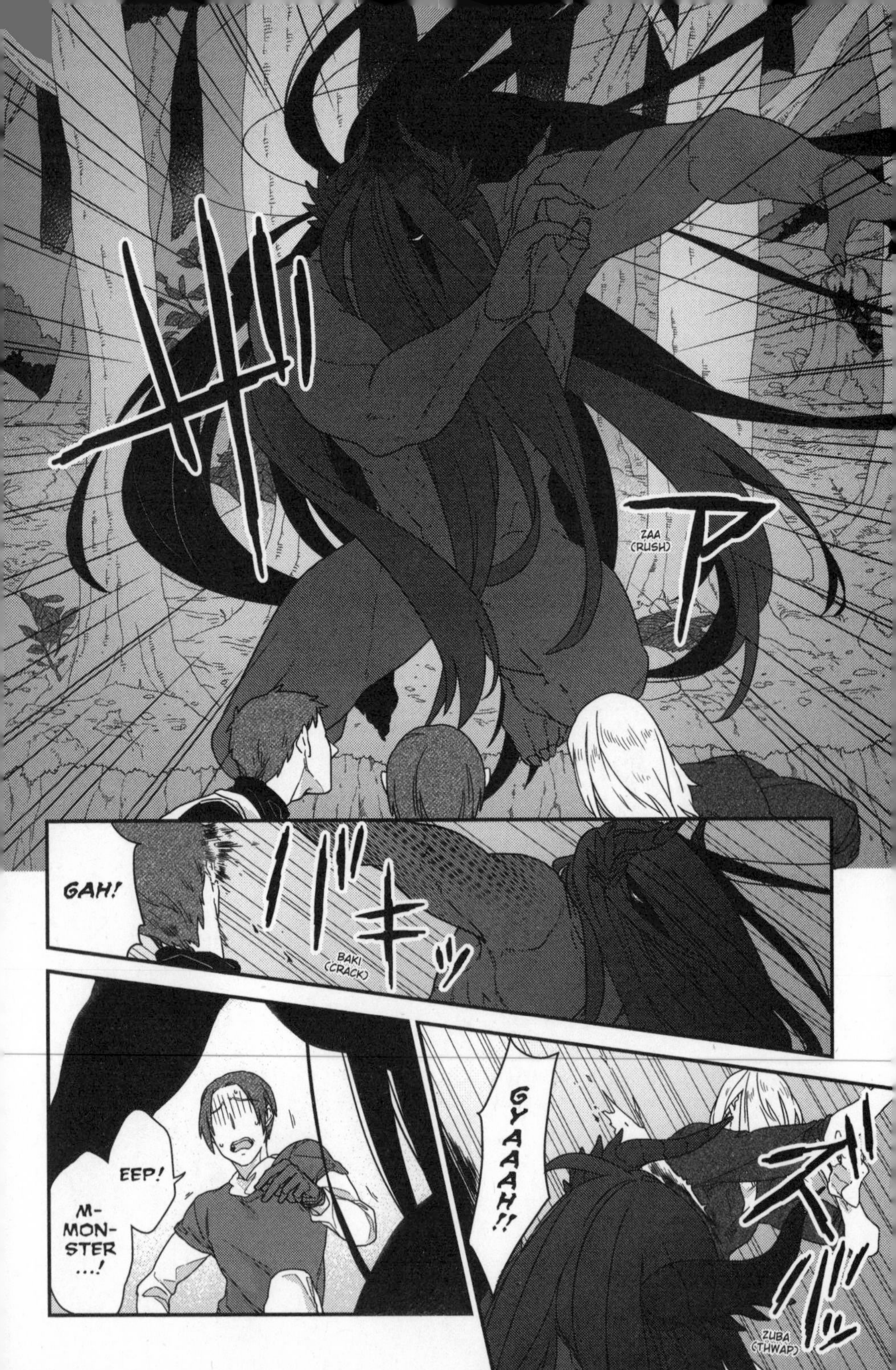
ZAA (RUSH)
GAH!
BAKI (CRACK)
GYAAAAH!!
ZUBA (THWAP)
EEP!
M-MONSTER ...!

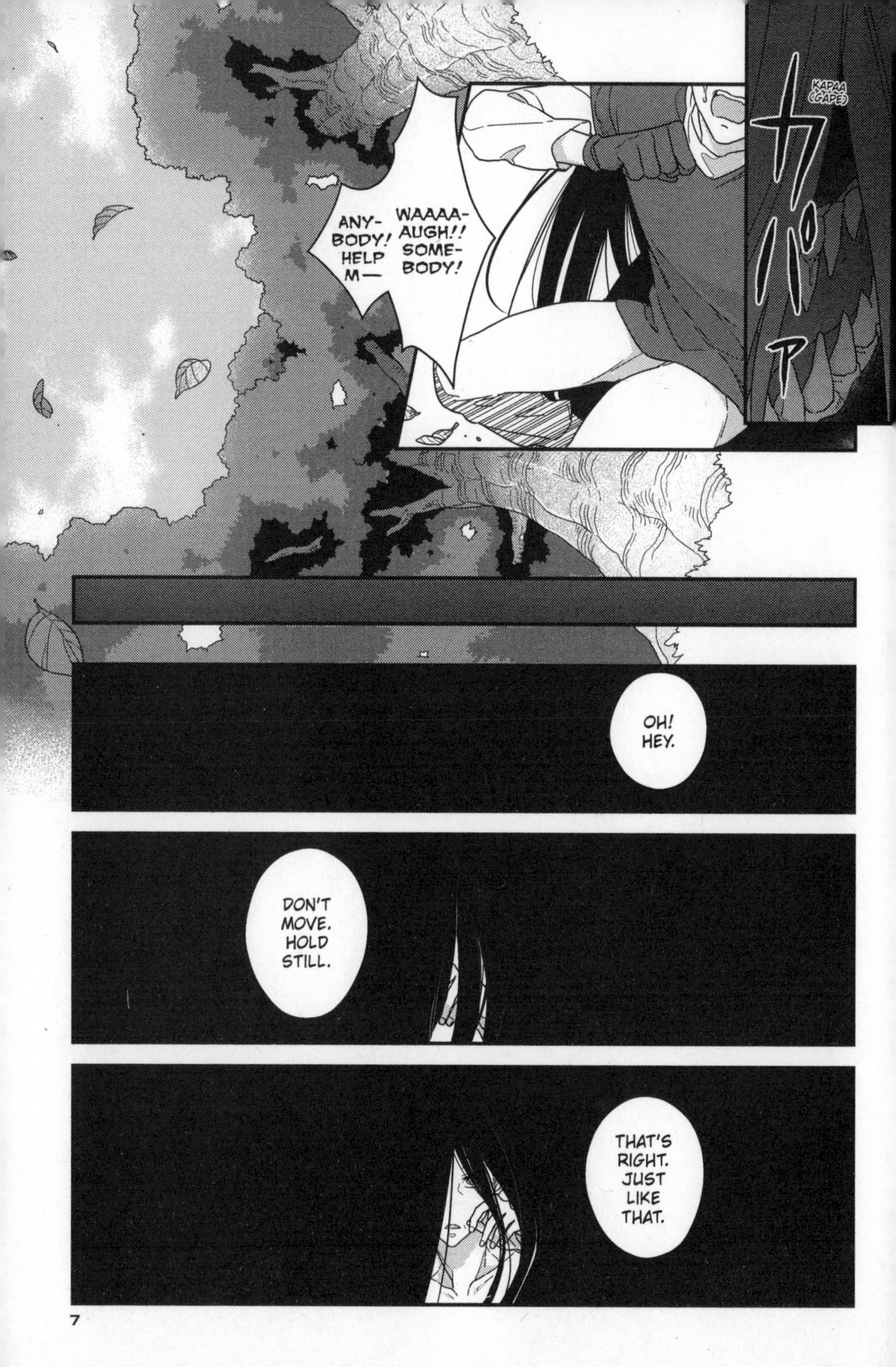
カパァ
KAPAA (GAPE)
WAAAA-AUGH!! SOME-BODY!
ANY-BODY! HELP M—
OH! HEY.
DON'T MOVE. HOLD STILL.
THAT'S RIGHT. JUST LIKE THAT.

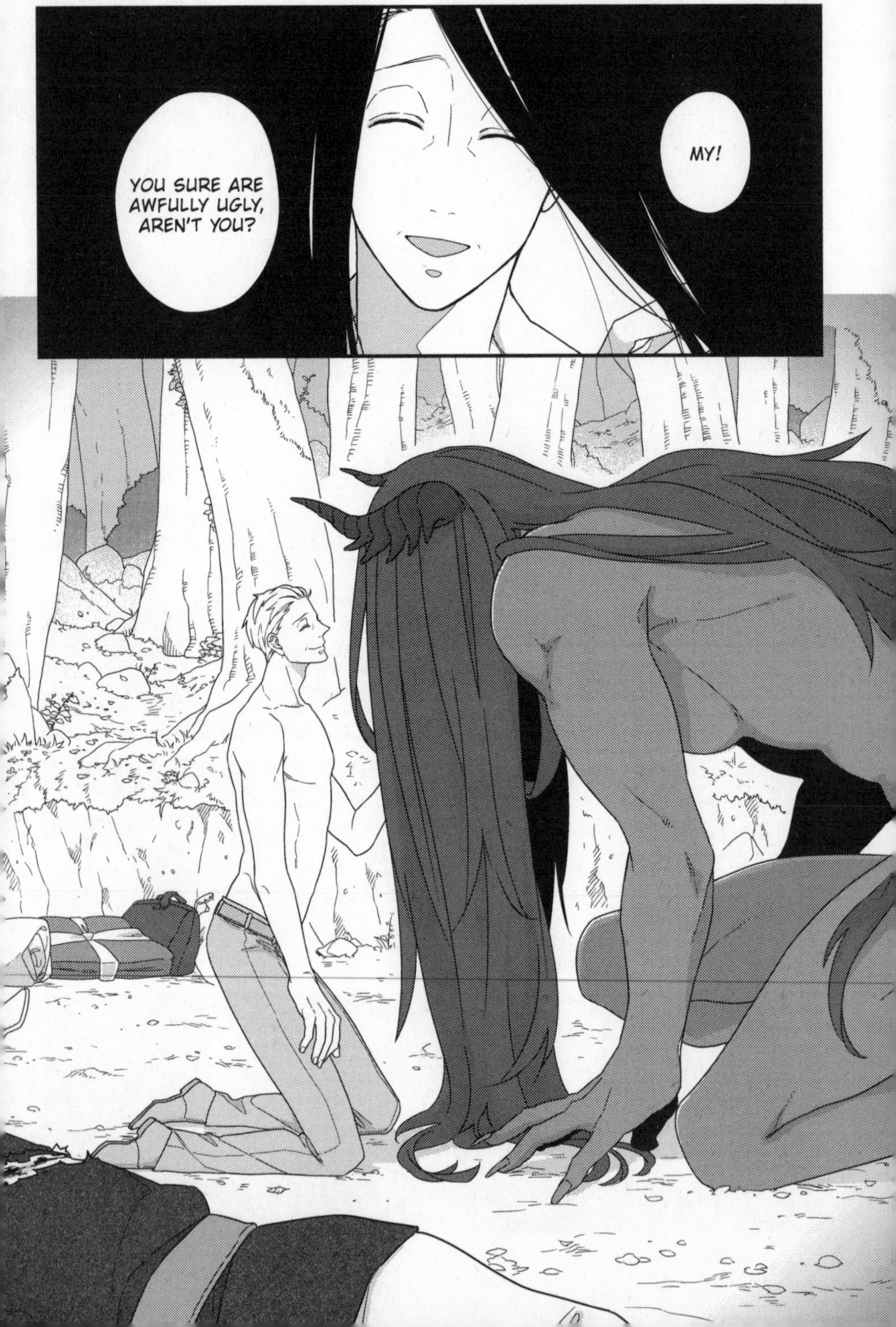
MY!
YOU SURE ARE AWFULLY UGLY, AREN'T YOU?

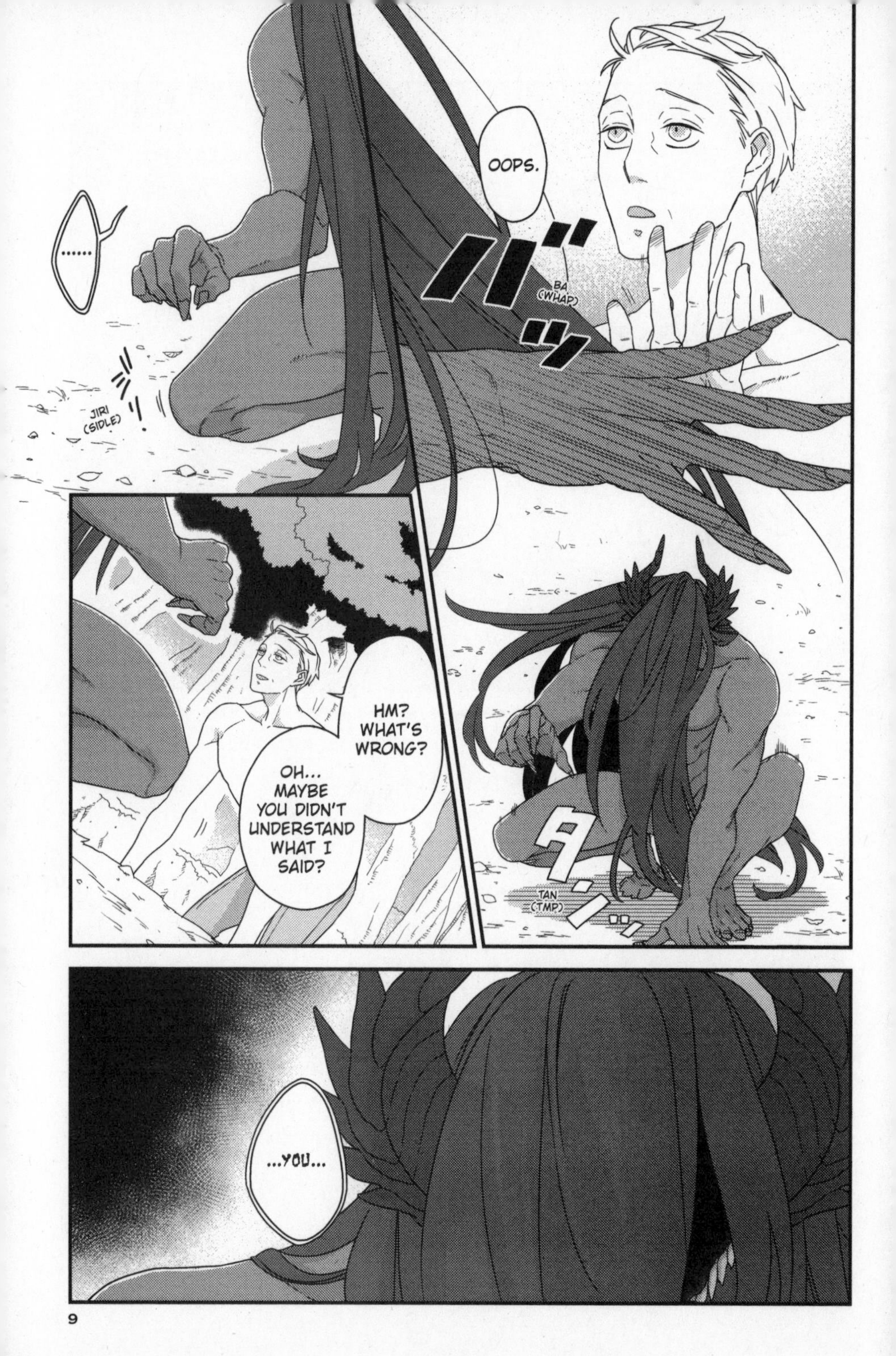
OOPS.
BA (WHAP)
......
JIRI (SIDLE)
TAN (TMP)
HM? WHAT'S WRONG?
OH... MAYBE YOU DIDN'T UNDERSTAND WHAT I SAID?
...YOU...

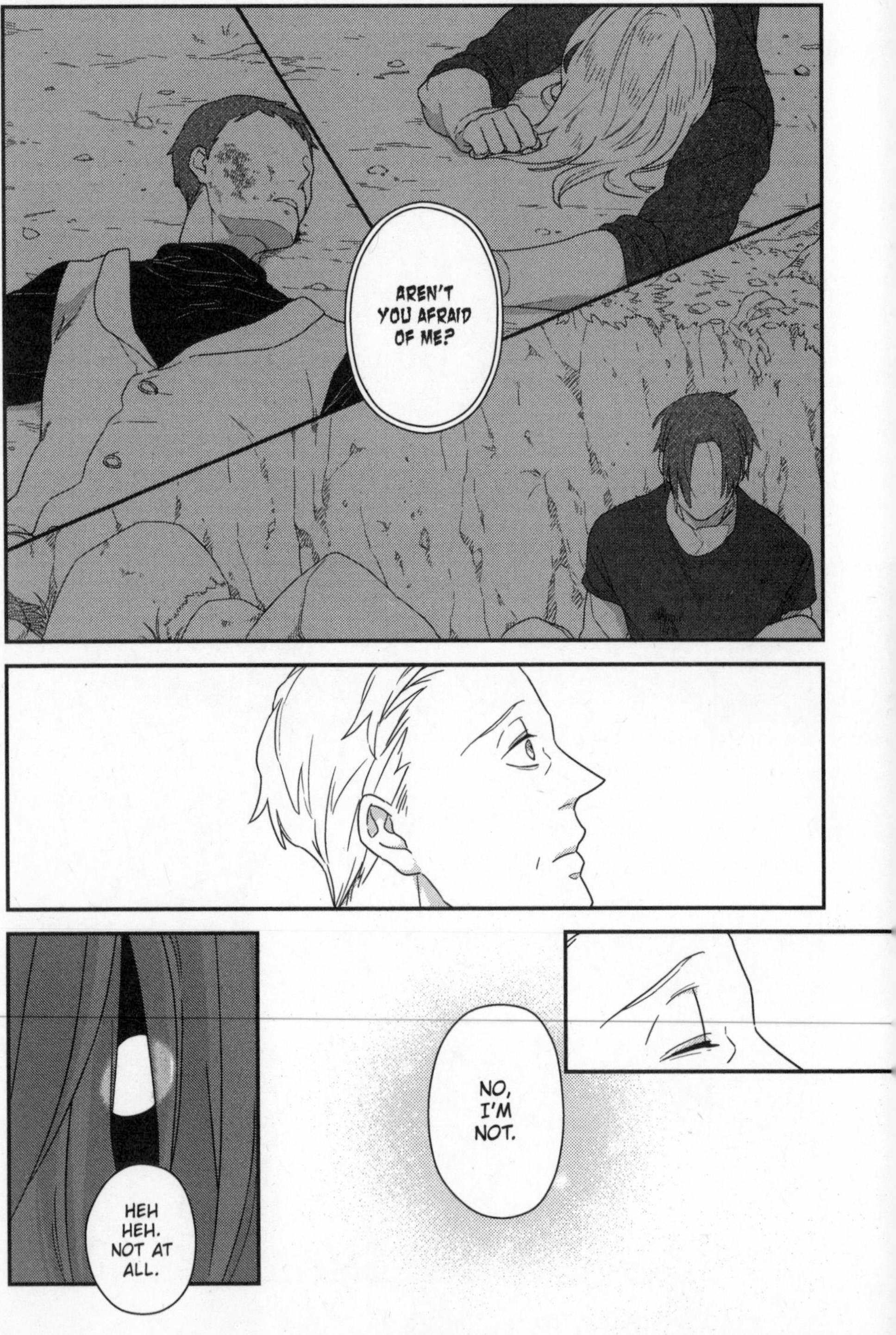
AREN'T YOU AFRAID OF ME?
NO, I'M NOT.
HEH HEH. NOT AT ALL.

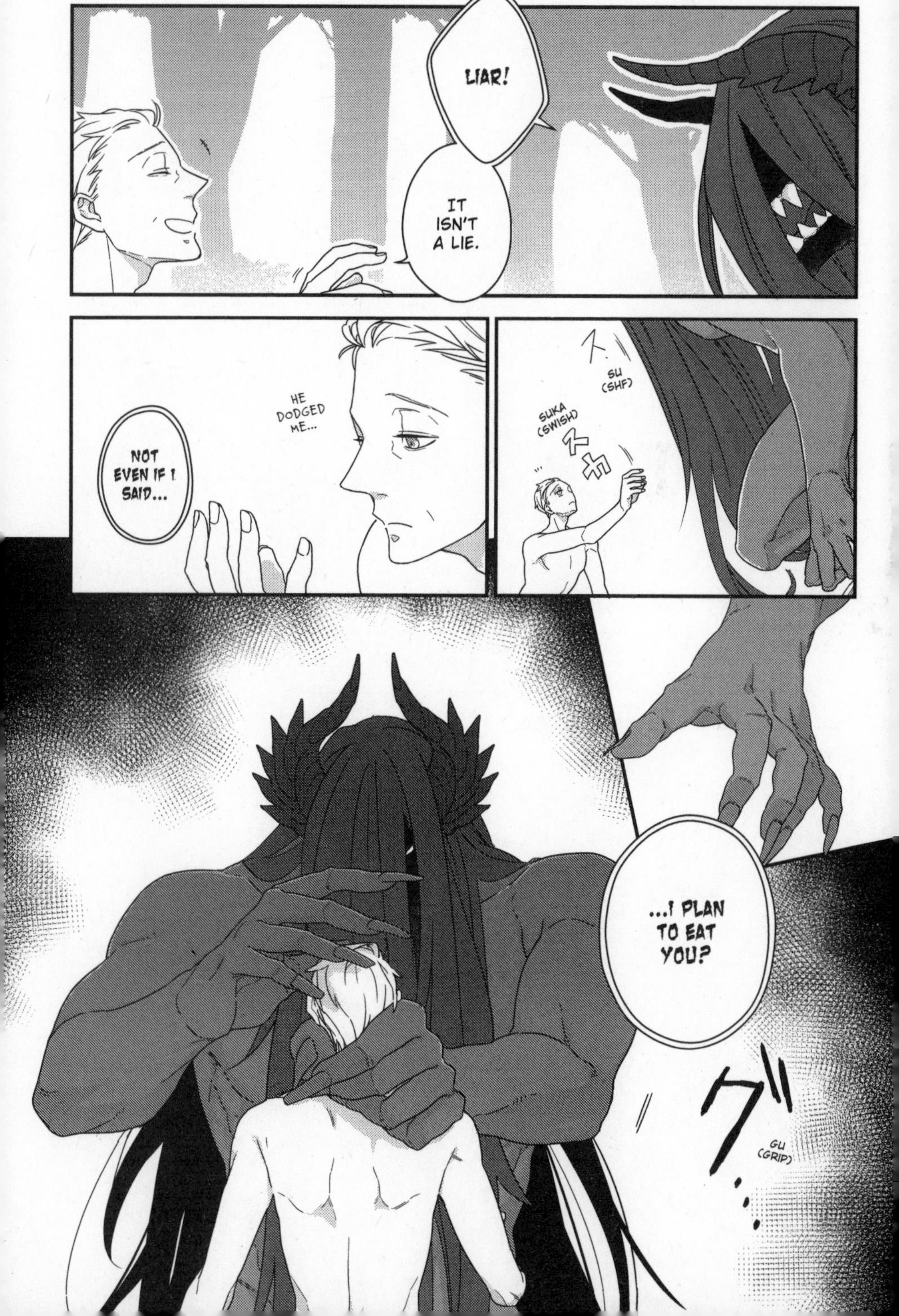
LIAR!
IT ISN'T A LIE.
ス
SU (SHF)
スカ
SUKA (SWISH)
HE DODGED ME...
NOT EVEN IF I SAID...
...I PLAN TO EAT YOU?
グ
GU (GRIP)

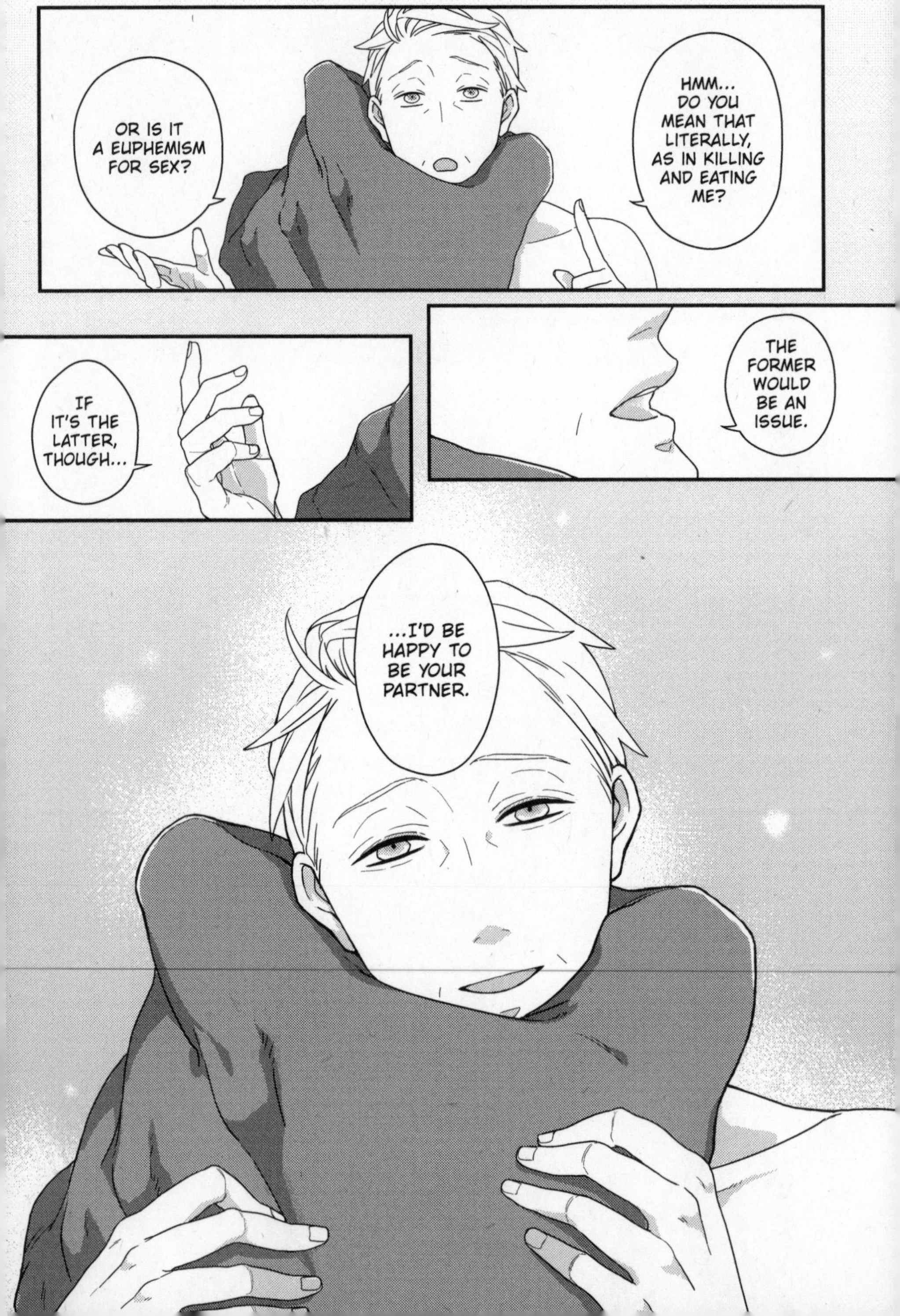
HMM... DO YOU MEAN THAT LITERALLY, AS IN KILLING AND EATING ME?
OR IS IT A EUPHEMISM FOR SEX?
THE FORMER WOULD BE AN ISSUE.
IF IT'S THE LATTER, THOUGH...
...I'D BE HAPPY TO BE YOUR PARTNER.

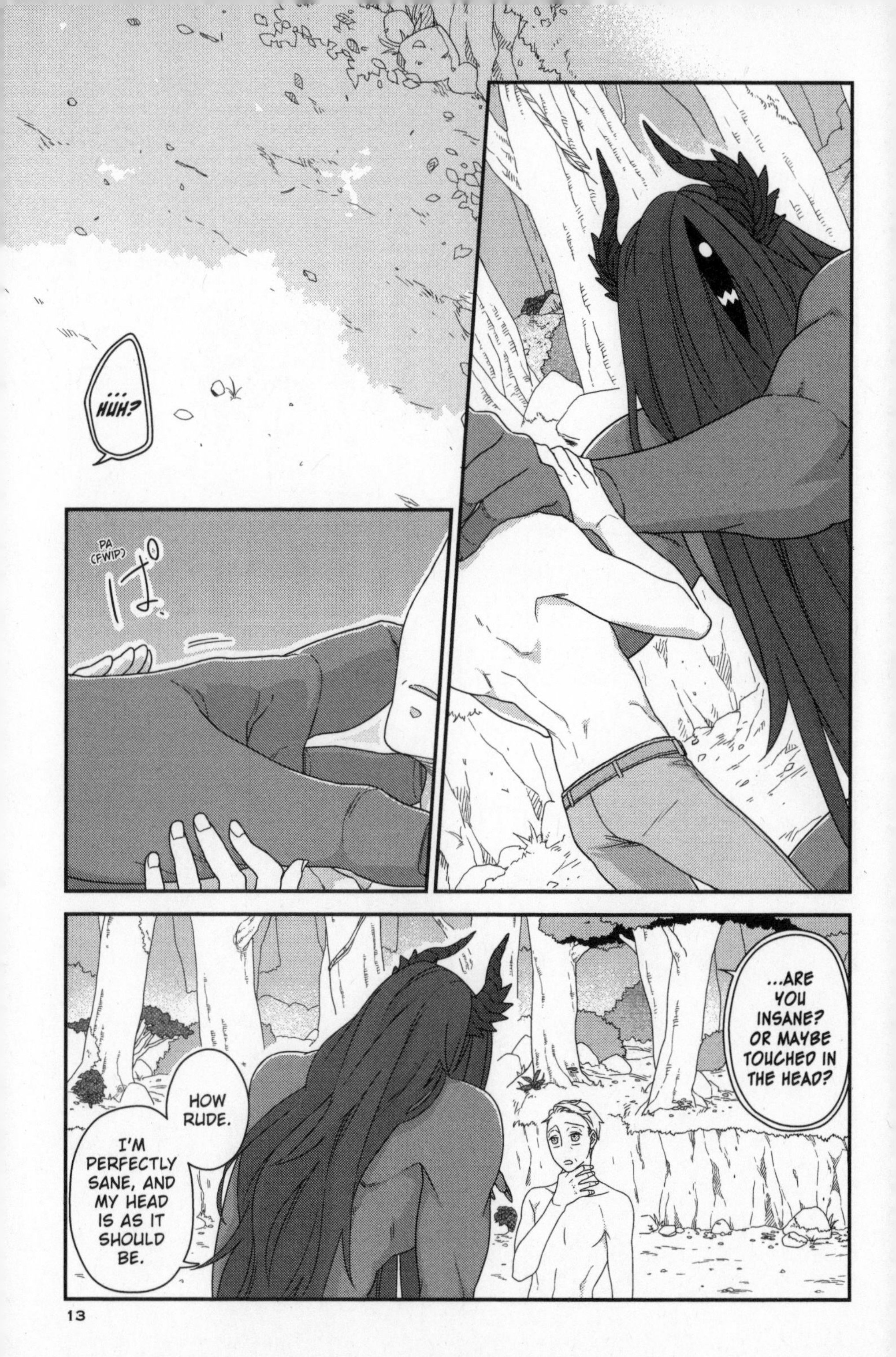
...HUH?
PA (FWIP)
ぱ
...ARE YOU INSANE? OR MAYBE TOUCHED IN THE HEAD?
HOW RUDE.
I'M PERFECTLY SANE, AND MY HEAD IS AS IT SHOULD BE.

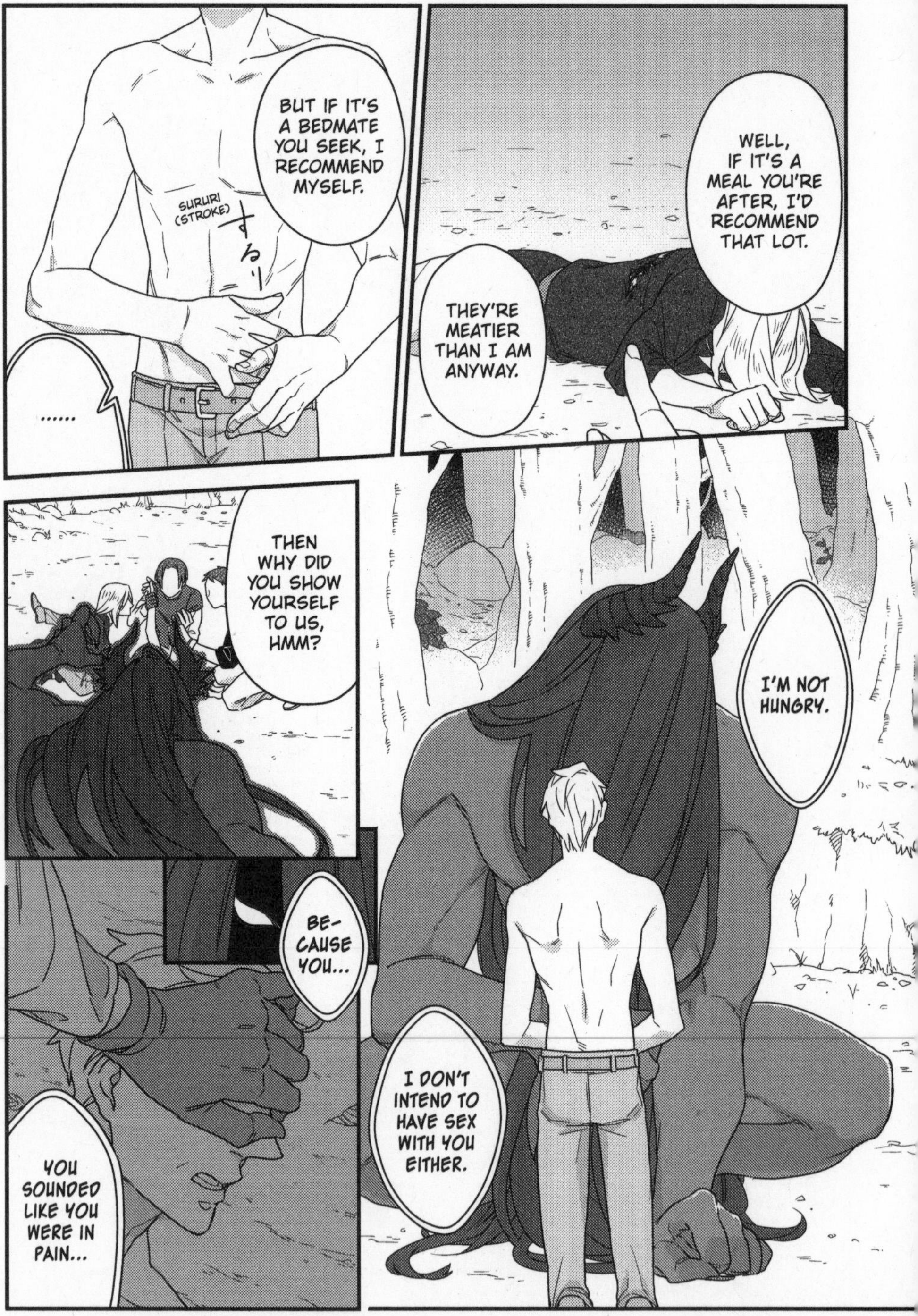
WELL, IF IT'S A MEAL YOU'RE AFTER, I'D RECOMMEND THAT LOT.
THEY'RE MEATIER THAN I AM ANYWAY.
BUT IF IT'S A BEDMATE YOU SEEK, I RECOMMEND MYSELF.
SURURI (STROKE)
するり
......
I'M NOT HUNGRY.
I DON'T INTEND TO HAVE SEX WITH YOU EITHER.
THEN WHY DID YOU SHOW YOURSELF TO US, HMM?
BE-CAUSE YOU...
YOU SOUNDED LIKE YOU WERE IN PAIN...

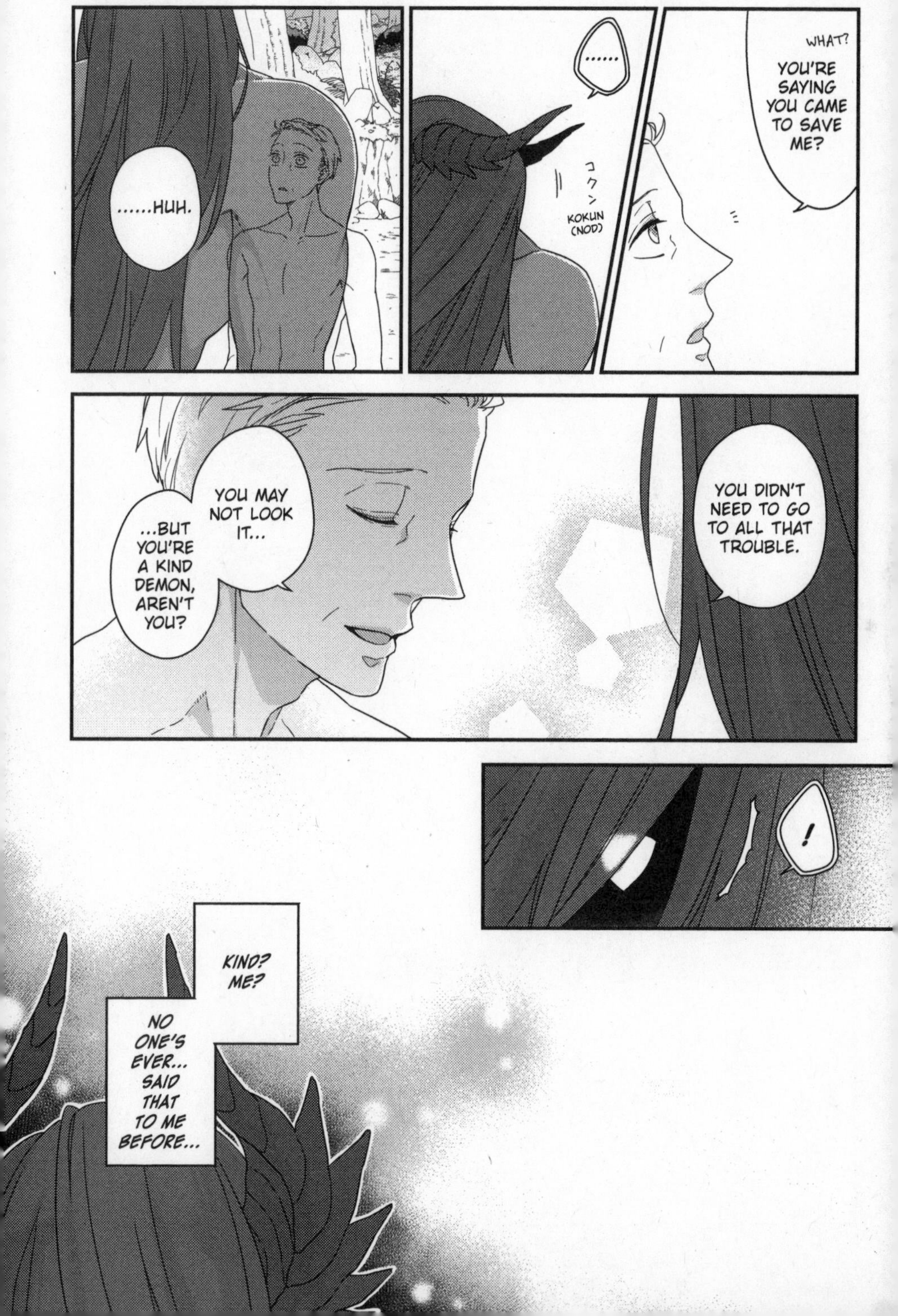
WHAT?
YOU'RE SAYING YOU CAME TO SAVE ME?
......
コクン
KOKUN (NOD)
......HUH.
YOU DIDN'T NEED TO GO TO ALL THAT TROUBLE.
YOU MAY NOT LOOK IT...
...BUT YOU'RE A KIND DEMON, AREN'T YOU?
!
KIND? ME?
NO ONE'S EVER... SAID THAT TO ME BEFORE...

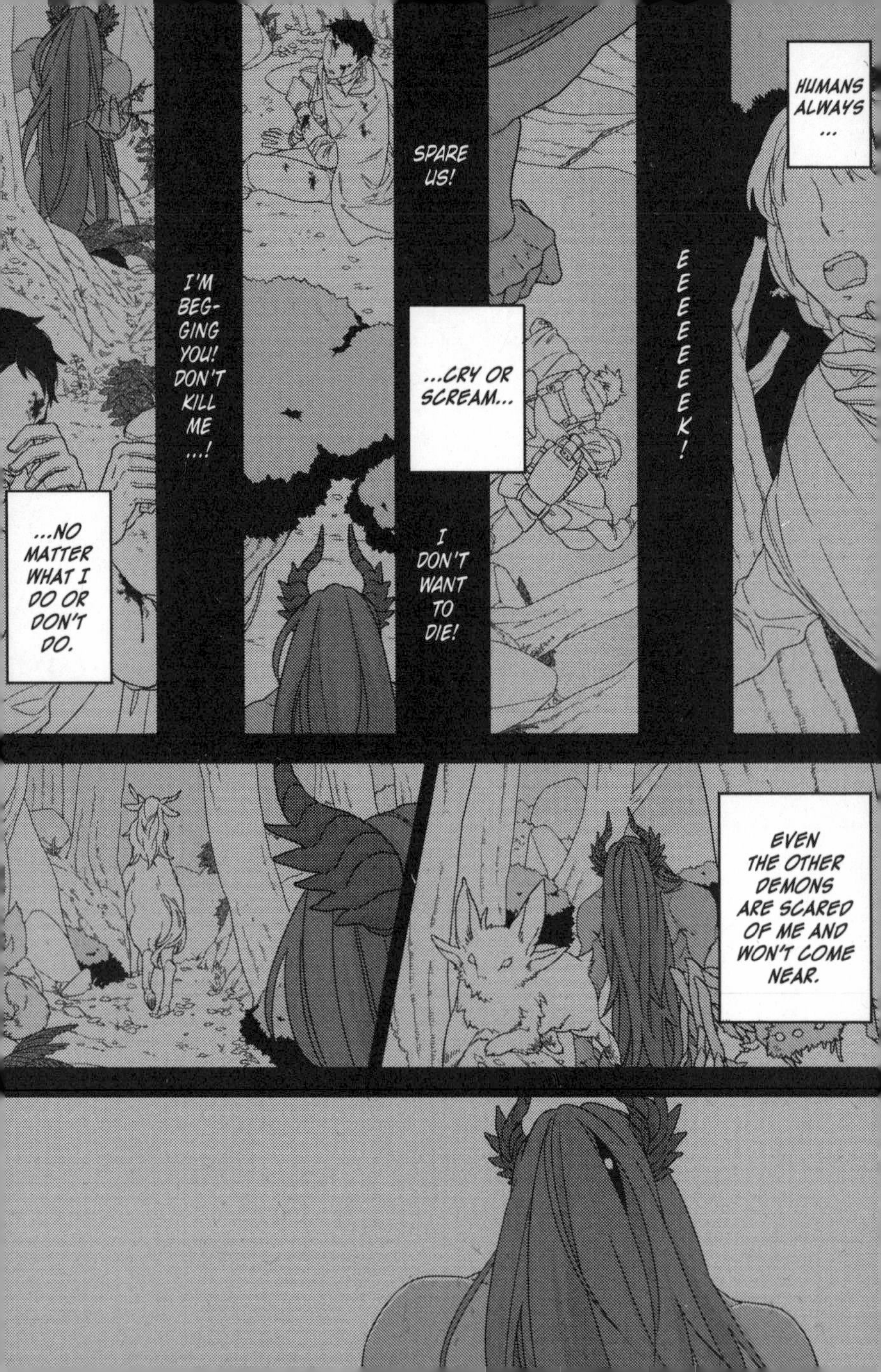
HUMANS ALWAYS ...
EEEEEEEK!
...CRY OR SCREAM...
SPARE US!
I DON'T WANT TO DIE!
I'M BEGGING YOU! DON'T KILL ME ...!
...NO MATTER WHAT I DO OR DON'T DO.
EVEN THE OTHER DEMONS ARE SCARED OF ME AND WON'T COME NEAR.

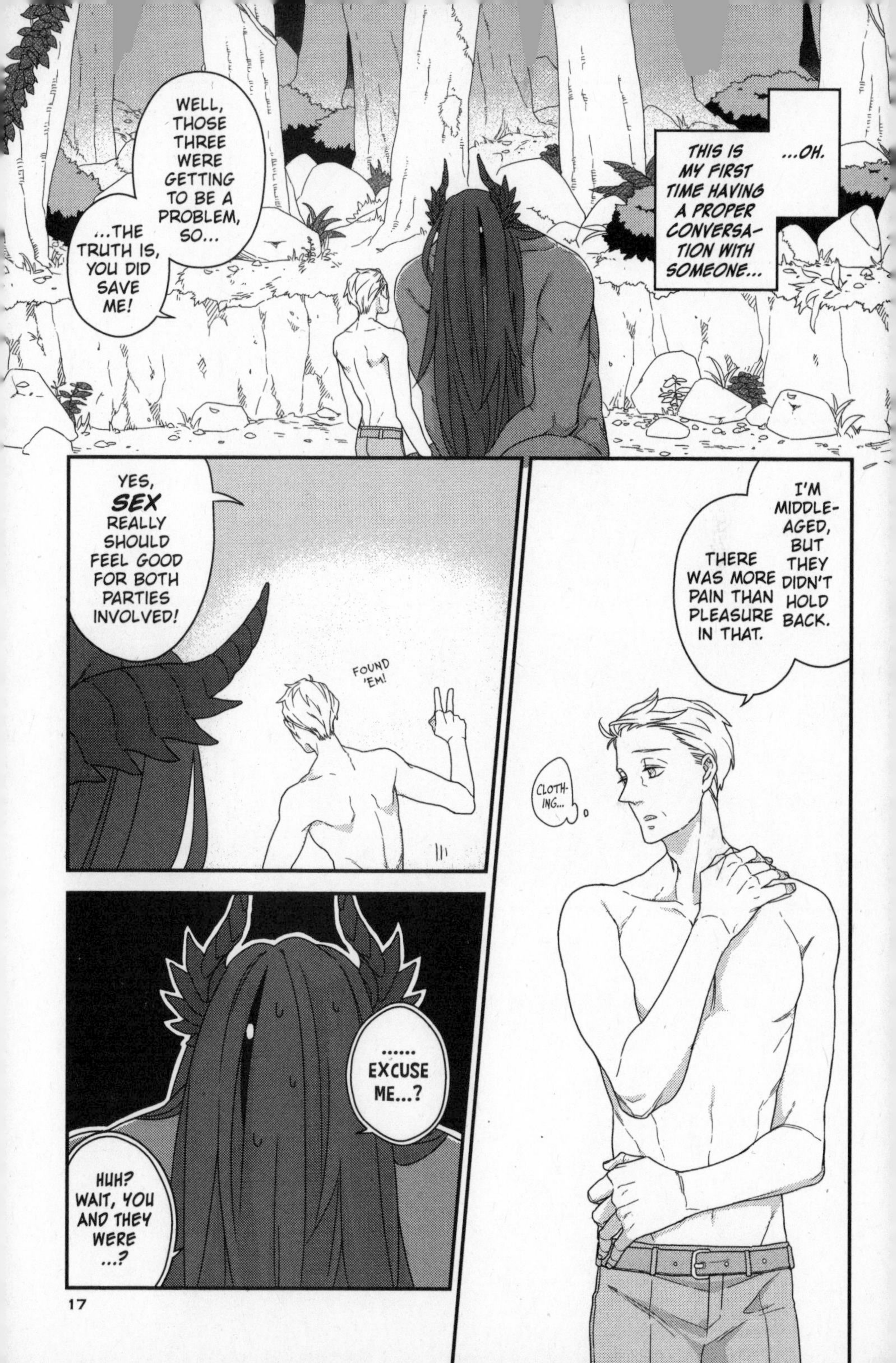
...OH.
THIS IS MY FIRST TIME HAVING A PROPER CONVERSATION WITH SOMEONE...
WELL, THOSE THREE WERE GETTING TO BE A PROBLEM, SO...
...THE TRUTH IS, YOU DID SAVE ME!
I'M MIDDLE-AGED, BUT THEY DIDN'T HOLD BACK.
THERE WAS MORE PAIN THAN PLEASURE IN THAT.
CLOTHING...
YES, SEX REALLY SHOULD FEEL GOOD FOR BOTH PARTIES INVOLVED!
FOUND 'EM!
......EXCUSE ME...?
HUH? WAIT, YOU AND THEY WERE ...?

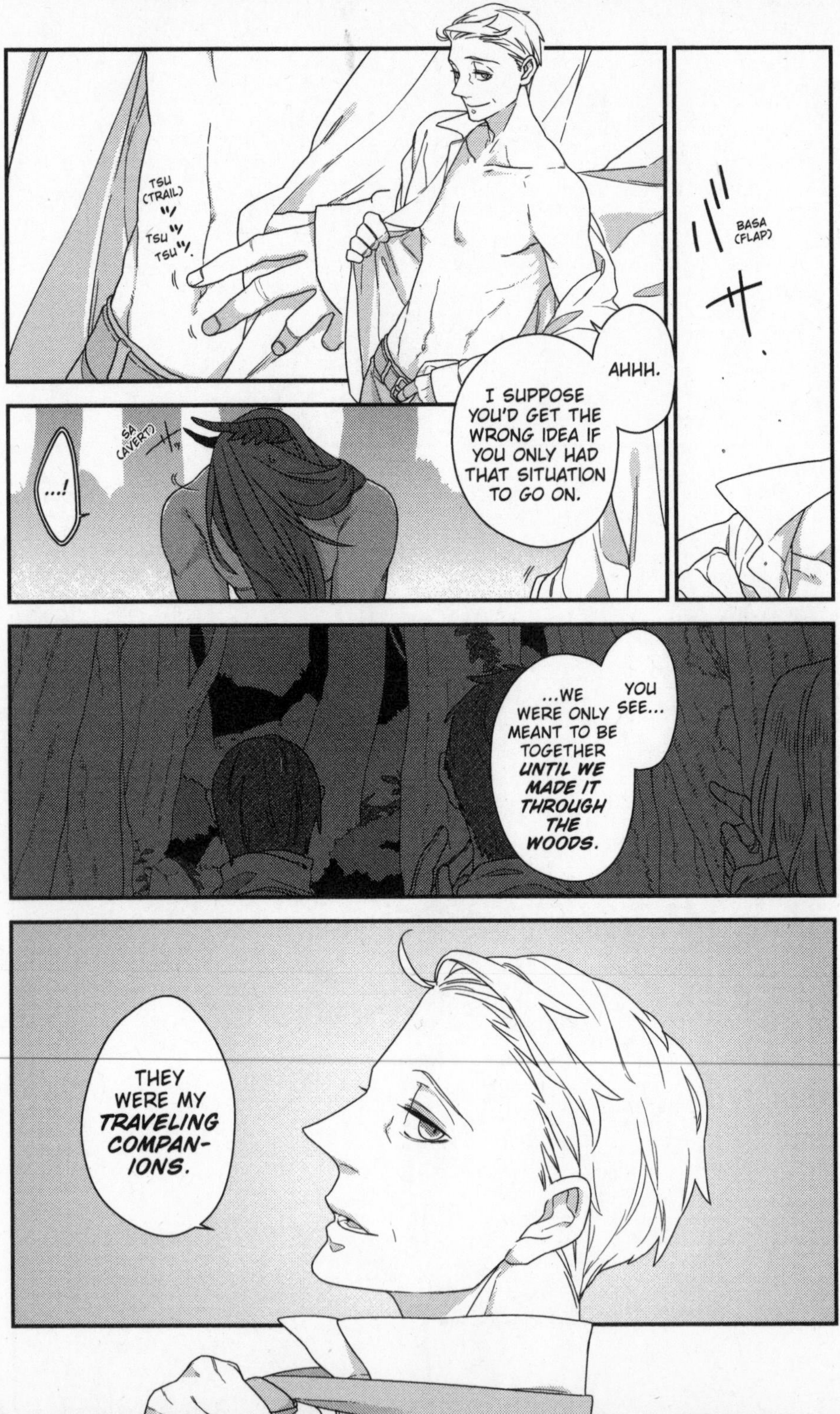
BASA (FLAP)
TSU (TRAIL) TSU TSU
AHHH.
I SUPPOSE YOU'D GET THE WRONG IDEA IF YOU ONLY HAD THAT SITUATION TO GO ON.
SA (AVERT)
...!
YOU SEE... ...WE WERE ONLY MEANT TO BE TOGETHER *UNTIL WE MADE IT THROUGH THE WOODS*.
THEY WERE MY *TRAVELING COMPAN-IONS*.

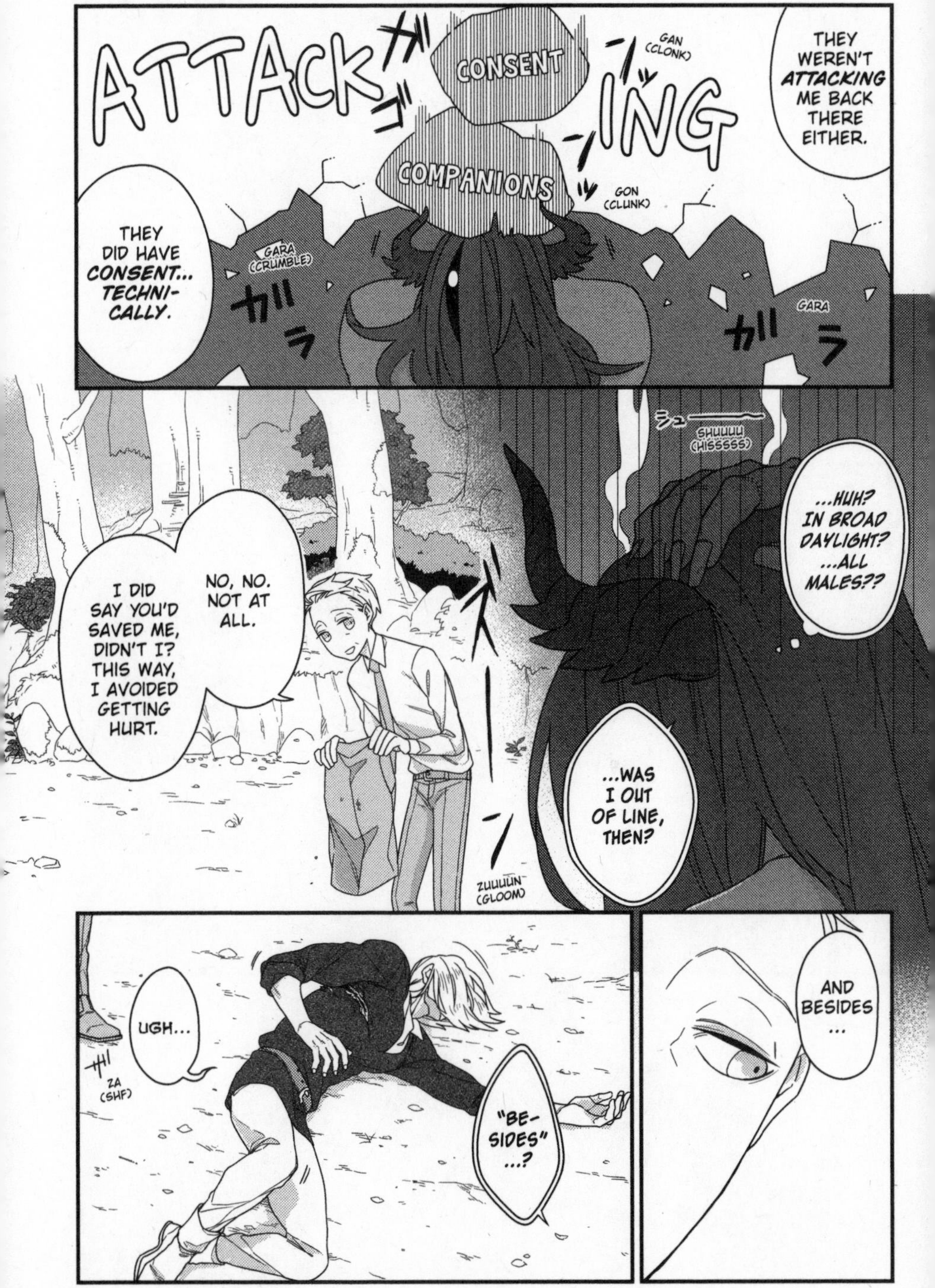
THEY WEREN'T ATTACKING ME BACK THERE EITHER.
GAN (CLONK)
ATTACK-ING
CONSENT
COMPANIONS
GON (CLUNK)
GARA
THEY DID HAVE CONSENT... TECHNI-CALLY.
GARA (CRUMBLE)
SHUUUU (HISSSSS)
...HUH? IN BROAD DAYLIGHT? ...ALL MALES??
...WAS I OUT OF LINE, THEN?
ZUUUUN (GLOOM)
NO, NO. NOT AT ALL.
I DID SAY YOU'D SAVED ME, DIDN'T I? THIS WAY, I AVOIDED GETTING HURT.
AND BESIDES ...
"BE-SIDES" ...?
UGH...
ZA (SHF)

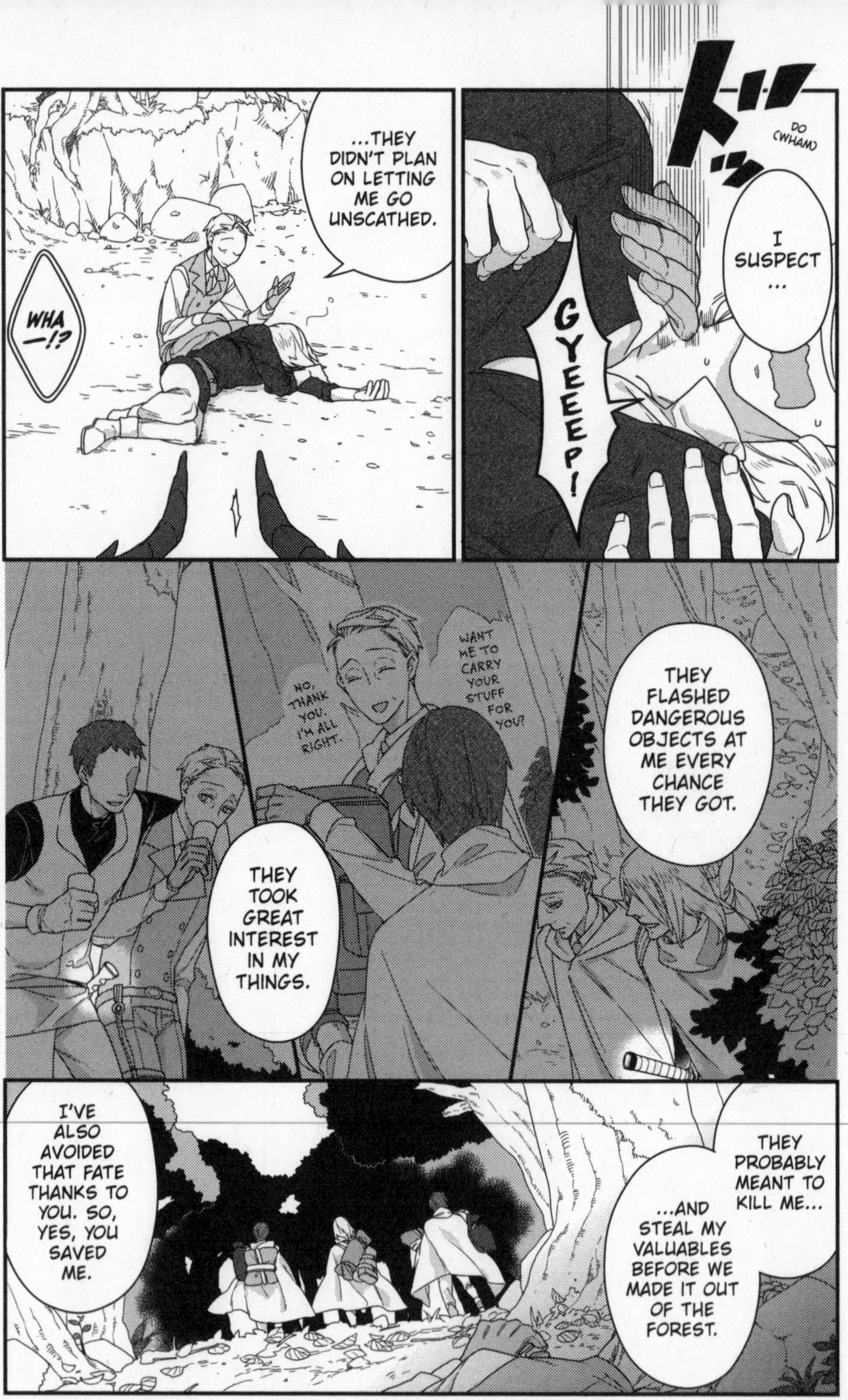
ドッ
DO (WHAM)
I SUSPECT...
GYEEEP!
...THEY DIDN'T PLAN ON LETTING ME GO UNSCATHED.
WHA—!?
THEY FLASHED DANGEROUS OBJECTS AT ME EVERY CHANCE THEY GOT.
WANT ME TO CARRY YOUR STUFF FOR YOU?
NO, THANK YOU. I'M ALL RIGHT.
THEY TOOK GREAT INTEREST IN MY THINGS.
THEY PROBABLY MEANT TO KILL ME...
...AND STEAL MY VALUABLES BEFORE WE MADE IT OUT OF THE FOREST.
I'VE ALSO AVOIDED THAT FATE THANKS TO YOU. SO, YES, YOU SAVED ME.

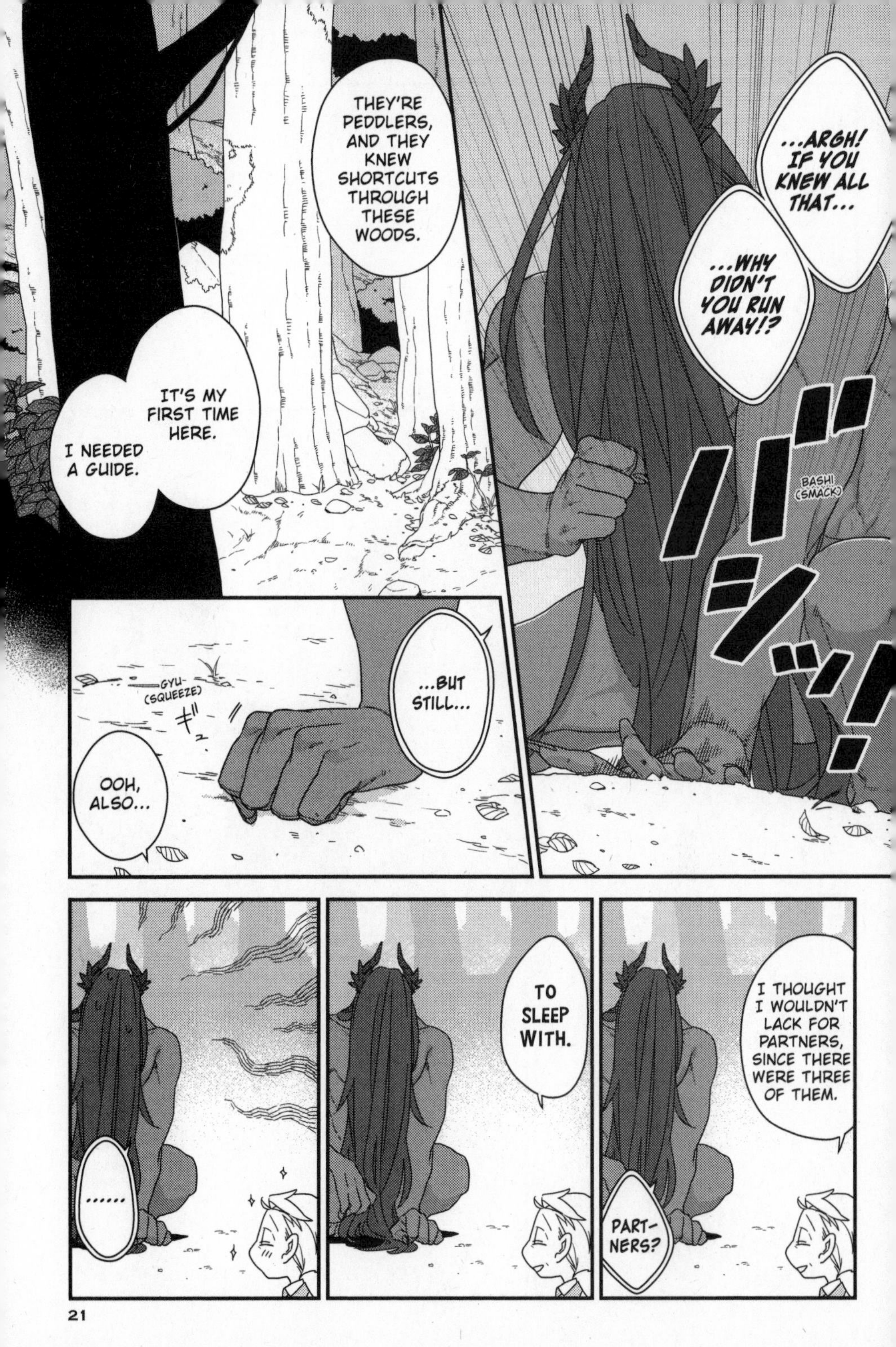

...ARGH! IF YOU KNEW ALL THAT...
...WHY DIDN'T YOU RUN AWAY!?
BASHI (SMACK)
THEY'RE PEDDLERS, AND THEY KNEW SHORTCUTS THROUGH THESE WOODS.
IT'S MY FIRST TIME HERE.
I NEEDED A GUIDE.
...BUT STILL...
GYU- (SQUEEZE)
OOH, ALSO...
I THOUGHT I WOULDN'T LACK FOR PARTNERS, SINCE THERE WERE THREE OF THEM.
PART-NERS?
TO SLEEP WITH.
......

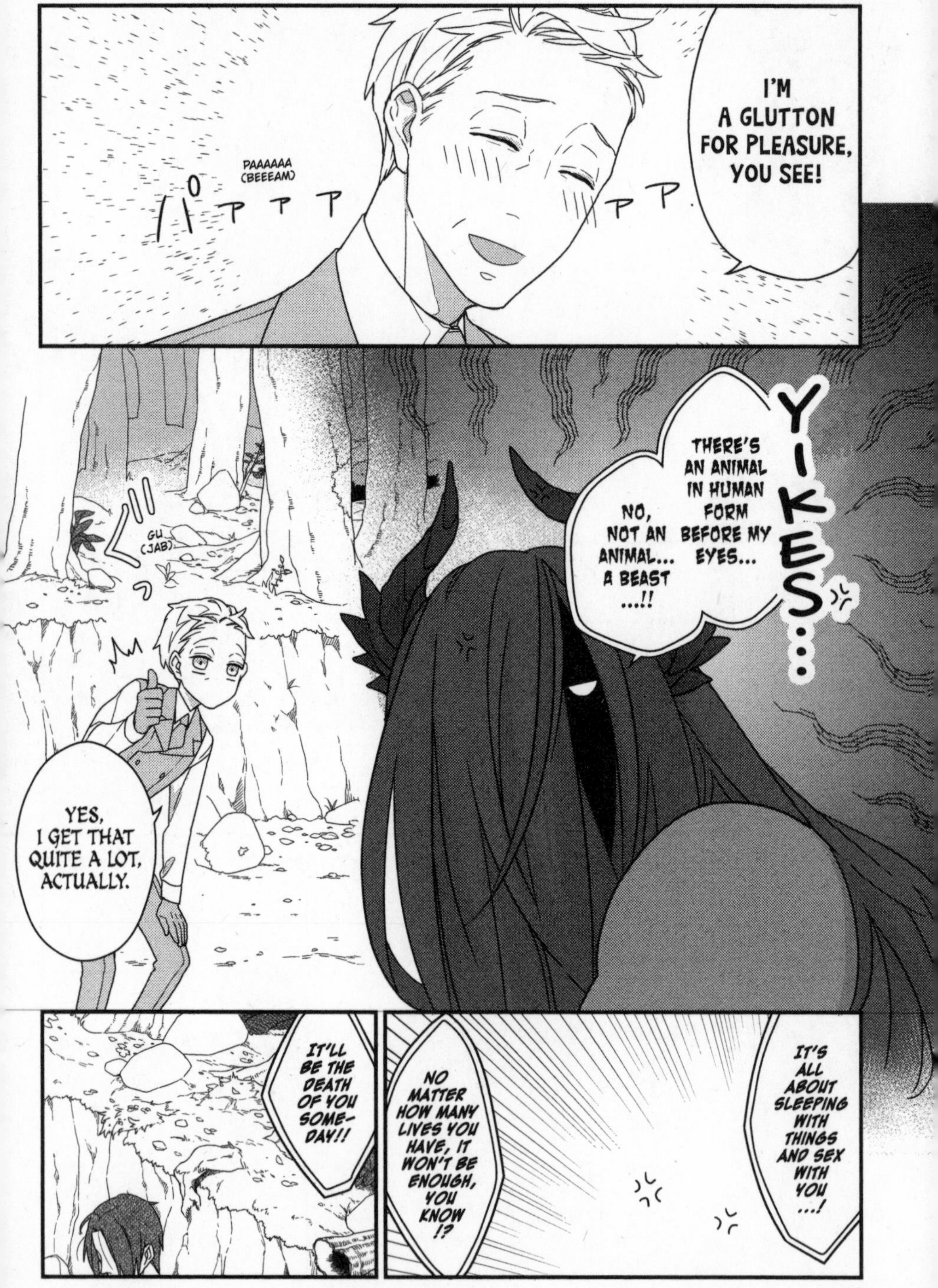
I'M A GLUTTON FOR PLEASURE, YOU SEE!
PAAAAAA (BEEEAM)
YIKES...
THERE'S AN ANIMAL IN HUMAN FORM BEFORE MY EYES...
NO, NOT AN ANIMAL... A BEAST ...!!
GU (JAB)
YES, I GET THAT QUITE A LOT, ACTUALLY.
IT'S ALL ABOUT SLEEPING WITH THINGS AND SEX WITH YOU ...!
NO MATTER HOW MANY LIVES YOU HAVE, IT WON'T BE ENOUGH, YOU KNOW !?
IT'LL BE THE DEATH OF YOU SOME-DAY!!

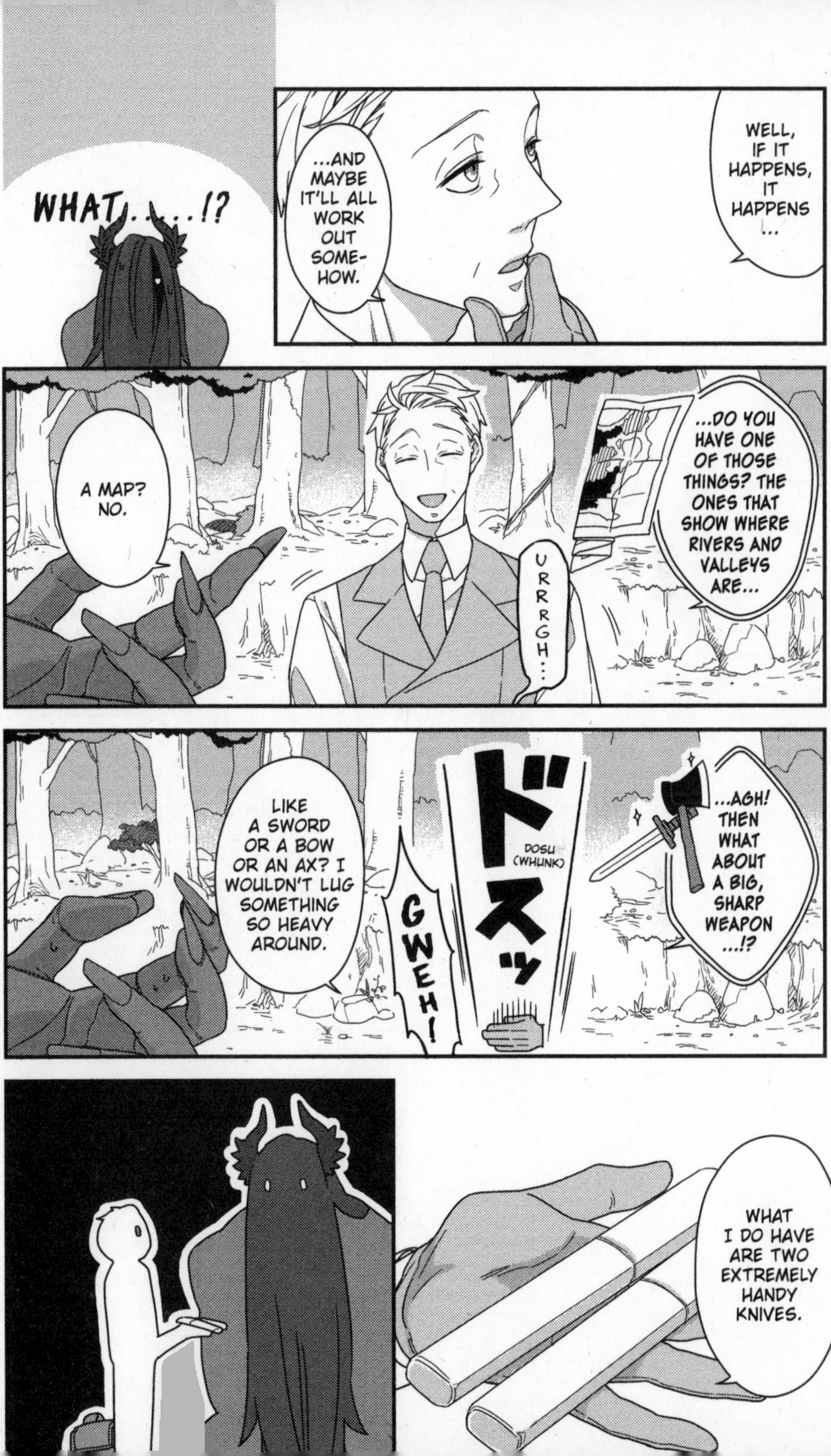
WELL, IF IT HAPPENS, IT HAPPENS...
...AND MAYBE IT'LL ALL WORK OUT SOMEHOW.
WHAT......!?
...DO YOU HAVE ONE OF THOSE THINGS? THE ONES THAT SHOW WHERE RIVERS AND VALLEYS ARE...
URRRGH...
A MAP? NO.
...AGH! THEN WHAT ABOUT A BIG, SHARP WEAPON...!?
ドスッ
DOSU (WHUNK)
GWEH!
LIKE A SWORD OR A BOW OR AN AX? I WOULDN'T LUG SOMETHING SO HEAVY AROUND.
WHAT I DO HAVE ARE TWO EXTREMELY HANDY KNIVES.

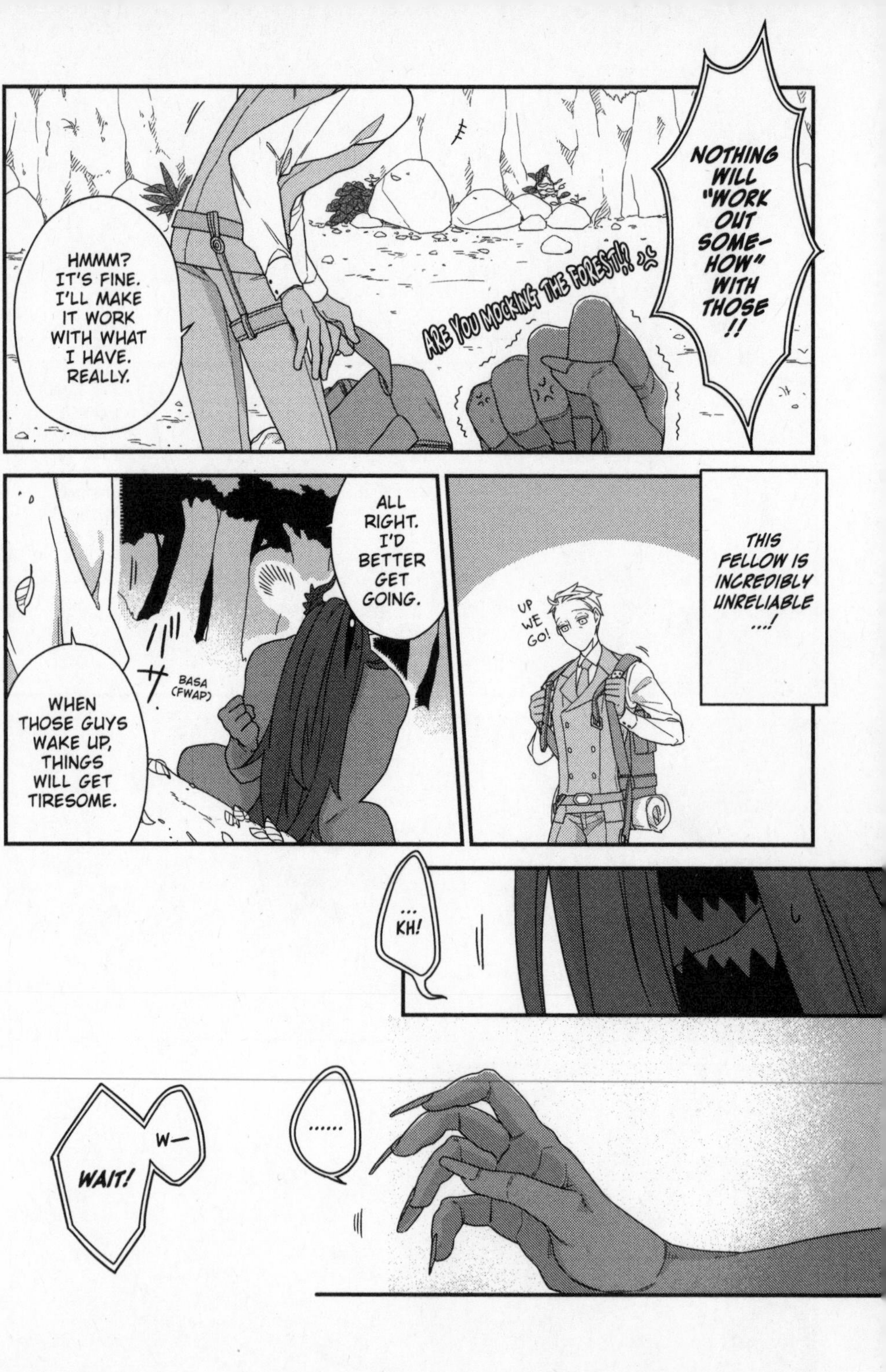
NOTHING WILL "WORK OUT SOME-HOW" WITH THOSE!!
ARE YOU MOCKING THE FOREST!?
HMMM? IT'S FINE. I'LL MAKE IT WORK WITH WHAT I HAVE. REALLY.
THIS FELLOW IS INCREDIBLY UNRELIABLE...!
UP WE GO!
ALL RIGHT. I'D BETTER GET GOING.
BASA (FWAP)
WHEN THOSE GUYS WAKE UP, THINGS WILL GET TIRESOME.
...KH!
......
W— WAIT!

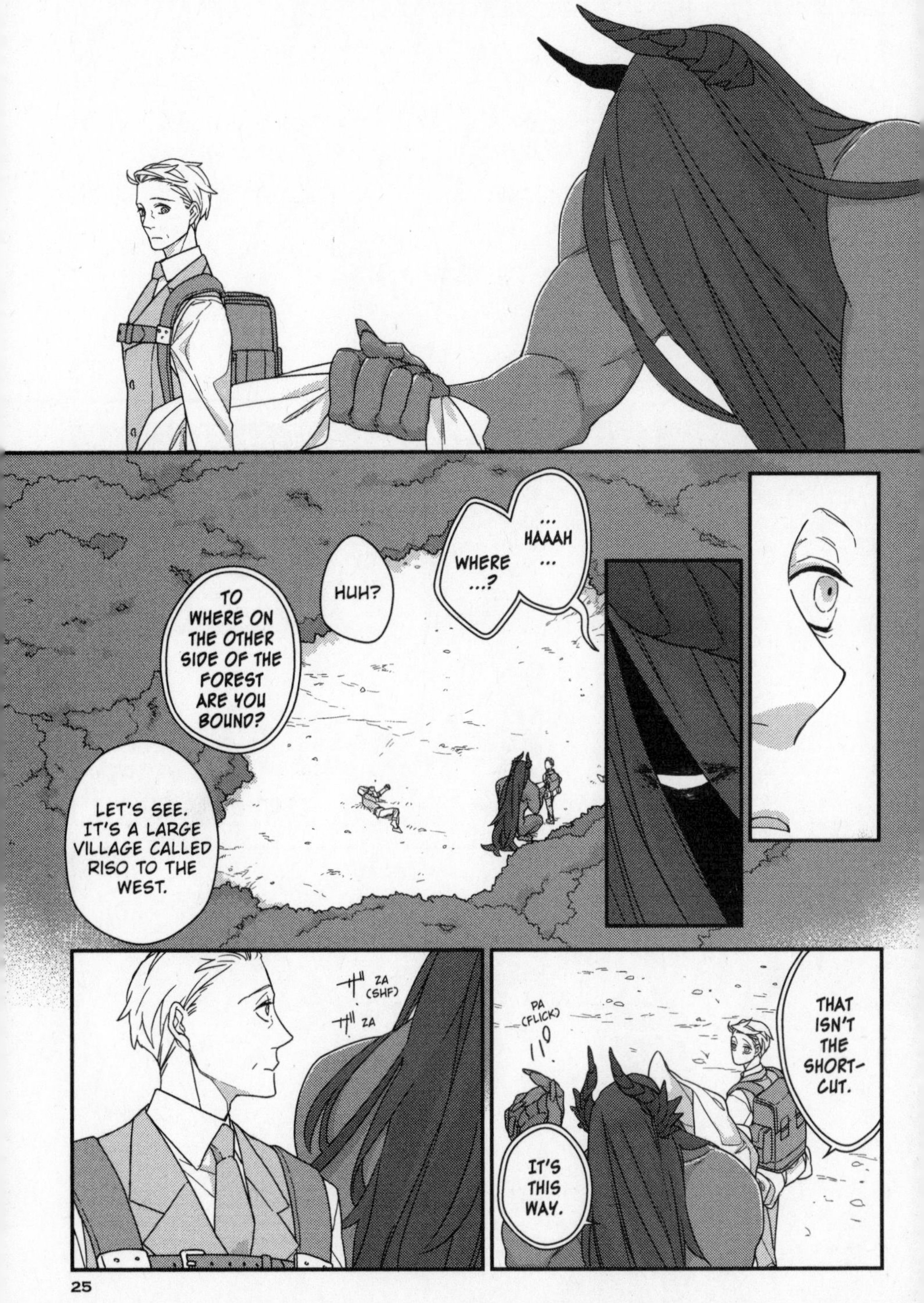
... HAAAH ...
WHERE ...?
HUH?
TO WHERE ON THE OTHER SIDE OF THE FOREST ARE YOU BOUND?
LET'S SEE. IT'S A LARGE VILLAGE CALLED RISO TO THE WEST.
THAT ISN'T THE SHORT-CUT.
PA (FLICK)
IT'S THIS WAY.
ZA (SHF)
ZA

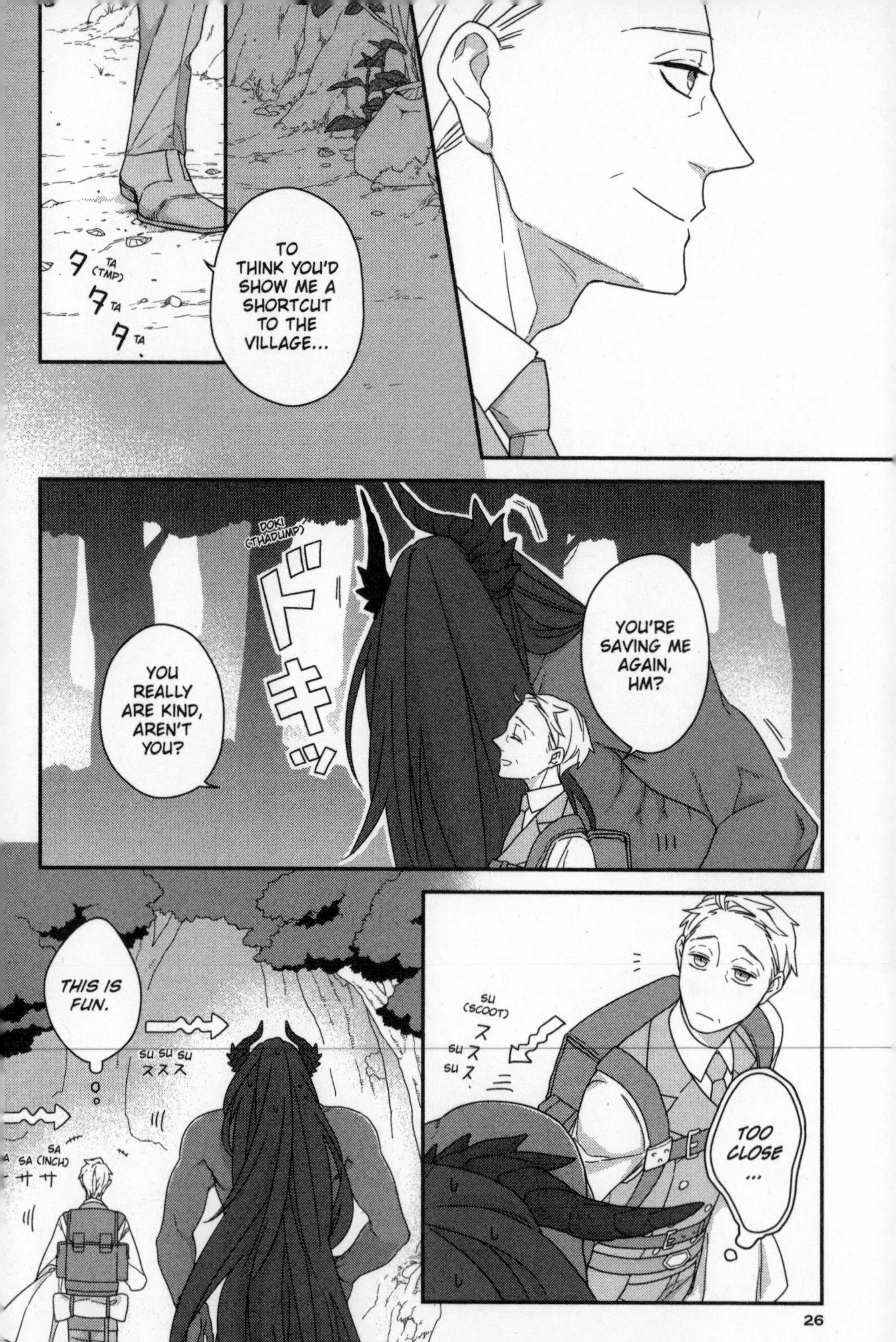
TO THINK YOU'D SHOW ME A SHORTCUT TO THE VILLAGE...
TA (TMP) TA TA
YOU'RE SAVING ME AGAIN, HM?
DOKI (THADUMP)
YOU REALLY ARE KIND, AREN'T YOU?
SU (SCOOT) SU SU
TOO CLOSE...
THIS IS FUN.
SU SU SU
SA SA (INCH)

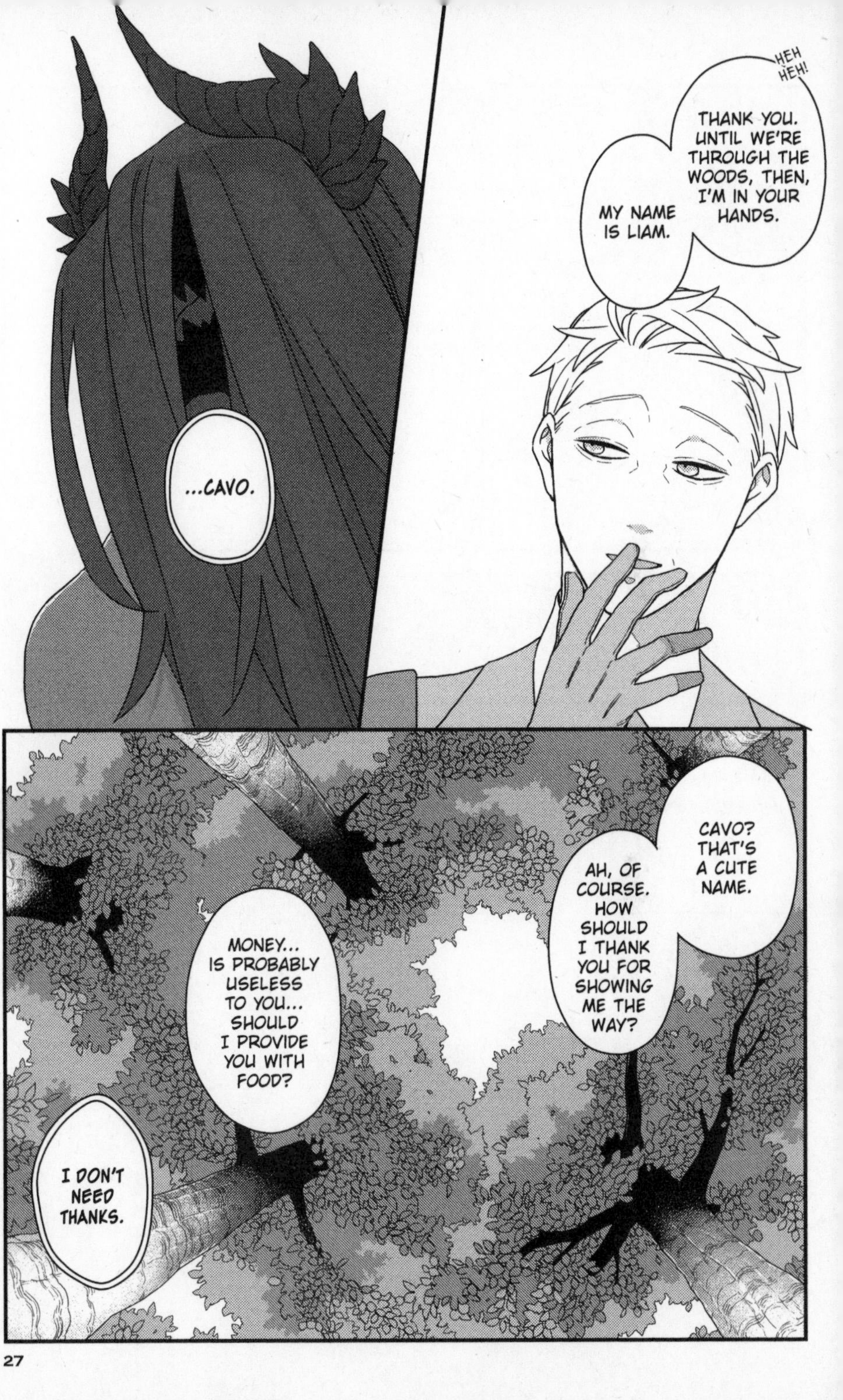
HEH HEH!
THANK YOU. UNTIL WE'RE THROUGH THE WOODS, THEN, I'M IN YOUR HANDS.
MY NAME IS LIAM.
...CAVO.
CAVO? THAT'S A CUTE NAME.
AH, OF COURSE. HOW SHOULD I THANK YOU FOR SHOWING ME THE WAY?
MONEY... IS PROBABLY USELESS TO YOU... SHOULD I PROVIDE YOU WITH FOOD?
I DON'T NEED THANKS.

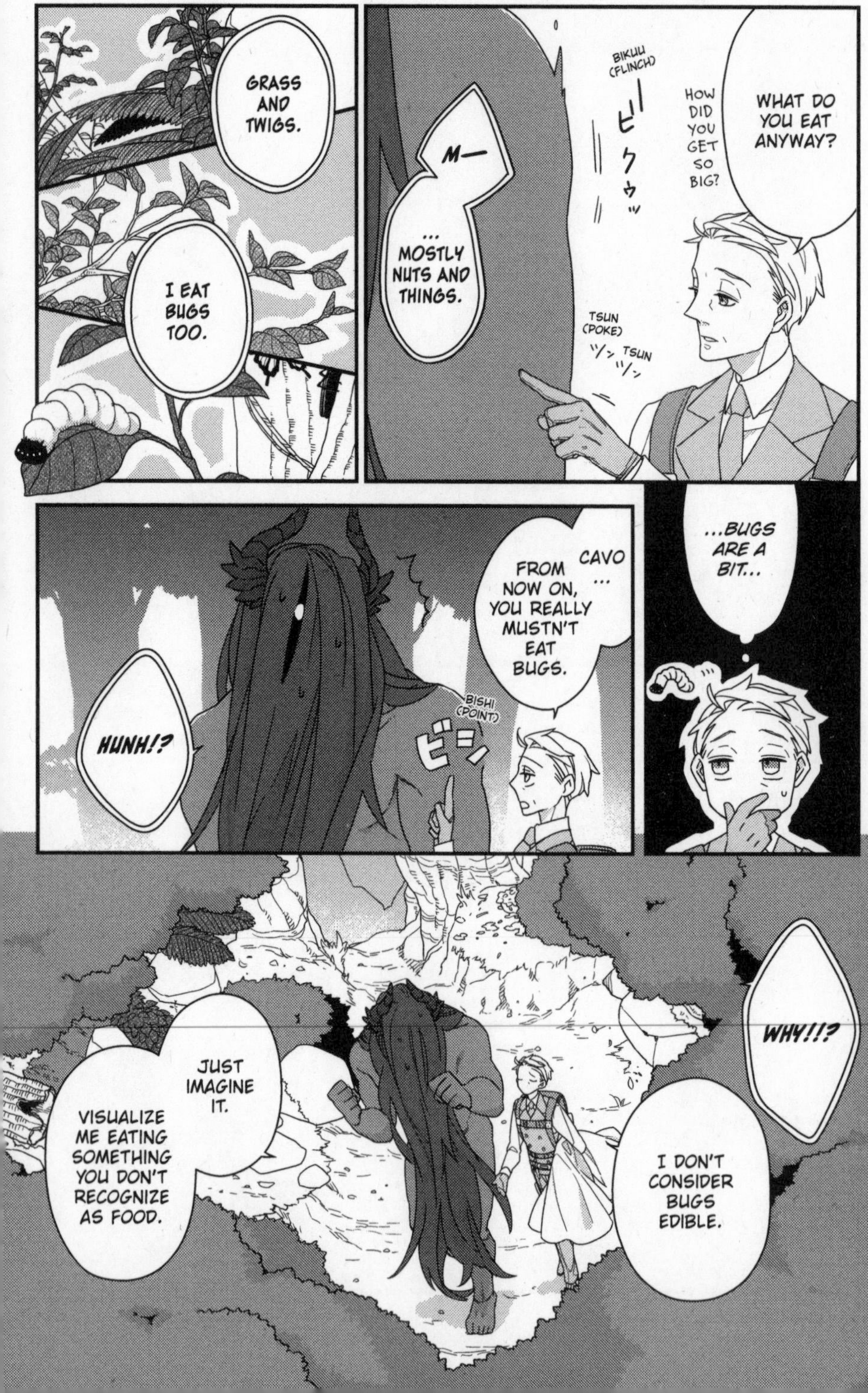
WHAT DO YOU EAT ANYWAY?
HOW DID YOU GET SO BIG?
BIKUU (FLINCH)
M—
TSUN (POKE) TSUN
...MOSTLY NUTS AND THINGS.
GRASS AND TWIGS.
I EAT BUGS TOO.
...BUGS ARE A BIT...
CAVO... FROM NOW ON, YOU REALLY MUSTN'T EAT BUGS.
BISHI (POINT)
HUNH!?
WHY!!?
I DON'T CONSIDER BUGS EDIBLE.
JUST IMAGINE IT.
VISUALIZE ME EATING SOMETHING YOU DON'T RECOGNIZE AS FOOD.

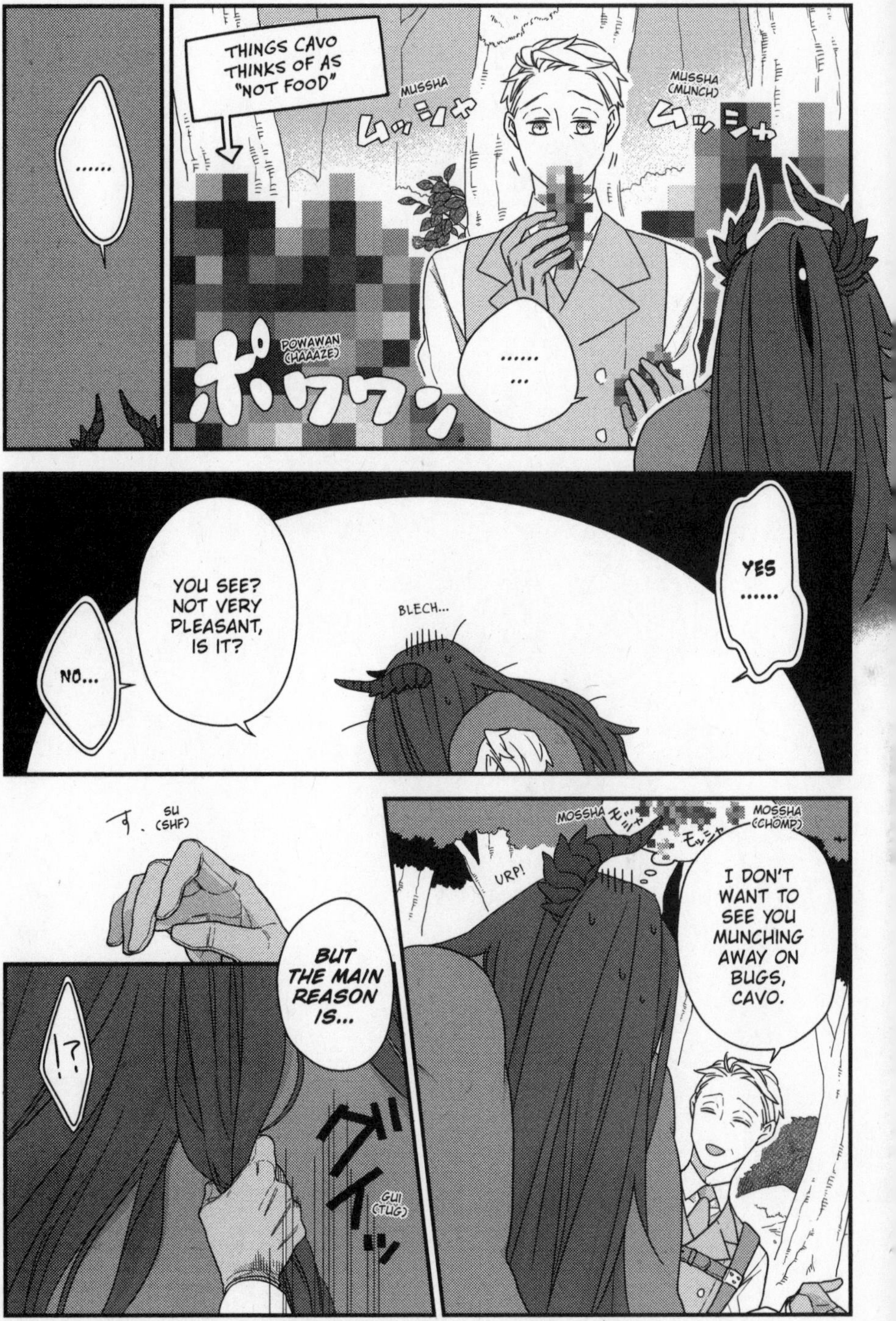
MUSSHA (MUNCH)
ムッシャ
MUSSHA
ムッシャ
THINGS CAVO THINKS OF AS "NOT FOOD"
POWAWAN (HAAAZE)
ポワワン
....
......
YES ......
BLECH...
YOU SEE? NOT VERY PLEASANT, IS IT?
NO...
MOSSHA (CHOMP)
モッシャ
MOSSHA
モッシャ
URP!
I DON'T WANT TO SEE YOU MUNCHING AWAY ON BUGS, CAVO.
す
SU (SHF)
BUT THE MAIN REASON IS...
GUI (TUG)
!?

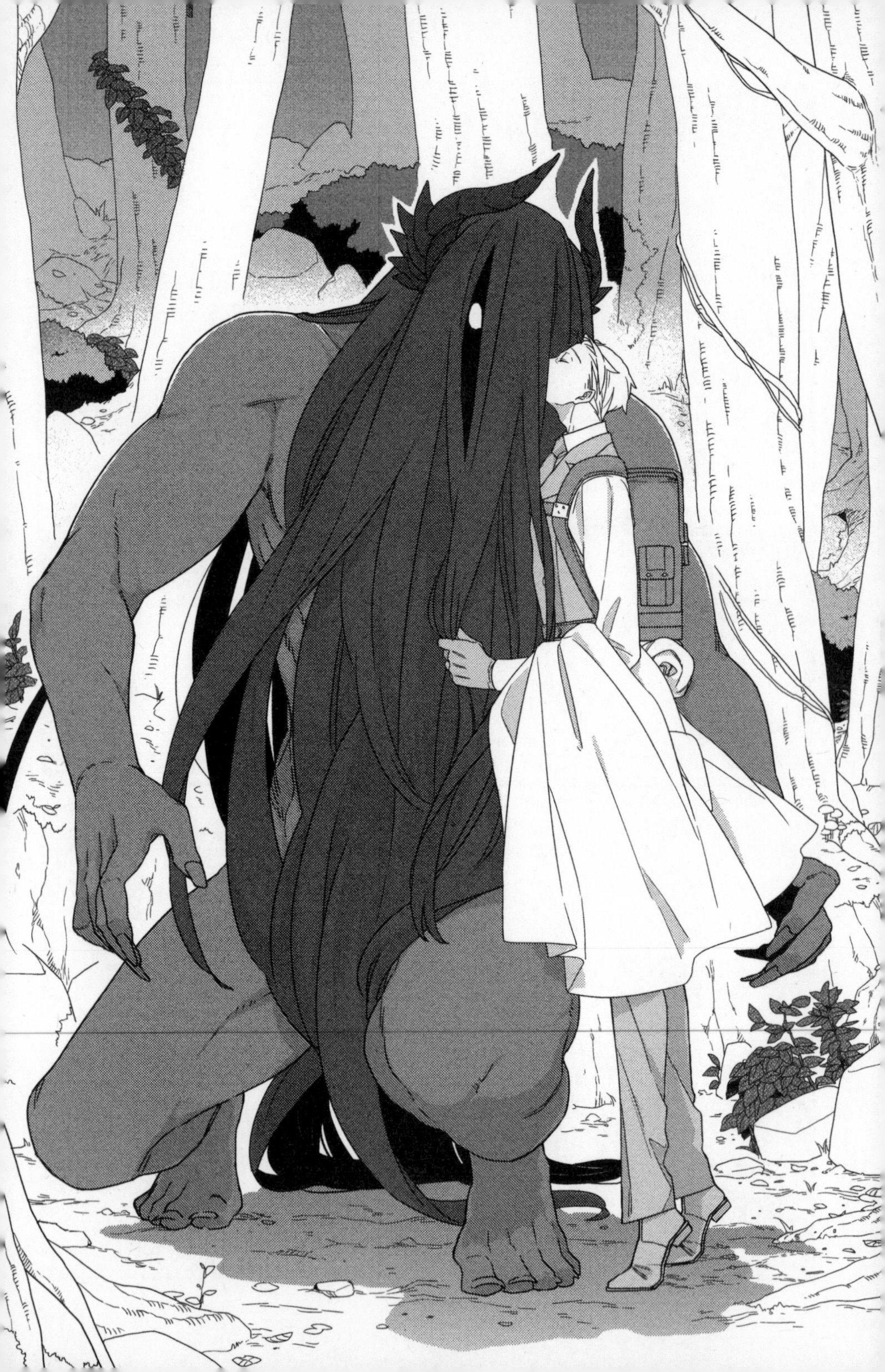

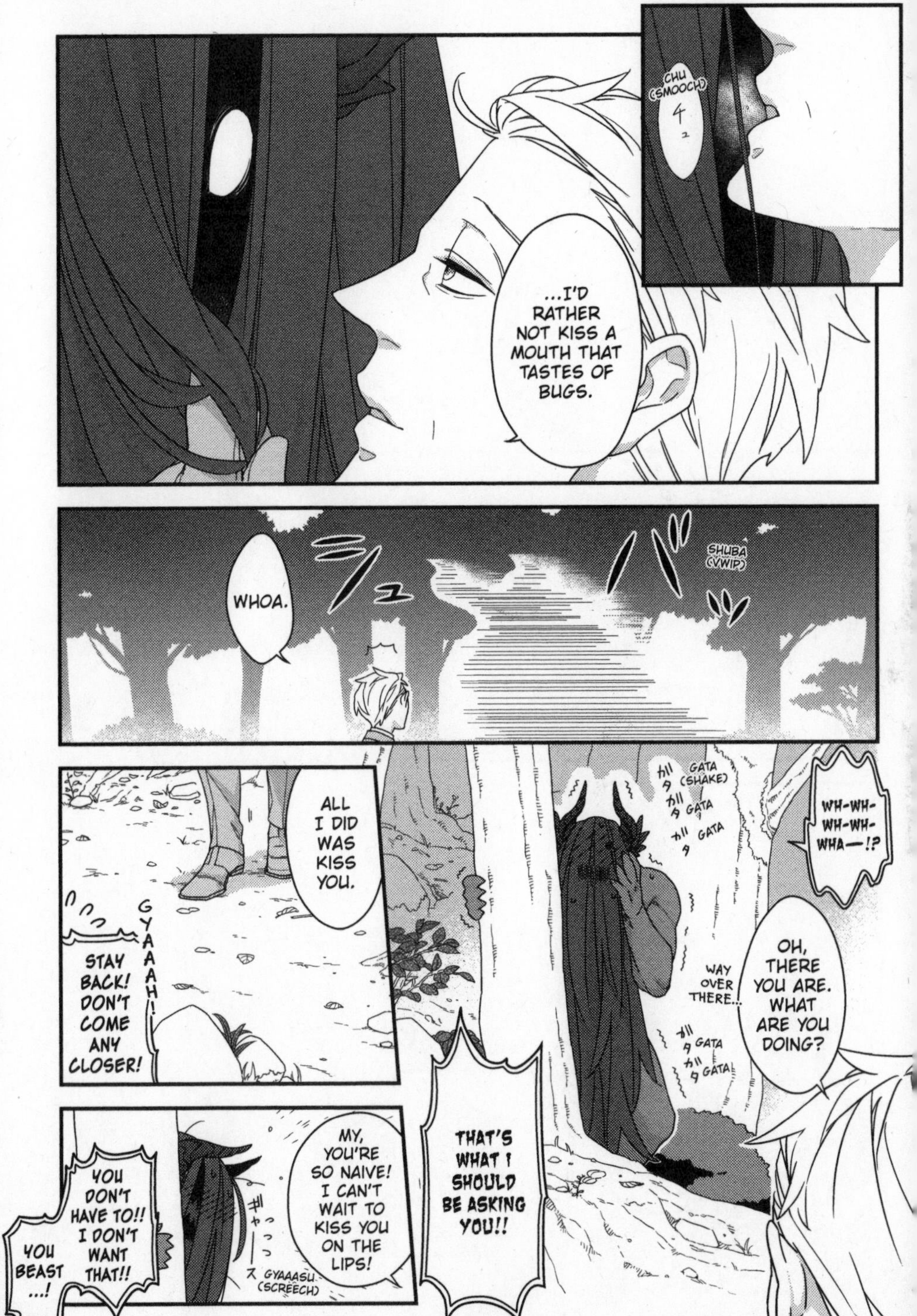
CHU (SMOOCH)
...I'D RATHER NOT KISS A MOUTH THAT TASTES OF BUGS.
SHUBA (VWIP)
WHOA.
WH-WH-WH-WH-WHA—!?
GATA (SHAKE) GATA GATA
OH, THERE YOU ARE. WHAT ARE YOU DOING?
WAY OVER THERE...
GATA GATA
THAT'S WHAT I SHOULD BE ASKING YOU!!
ALL I DID WAS KISS YOU.
GYAAAH!
STAY BACK! DON'T COME ANY CLOSER!
MY, YOU'RE SO NAIVE! I CAN'T WAIT TO KISS YOU ON THE LIPS!
GYAAASU (SCREECH)
YOU DON'T HAVE TO!! I DON'T WANT THAT!!
YOU BEAST ...!

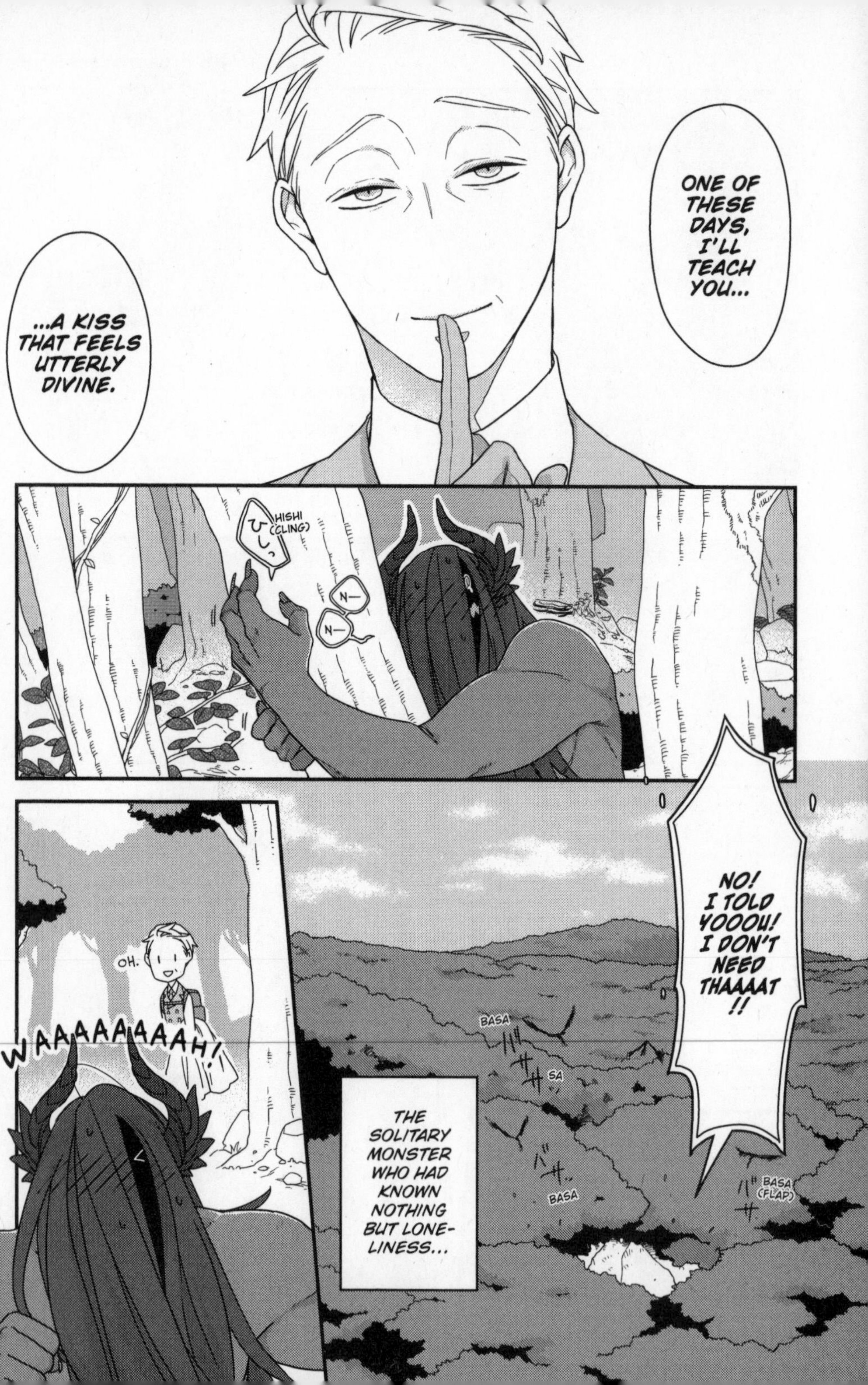
ONE OF THESE DAYS, I'LL TEACH YOU...
...A KISS THAT FEELS UTTERLY DIVINE.
ひしっ
HISHI (CLING)
N—
N—
NO! I TOLD YOOOU! I DON'T NEED THAAAAT!!
BASA
SA
BASA
BASA (FLAP)
THE SOLITARY MONSTER WHO HAD KNOWN NOTHING BUT LONE-LINESS...
OH.
WAAAAAAAAH!

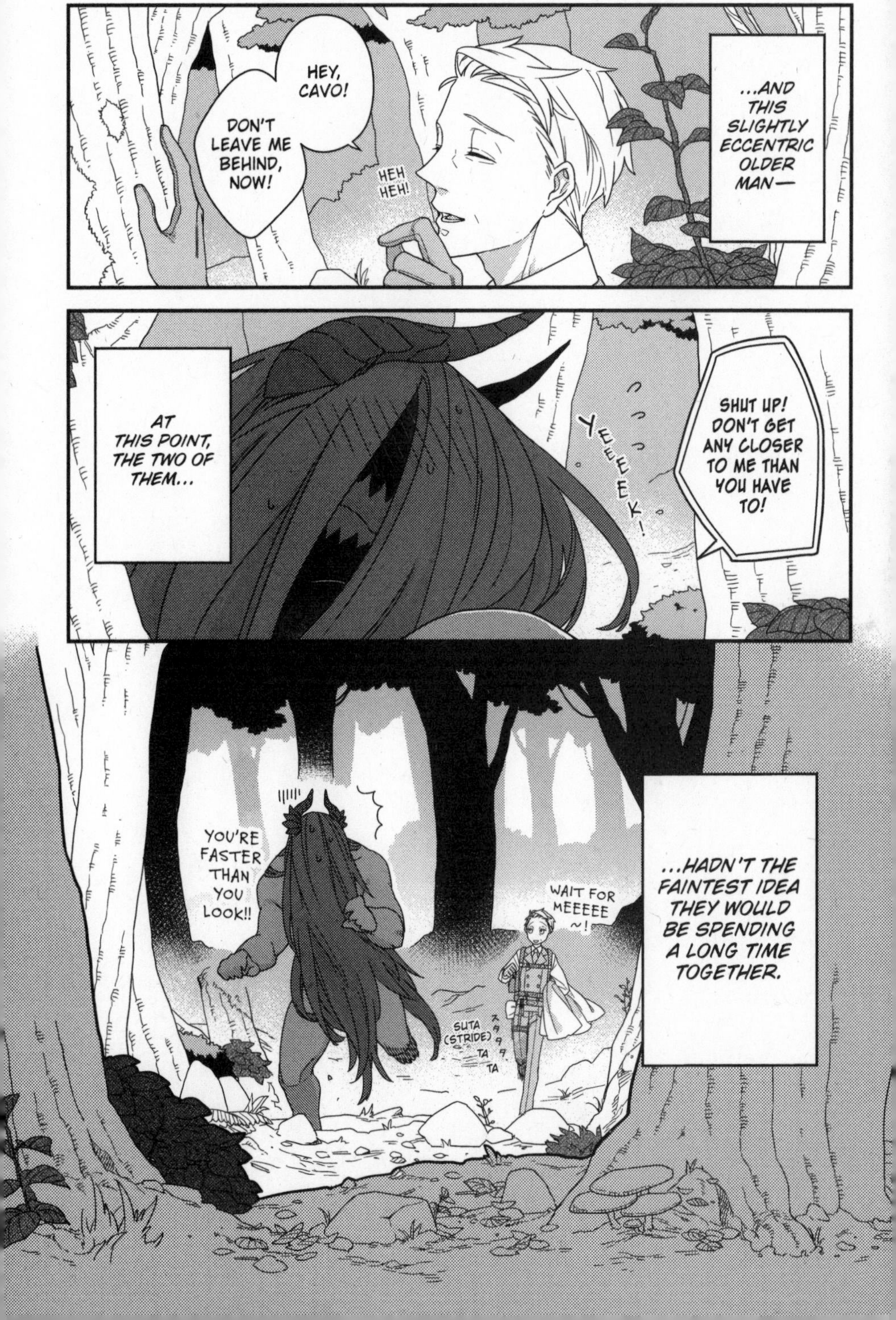
...AND THIS SLIGHTLY ECCENTRIC OLDER MAN—
HEY, CAVO! DON'T LEAVE ME BEHIND, NOW!
HEH HEH!
SHUT UP! DON'T GET ANY CLOSER TO ME THAN YOU HAVE TO!
YEEEEK!
AT THIS POINT, THE TWO OF THEM...
...HADN'T THE FAINTEST IDEA THEY WOULD BE SPENDING A LONG TIME TOGETHER.
WAIT FOR MEEEEE ~!
YOU'RE FASTER THAN YOU LOOK!!
SUTA (STRIDE)
TA TA

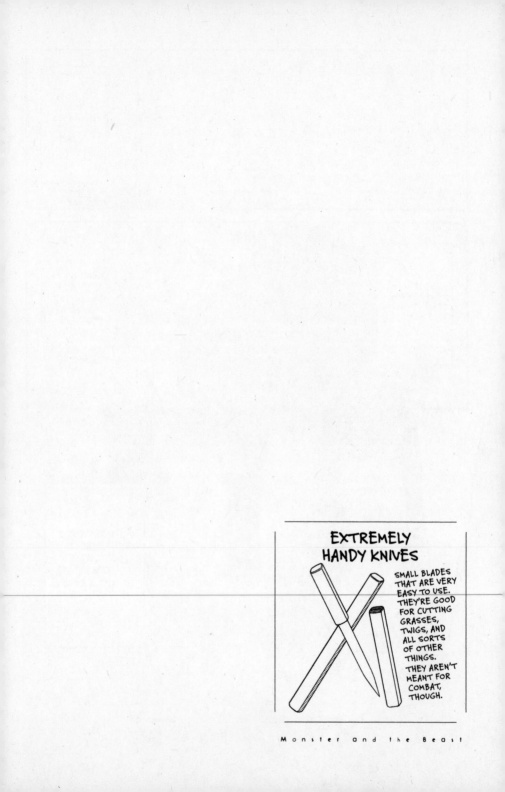

EXTREMELY
HANDY KNIVES

SMALL BLADES
THAT ARE VERY
EASY TO USE.
THEY'RE GOOD
FOR CUTTING
GRASSES,
TWIGS, AND
ALL SORTS
OF OTHER
THINGS.

THEY AREN'T
MEANT FOR
COMBAT,
THOUGH.

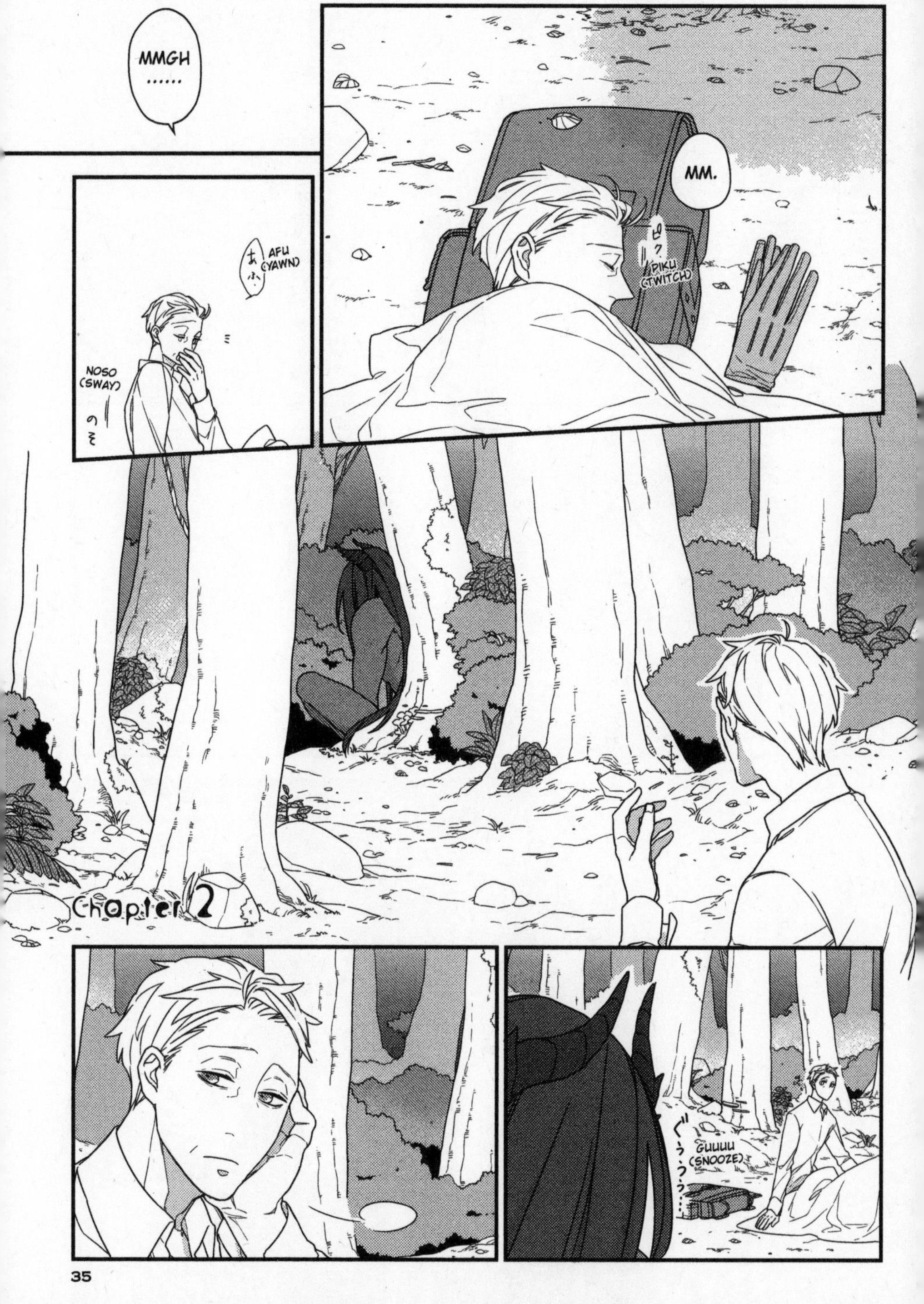
MM.
ピク
PIKU (TWITCH)
MMGH ......
あふ
AFU (YAWN)
NOSO (SWAY)
のそ
Chapter 2
ぐぅぅぅ……
GUUUU (SNOOZE)

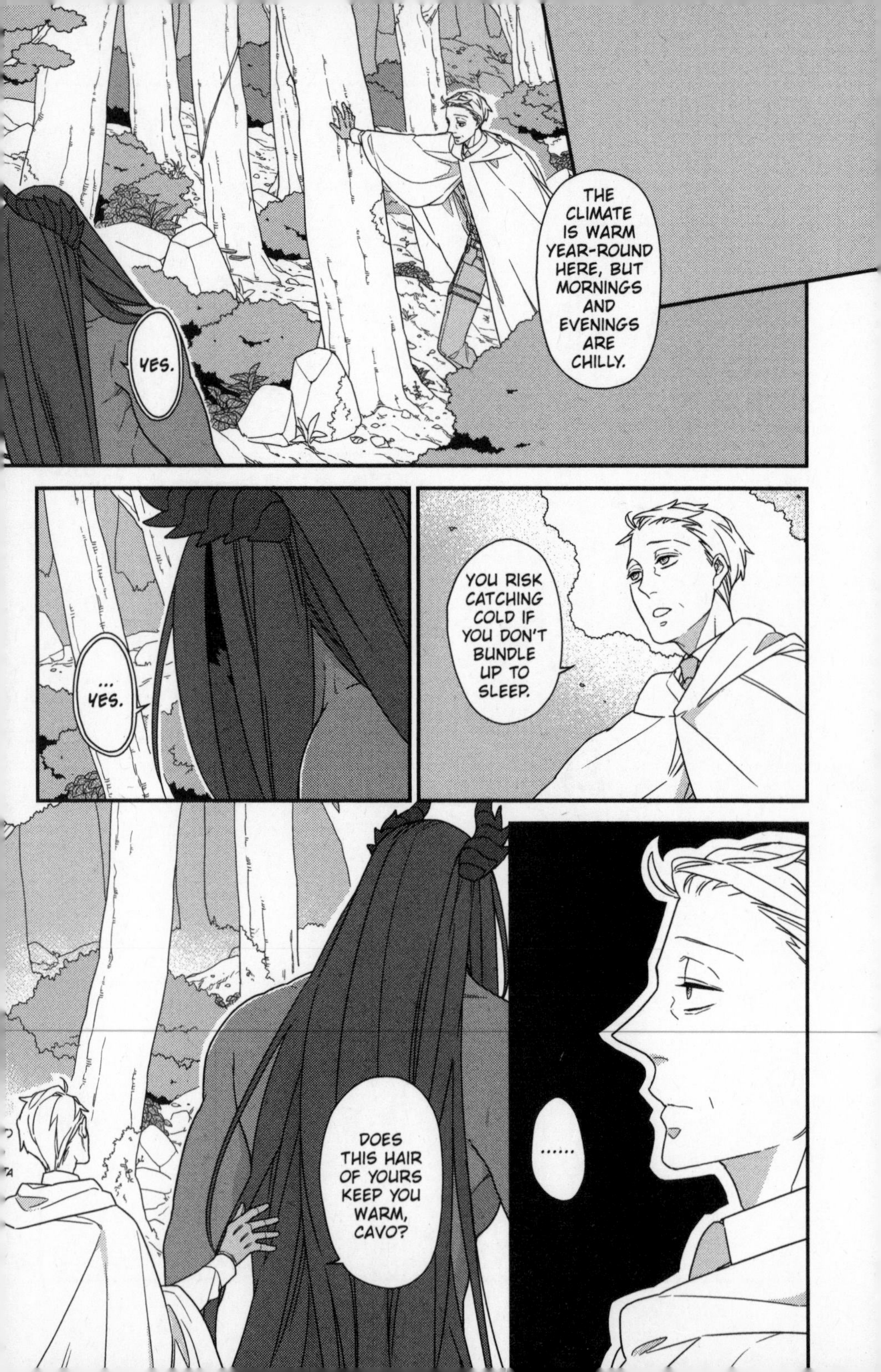
THE CLIMATE IS WARM YEAR-ROUND HERE, BUT MORNINGS AND EVENINGS ARE CHILLY.
YES.
YOU RISK CATCHING COLD IF YOU DON'T BUNDLE UP TO SLEEP.
... YES.
......
DOES THIS HAIR OF YOURS KEEP YOU WARM, CAVO?

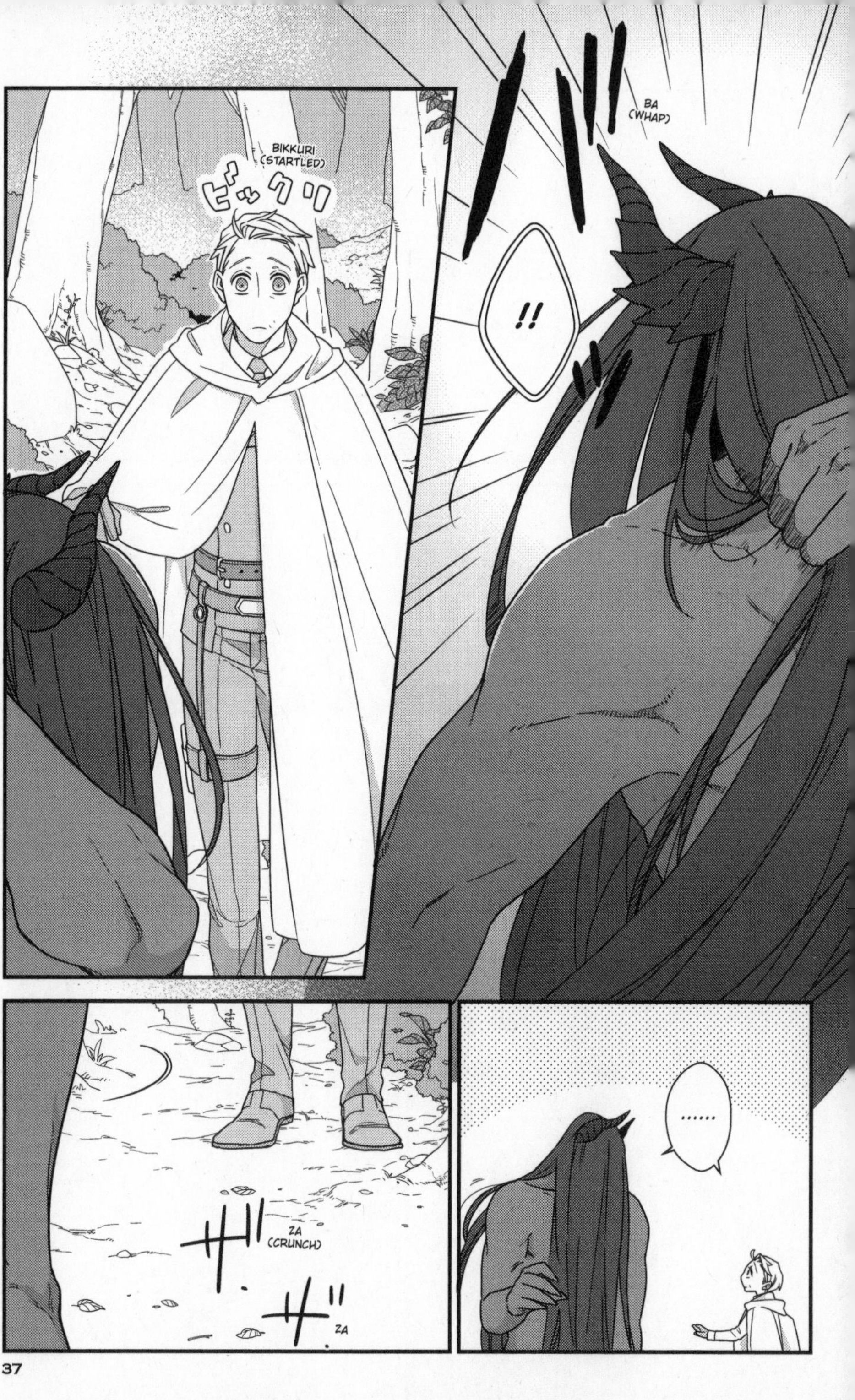
BA (WHAP)
!!
BIKKURI (STARTLED)
ビックリ
......
ZA (CRUNCH)
ZA

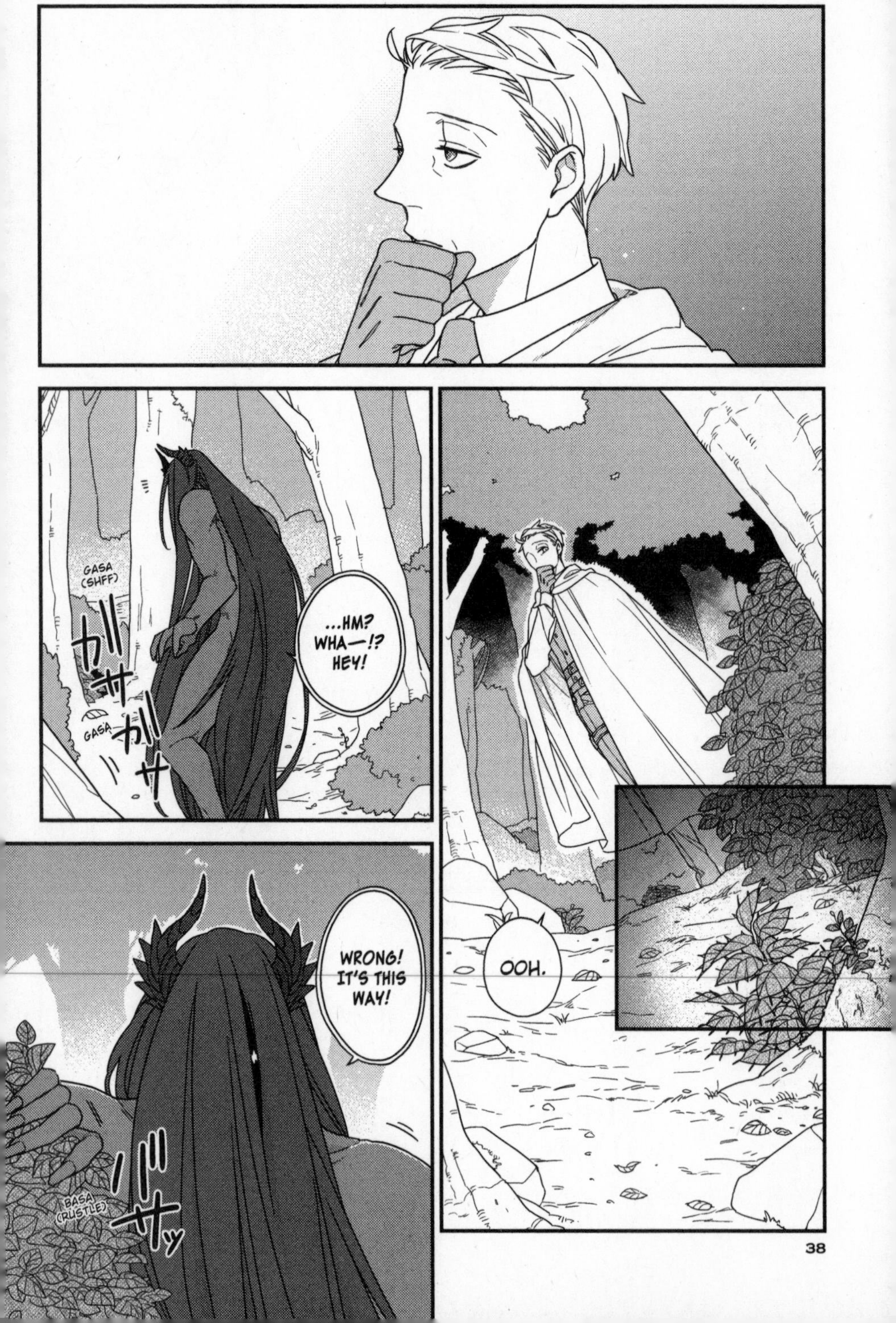
OOH.
...HM? WHA—!? HEY!
GASA (SHFF)
ガサ
GASA
ガサ
WRONG! IT'S THIS WAY!
BASA (RUSTLE)
バサッ

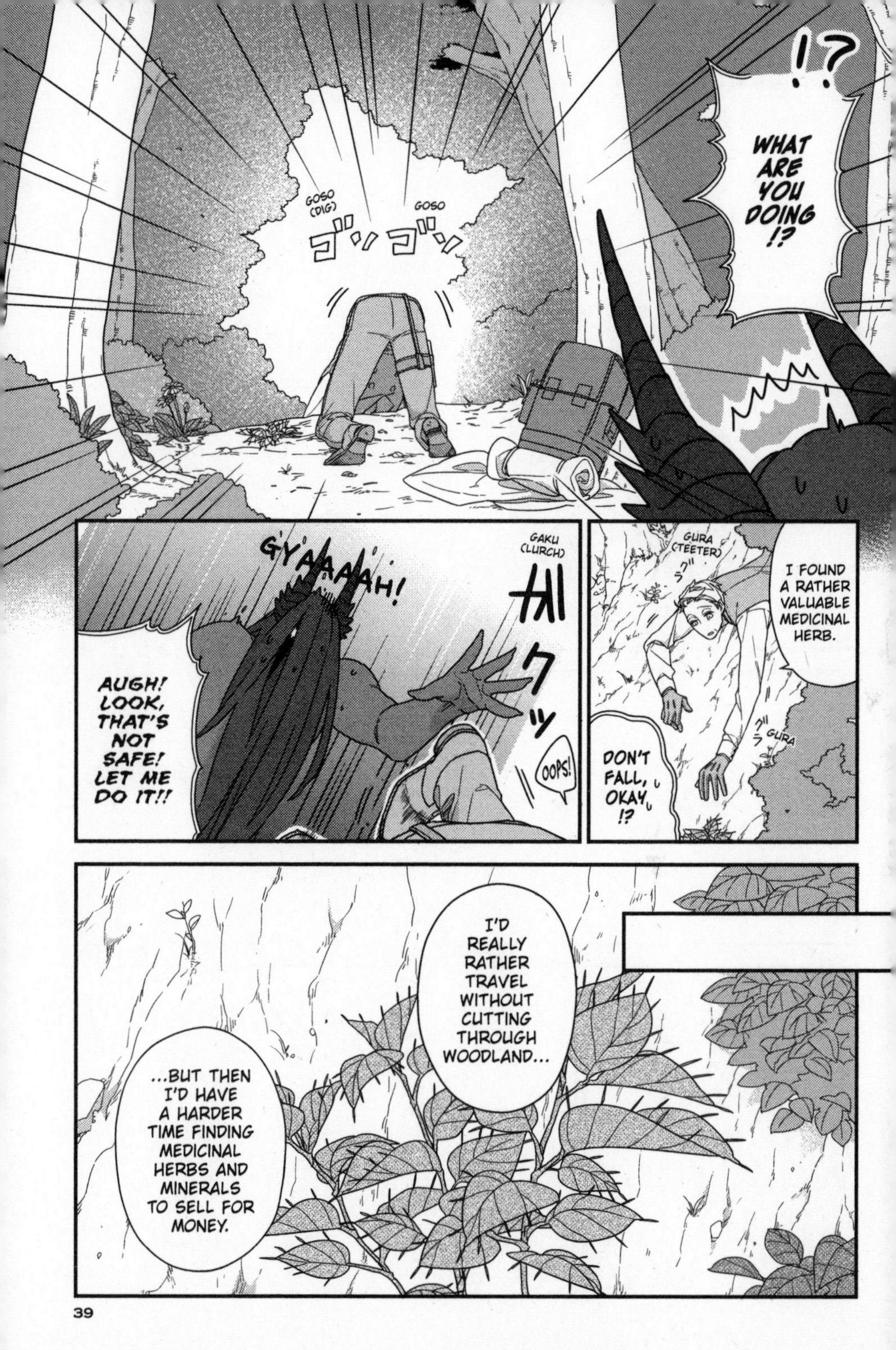
!?
WHAT ARE YOU DOING !?
GOSO (DIG) GOSO
ゴソゴソ
I FOUND A RATHER VALUABLE MEDICINAL HERB.
GURA (TEETER)
GURA
DON'T FALL, OKAY !?
GAKU (LURCH)
ガクッ
GYAAAAAH!
OOPS!
AUGH! LOOK, THAT'S NOT SAFE! LET ME DO IT!!
I'D REALLY RATHER TRAVEL WITHOUT CUTTING THROUGH WOODLAND...
...BUT THEN I'D HAVE A HARDER TIME FINDING MEDICINAL HERBS AND MINERALS TO SELL FOR MONEY.

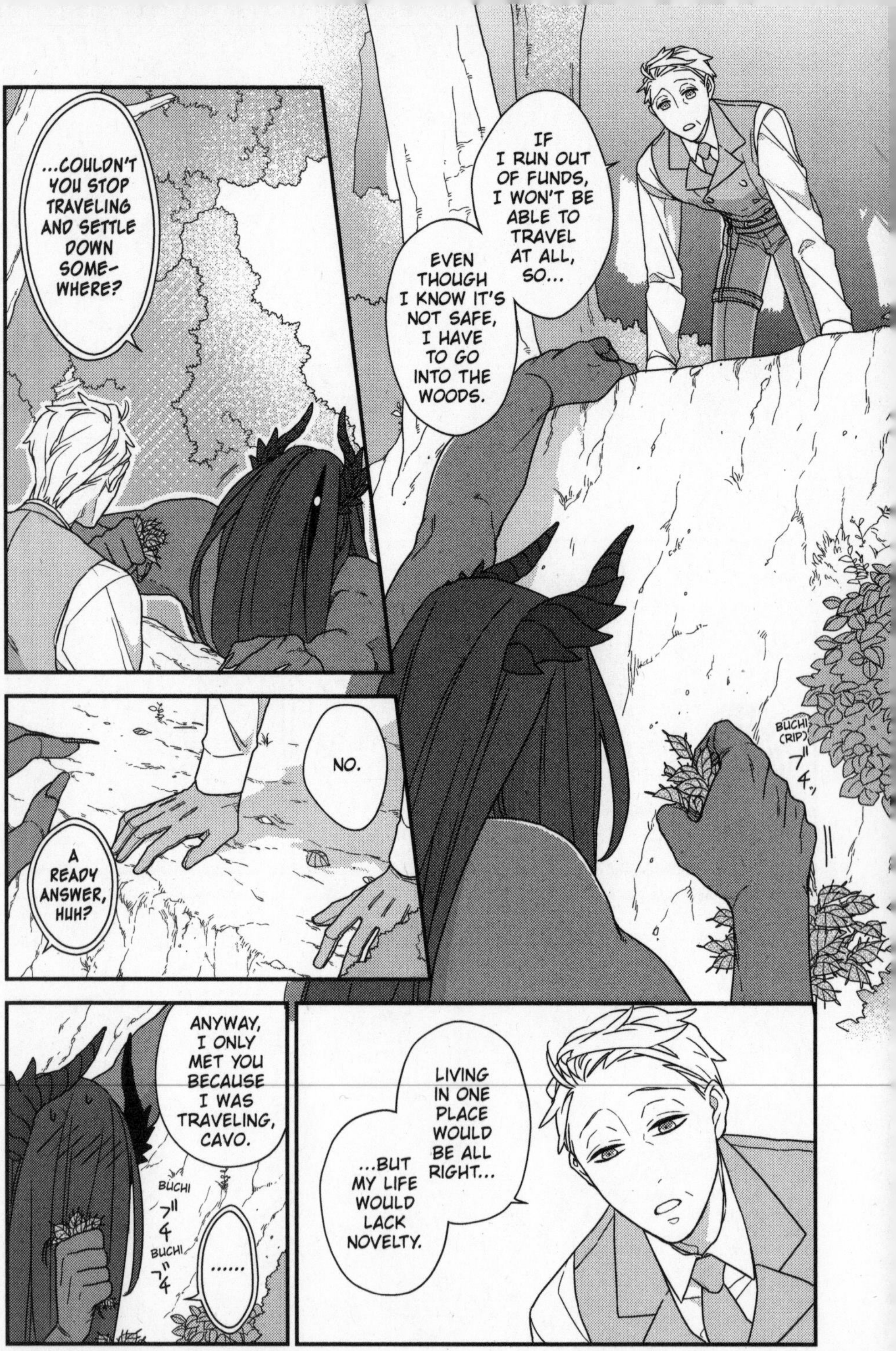
IF I RUN OUT OF FUNDS, I WON'T BE ABLE TO TRAVEL AT ALL, SO...
EVEN THOUGH I KNOW IT'S NOT SAFE, I HAVE TO GO INTO THE WOODS.
BUCHI (RIP)
ブチッ
...COULDN'T YOU STOP TRAVELING AND SETTLE DOWN SOME-WHERE?
NO.
A READY ANSWER, HUH?
LIVING IN ONE PLACE WOULD BE ALL RIGHT...
...BUT MY LIFE WOULD LACK NOVELTY.
ANYWAY, I ONLY MET YOU BECAUSE I WAS TRAVELING, CAVO.
BUCHI
ブチ
BUCHI
ブチ
......

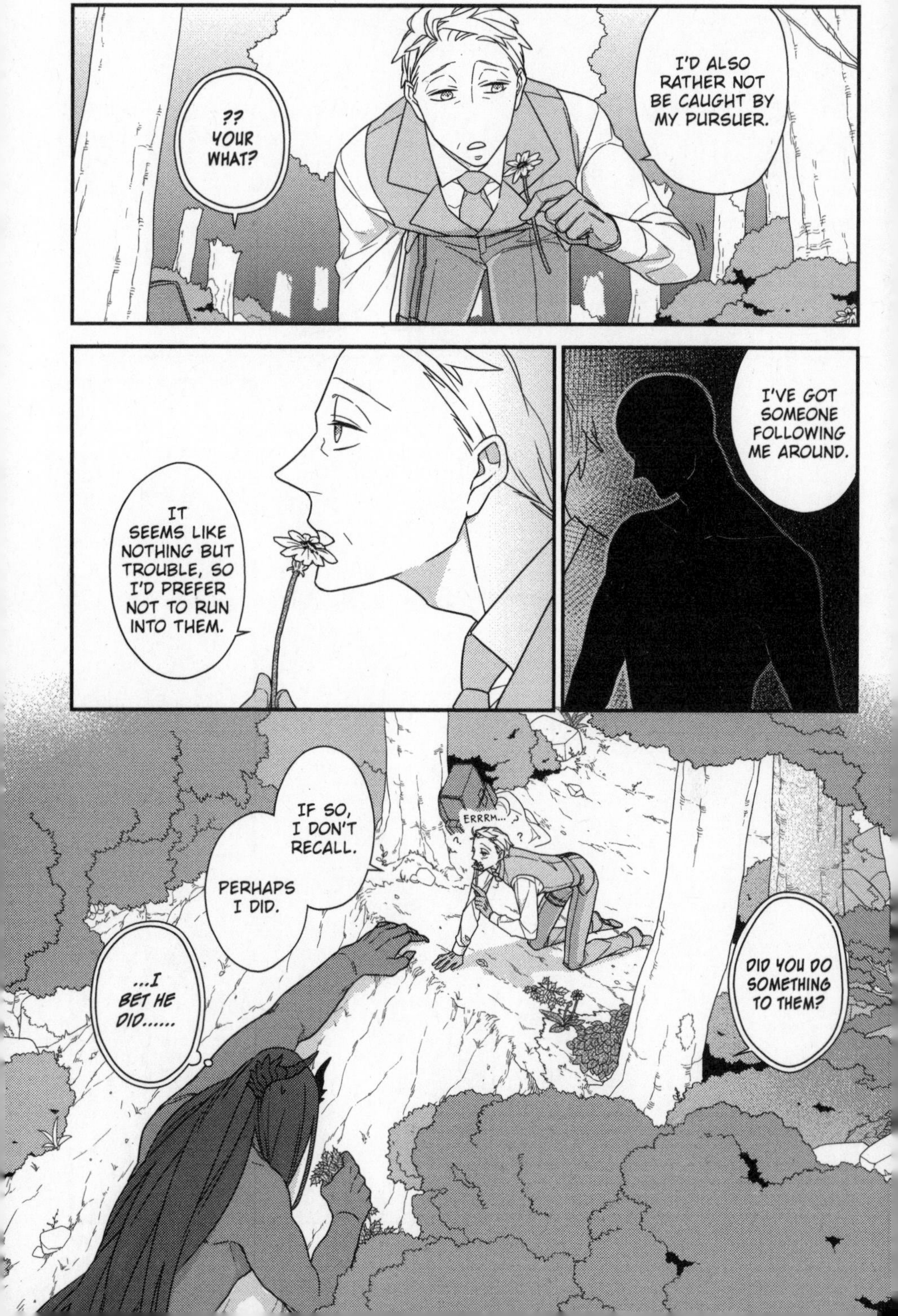
I'D ALSO RATHER NOT BE CAUGHT BY MY PURSUER.
?? YOUR WHAT?
I'VE GOT SOMEONE FOLLOWING ME AROUND.
IT SEEMS LIKE NOTHING BUT TROUBLE, SO I'D PREFER NOT TO RUN INTO THEM.
DID YOU DO SOMETHING TO THEM?
IF SO, I DON'T RECALL.
PERHAPS I DID.
ERRRM...
...I BET HE DID......

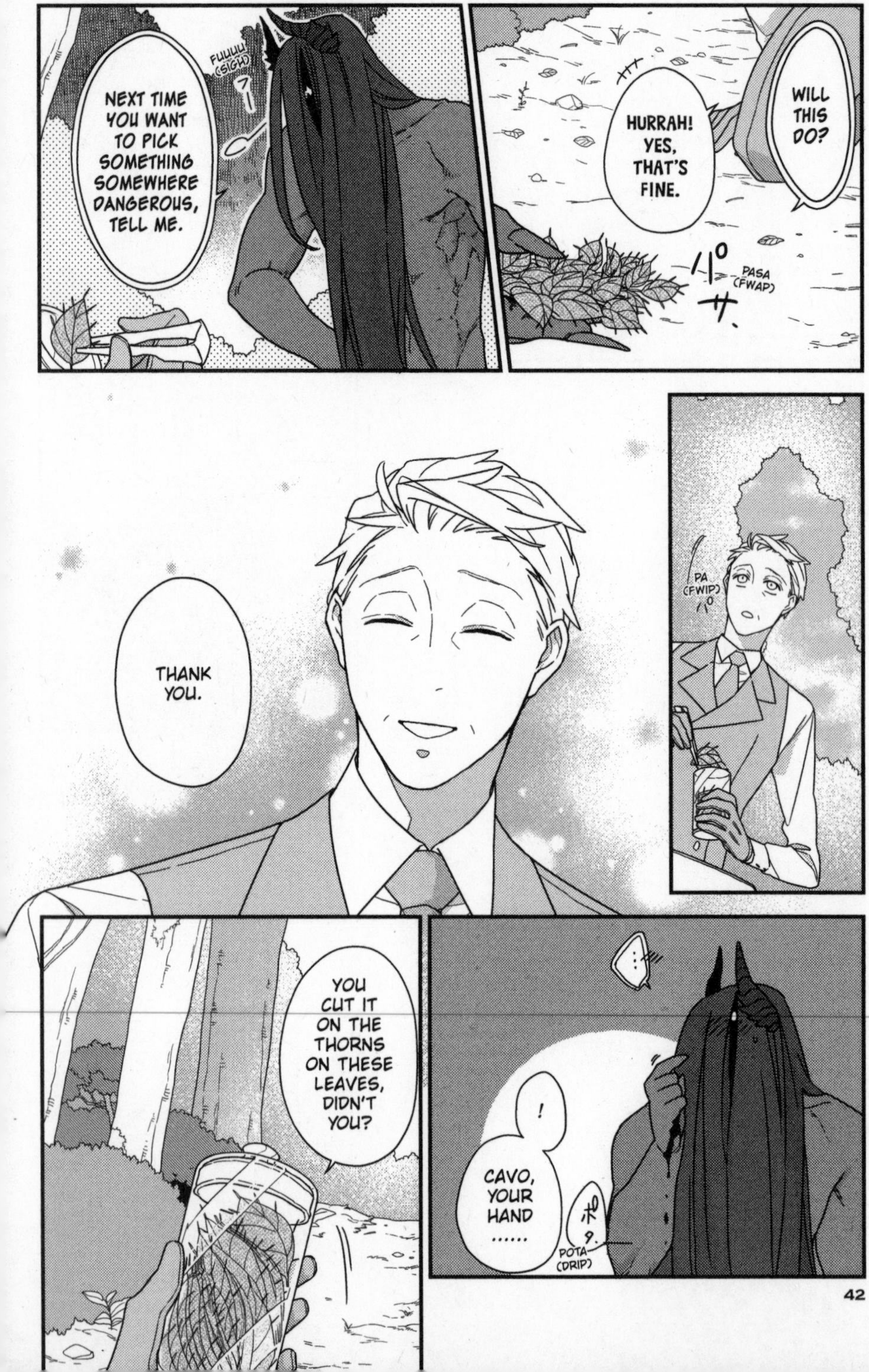
WILL THIS DO?
HURRAH! YES, THAT'S FINE.
PASA (FWAP)
FUUUUU (SIGH)
NEXT TIME YOU WANT TO PICK SOMETHING SOMEWHERE DANGEROUS, TELL ME.
PA (FWIP)
THANK YOU.
......
!
CAVO, YOUR HAND ......
POTA (DRIP)
YOU CUT IT ON THE THORNS ON THESE LEAVES, DIDN'T YOU?

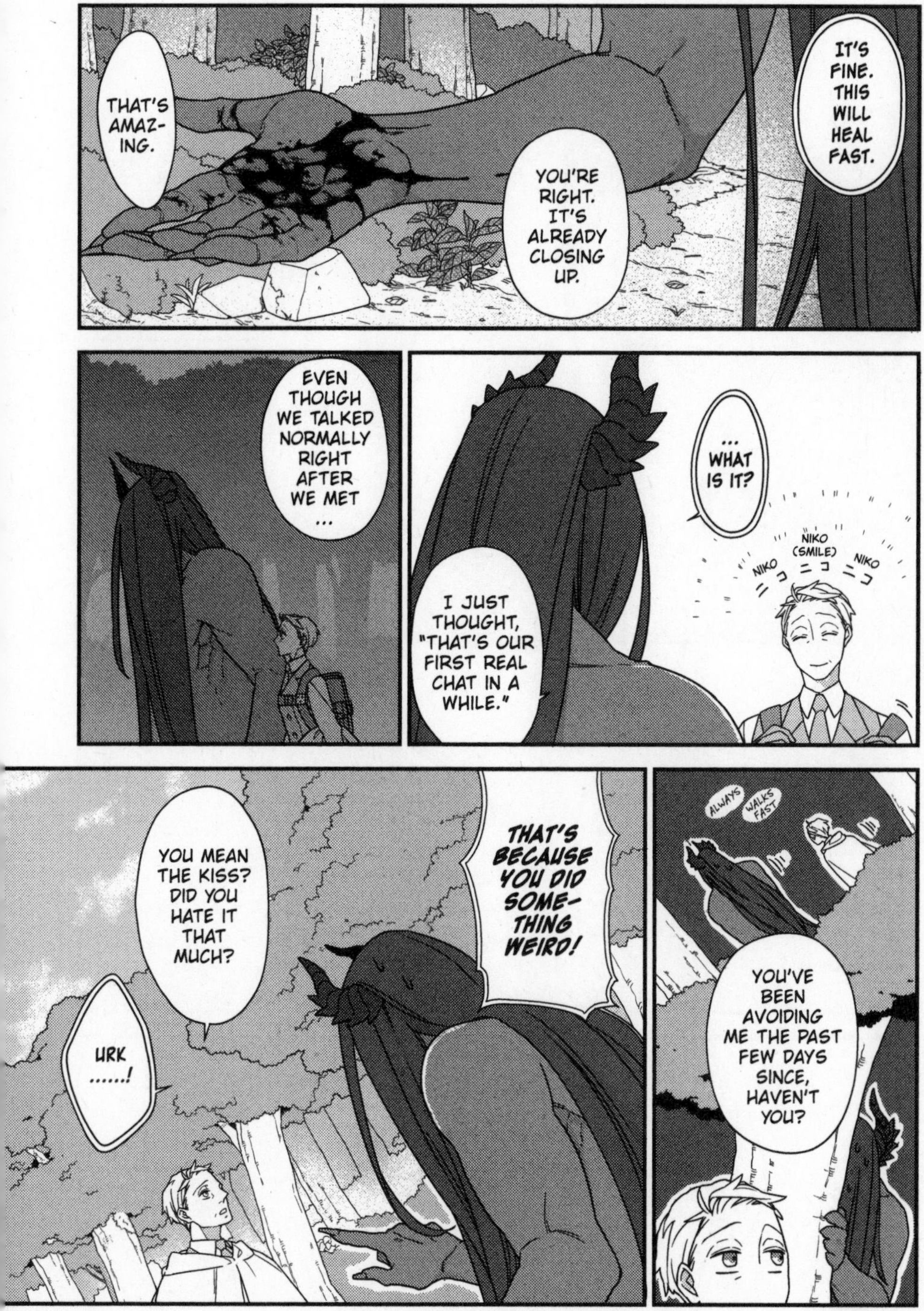
IT'S FINE. THIS WILL HEAL FAST.
YOU'RE RIGHT. IT'S ALREADY CLOSING UP.
THAT'S AMAZ-ING.
... WHAT IS IT?
NIKO ニコ
NIKO (SMILE) ニコ
NIKO ニコ
I JUST THOUGHT, "THAT'S OUR FIRST REAL CHAT IN A WHILE."
EVEN THOUGH WE TALKED NORMALLY RIGHT AFTER WE MET ...
ALWAYS WALKS FAST
YOU'VE BEEN AVOIDING ME THE PAST FEW DAYS SINCE, HAVEN'T YOU?
THAT'S BECAUSE YOU DID SOME-THING WEIRD!
YOU MEAN THE KISS? DID YOU HATE IT THAT MUCH?
URK ......!

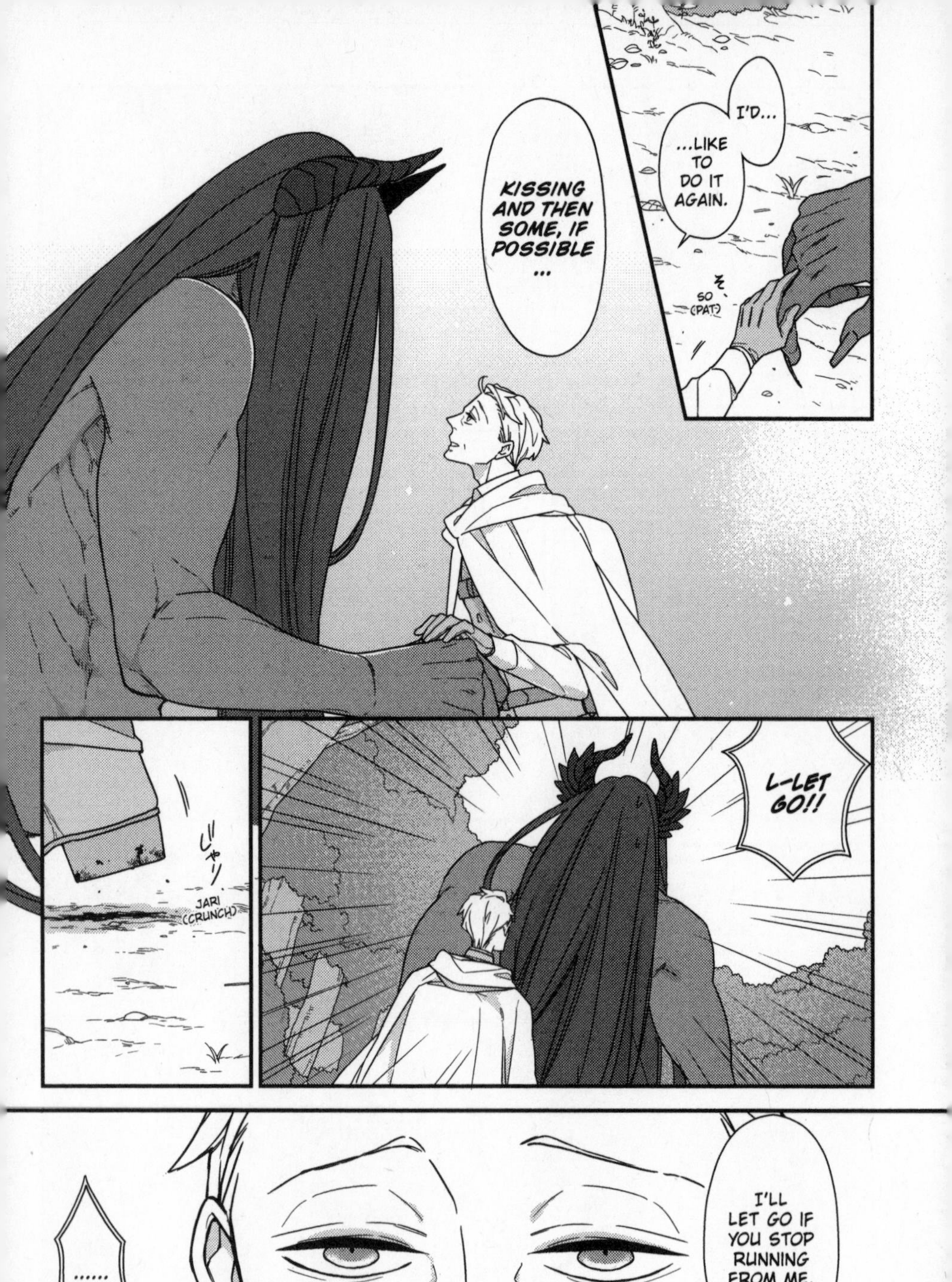
I'D...
...LIKE TO DO IT AGAIN.
SO (PAT)
KISSING AND THEN SOME, IF POSSIBLE ...
L-LET GO!!
じゃり
JARI (CRUNCH)
I'LL LET GO IF YOU STOP RUNNING FROM ME.
......RGH!

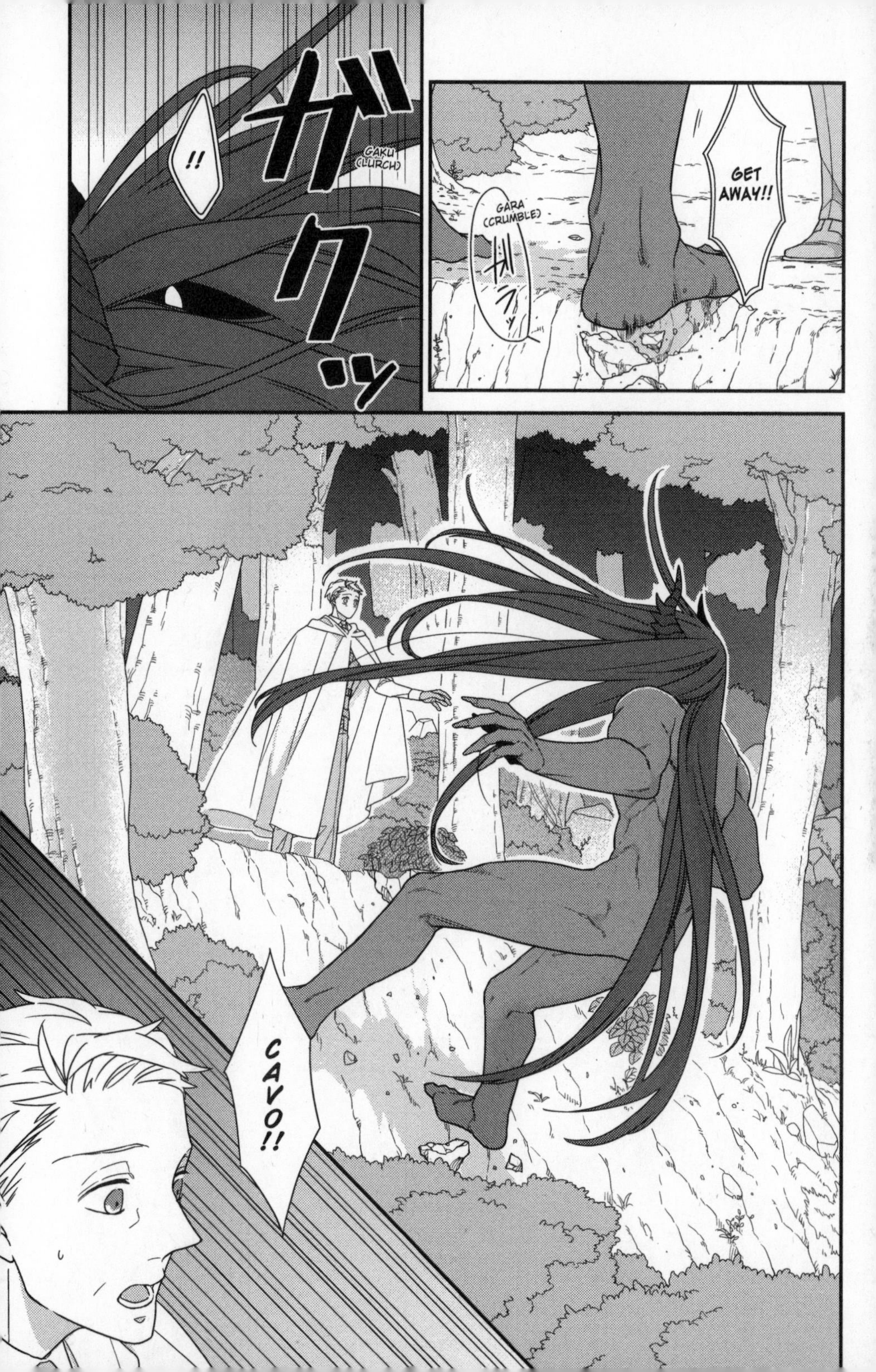
GET AWAY!!
GARA (CRUMBLE)
ガラッ
!!
ガクッ
GAKU (LURCH)
CAVO!!

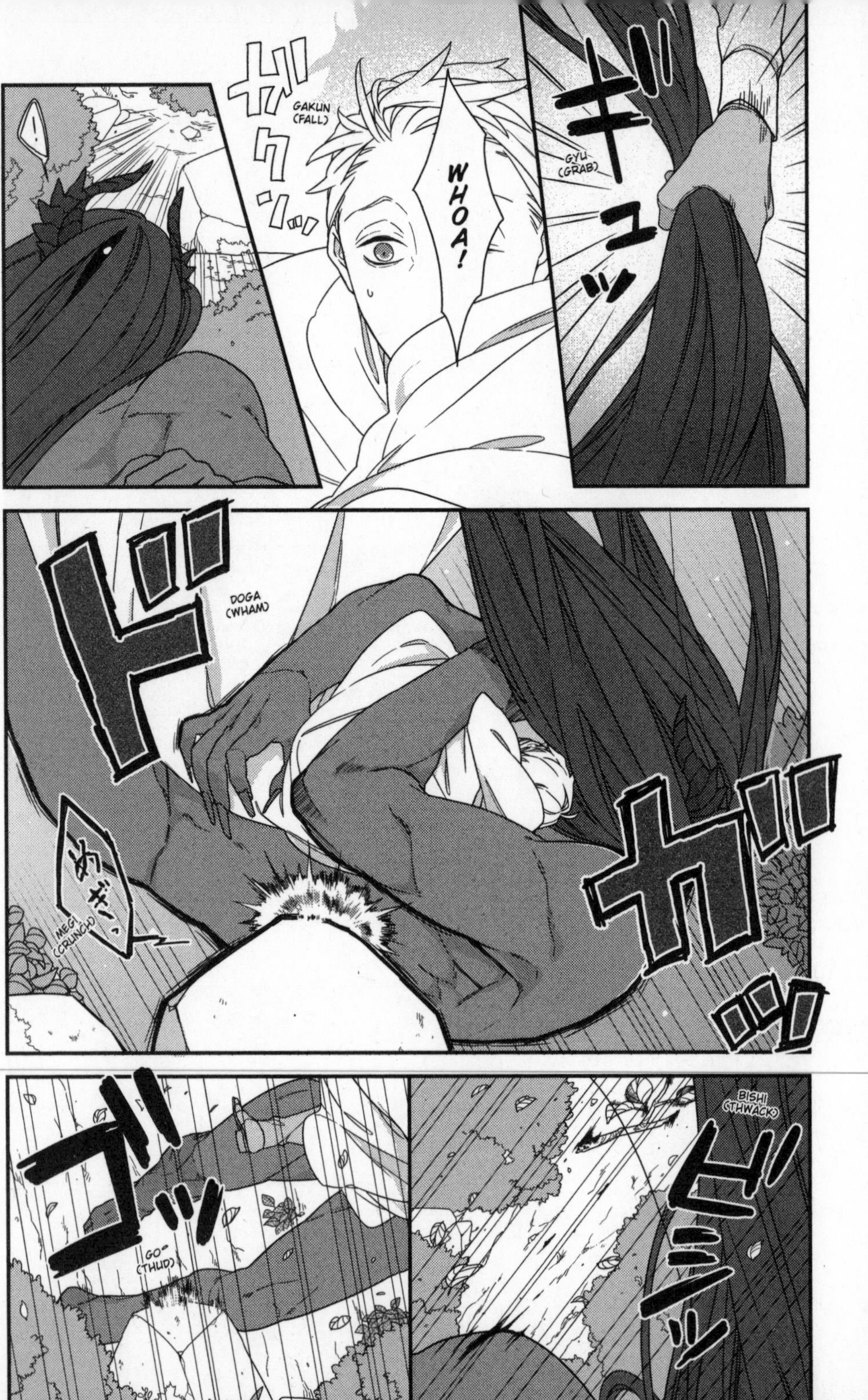
GYU
(GRAB)
GAKUN
(FALL)
WHOA!
!
DOGA
(WHAM)
MEGI
(CRUNCH)
BISHI
(THWACK)
GO
(THUD)

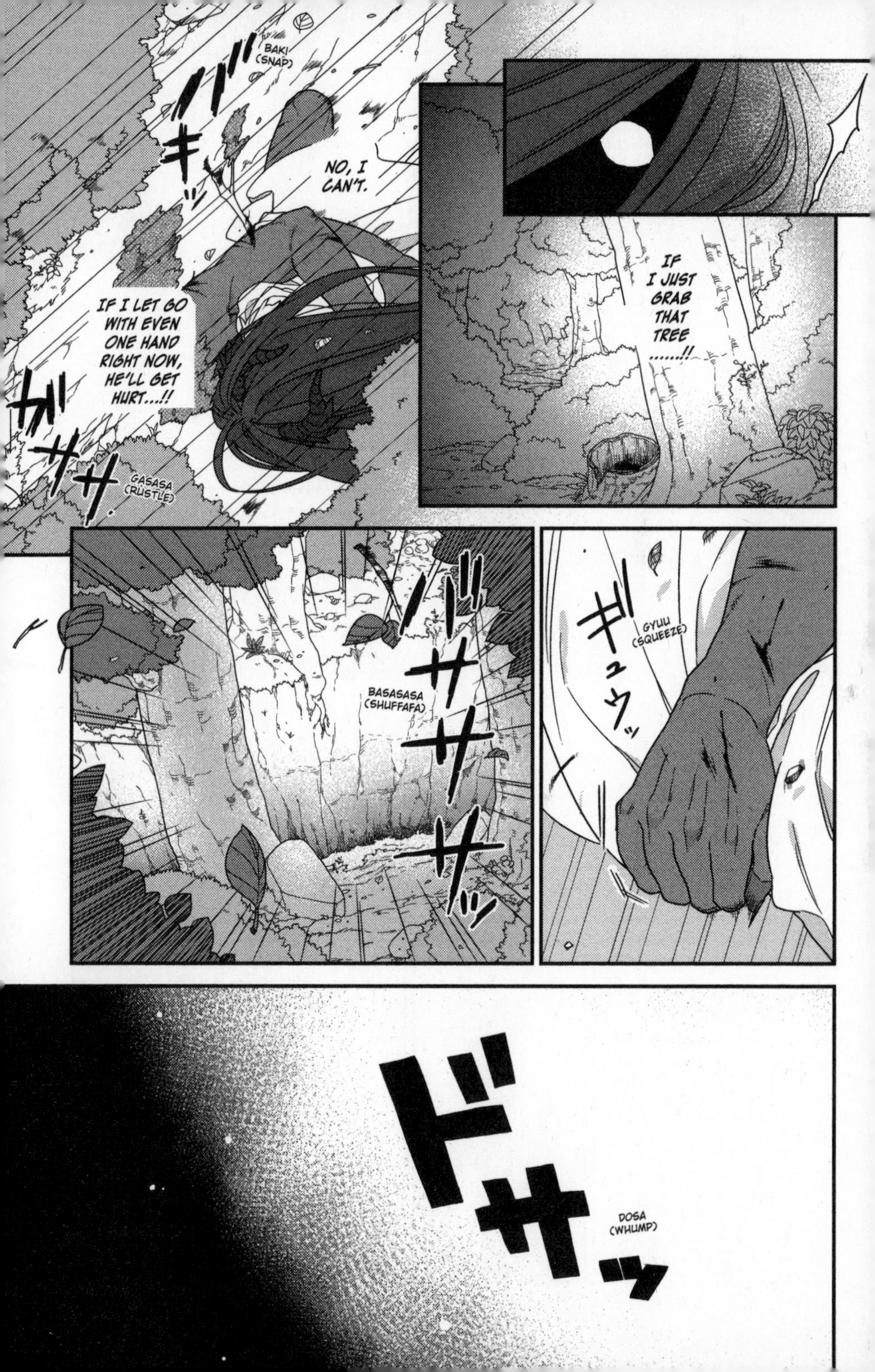
IF I JUST GRAB THAT TREE......!!
バキッ
BAKI (SNAP)
NO, I CAN'T.
IF I LET GO WITH EVEN ONE HAND RIGHT NOW, HE'LL GET HURT...!!
ガササ
GASASA (RUSTLE)
ギュウッ
GYUU (SQUEEZE)
バササササッ
BASASASA (SHUFFAFA)
ドサッ
DOSA (WHUMP)

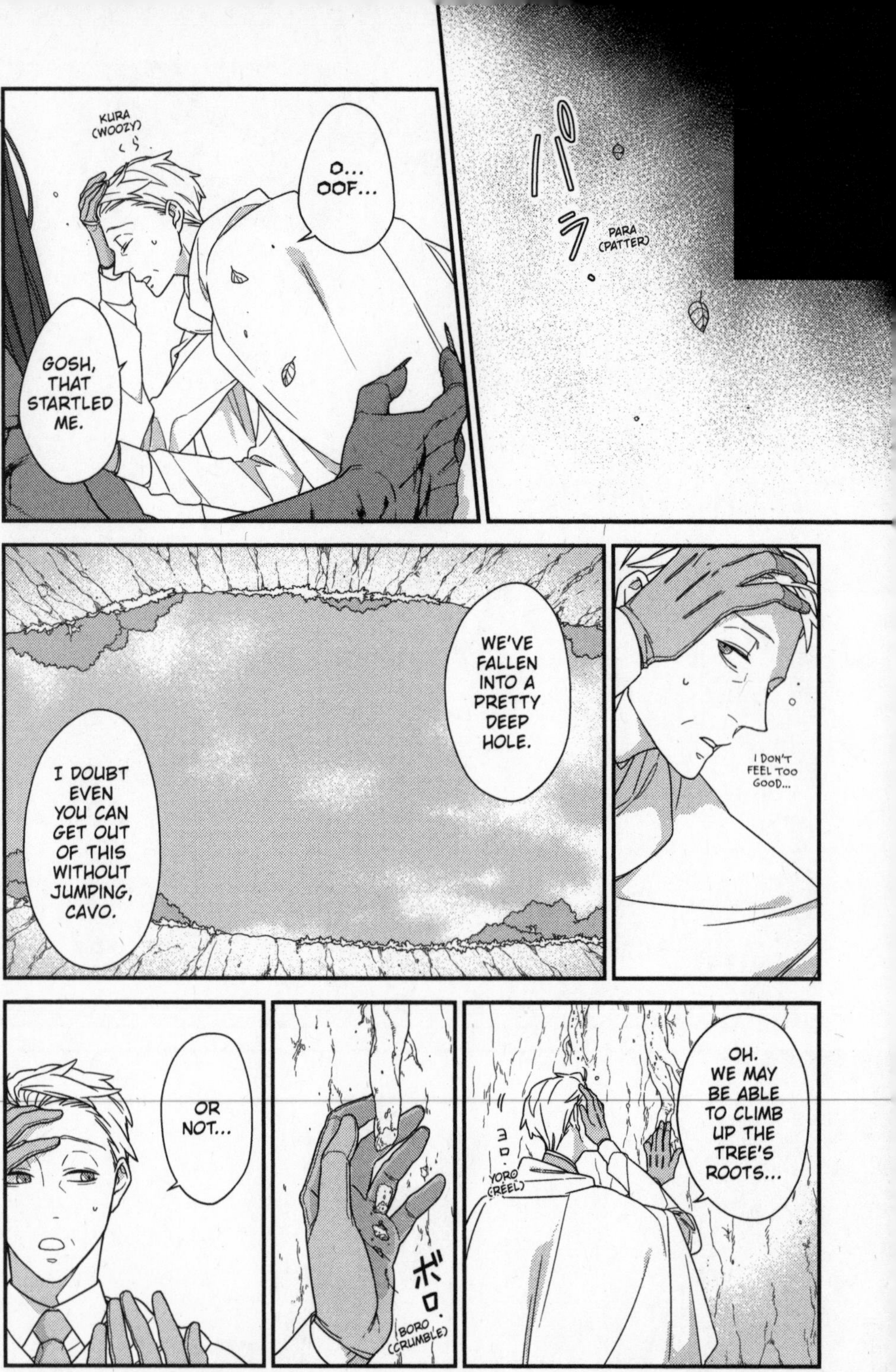
パラ
PARA (PATTER)
KURA (WOOZY)
くら
O... OOF...
GOSH, THAT STARTLED ME.
I DON'T FEEL TOO GOOD...
WE'VE FALLEN INTO A PRETTY DEEP HOLE.
I DOUBT EVEN YOU CAN GET OUT OF THIS WITHOUT JUMPING, CAVO.
OH. WE MAY BE ABLE TO CLIMB UP THE TREE'S ROOTS...
ヨロ
YORO (REEL)
ボロ
BORO (CRUMBLE)
OR NOT...

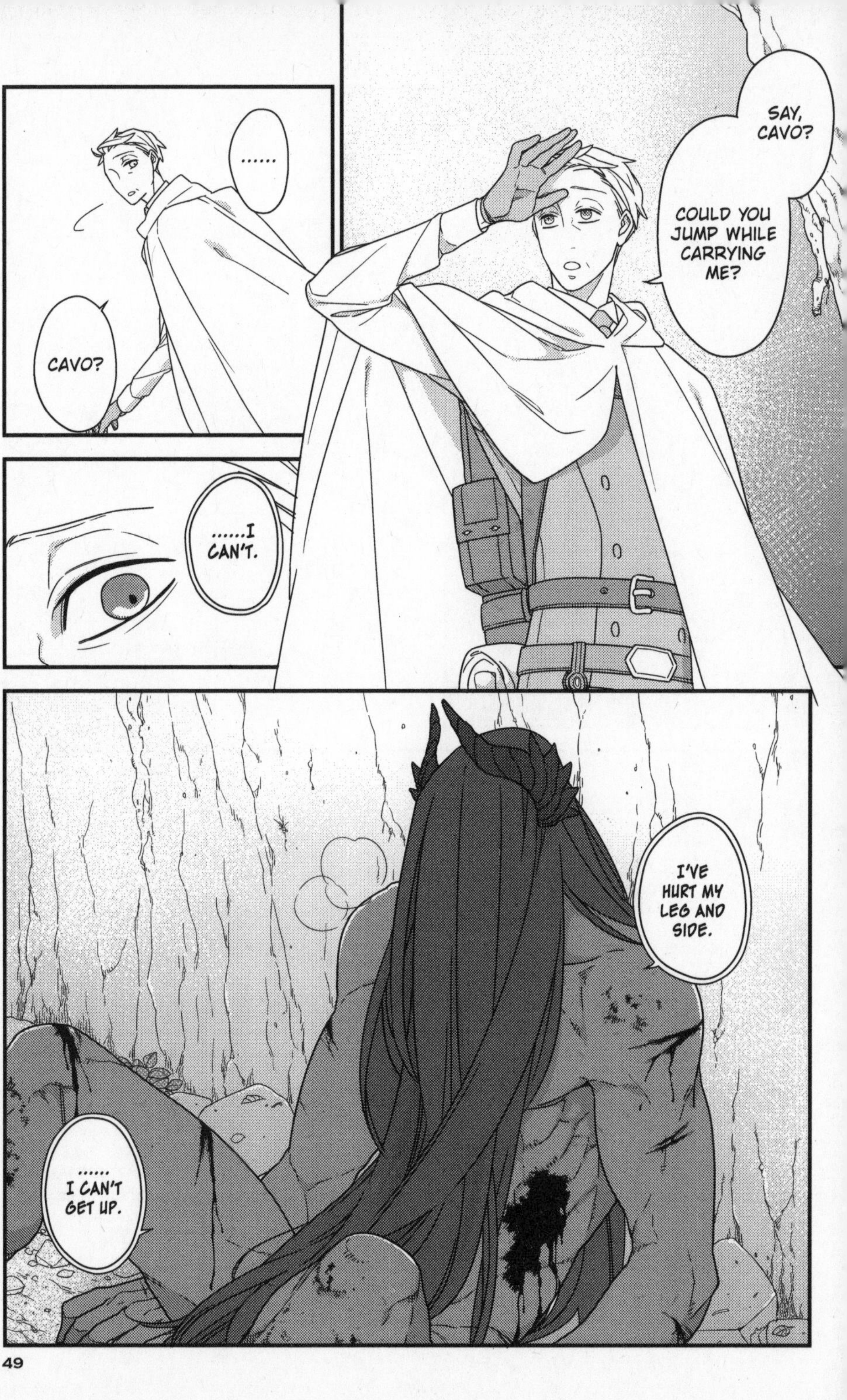
SAY, CAVO?
COULD YOU JUMP WHILE CARRYING ME?
......
CAVO?
......I CAN'T.
I'VE HURT MY LEG AND SIDE.
...... I CAN'T GET UP.

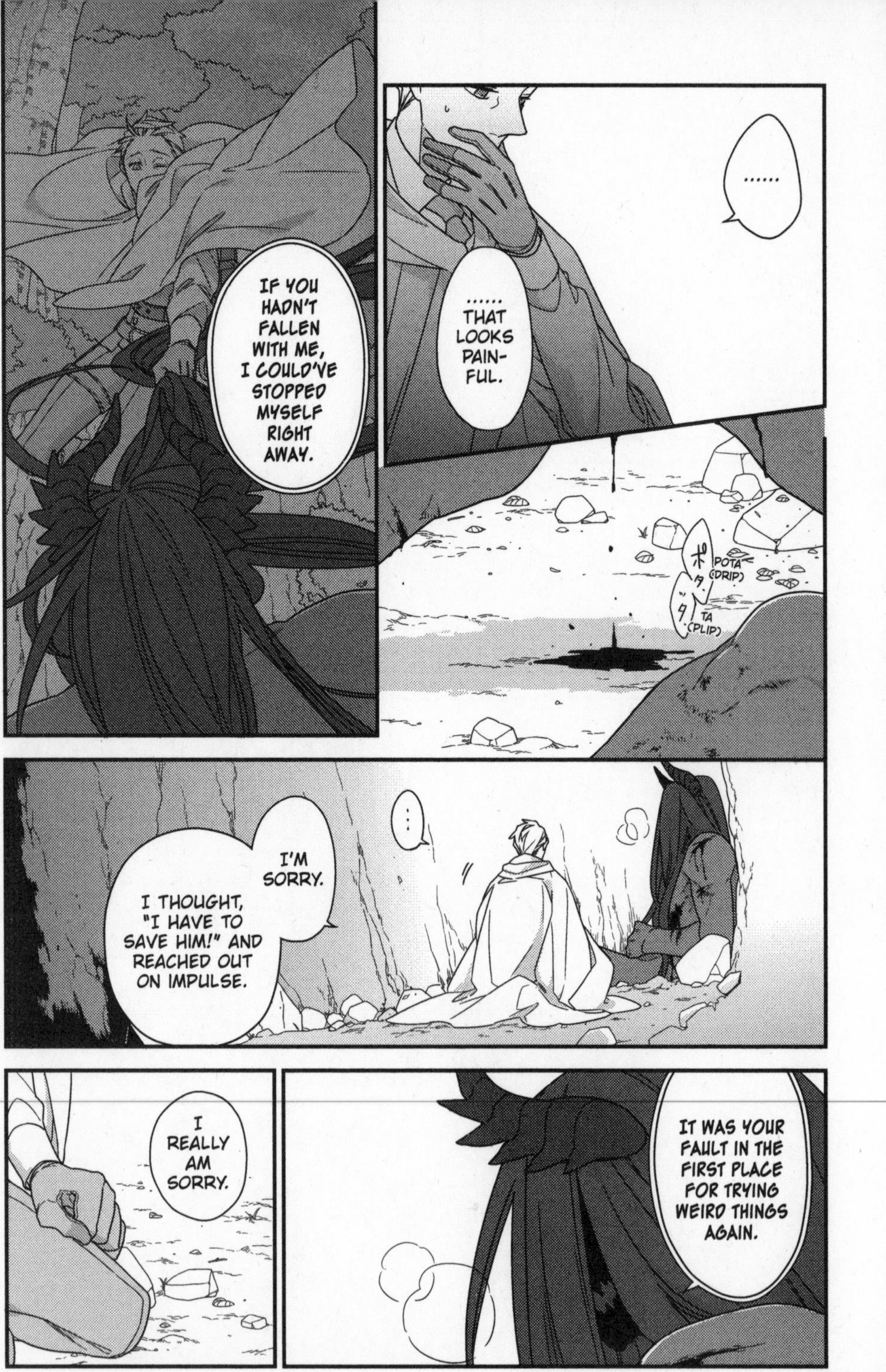
......
...... THAT LOOKS PAIN-FUL.
ポタッ POTA (DRIP)
タ TA (PLIP)
IF YOU HADN'T FALLEN WITH ME, I COULD'VE STOPPED MYSELF RIGHT AWAY.
...
I'M SORRY.
I THOUGHT, "I HAVE TO SAVE HIM!" AND REACHED OUT ON IMPULSE.
IT WAS YOUR FAULT IN THE FIRST PLACE FOR TRYING WEIRD THINGS AGAIN.
I REALLY AM SORRY.

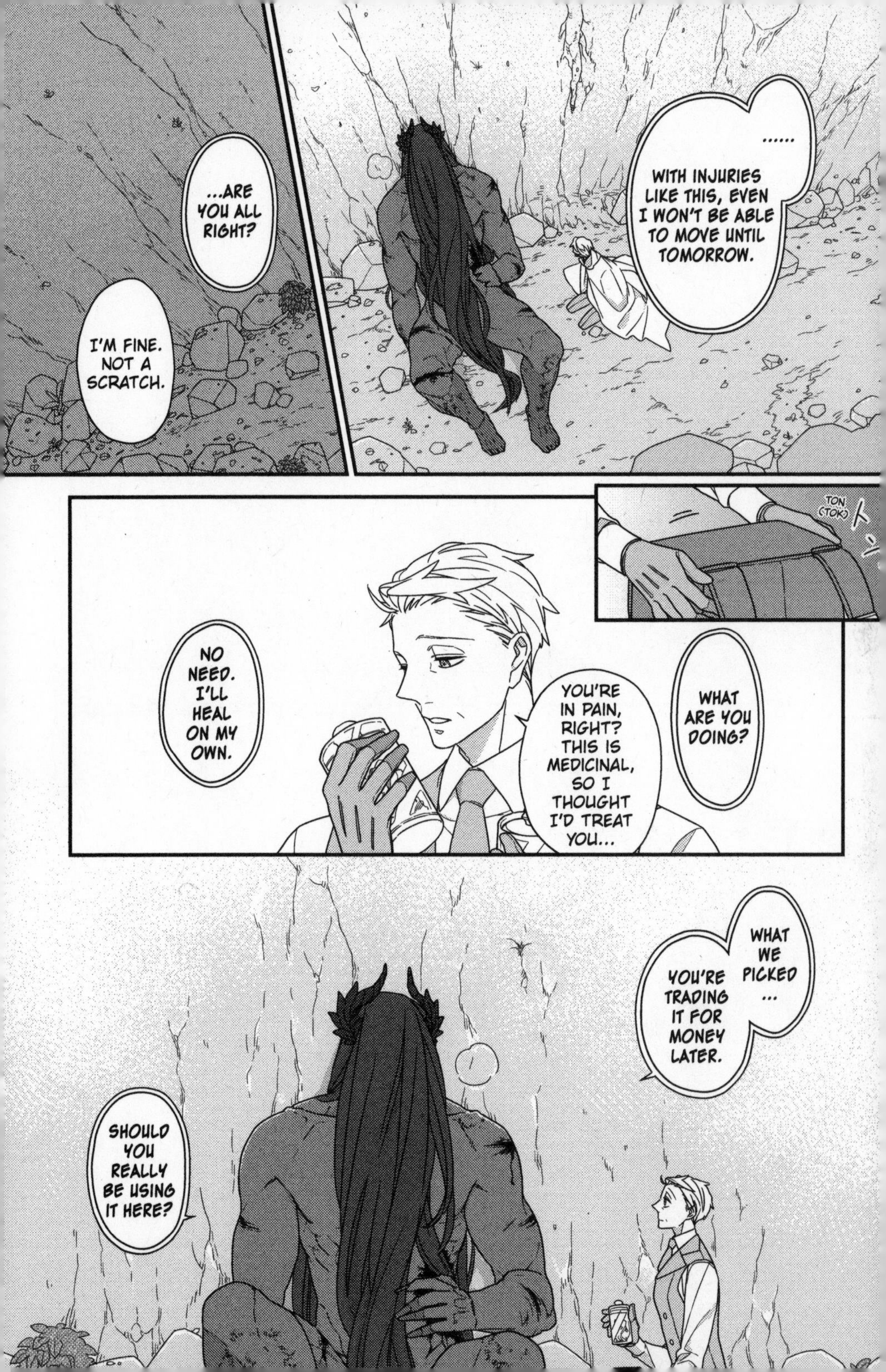
......
WITH INJURIES LIKE THIS, EVEN I WON'T BE ABLE TO MOVE UNTIL TOMORROW.
...ARE YOU ALL RIGHT?
I'M FINE. NOT A SCRATCH.
TON (TOK)
WHAT ARE YOU DOING?
YOU'RE IN PAIN, RIGHT? THIS IS MEDICINAL, SO I THOUGHT I'D TREAT YOU...
NO NEED. I'LL HEAL ON MY OWN.
WHAT WE PICKED...
YOU'RE TRADING IT FOR MONEY LATER.
SHOULD YOU REALLY BE USING IT HERE?

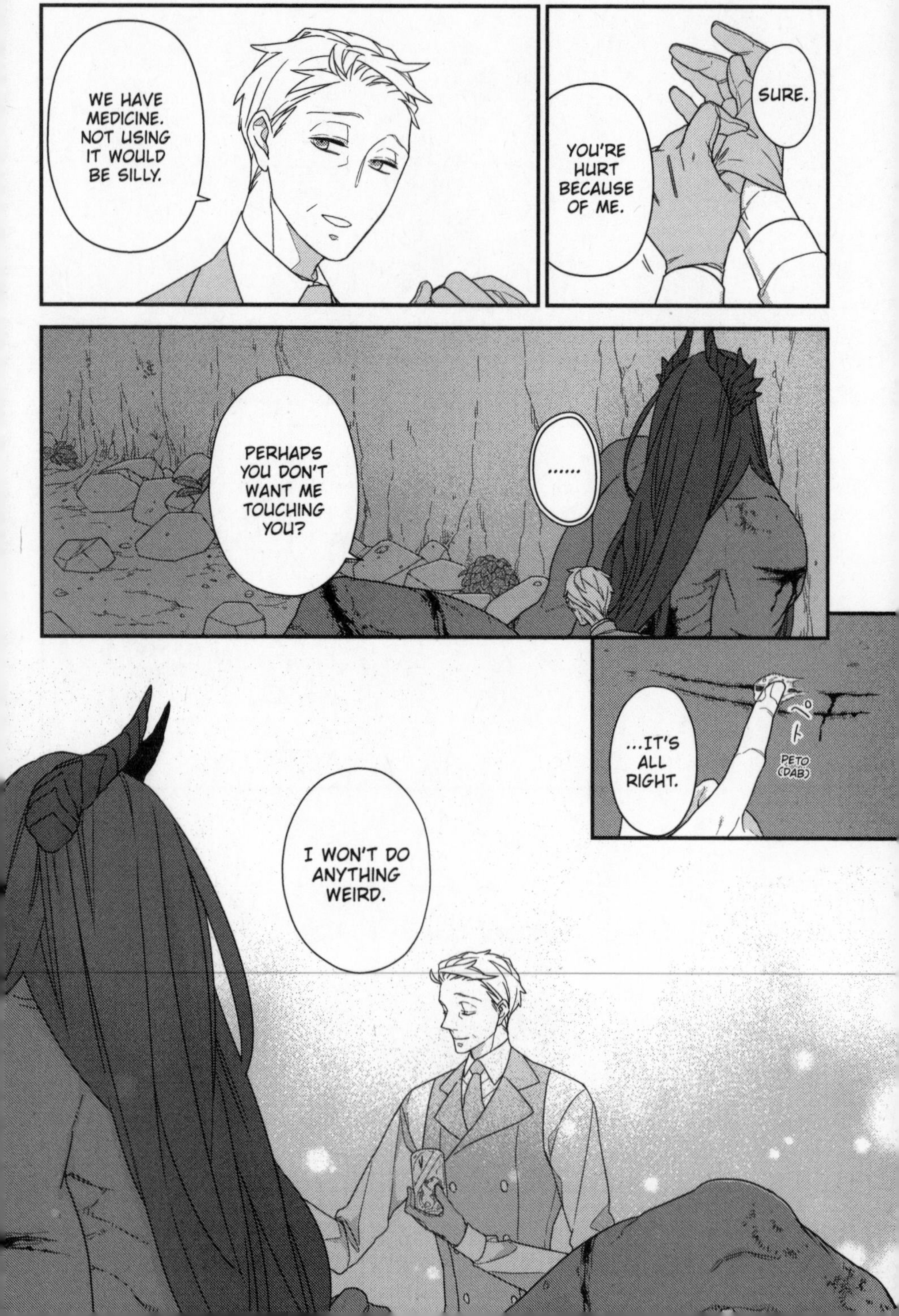
SURE.
YOU'RE HURT BECAUSE OF ME.
WE HAVE MEDICINE. NOT USING IT WOULD BE SILLY.
......
PERHAPS YOU DON'T WANT ME TOUCHING YOU?
ペト
PETO (DAB)
...IT'S ALL RIGHT.
I WON'T DO ANYTHING WEIRD.

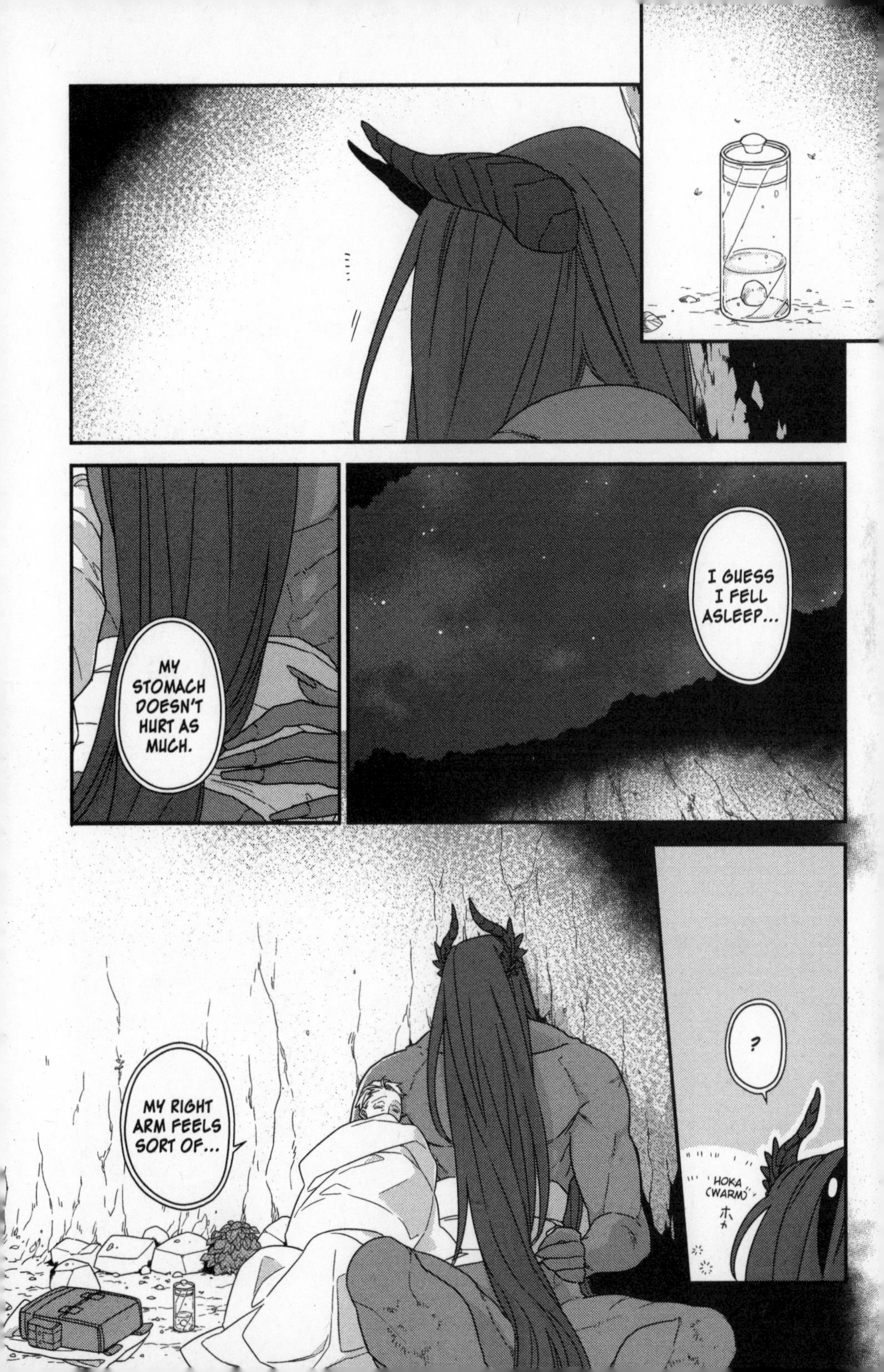
......
I GUESS I FELL ASLEEP...
MY STOMACH DOESN'T HURT AS MUCH.
?
HOKA (WARM)
MY RIGHT ARM FEELS SORT OF...

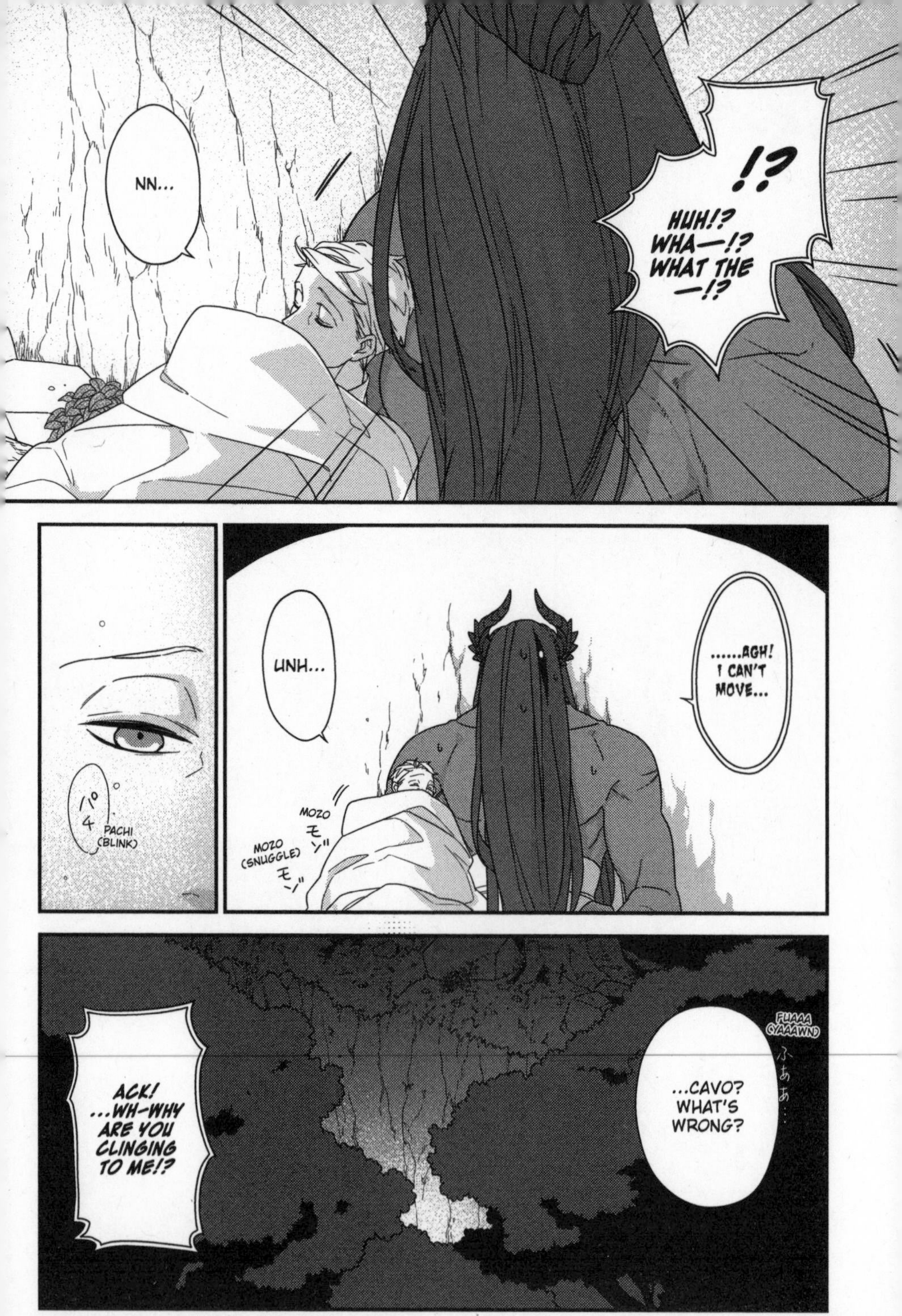
!?
HUH!? WHA—!? WHAT THE —!?
NN...
......AGH! I CAN'T MOVE...
UNH...
MOZO MOZO (SNUGGLE)
モゾモゾ
PACHI (BLINK)
パチ
FUAAA (YAAAWN)
ふぁあ…
...CAVO? WHAT'S WRONG?
ACK! ...WH-WHY ARE YOU CLINGING TO ME!?

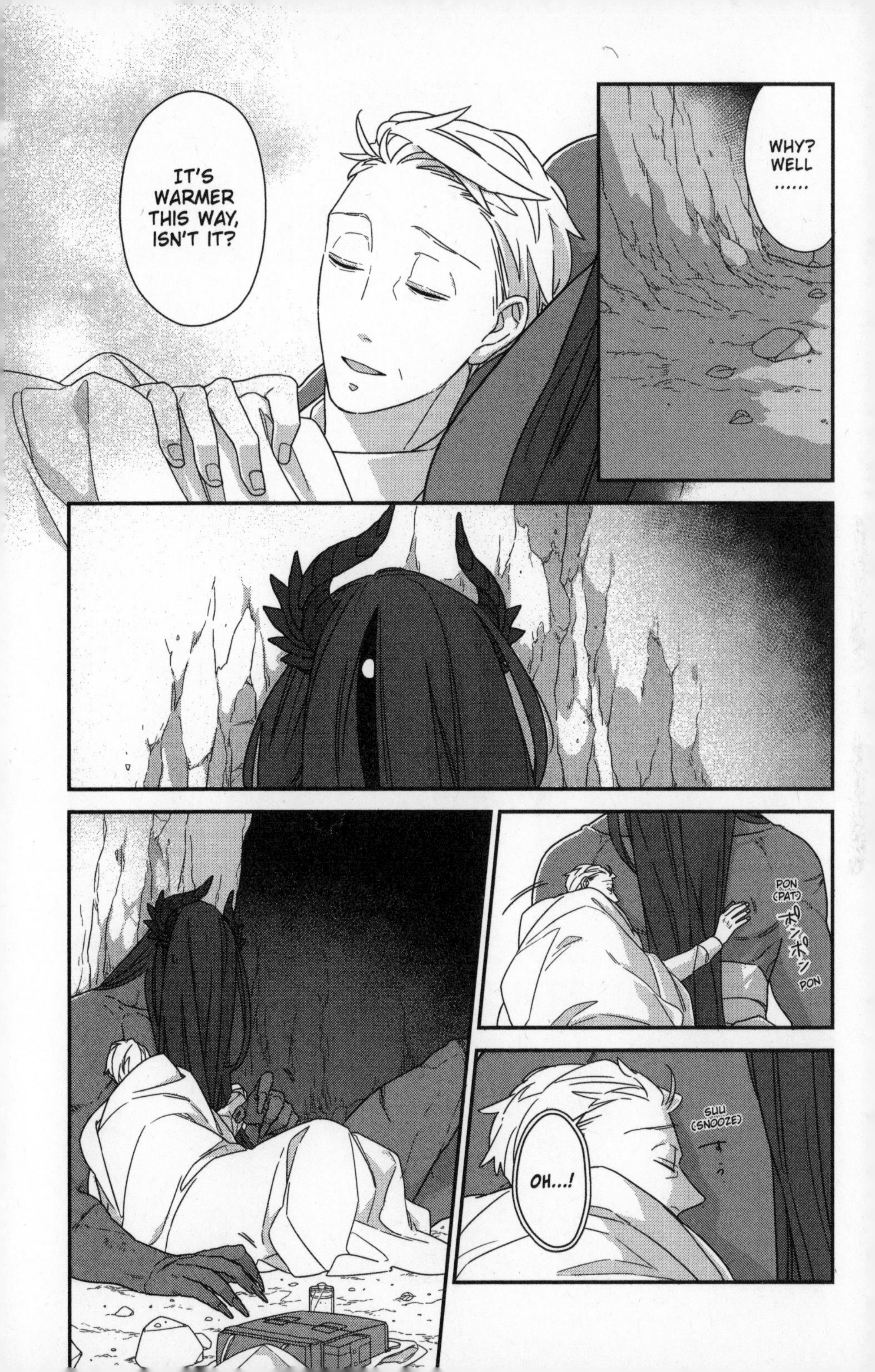
WHY? WELL ......
IT'S WARMER THIS WAY, ISN'T IT?
PON (PAT)
ポンポン
PON
SUU (SNOOZE)
OH...!

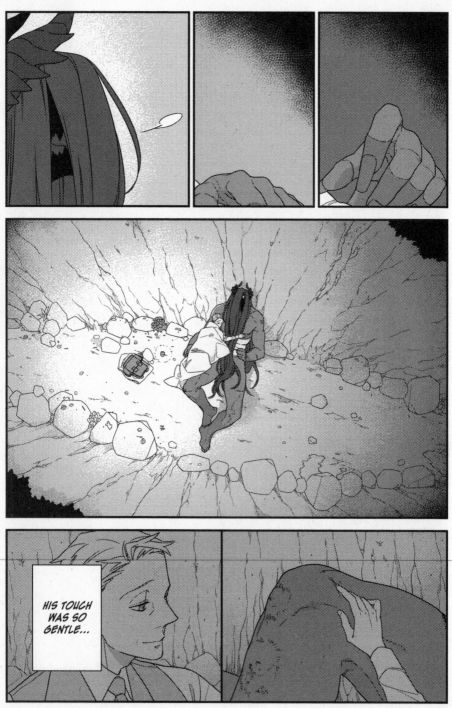

HIS TOUCH
WAS SO
GENTLE...

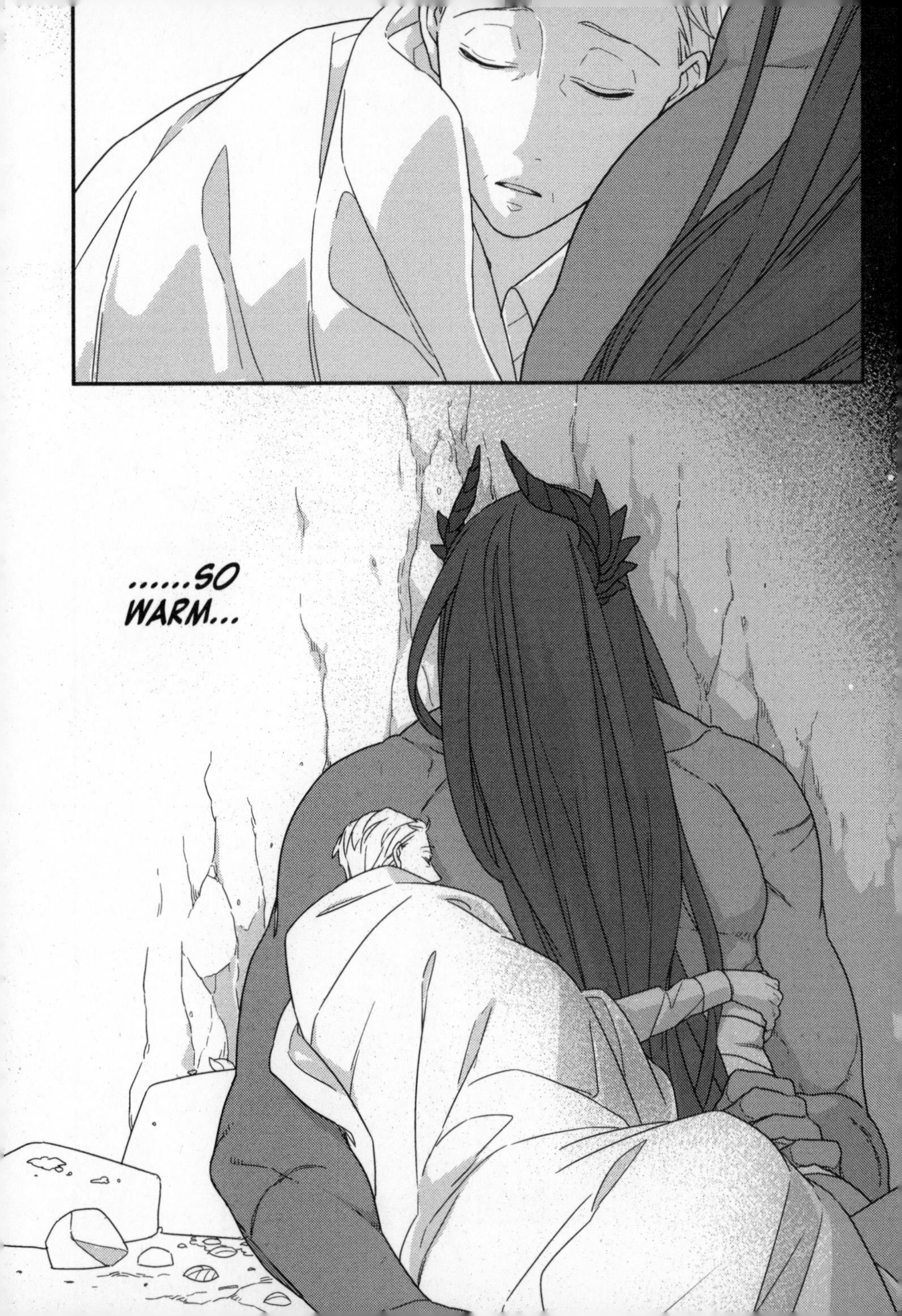
......SO WARM...

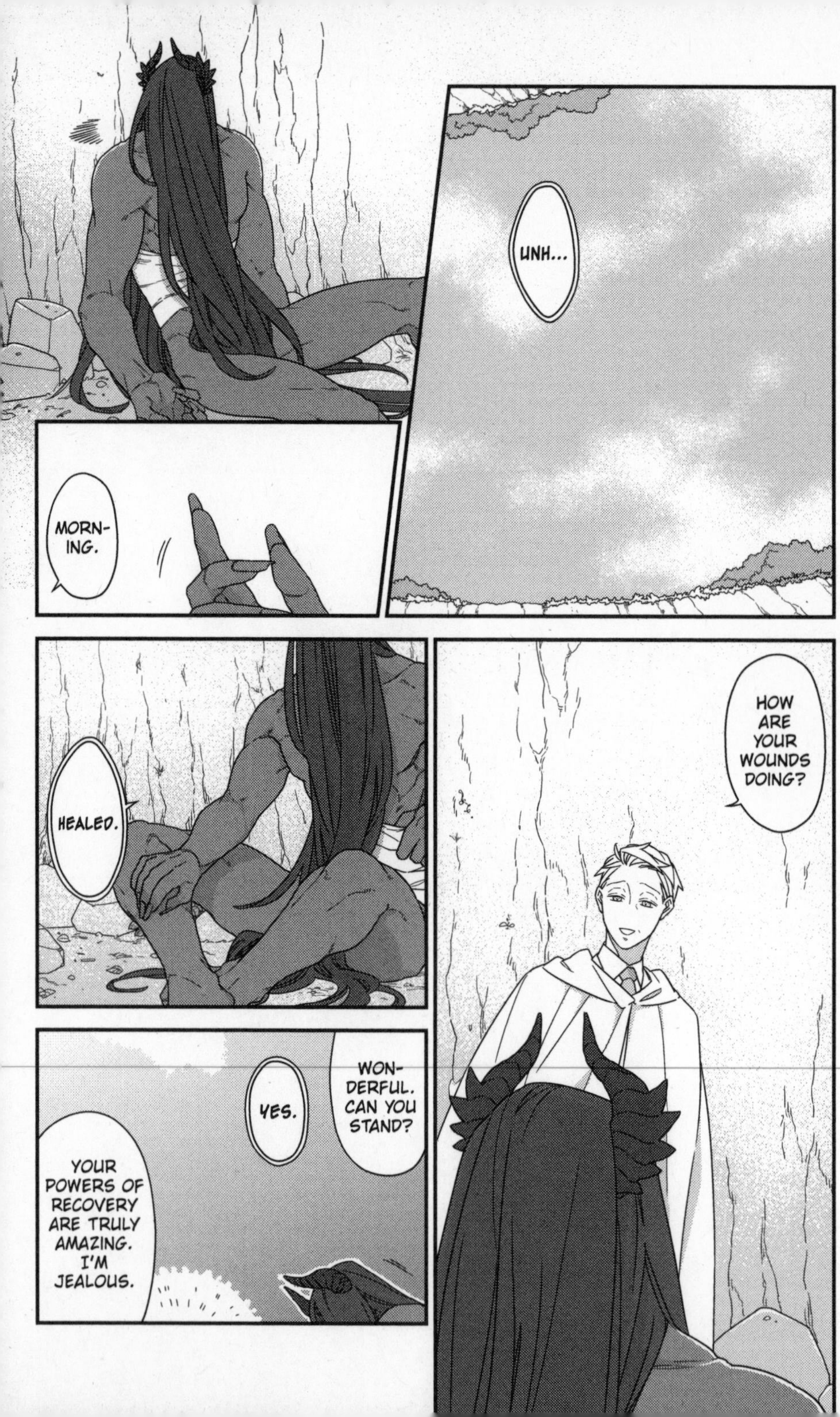
UNH...
MORN-ING.
HOW ARE YOUR WOUNDS DOING?
HEALED.
WON-DERFUL. CAN YOU STAND?
YES.
YOUR POWERS OF RECOVERY ARE TRULY AMAZING. I'M JEALOUS.

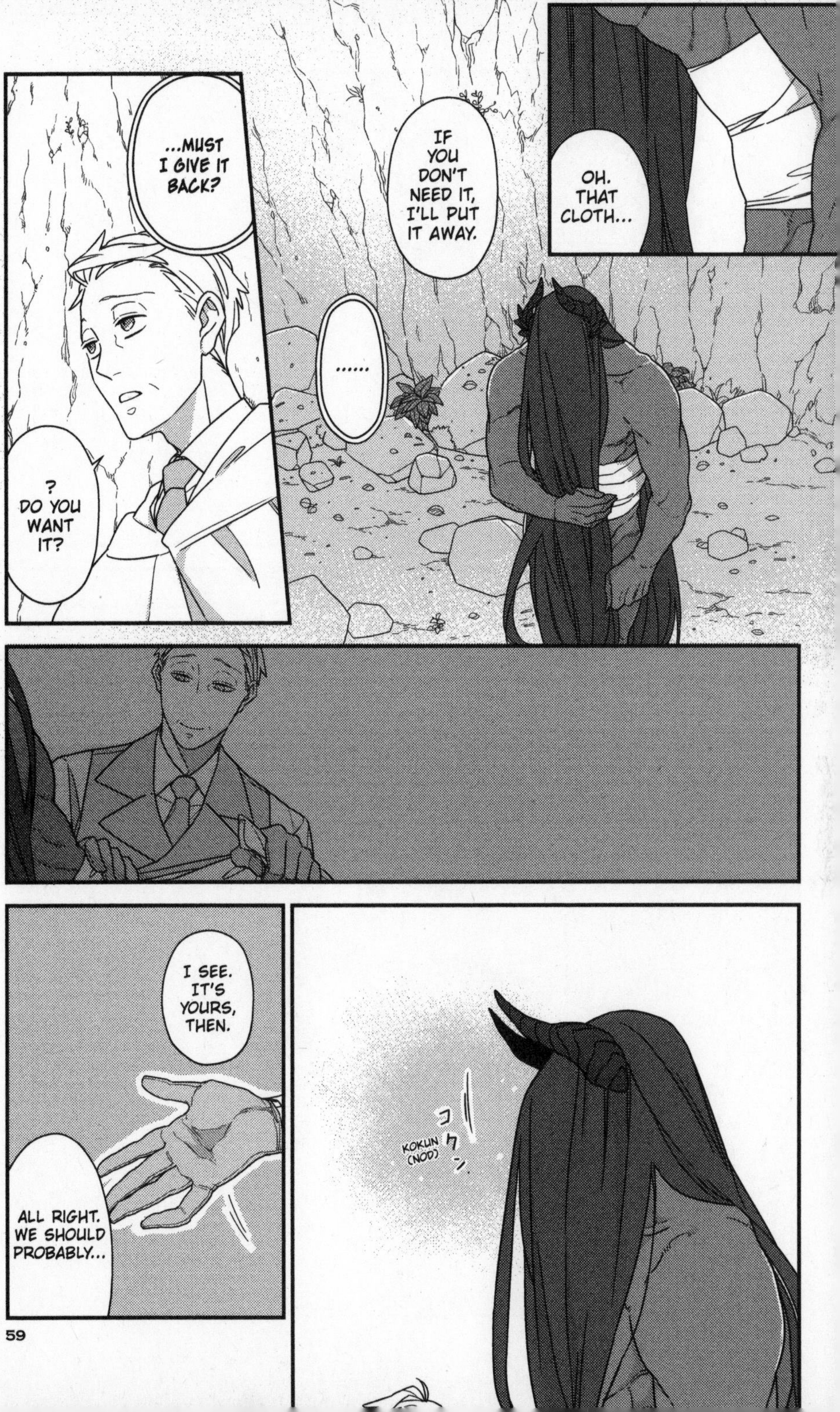
OH. THAT CLOTH...
IF YOU DON'T NEED IT, I'LL PUT IT AWAY.
......
...MUST I GIVE IT BACK?
? DO YOU WANT IT?
KOKUN (NOD)
I SEE. IT'S YOURS, THEN.
ALL RIGHT. WE SHOULD PROBABLY...

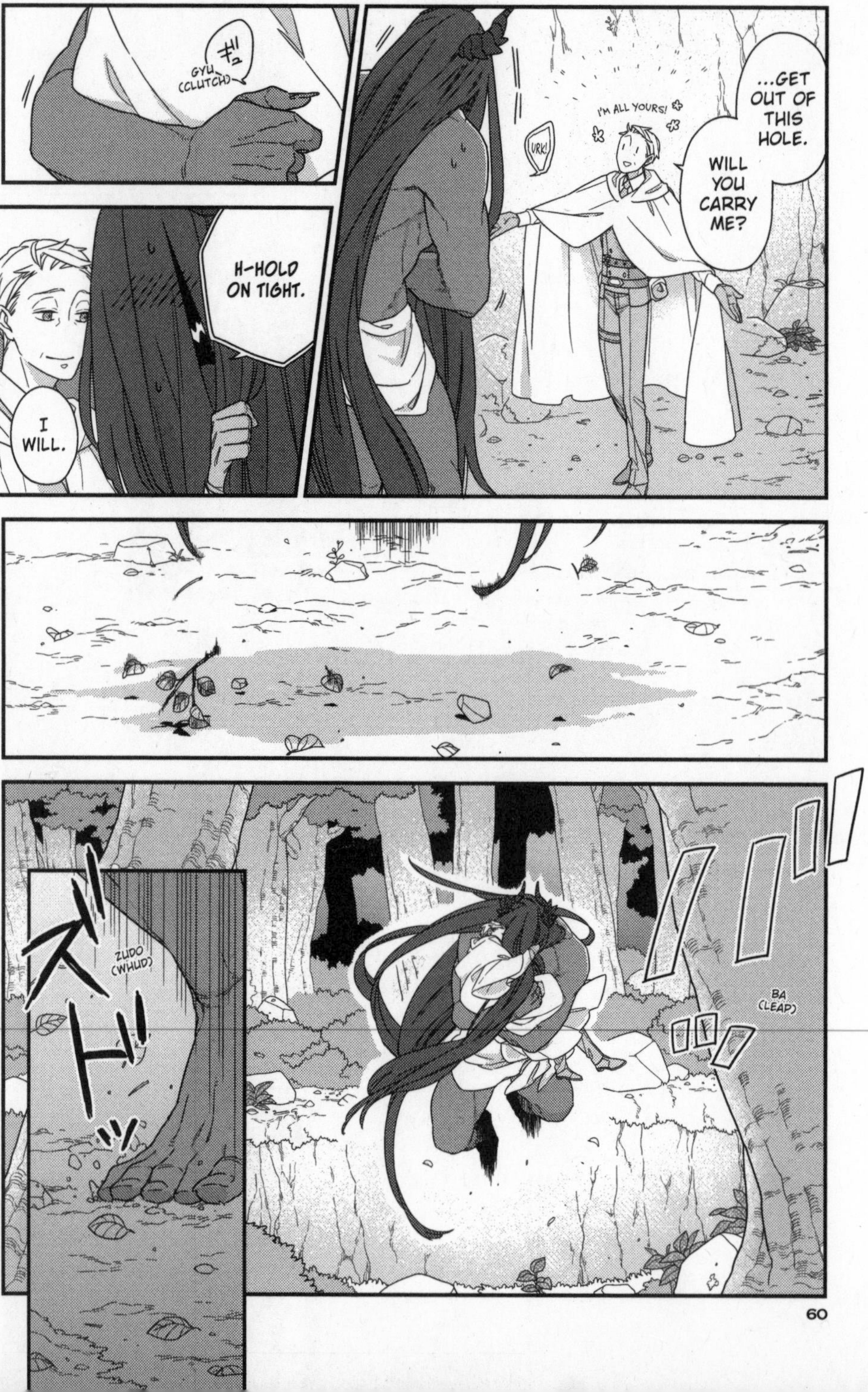
...GET OUT OF THIS HOLE. WILL YOU CARRY ME?
I'M ALL YOURS!
URK!
ギュ
GYU (CLUTCH)
H-HOLD ON TIGHT.
I WILL.
BA (LEAP)
ZUDO (WHUD)

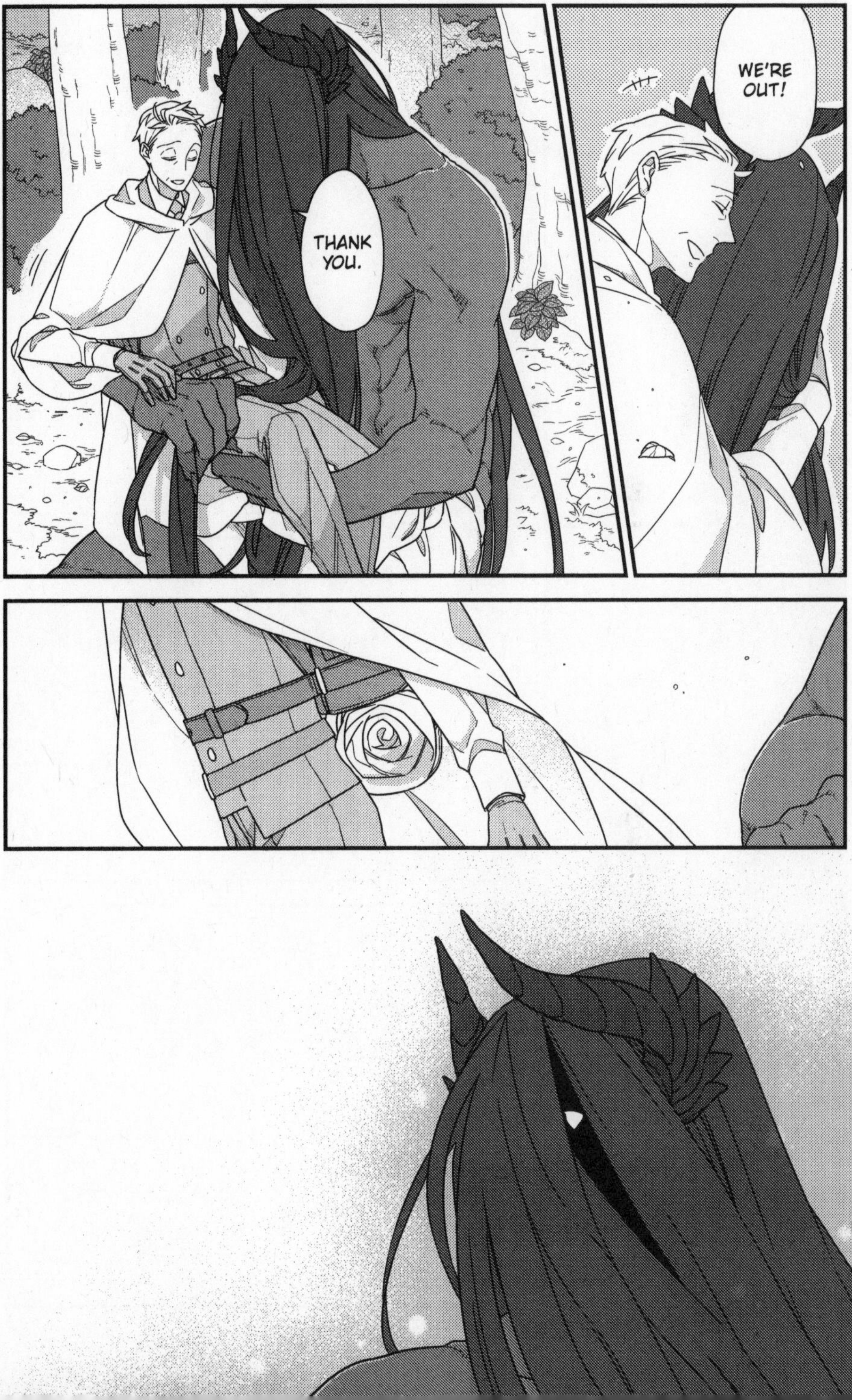
WE'RE OUT!
THANK YOU.

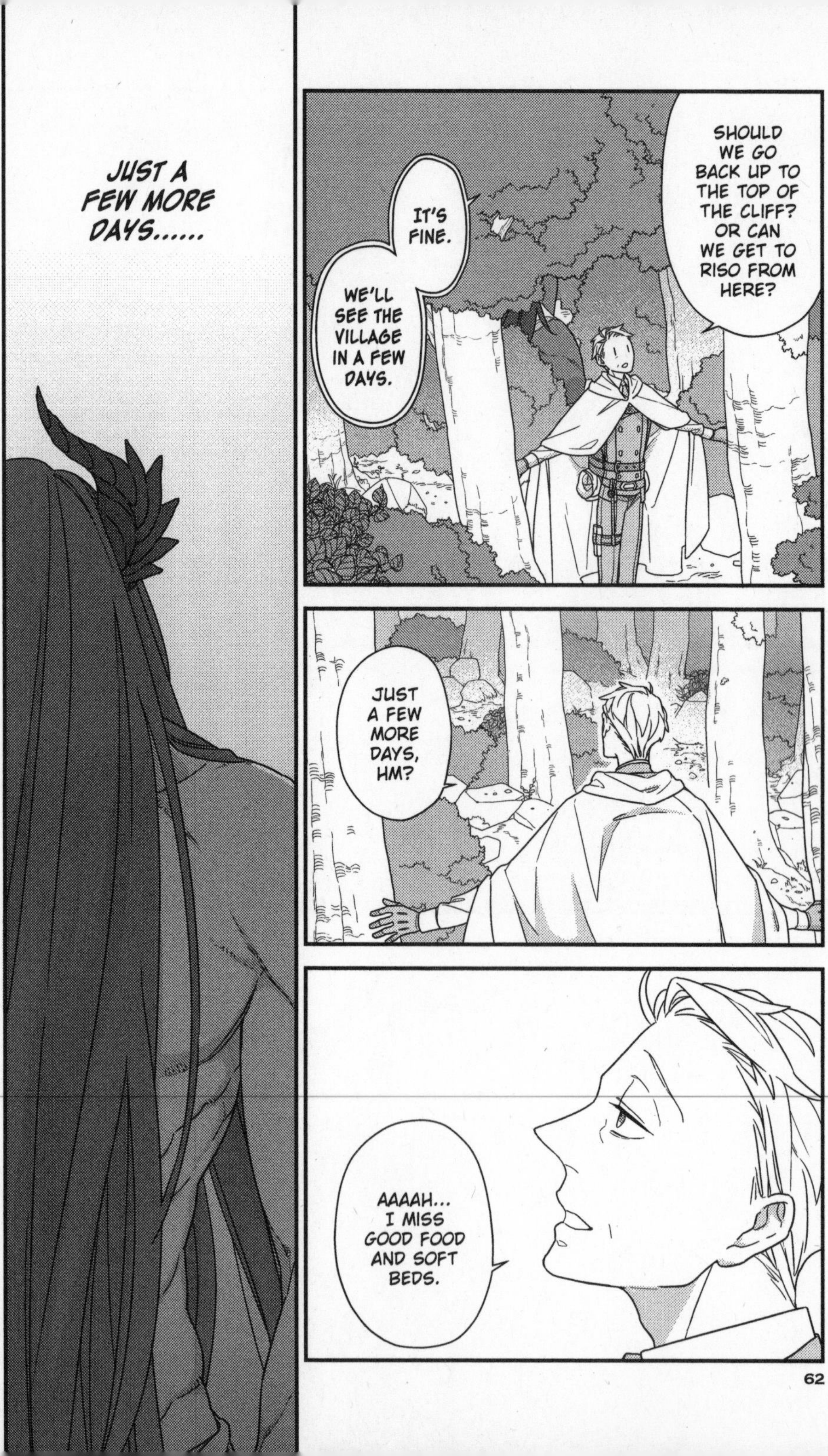
SHOULD WE GO BACK UP TO THE TOP OF THE CLIFF? OR CAN WE GET TO RISO FROM HERE?
IT'S FINE.
WE'LL SEE THE VILLAGE IN A FEW DAYS.
JUST A FEW MORE DAYS, HM?
AAAAH... I MISS GOOD FOOD AND SOFT BEDS.
JUST A FEW MORE DAYS......

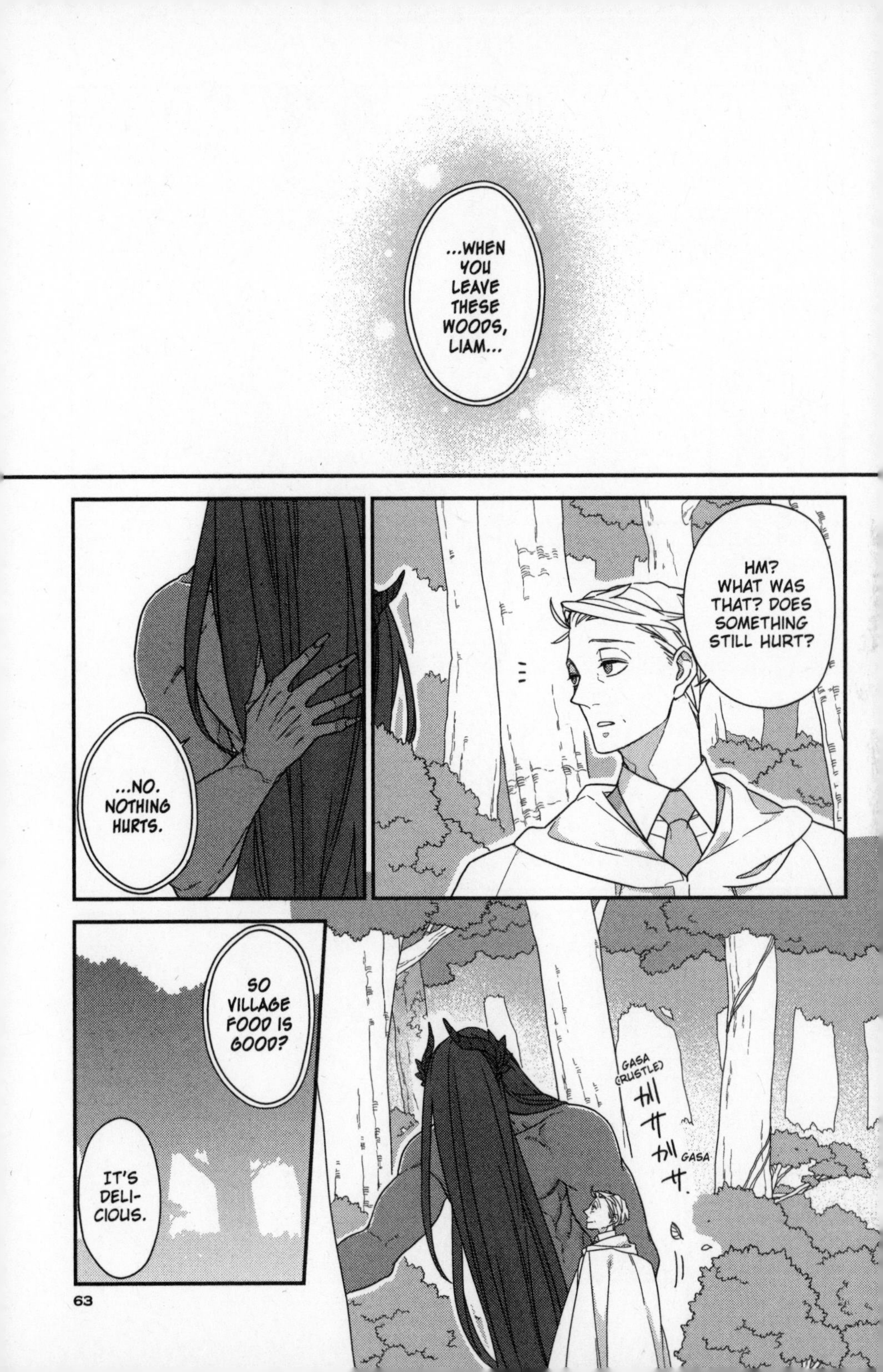
...WHEN YOU LEAVE THESE WOODS, LIAM...
HM? WHAT WAS THAT? DOES SOMETHING STILL HURT?
...NO. NOTHING HURTS.
GASA (RUSTLE)
GASA
SO VILLAGE FOOD IS GOOD?
IT'S DELICIOUS.

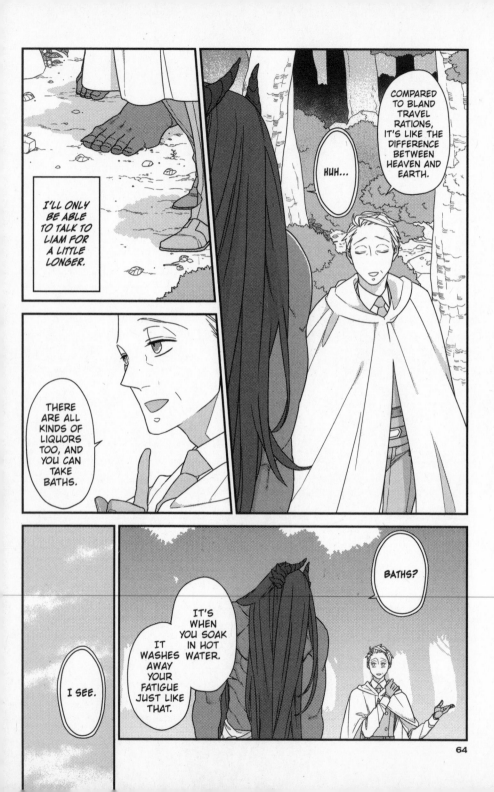

COMPARED TO BLAND TRAVEL RATIONS, IT'S LIKE THE DIFFERENCE BETWEEN HEAVEN AND EARTH.

HUH...

I'LL ONLY BE ABLE TO TALK TO LIAM FOR A LITTLE LONGER.

THERE ARE ALL KINDS OF LIQUORS TOO, AND YOU CAN TAKE BATHS.

BATHS?

IT'S WHEN YOU SOAK IN HOT WATER. IT WASHES AWAY YOUR FATIGUE JUST LIKE THAT.

I SEE.

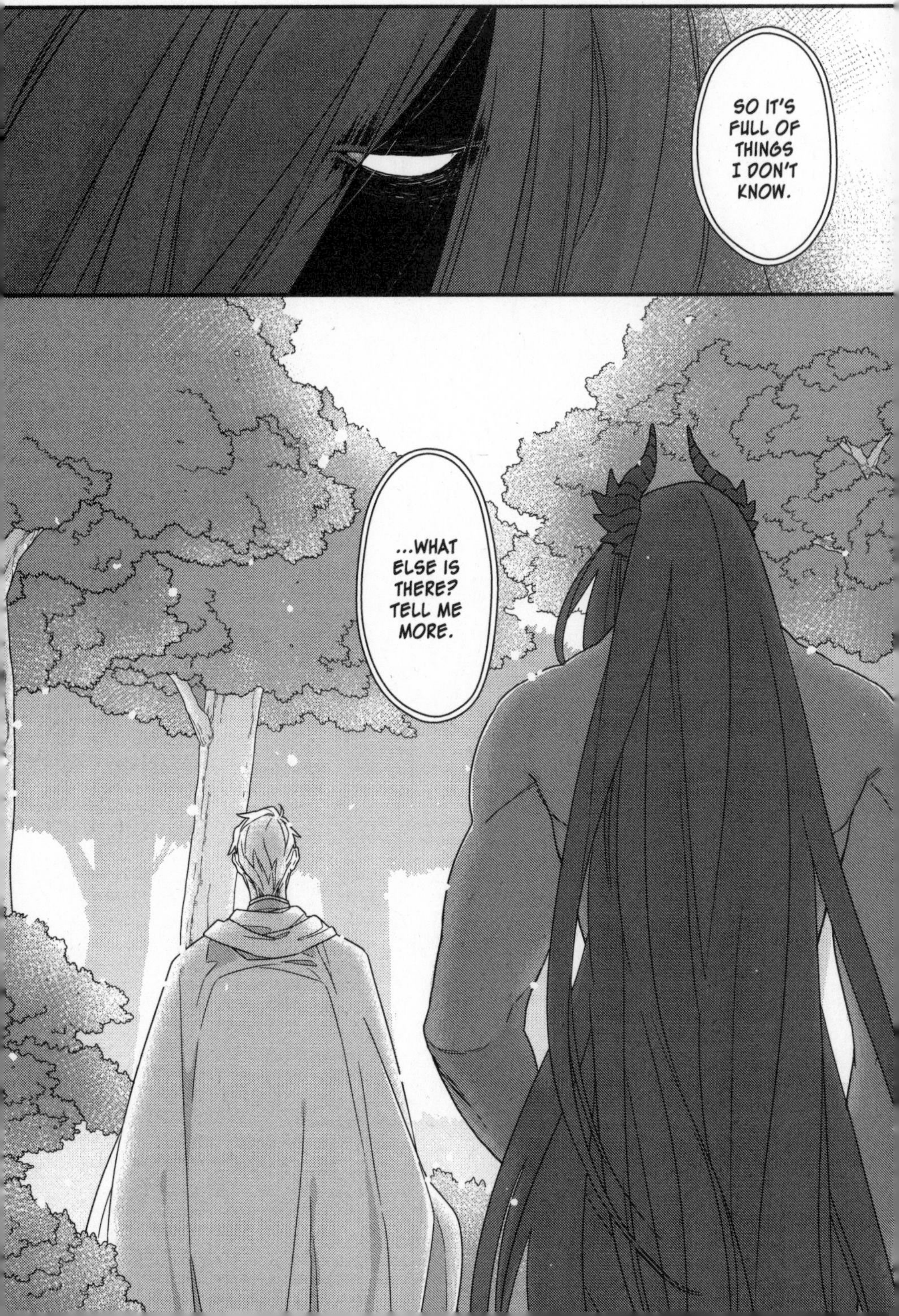
SO IT'S FULL OF THINGS I DON'T KNOW.
...WHAT ELSE IS THERE? TELL ME MORE.

LANTERN...?

A SIMPLE LANTERN MADE FROM A BOTTLE LIAM BROUGHT ALONG FOR MEDICINAL PLANTS AND MINERALS.

BOTTLE + WATER + A SPECIAL STONE THAT GLOWS WHEN WET.

THIS WAY, YOU CAN HAVE LIGHT EVEN IN PLACES WHERE YOU CAN'T BUILD A FIRE.

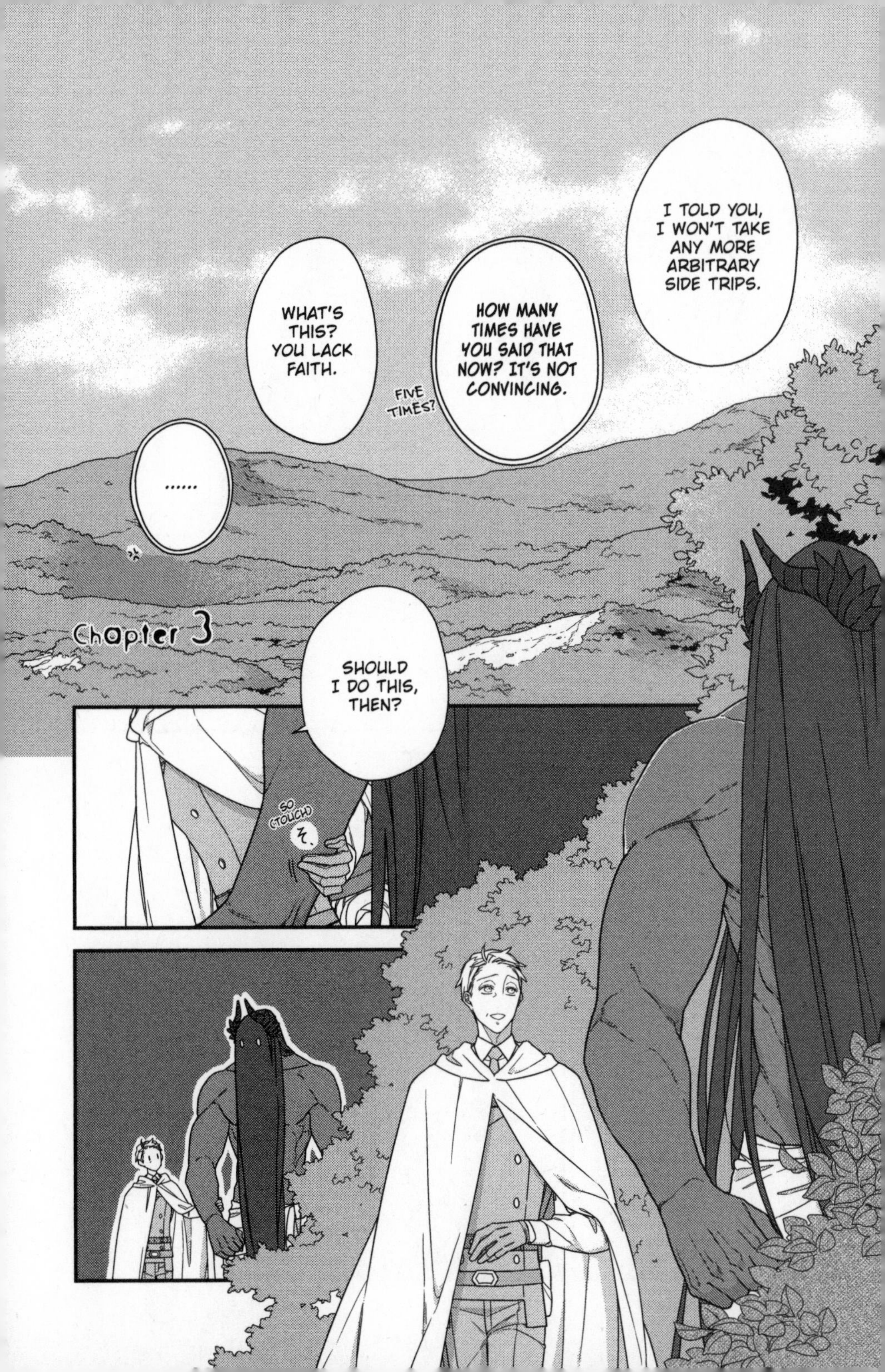
I TOLD YOU, I WON'T TAKE ANY MORE ARBITRARY SIDE TRIPS.
HOW MANY TIMES HAVE YOU SAID THAT NOW? IT'S NOT CONVINCING.
FIVE TIMES?
WHAT'S THIS? YOU LACK FAITH.
......
Chapter 3
SHOULD I DO THIS, THEN?
SO (TOUCH)

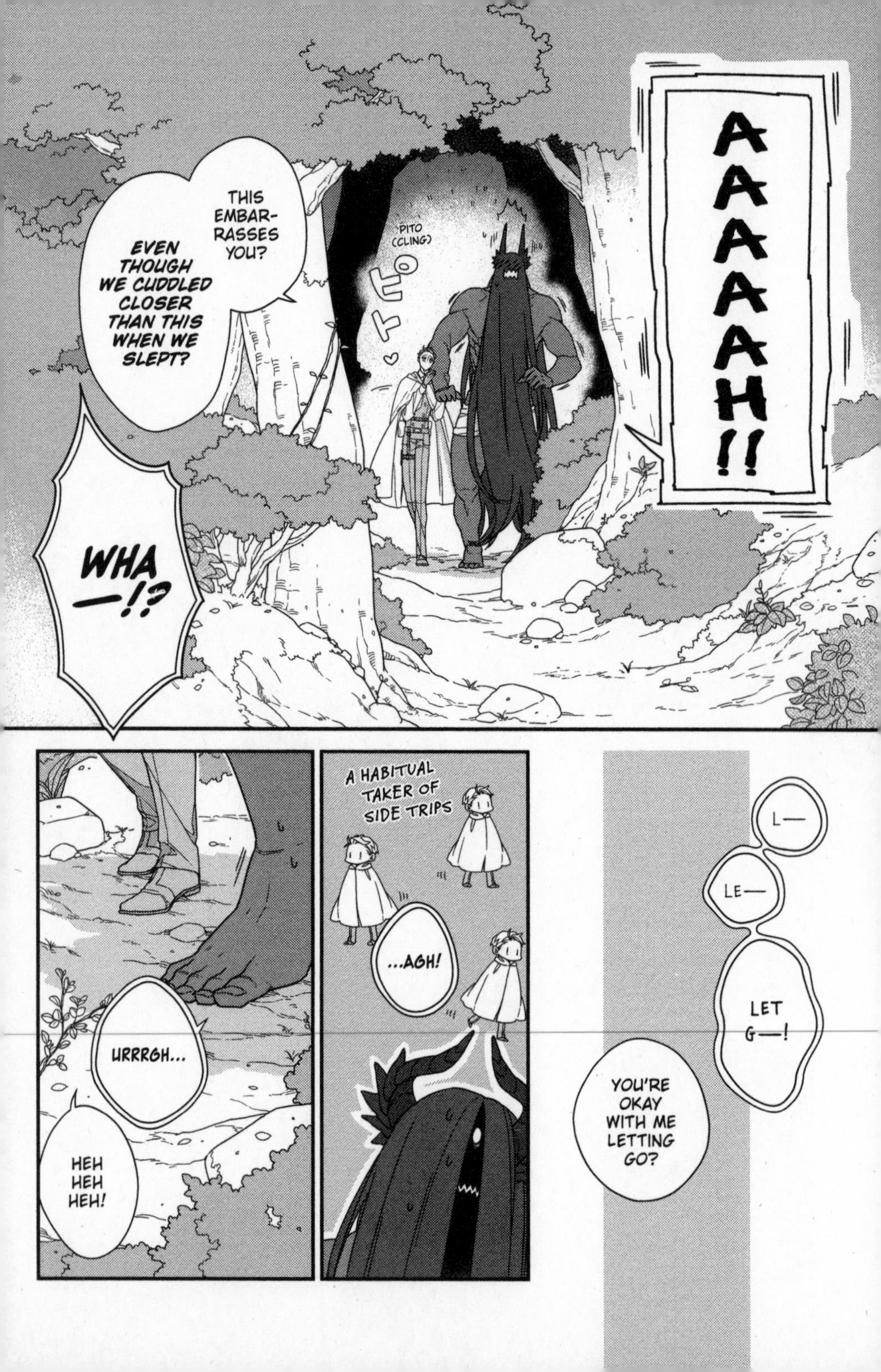
AAAAAH!!
PITO (CLING)
THIS EMBAR-RASSES YOU?
EVEN THOUGH WE CUDDLED CLOSER THAN THIS WHEN WE SLEPT?
WHA—!?
L—
LE—
LET G—!
YOU'RE OKAY WITH ME LETTING GO?
A HABITUAL TAKER OF SIDE TRIPS
...AGH!
URRRGH...
HEH HEH HEH!

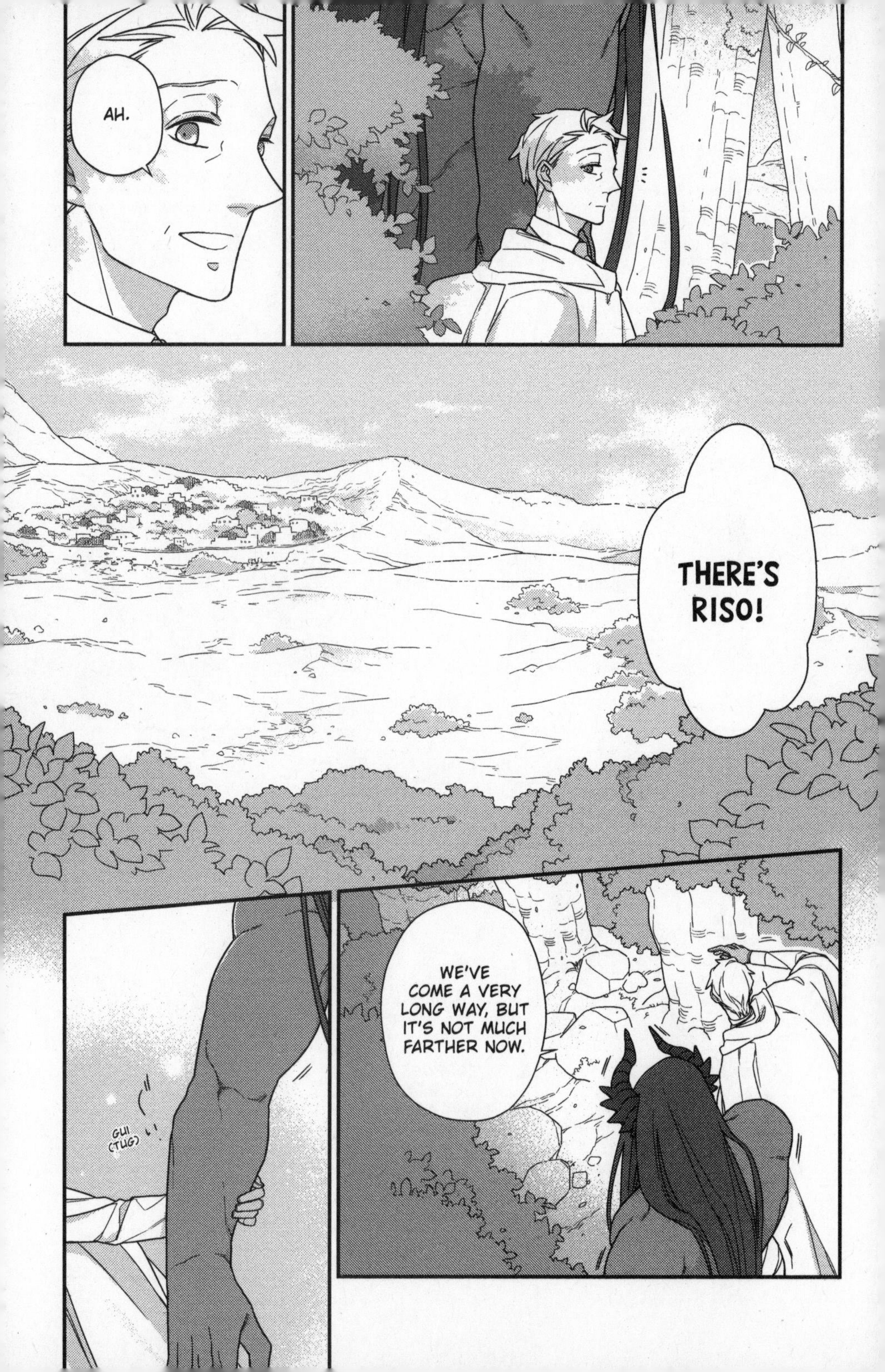
AH.
THERE'S RISO!
WE'VE COME A VERY LONG WAY, BUT IT'S NOT MUCH FARTHER NOW.
GUI (TUG)

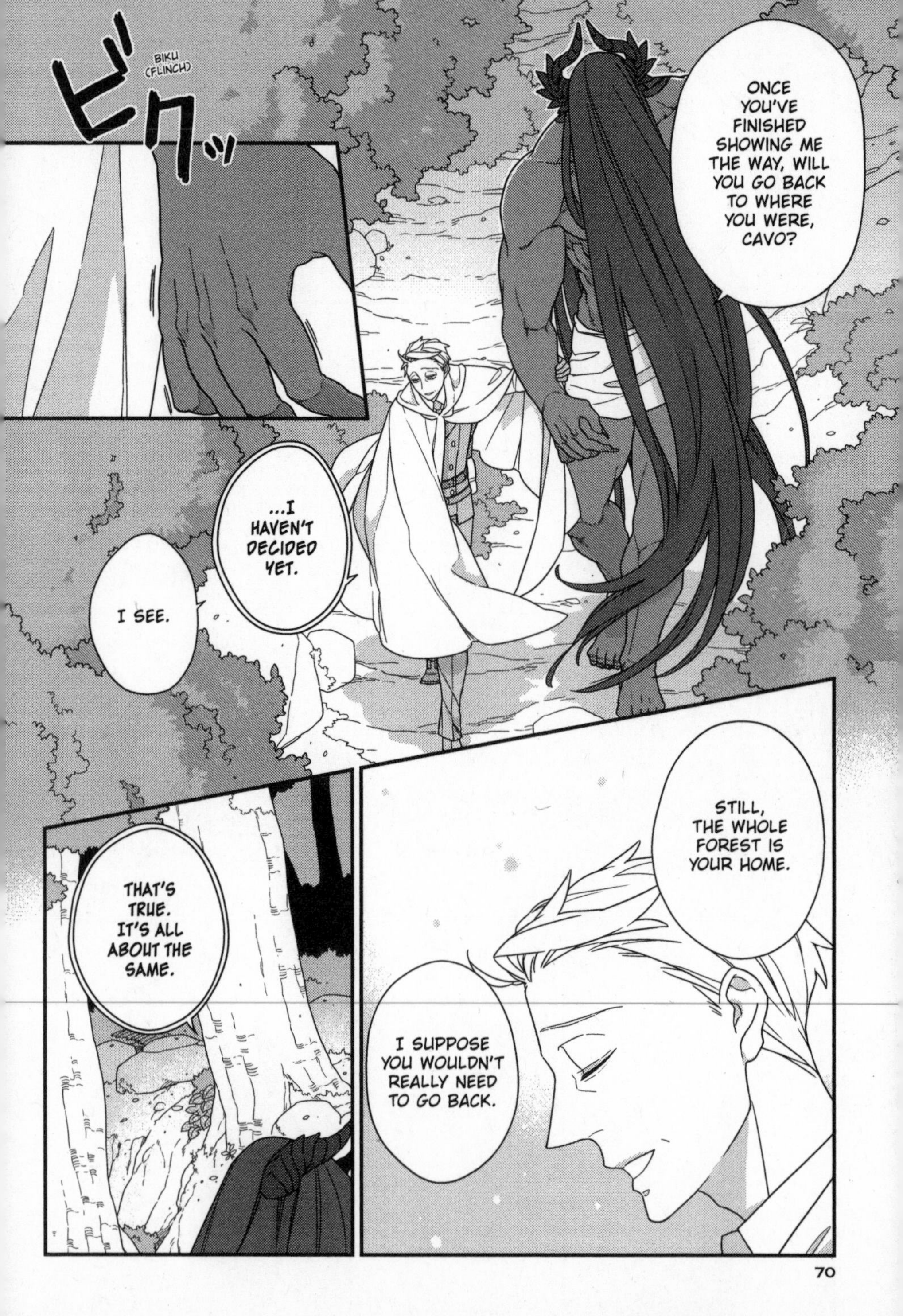
ONCE YOU'VE FINISHED SHOWING ME THE WAY, WILL YOU GO BACK TO WHERE YOU WERE, CAVO?
ビクッ
BIKU (FLINCH)
...I HAVEN'T DECIDED YET.
I SEE.
STILL, THE WHOLE FOREST IS YOUR HOME.
I SUPPOSE YOU WOULDN'T REALLY NEED TO GO BACK.
THAT'S TRUE. IT'S ALL ABOUT THE SAME.

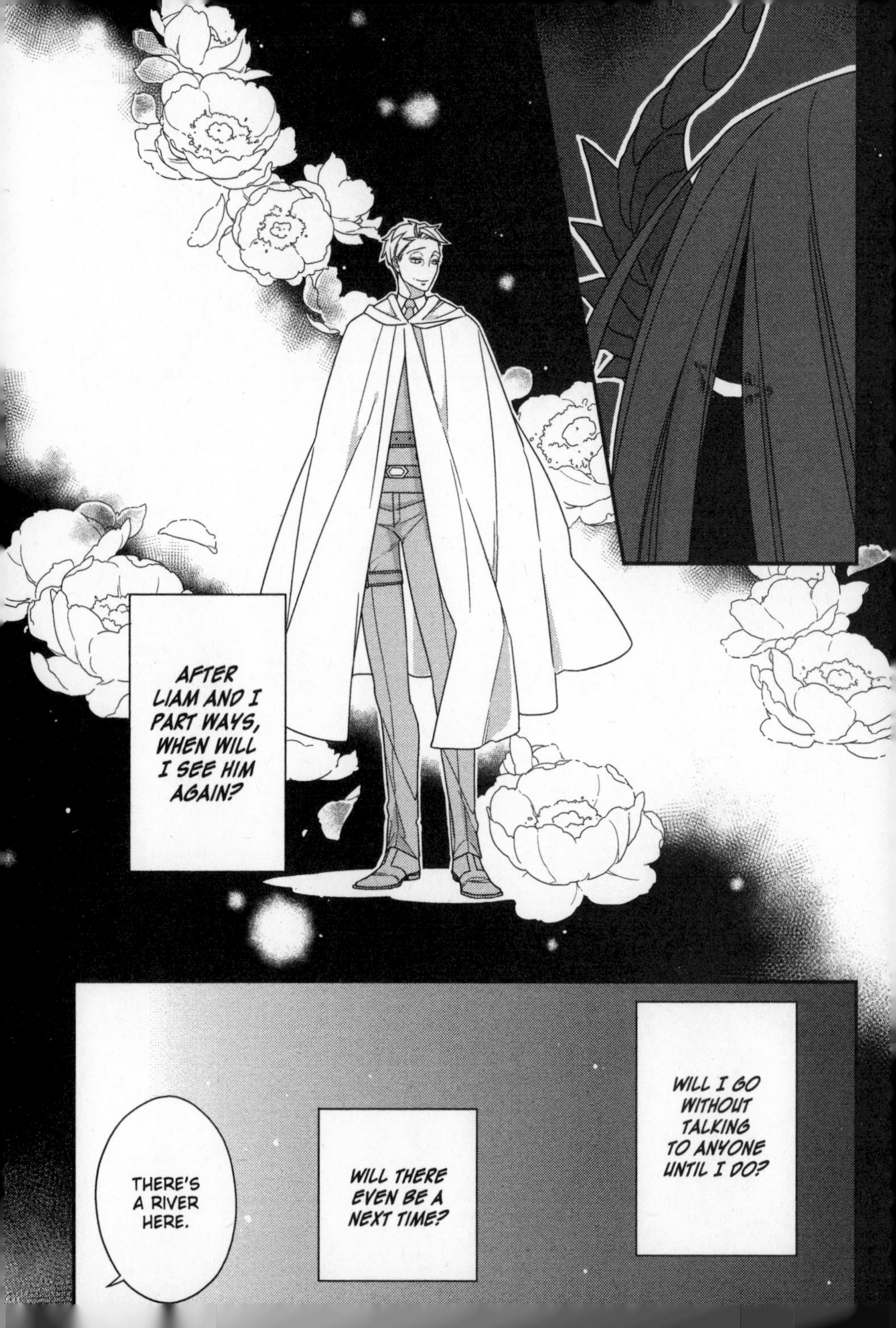
AFTER LIAM AND I PART WAYS, WHEN WILL I SEE HIM AGAIN?
WILL I GO WITHOUT TALKING TO ANYONE UNTIL I DO?
WILL THERE EVEN BE A NEXT TIME?
THERE'S A RIVER HERE.

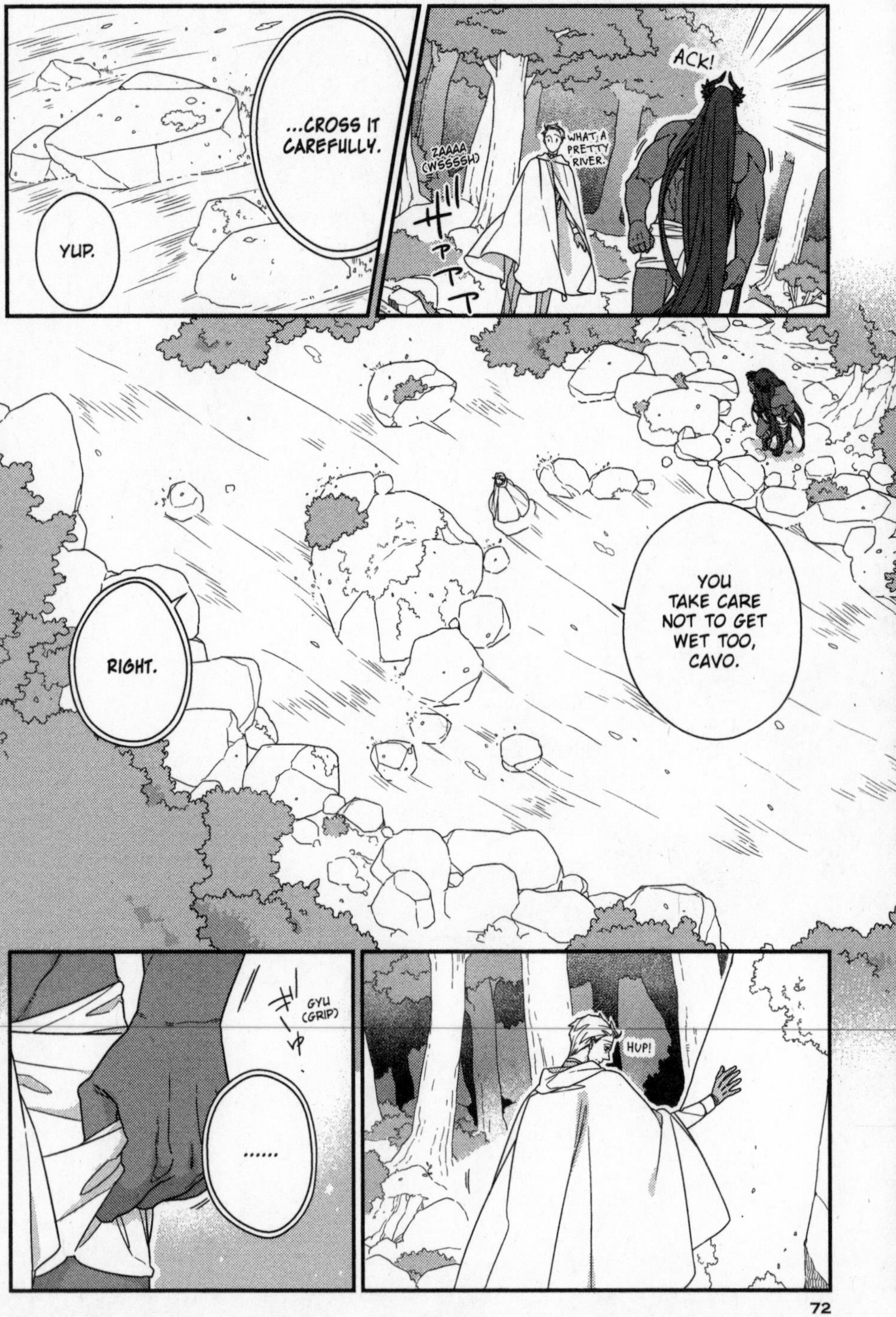
ACK!
WHAT A PRETTY RIVER.
ZAAAA (WSSSSH)
...CROSS IT CAREFULLY.
YUP.
YOU TAKE CARE NOT TO GET WET TOO, CAVO.
RIGHT.
HUP!
GYU (GRIP)
......

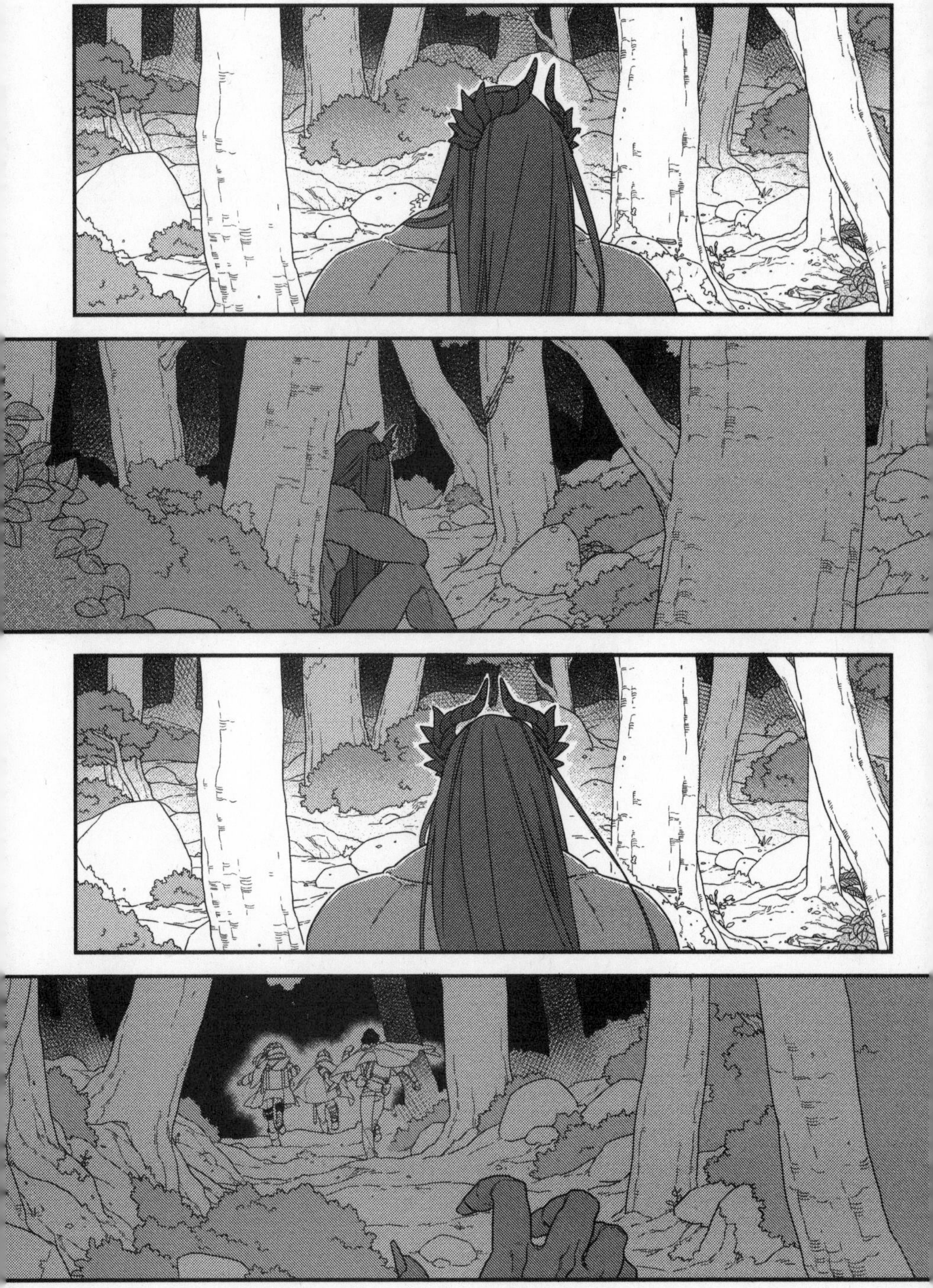

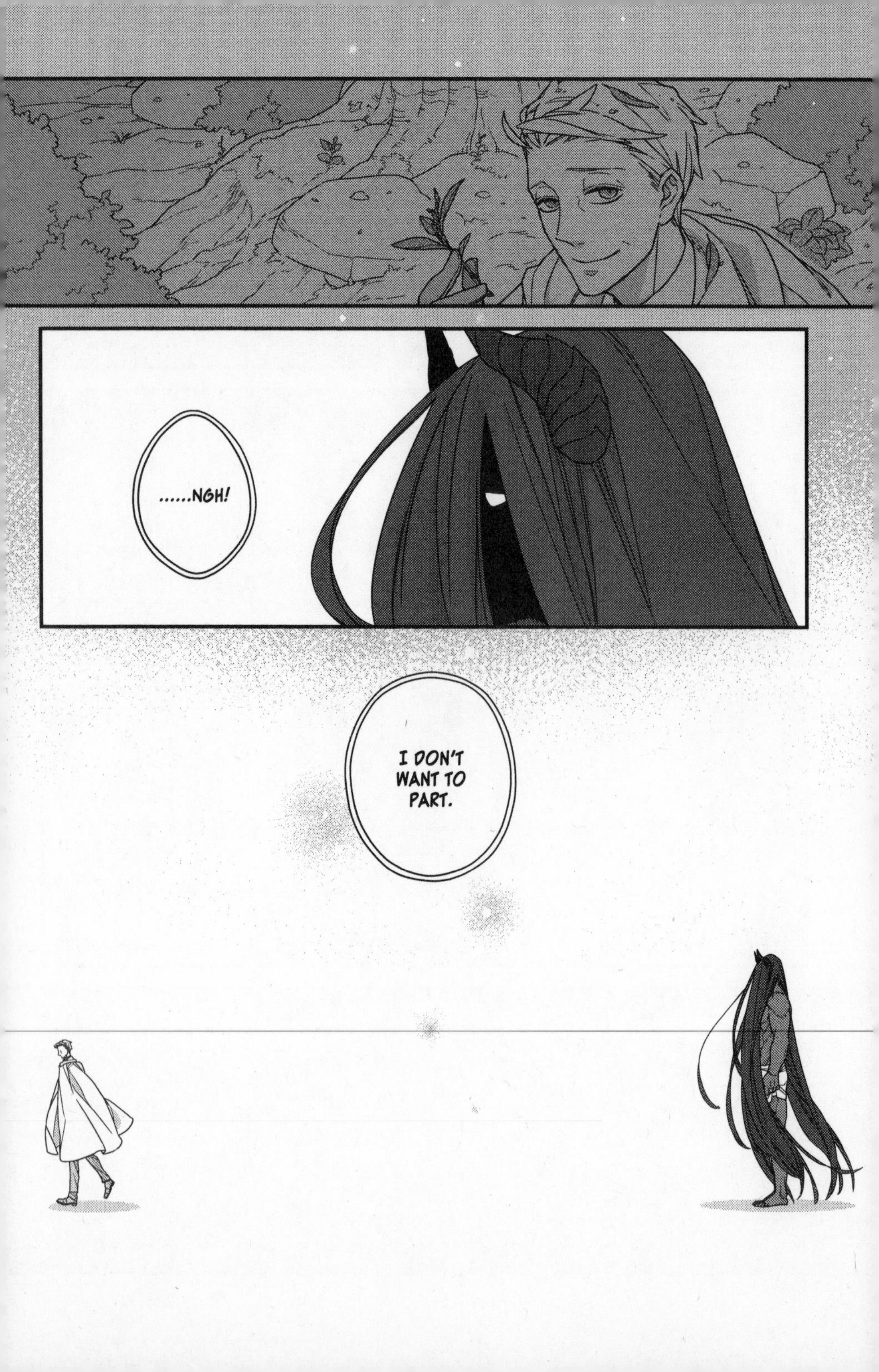
......NGH!
I DON'T WANT TO PART.

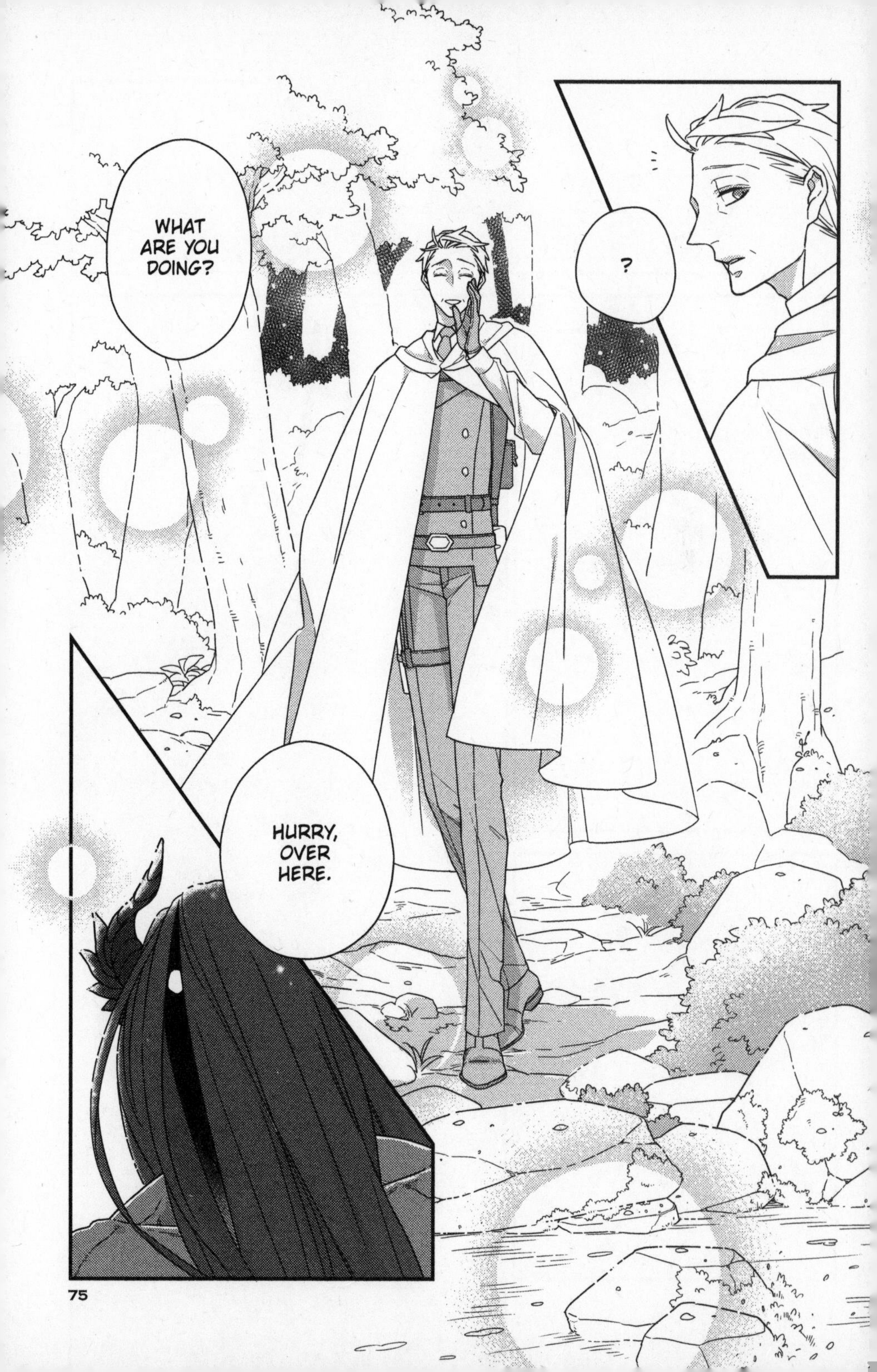
?
WHAT ARE YOU DOING?
HURRY, OVER HERE.

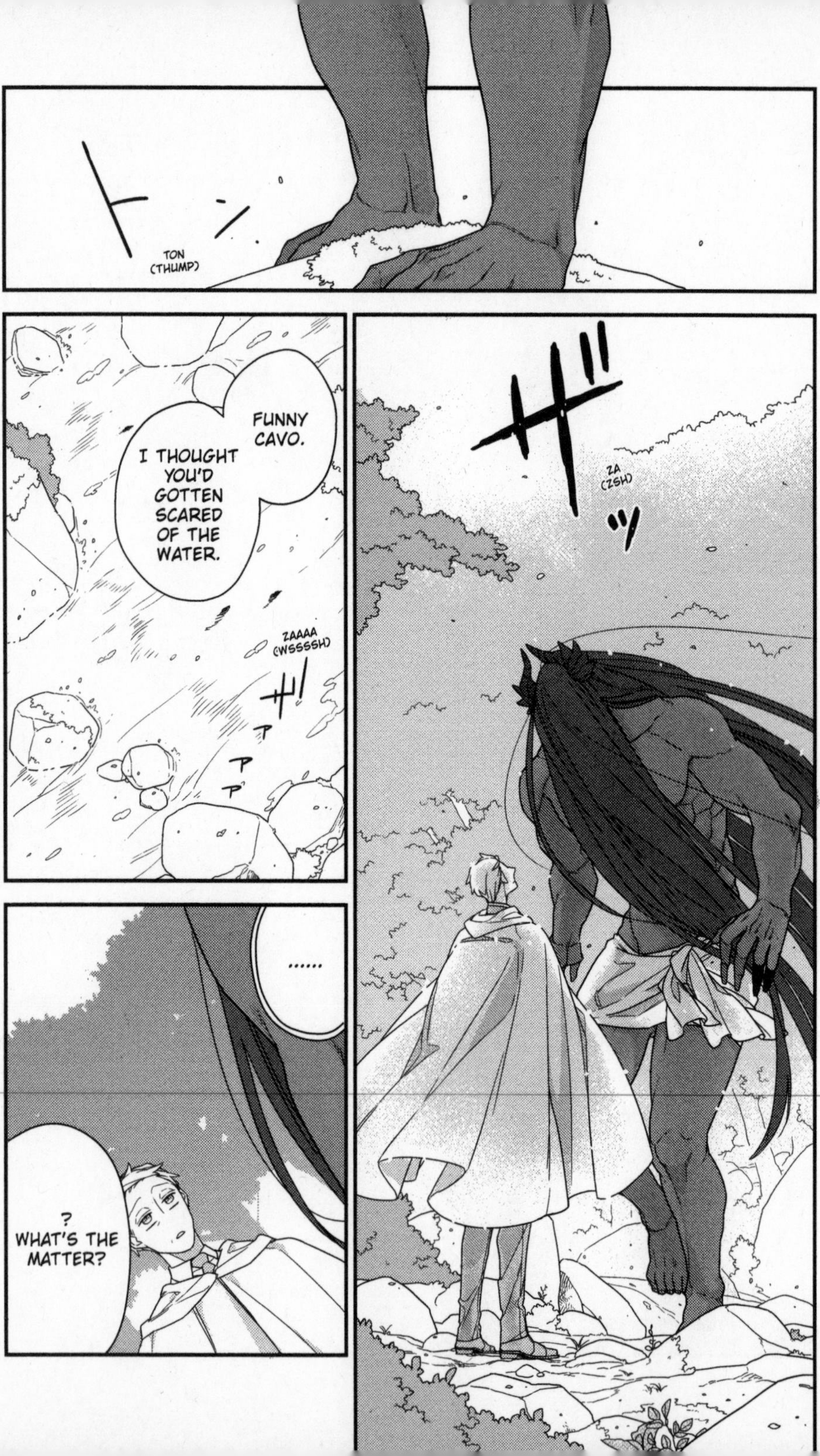
TON
(THUMP)
ZA
(ZSH)
FUNNY CAVO. I THOUGHT YOU'D GOTTEN SCARED OF THE WATER.
ZAAAA
(WSSSSH)
......
? WHAT'S THE MATTER?

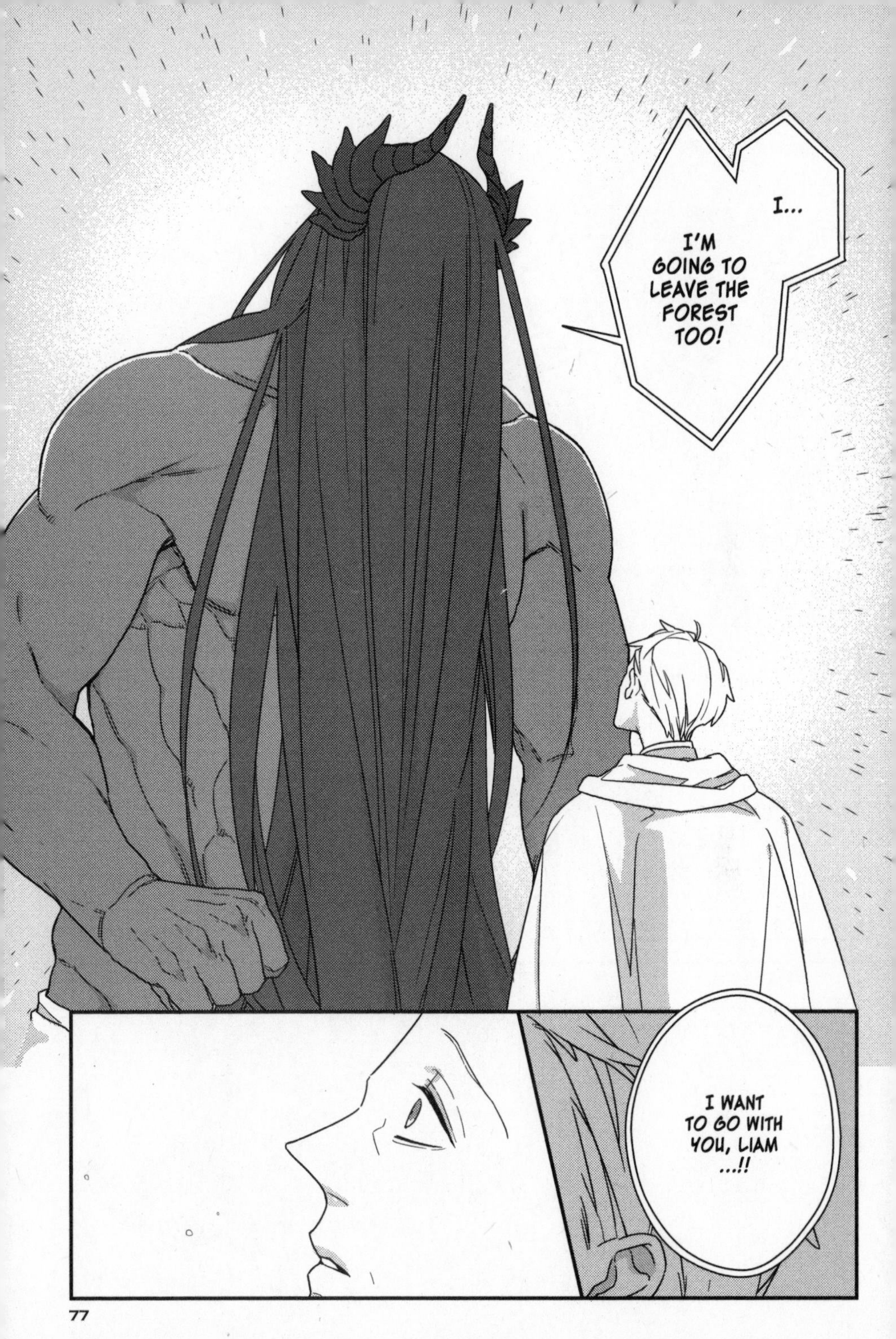
I...
I'M GOING TO LEAVE THE FOREST TOO!
I WANT TO GO WITH YOU, LIAM ...!!

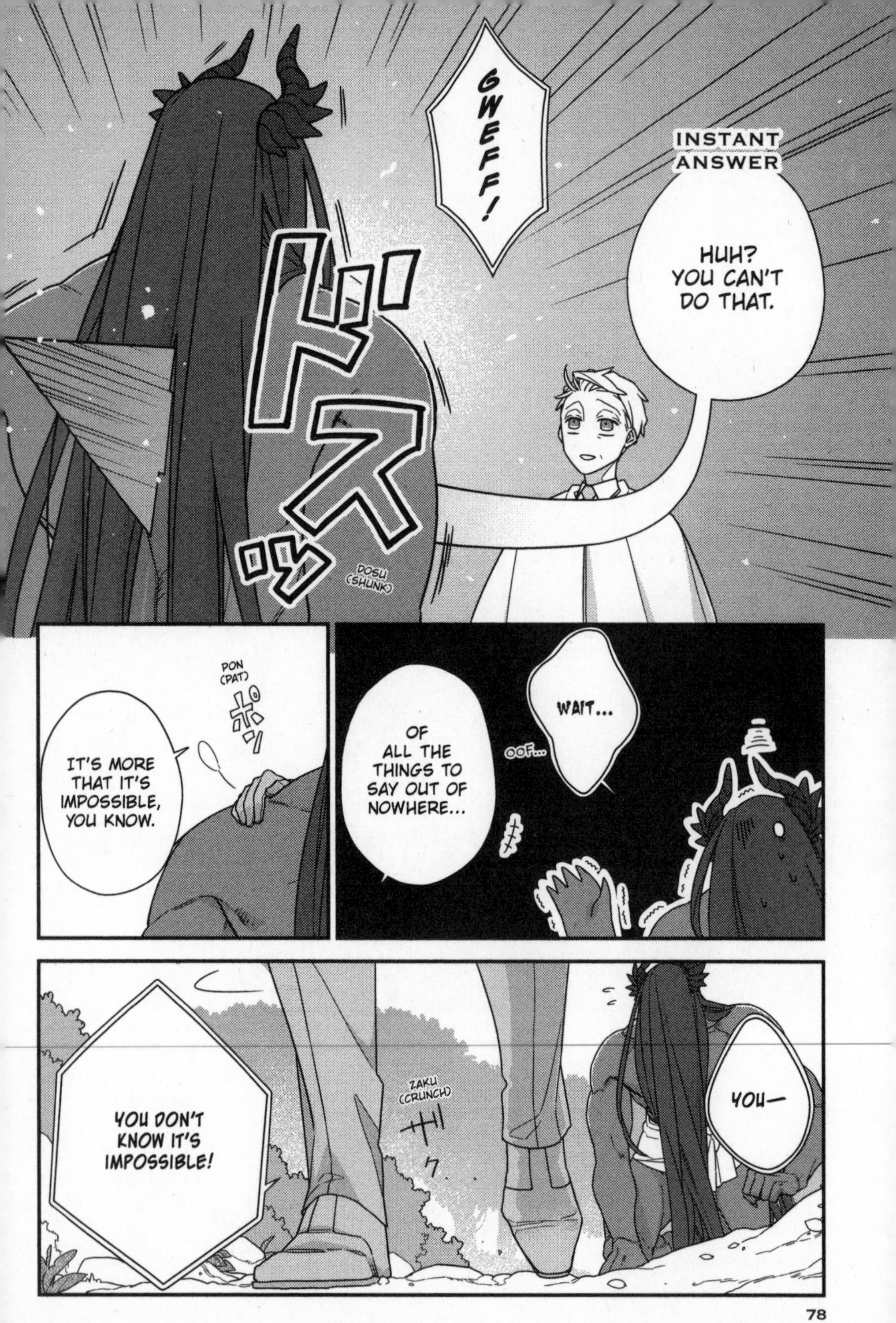
INSTANT ANSWER
HUH? YOU CAN'T DO THAT.
GWEFF!
DOSU (SHUNK)
WAIT...
OOF...
OF ALL THE THINGS TO SAY OUT OF NOWHERE...
PON (PAT)
IT'S MORE THAT IT'S IMPOSSIBLE, YOU KNOW.
YOU—
ZAKU (CRUNCH)
YOU DON'T KNOW IT'S IMPOSSIBLE!

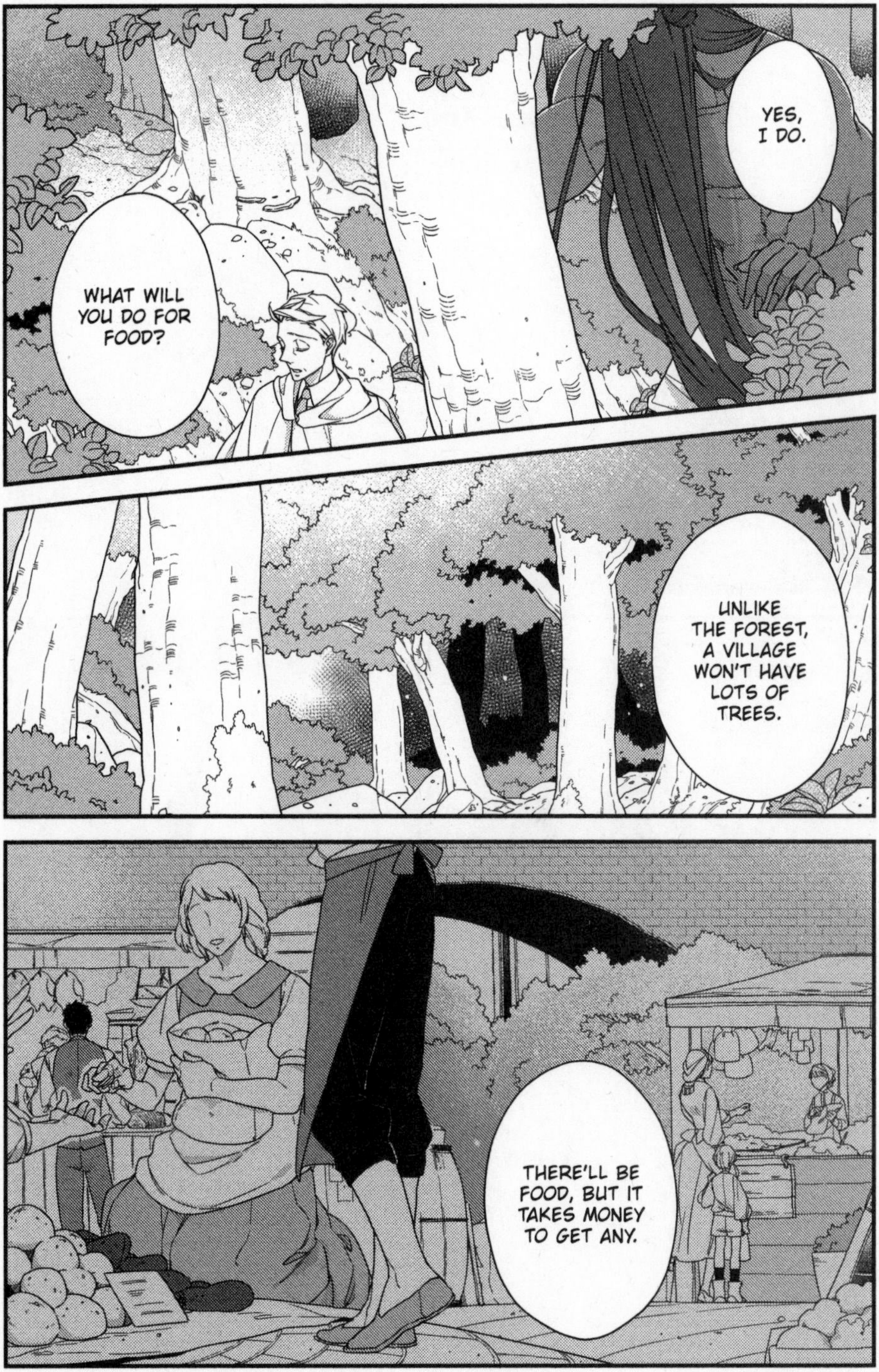
YES, I DO.
WHAT WILL YOU DO FOR FOOD?
UNLIKE THE FOREST, A VILLAGE WON'T HAVE LOTS OF TREES.
THERE'LL BE FOOD, BUT IT TAKES MONEY TO GET ANY.

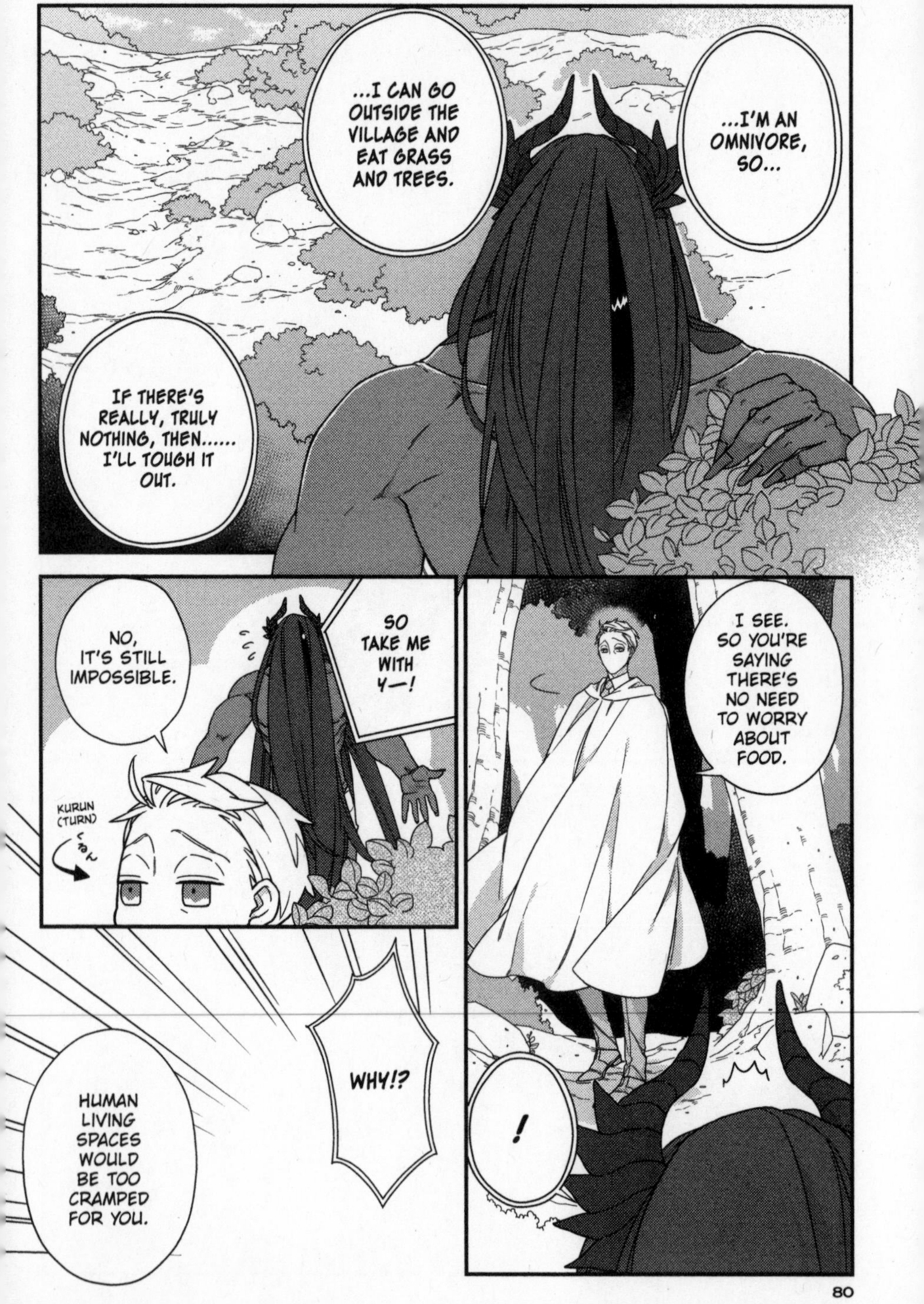
...I'M AN OMNIVORE, SO...
...I CAN GO OUTSIDE THE VILLAGE AND EAT GRASS AND TREES.
IF THERE'S REALLY, TRULY NOTHING, THEN...... I'LL TOUGH IT OUT.
I SEE. SO YOU'RE SAYING THERE'S NO NEED TO WORRY ABOUT FOOD.
!
SO TAKE ME WITH Y—!
NO, IT'S STILL IMPOSSIBLE.
KURUN (TURN)
くるん
WHY!?
HUMAN LIVING SPACES WOULD BE TOO CRAMPED FOR YOU.

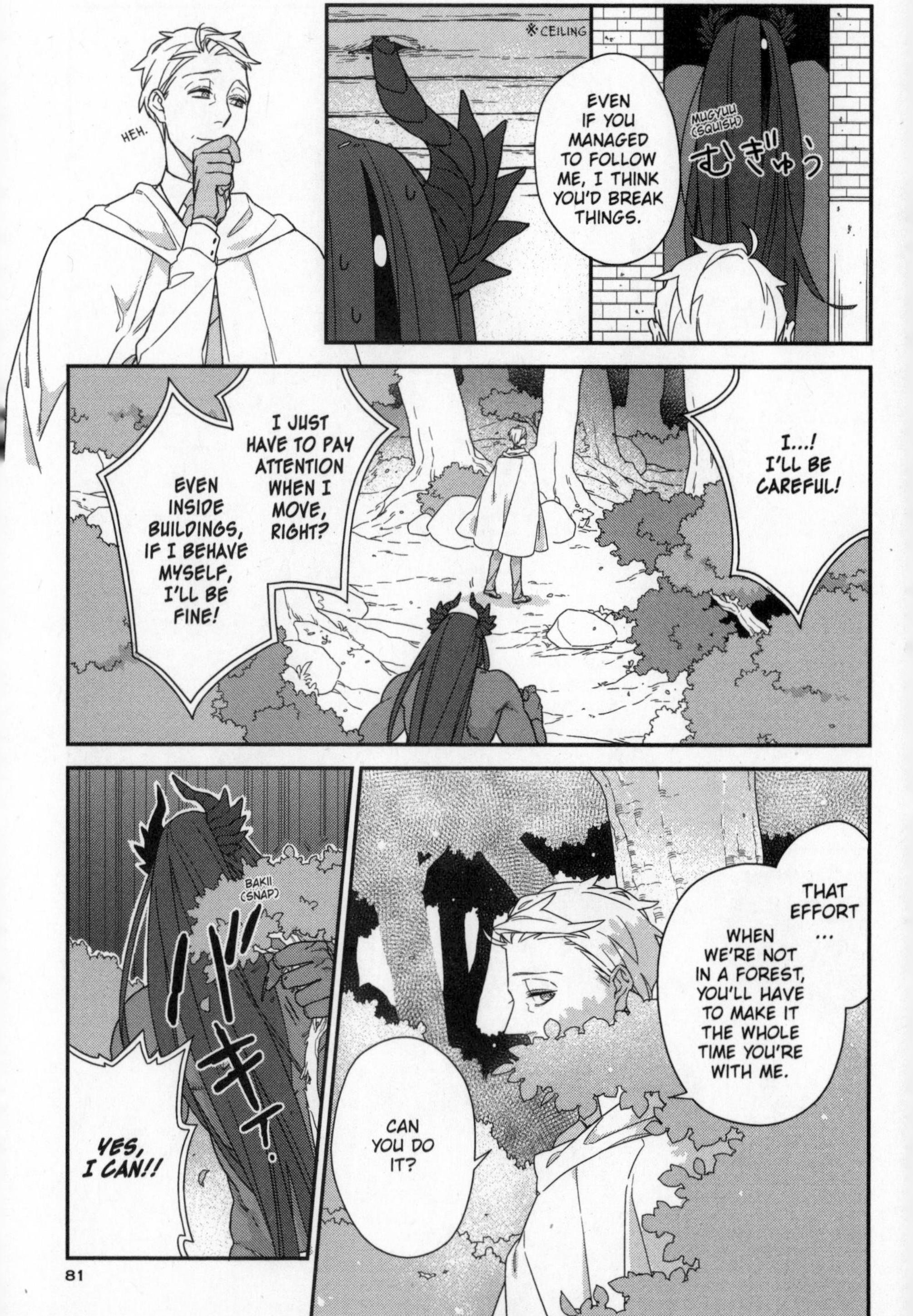
※CEILING
EVEN IF YOU MANAGED TO FOLLOW ME, I THINK YOU'D BREAK THINGS.
MUGYUU (SQUISH)
むぎゅう
HEH.
I...! I'LL BE CAREFUL!
I JUST HAVE TO PAY ATTENTION WHEN I MOVE, RIGHT?
EVEN INSIDE BUILDINGS, IF I BEHAVE MYSELF, I'LL BE FINE!
THAT EFFORT ...
WHEN WE'RE NOT IN A FOREST, YOU'LL HAVE TO MAKE IT THE WHOLE TIME YOU'RE WITH ME.
CAN YOU DO IT?
BAKII (SNAP)
バキィ。
YES, I CAN!!

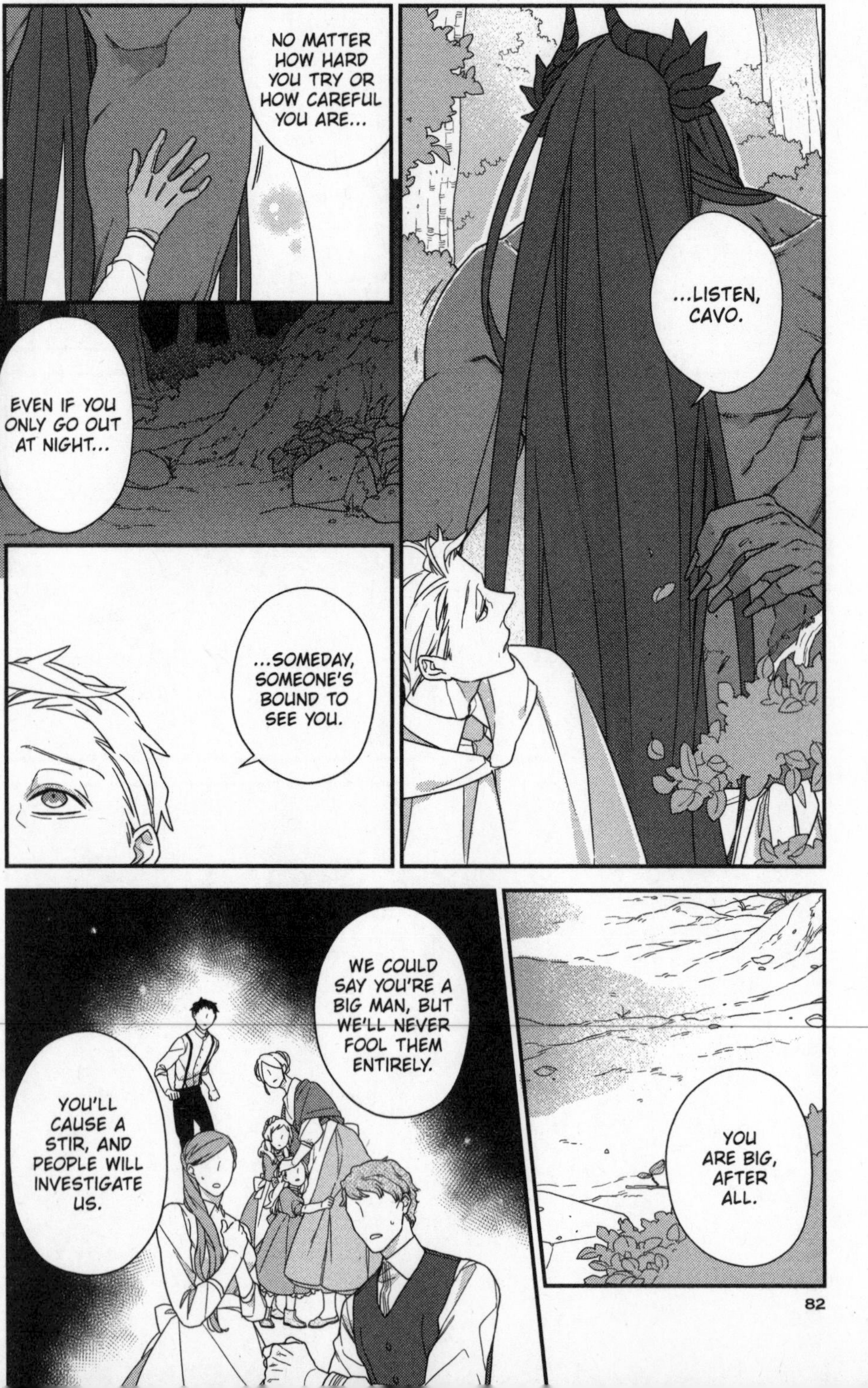
...LISTEN, CAVO.
NO MATTER HOW HARD YOU TRY OR HOW CAREFUL YOU ARE...
EVEN IF YOU ONLY GO OUT AT NIGHT...
...SOMEDAY, SOMEONE'S BOUND TO SEE YOU.
YOU ARE BIG, AFTER ALL.
WE COULD SAY YOU'RE A BIG MAN, BUT WE'LL NEVER FOOL THEM ENTIRELY.
YOU'LL CAUSE A STIR, AND PEOPLE WILL INVESTIGATE US.

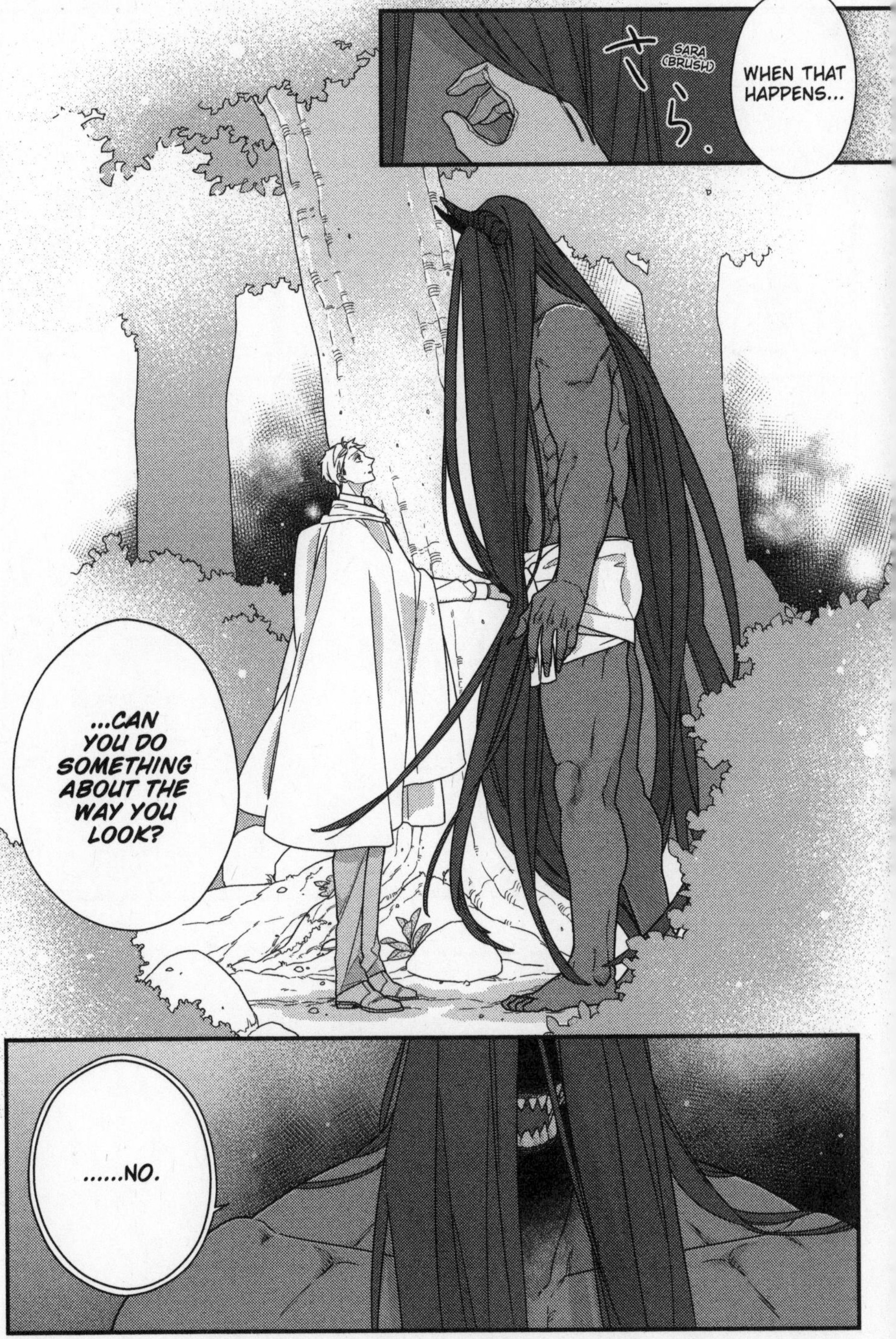
WHEN THAT HAPPENS...
さら
SARA (BRUSH)
...CAN YOU DO SOMETHING ABOUT THE WAY YOU LOOK?
......NO.

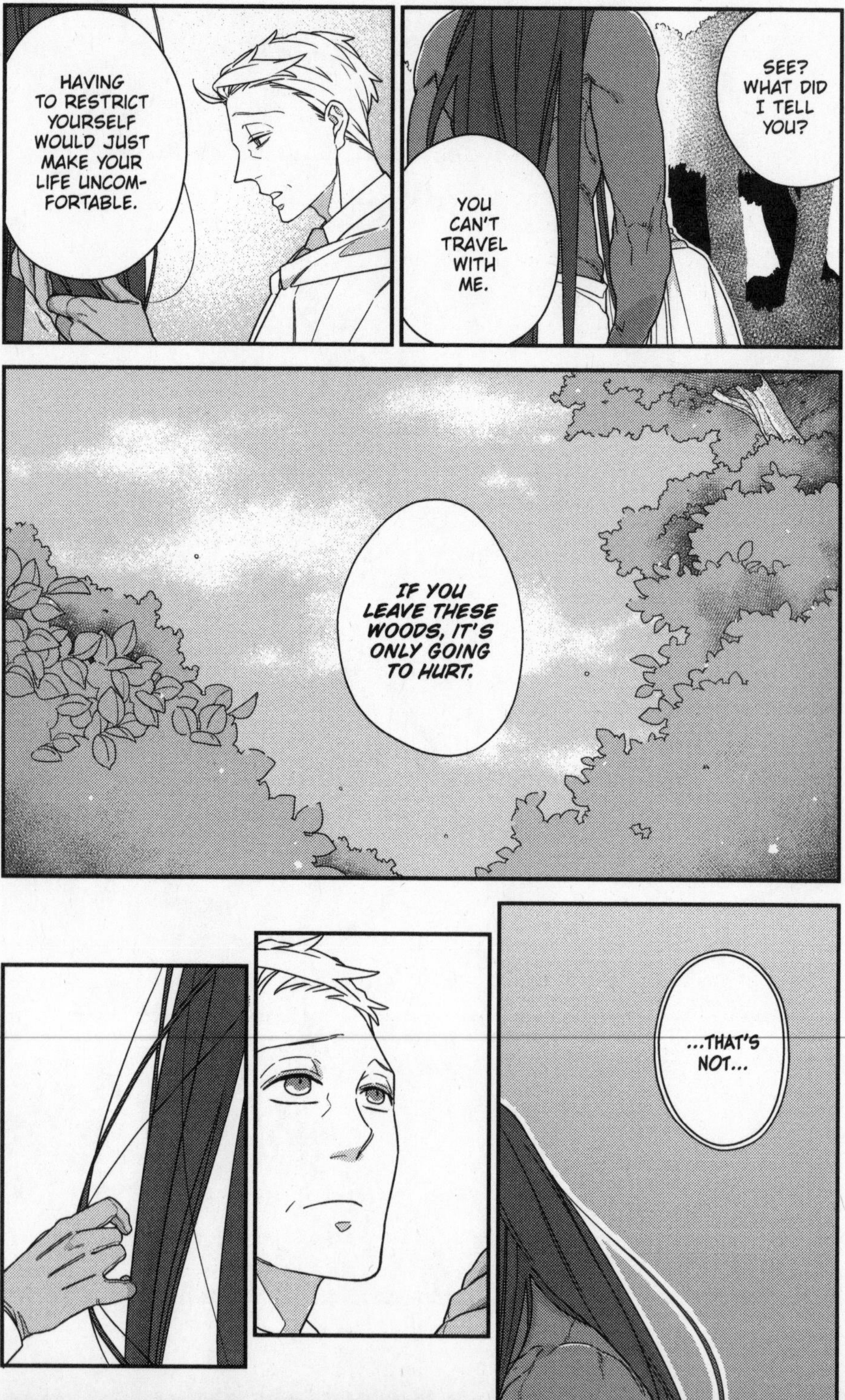
SEE? WHAT DID I TELL YOU?
YOU CAN'T TRAVEL WITH ME.
HAVING TO RESTRICT YOURSELF WOULD JUST MAKE YOUR LIFE UNCOM-FORTABLE.
IF YOU LEAVE THESE WOODS, IT'S ONLY GOING TO HURT.
...THAT'S NOT...

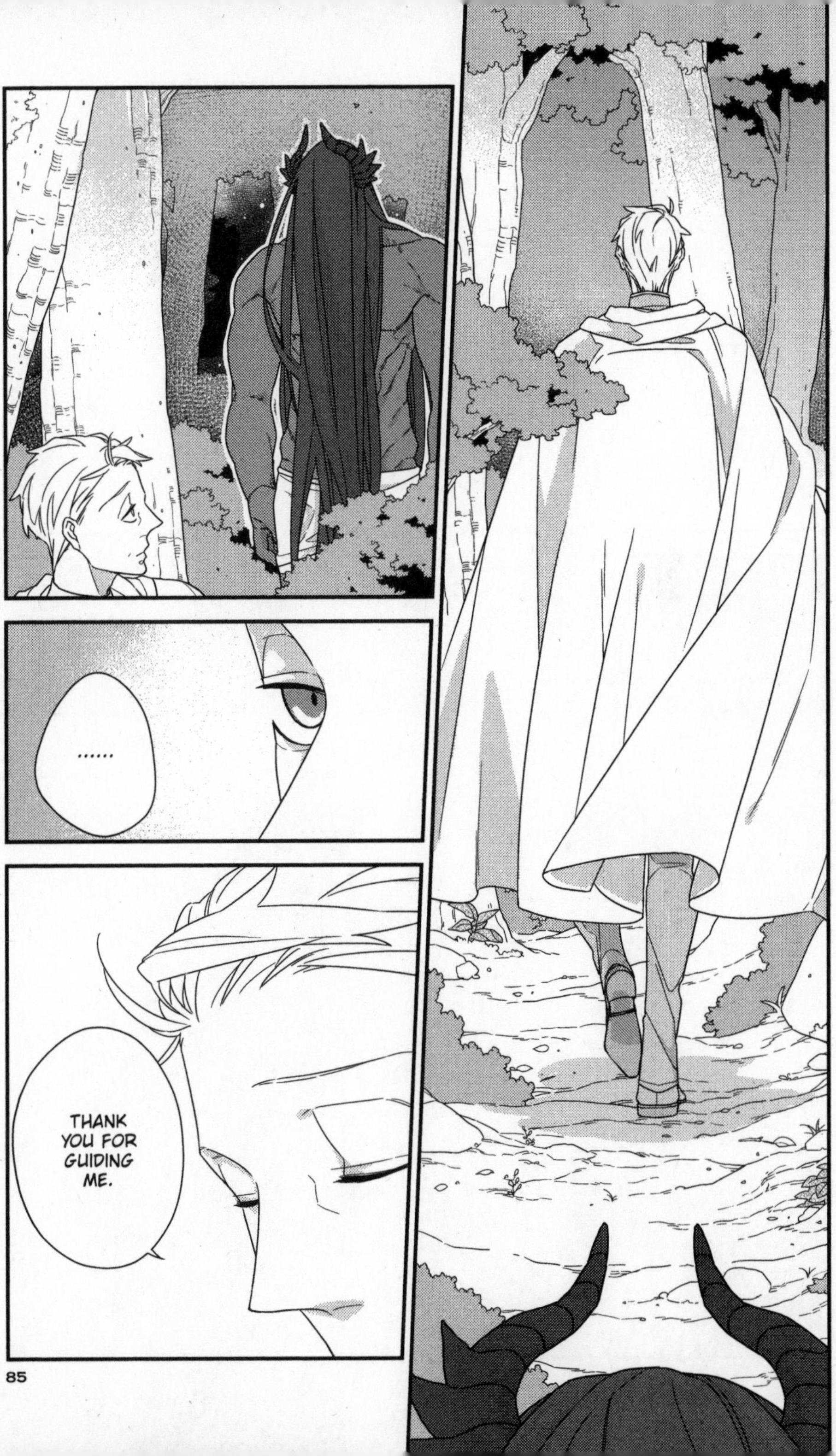
......
THANK YOU FOR GUIDING ME.

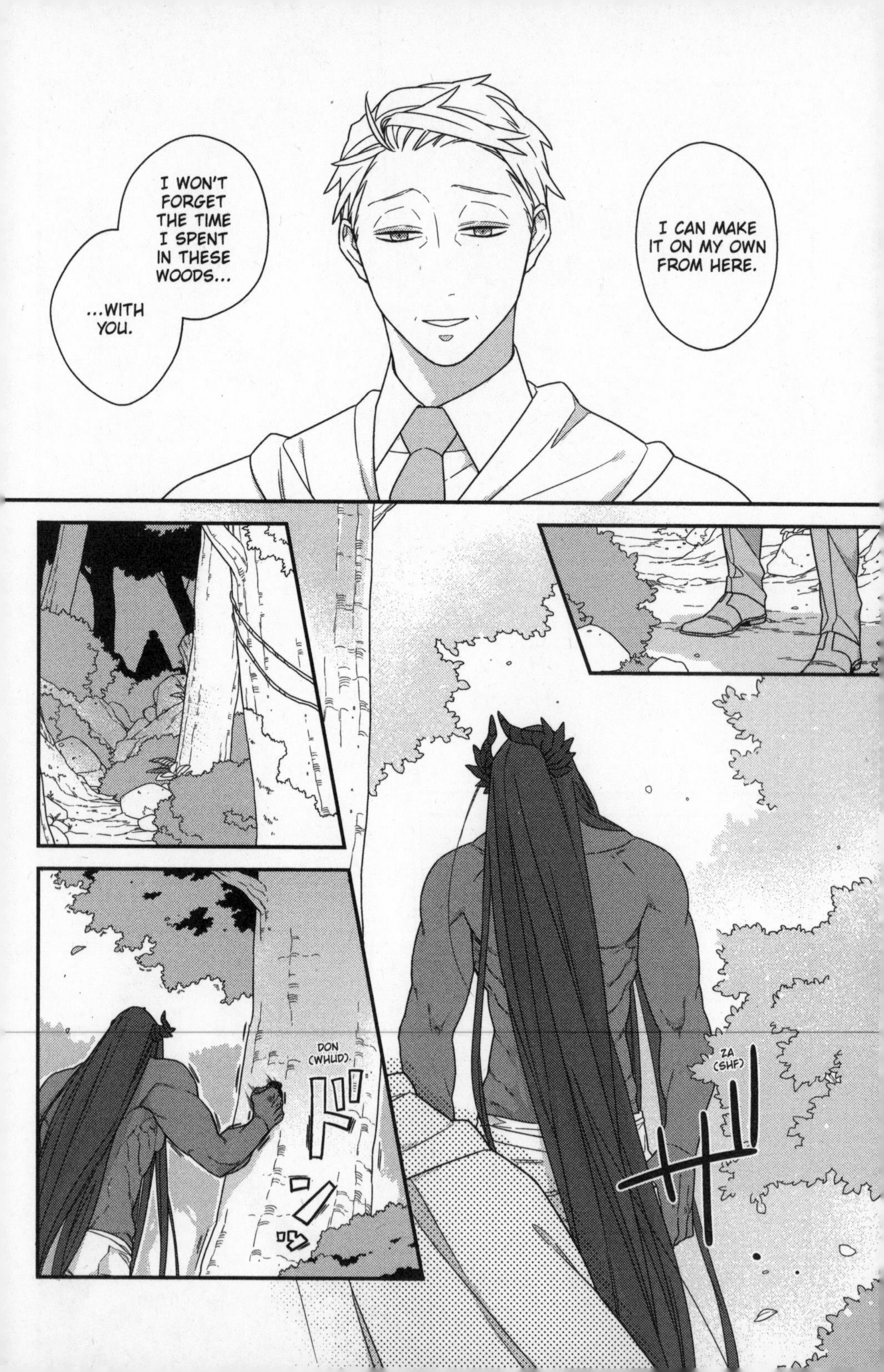
I CAN MAKE IT ON MY OWN FROM HERE.
I WON'T FORGET THE TIME I SPENT IN THESE WOODS...
...WITH YOU.
ZA (SHF)
DON (WHUD)

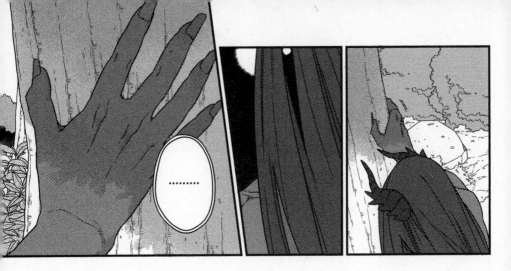

....

FU
(WSH)

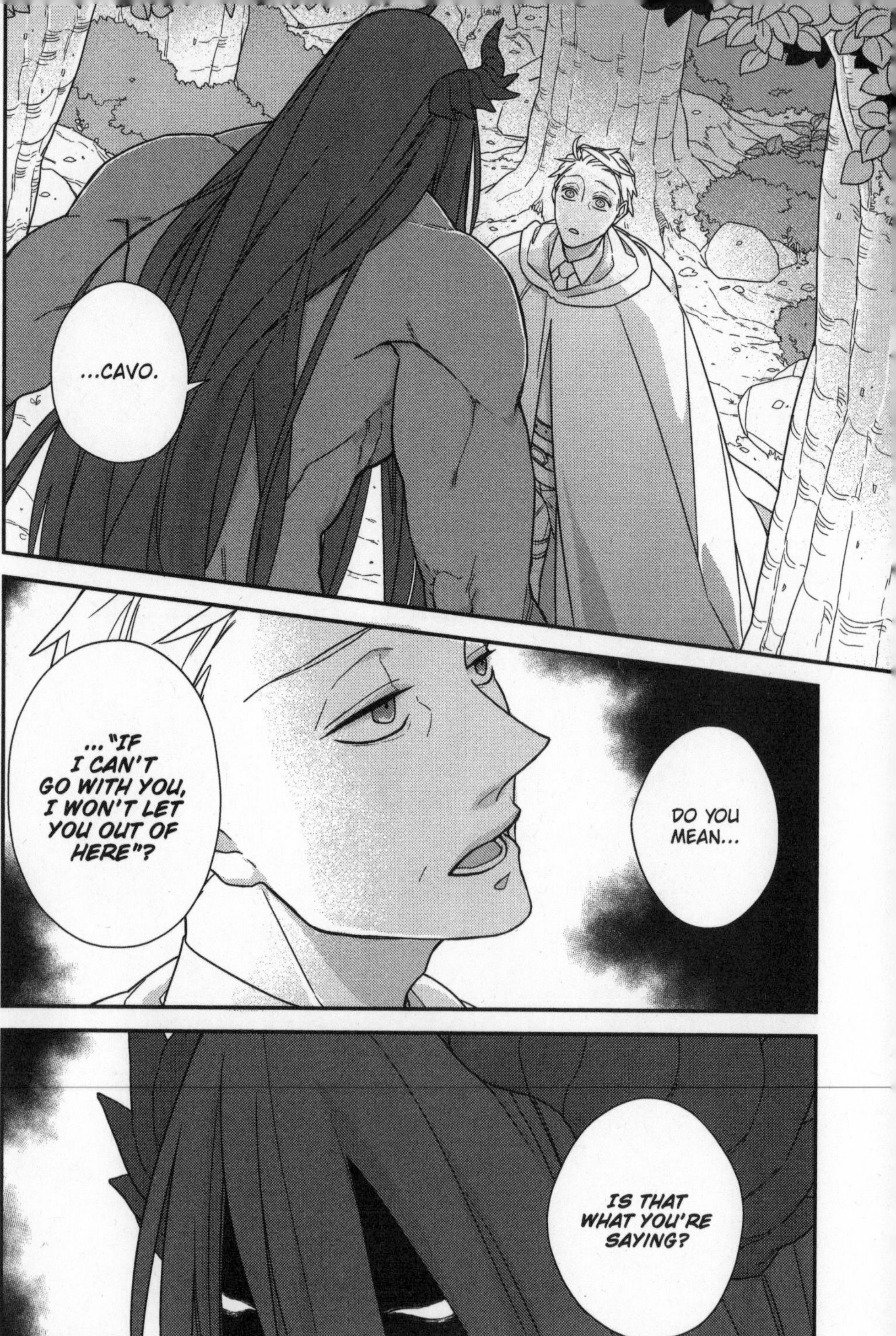
...CAVO.
DO YOU MEAN...
..."IF I CAN'T GO WITH YOU, I WON'T LET YOU OUT OF HERE"?
IS THAT WHAT YOU'RE SAYING?

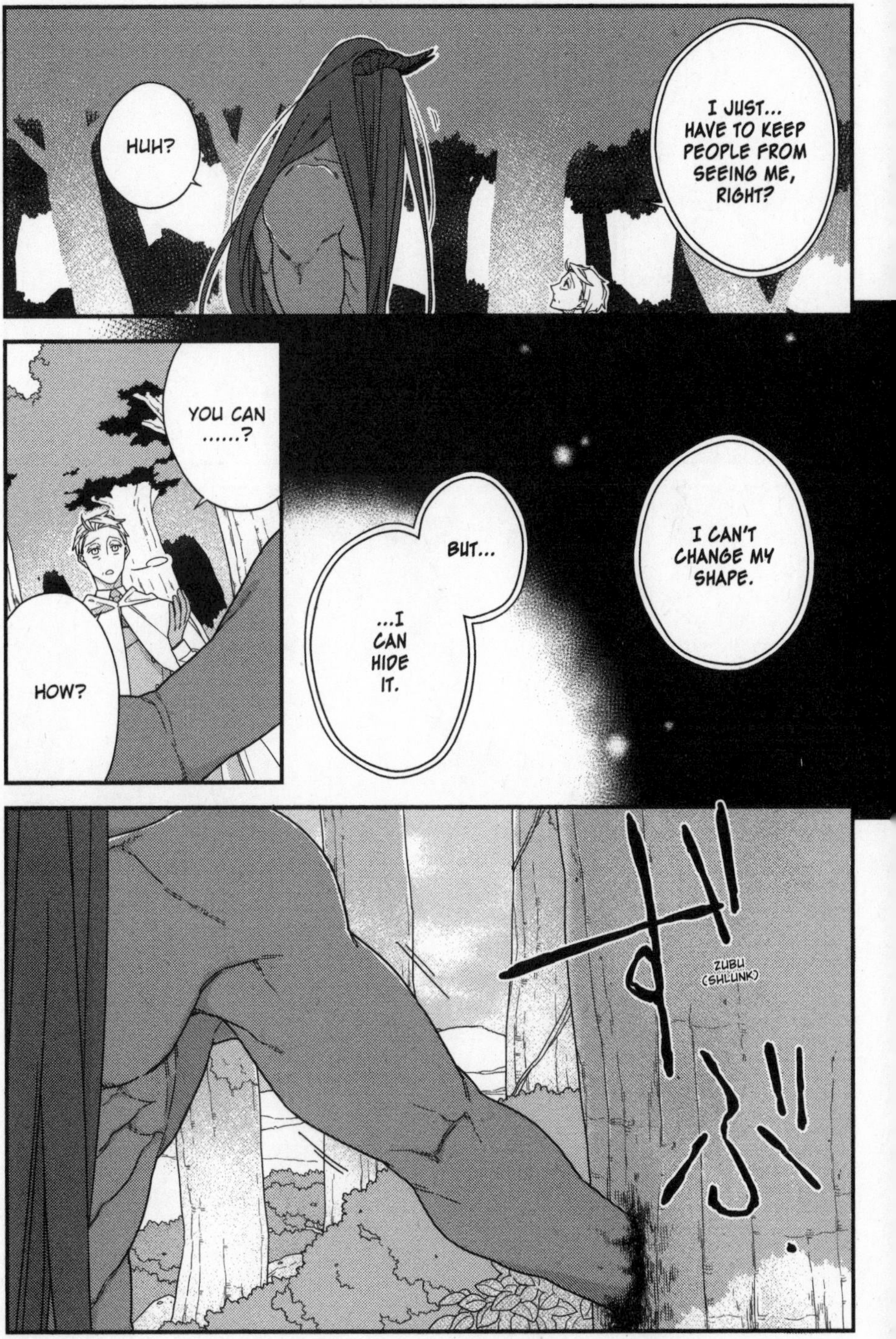
I JUST... HAVE TO KEEP PEOPLE FROM SEEING ME, RIGHT?
HUH?
I CAN'T CHANGE MY SHAPE.
BUT...
...I CAN HIDE IT.
YOU CAN ......?
HOW?
ずぶ
ZUBU (SHLUNK)

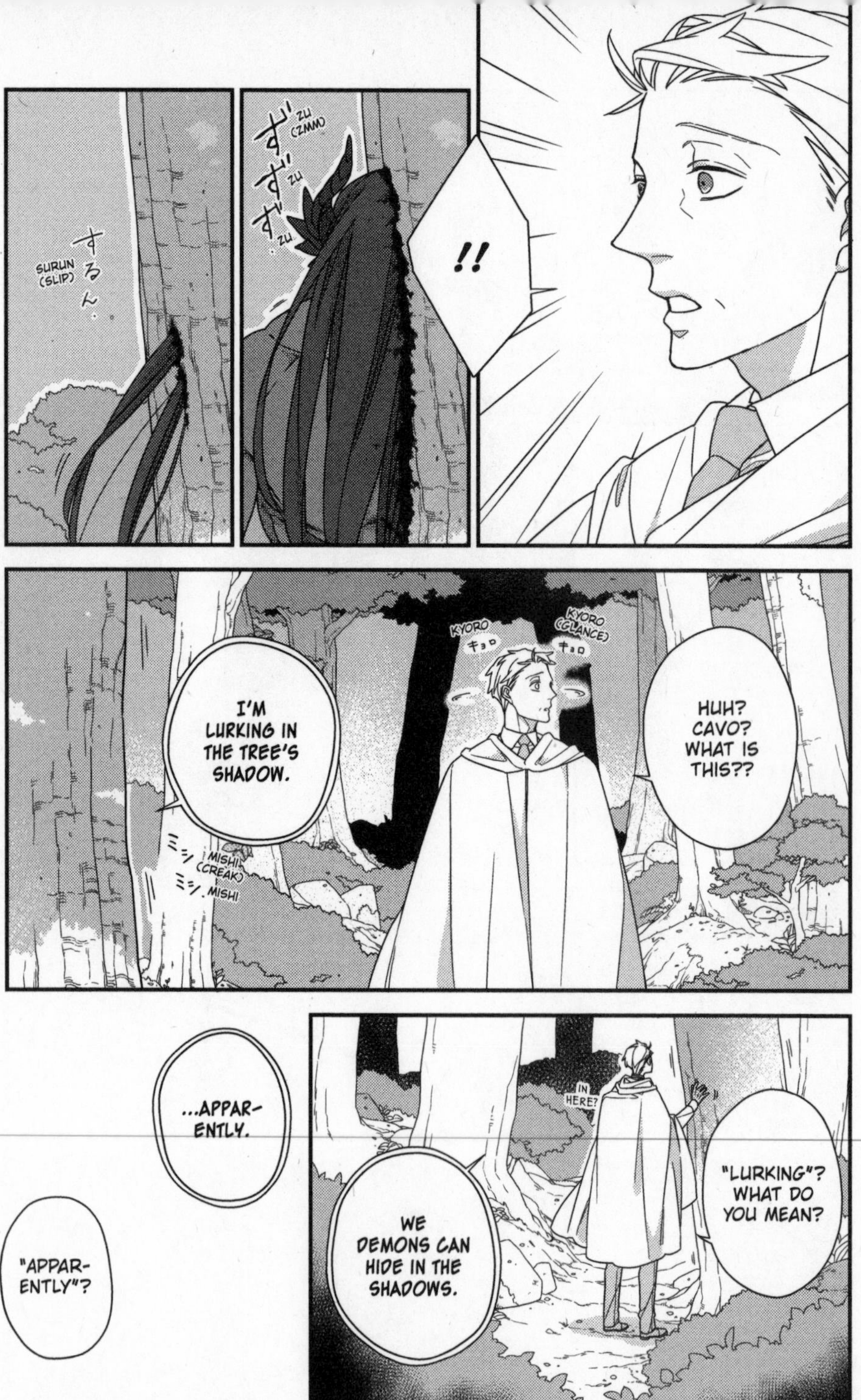
!!
ずずず
ZU (ZMM) ZU ZU
するん。
SURUN (SLIP)
HUH? CAVO? WHAT IS THIS??
キョロ キョロ
KYORO (GLANCE) KYORO
I'M LURKING IN THE TREE'S SHADOW.
ミシ ミシ
MISHI (CREAK) MISHI
"LURKING"? WHAT DO YOU MEAN?
IN HERE?
WE DEMONS CAN HIDE IN THE SHADOWS.
...APPARENTLY.
"APPARENTLY"?

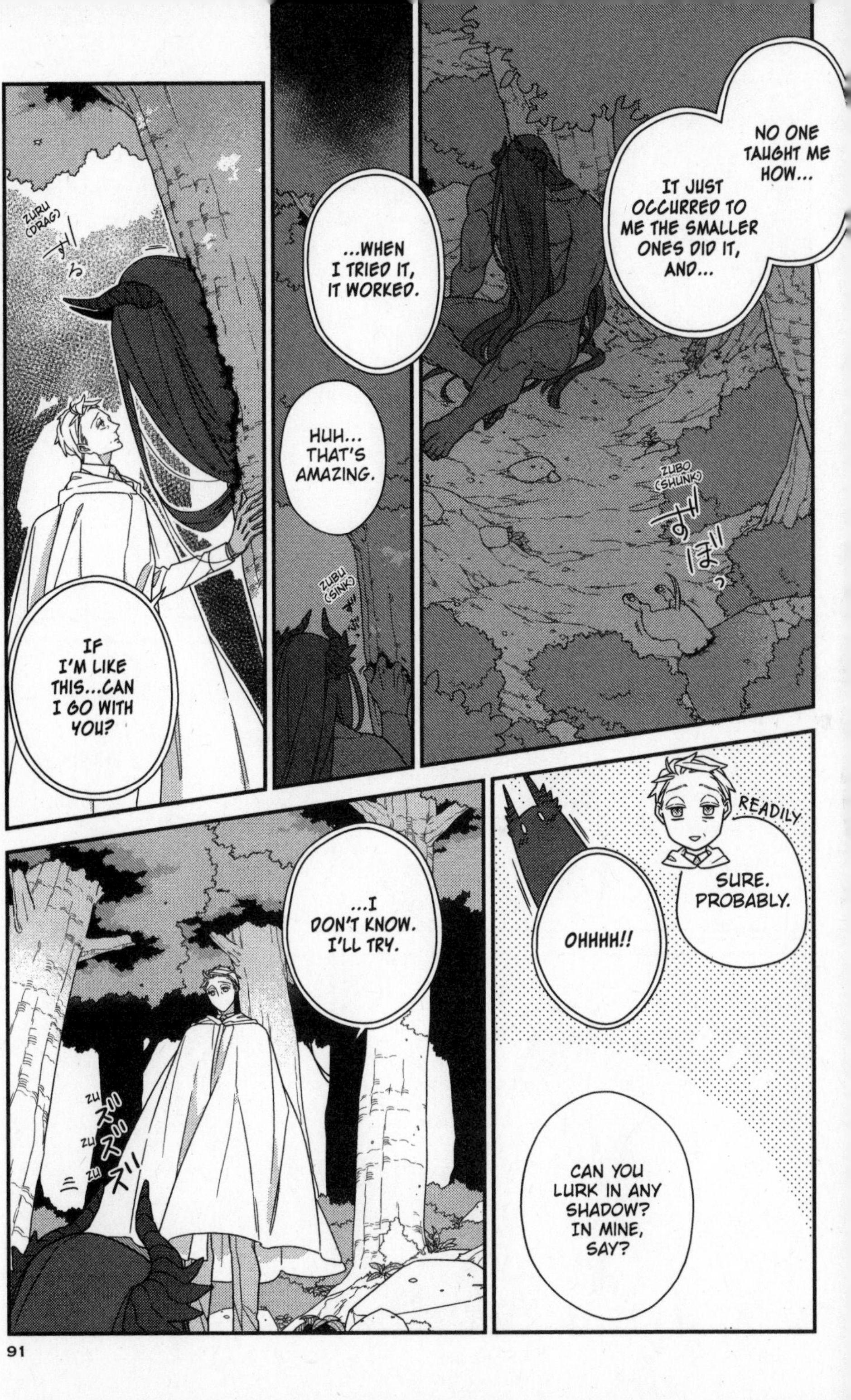
NO ONE TAUGHT ME HOW...
IT JUST OCCURRED TO ME THE SMALLER ONES DID IT, AND...
ZUBO (SHUNK)
...WHEN I TRIED IT, IT WORKED.
HUH... THAT'S AMAZING.
ZUBU (SINK)
ZURU (DRAG)
IF I'M LIKE THIS...CAN I GO WITH YOU?
READILY
SURE. PROBABLY.
OHHHH!!
CAN YOU LURK IN ANY SHADOW? IN MINE, SAY?
...I DON'T KNOW. I'LL TRY.
ZU ZU ZU

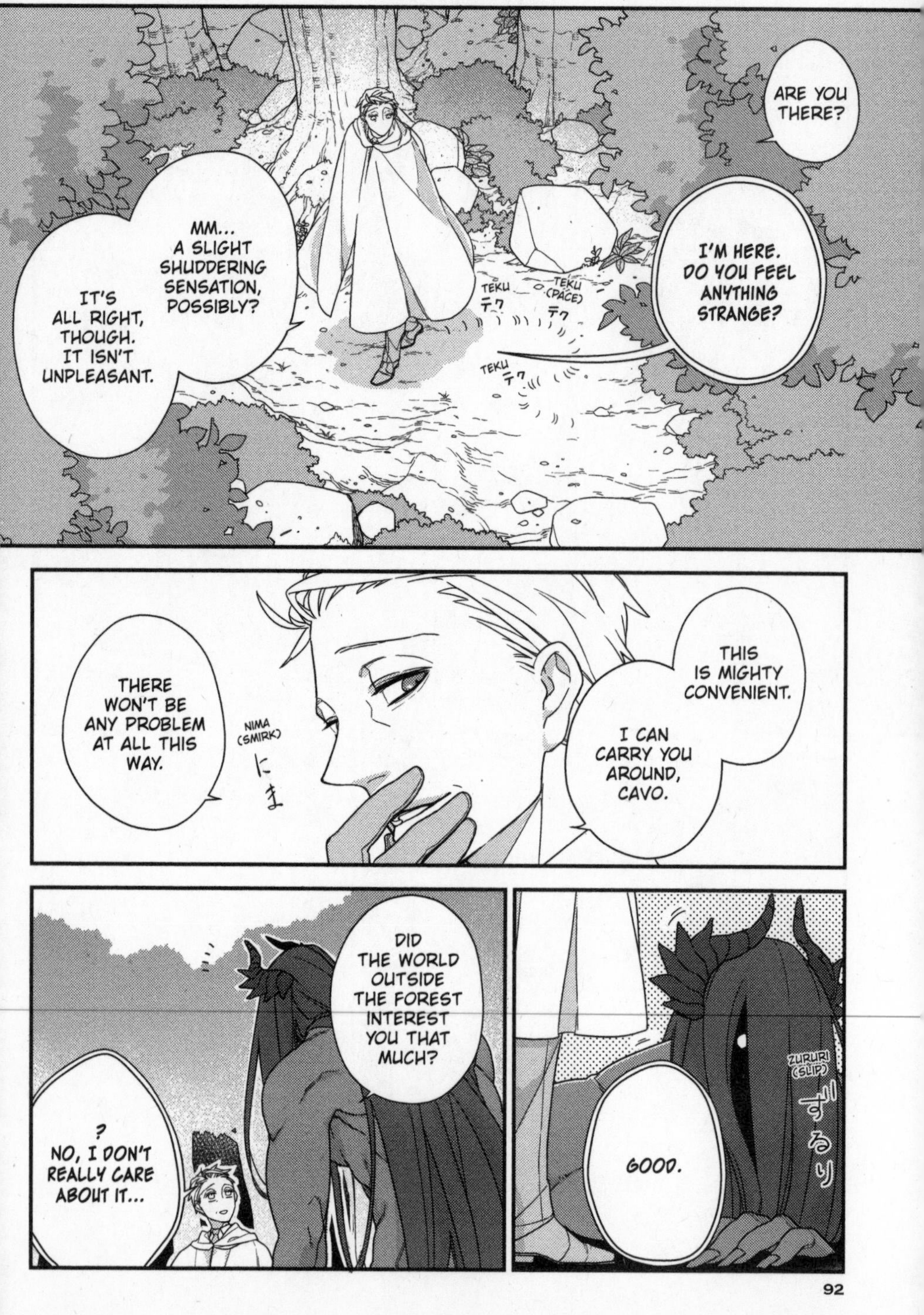
ARE YOU THERE?
I'M HERE. DO YOU FEEL ANYTHING STRANGE?
TEKU (PACE) テク
TEKU テク
TEKU テク
MM... A SLIGHT SHUDDERING SENSATION, POSSIBLY?
IT'S ALL RIGHT, THOUGH. IT ISN'T UNPLEASANT.
THIS IS MIGHTY CONVENIENT.
I CAN CARRY YOU AROUND, CAVO.
NIMA (SMIRK) にま
THERE WON'T BE ANY PROBLEM AT ALL THIS WAY.
ZURURI (SLIP) ずるり
GOOD.
DID THE WORLD OUTSIDE THE FOREST INTEREST YOU THAT MUCH?
? NO, I DON'T REALLY CARE ABOUT IT...

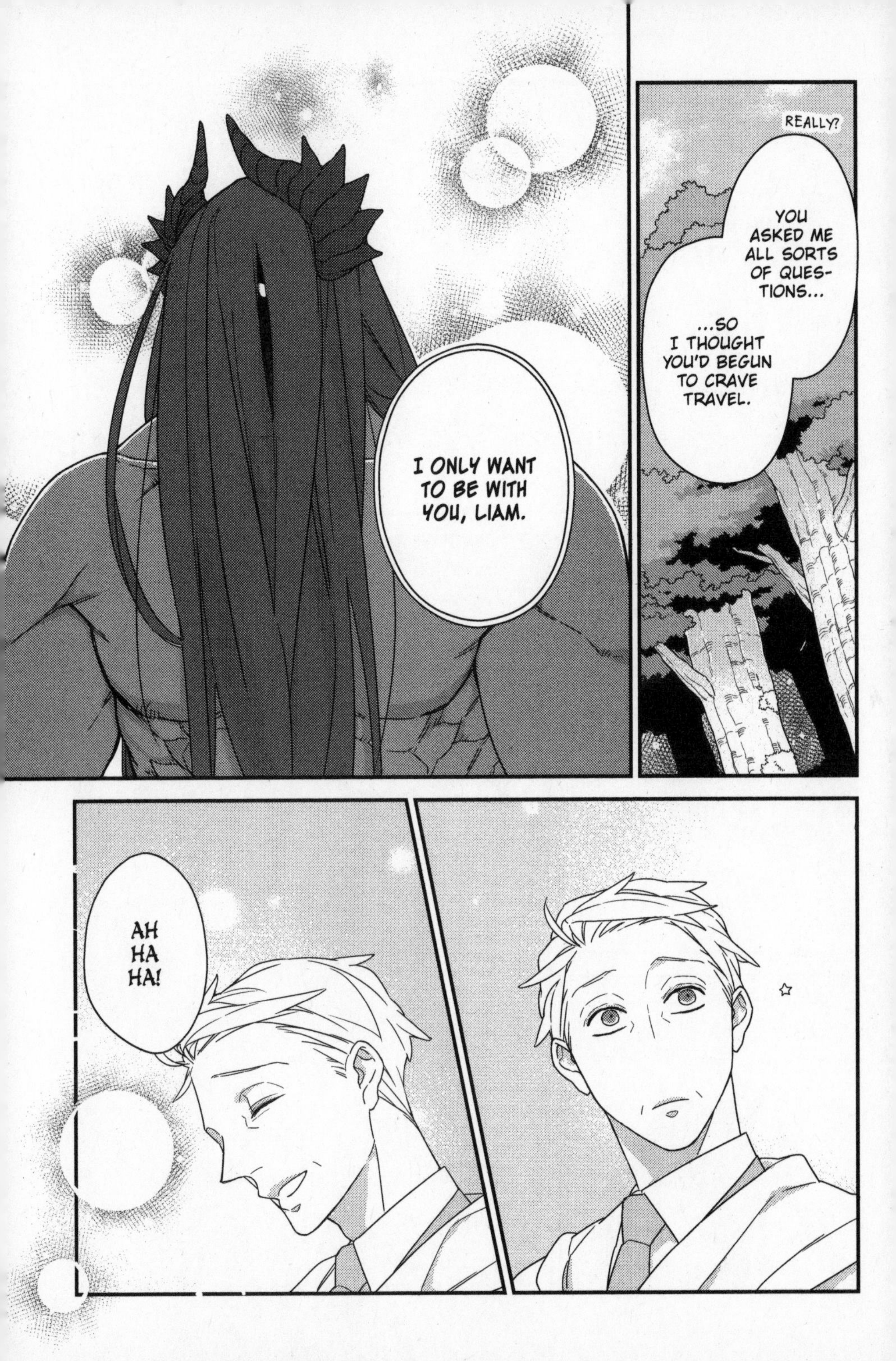
REALLY?
YOU ASKED ME ALL SORTS OF QUES-TIONS...
...SO I THOUGHT YOU'D BEGUN TO CRAVE TRAVEL.
I ONLY WANT TO BE WITH YOU, LIAM.
AH HA HA!

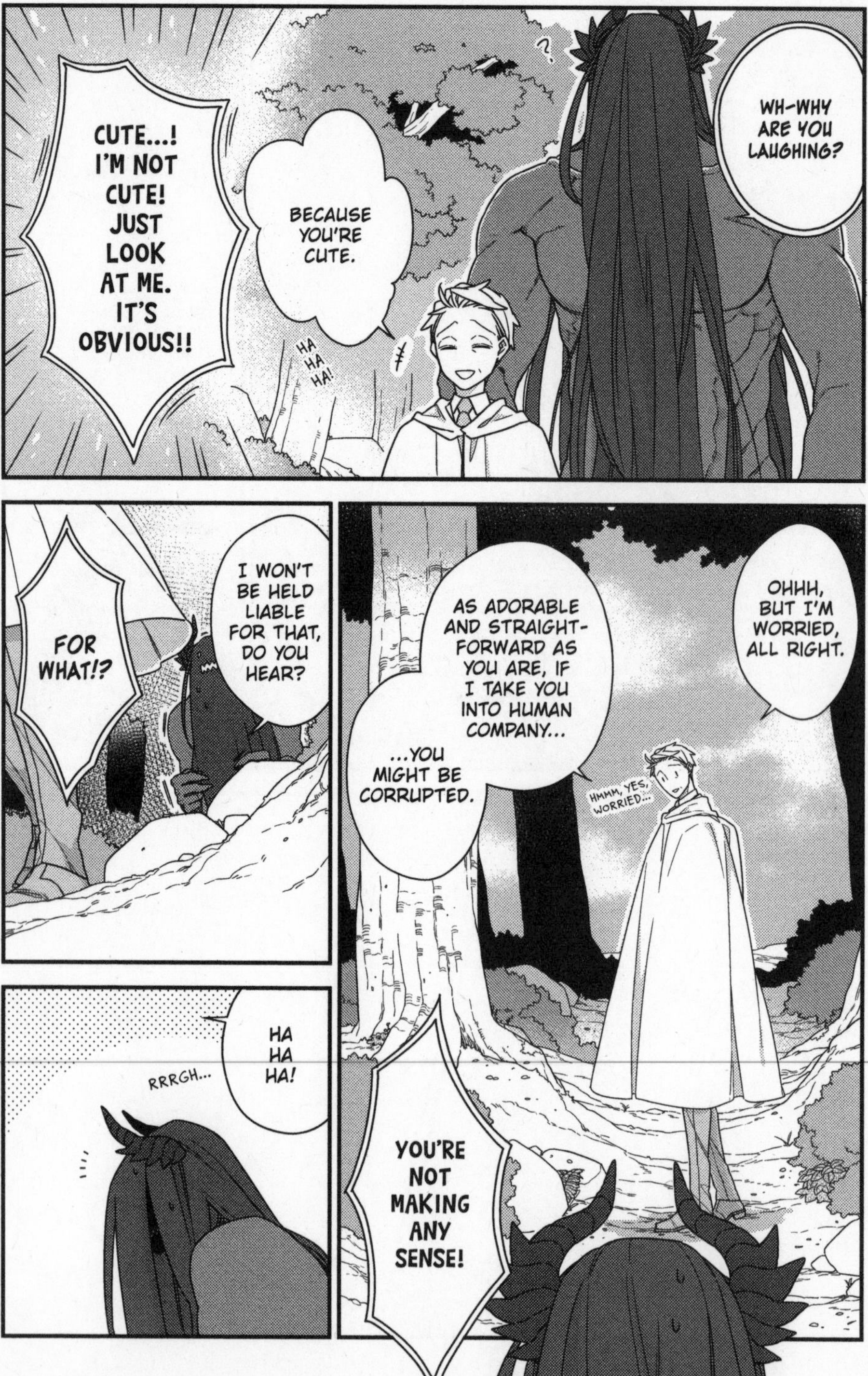
WH-WHY ARE YOU LAUGHING?
?
BECAUSE YOU'RE CUTE.
HA HA HA!
CUTE...! I'M NOT CUTE! JUST LOOK AT ME. IT'S OBVIOUS!!
OHHH, BUT I'M WORRIED, ALL RIGHT.
HMMM, YES, WORRIED...
AS ADORABLE AND STRAIGHT-FORWARD AS YOU ARE, IF I TAKE YOU INTO HUMAN COMPANY...
...YOU MIGHT BE CORRUPTED.
YOU'RE NOT MAKING ANY SENSE!
I WON'T BE HELD LIABLE FOR THAT, DO YOU HEAR?
FOR WHAT!?
HA HA HA!
RRRGH...

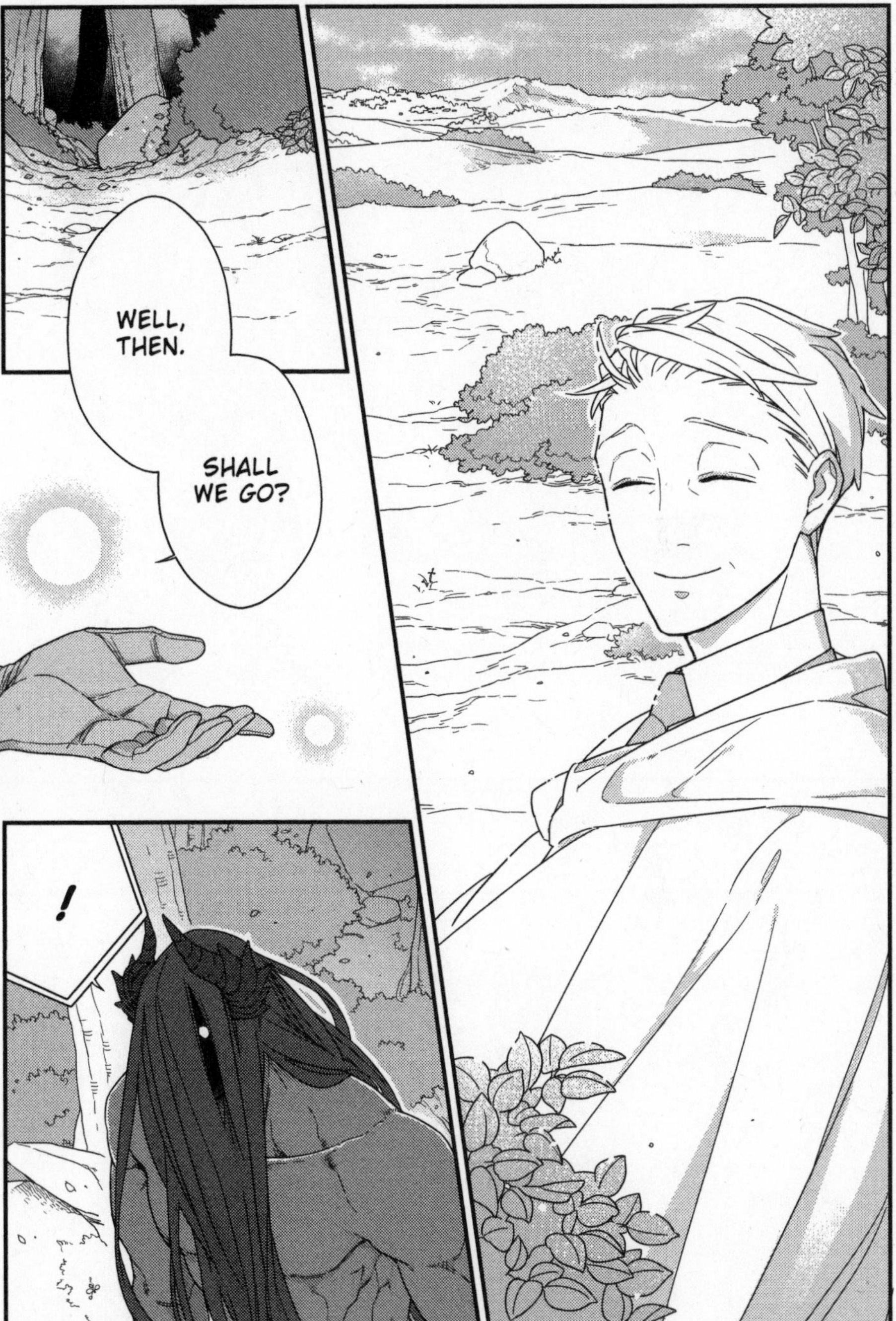
WELL, THEN.
SHALL WE GO?
!

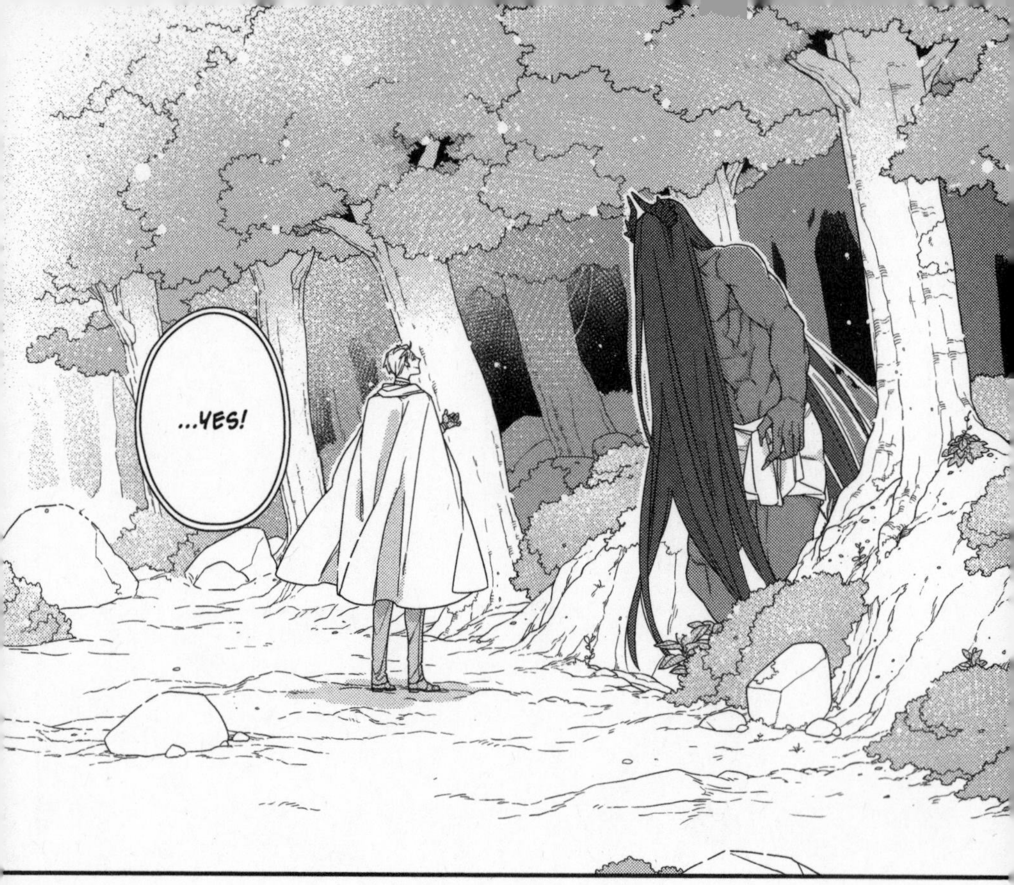
...YES!

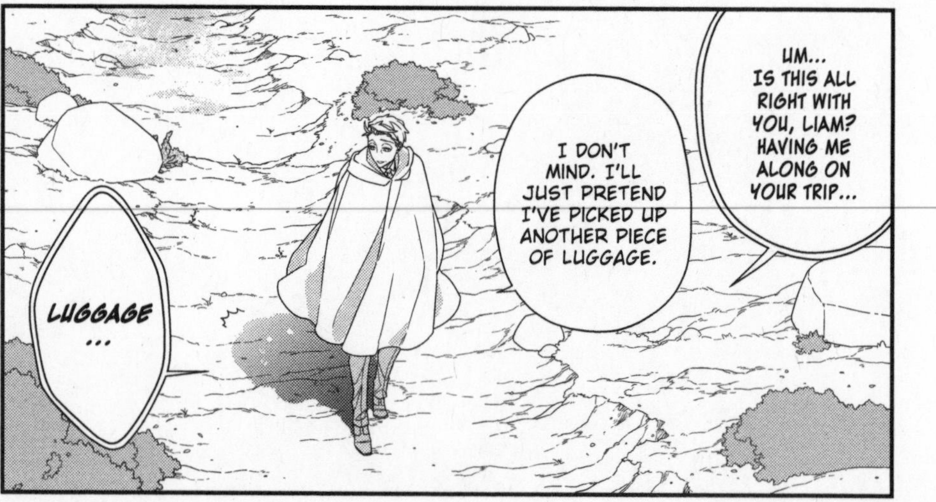
UM... IS THIS ALL RIGHT WITH YOU, LIAM? HAVING ME ALONG ON YOUR TRIP...
I DON'T MIND. I'LL JUST PRETEND I'VE PICKED UP ANOTHER PIECE OF LUGGAGE.
LUGGAGE...

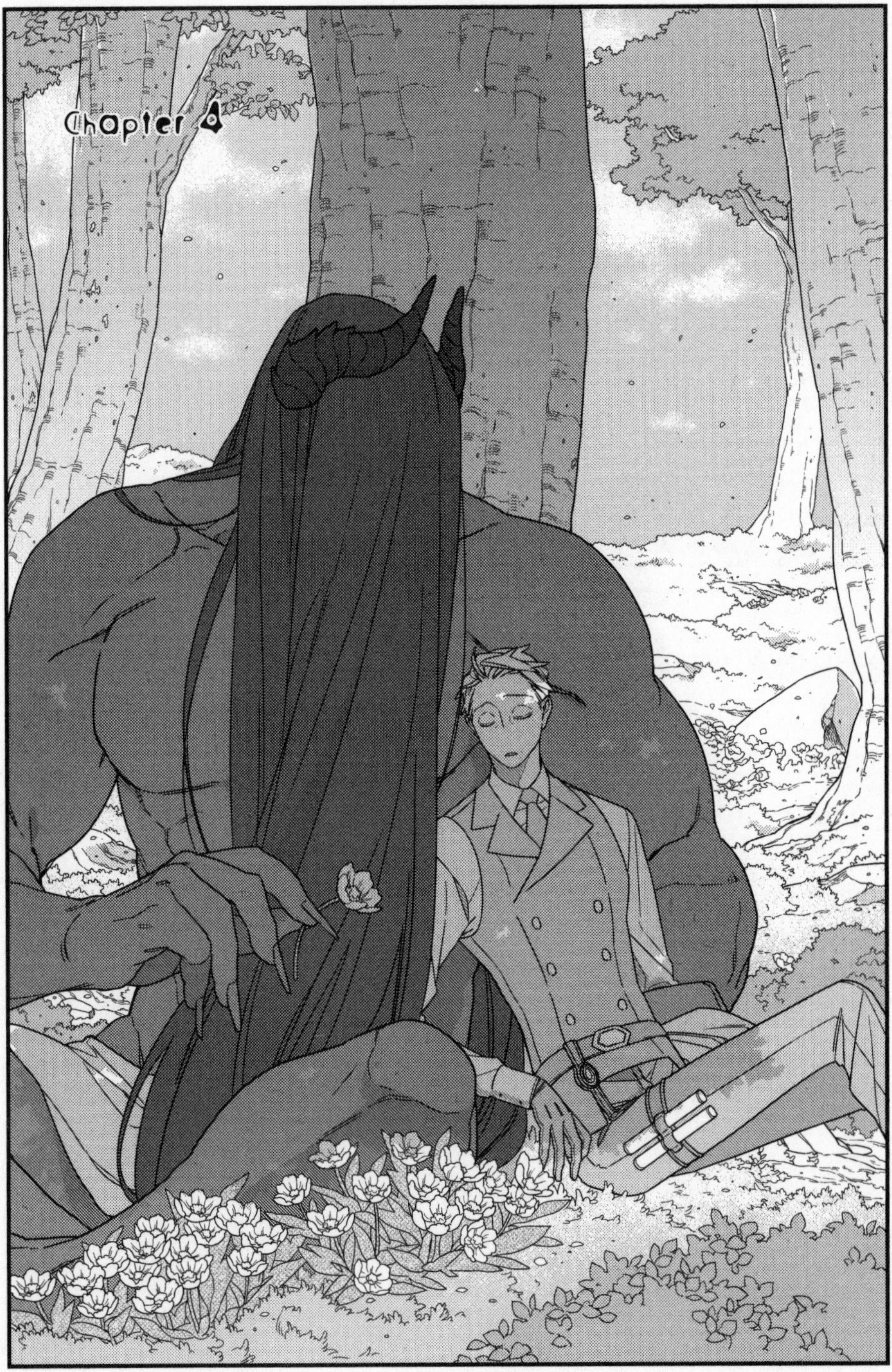
Chapter 4

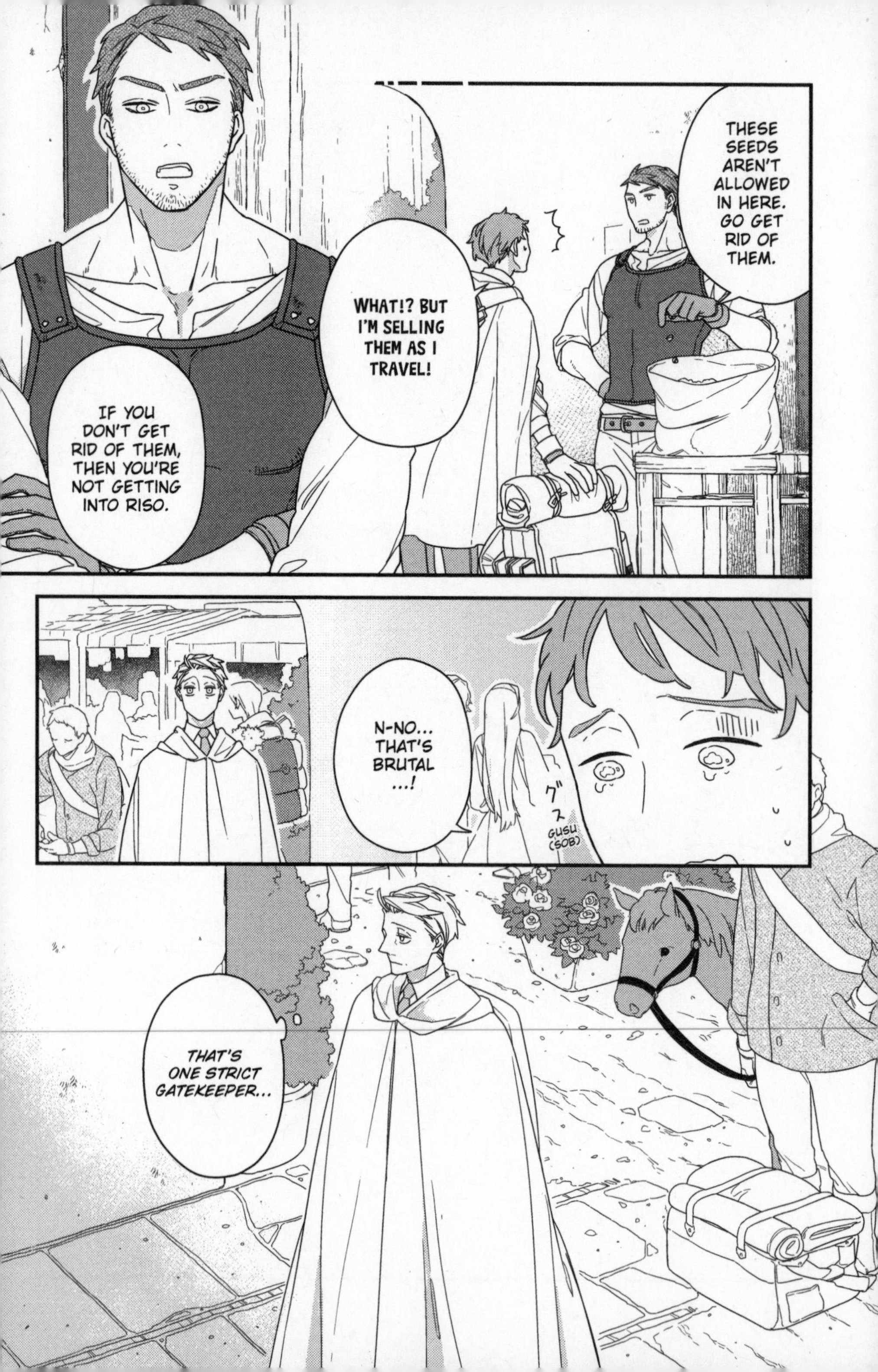
THESE SEEDS AREN'T ALLOWED IN HERE. GO GET RID OF THEM.
WHAT!? BUT I'M SELLING THEM AS I TRAVEL!
IF YOU DON'T GET RID OF THEM, THEN YOU'RE NOT GETTING INTO RISO.
N-NO... THAT'S BRUTAL ...!
グス
GUSU (SOB)
THAT'S ONE STRICT GATEKEEPER...

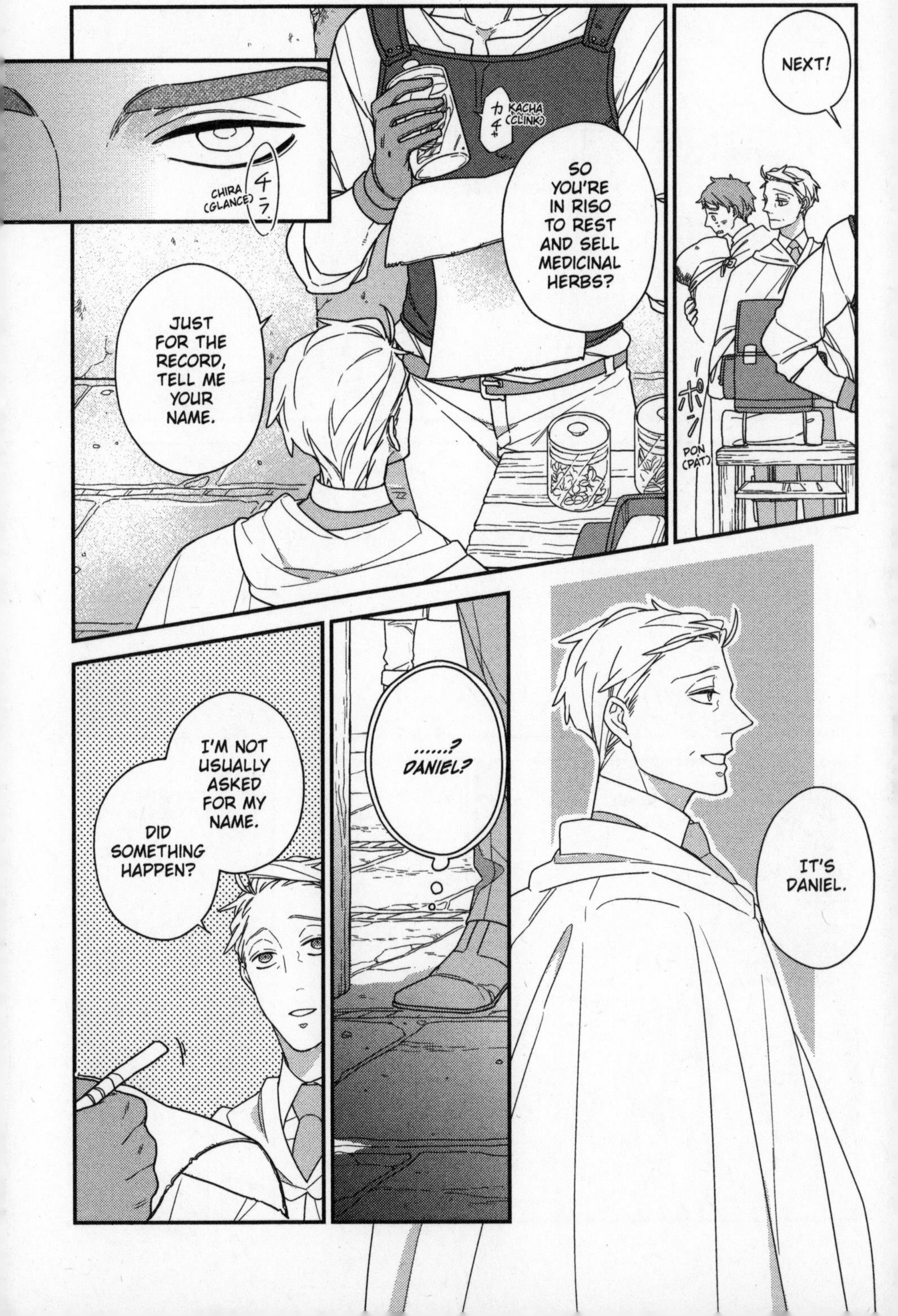
NEXT!
ポン
PON (PAT)
カチャ
KACHA (CLINK)
SO YOU'RE IN RISO TO REST AND SELL MEDICINAL HERBS?
チラ
CHIRA (GLANCE)
JUST FOR THE RECORD, TELL ME YOUR NAME.
IT'S DANIEL.
......? DANIEL?
I'M NOT USUALLY ASKED FOR MY NAME.
DID SOMETHING HAPPEN?

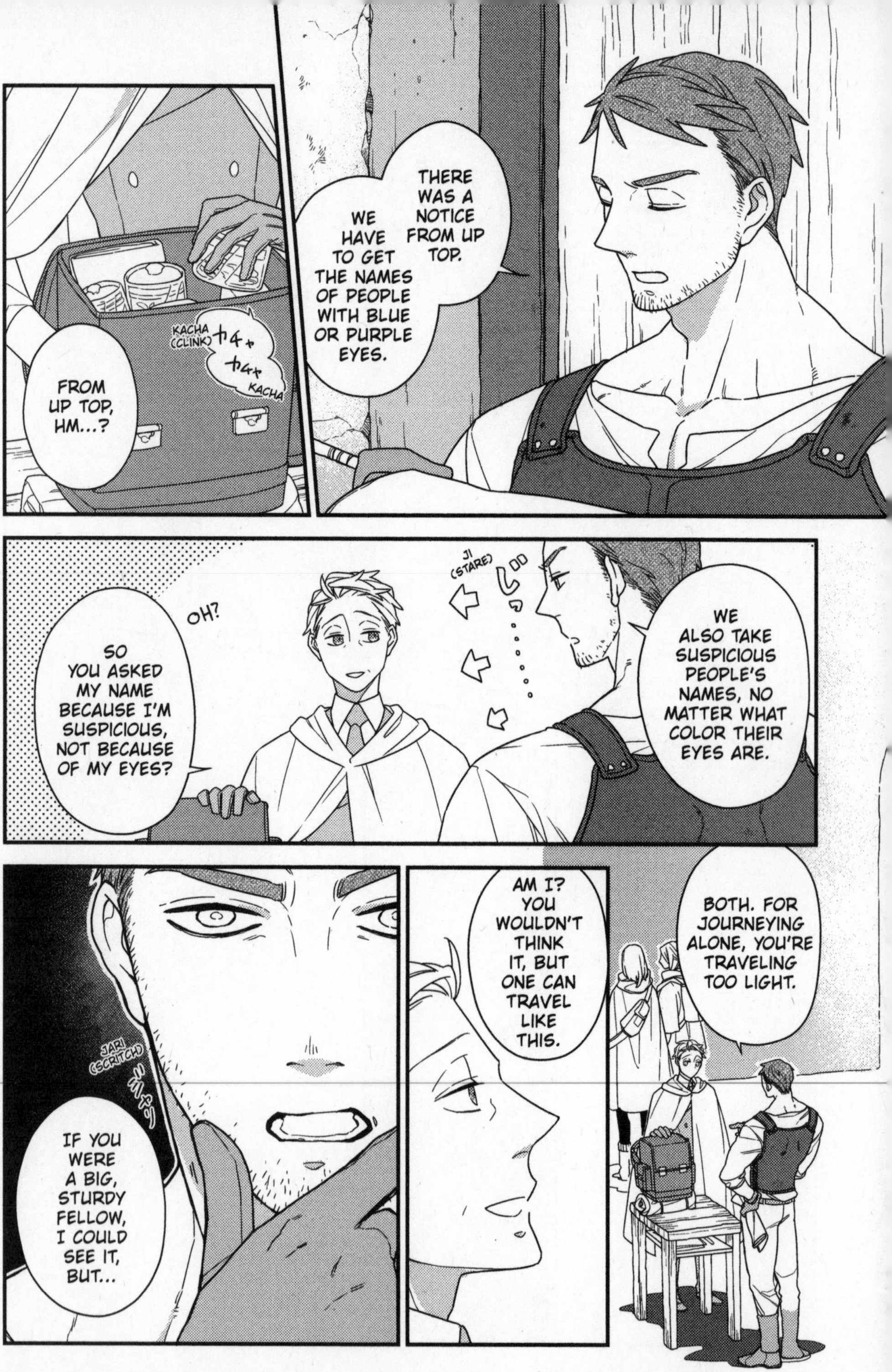
THERE WAS A NOTICE FROM UP TOP.
WE HAVE TO GET THE NAMES OF PEOPLE WITH BLUE OR PURPLE EYES.
KACHA (CLINK)
カチャ
カチャ
KACHA
FROM UP TOP, HM...?
JI (STARE)
じっ
WE ALSO TAKE SUSPICIOUS PEOPLE'S NAMES, NO MATTER WHAT COLOR THEIR EYES ARE.
OH?
SO YOU ASKED MY NAME BECAUSE I'M SUSPICIOUS, NOT BECAUSE OF MY EYES?
BOTH. FOR JOURNEYING ALONE, YOU'RE TRAVELING TOO LIGHT.
AM I? YOU WOULDN'T THINK IT, BUT ONE CAN TRAVEL LIKE THIS.
JARI (SCRITCH)
IF YOU WERE A BIG, STURDY FELLOW, I COULD SEE IT, BUT...

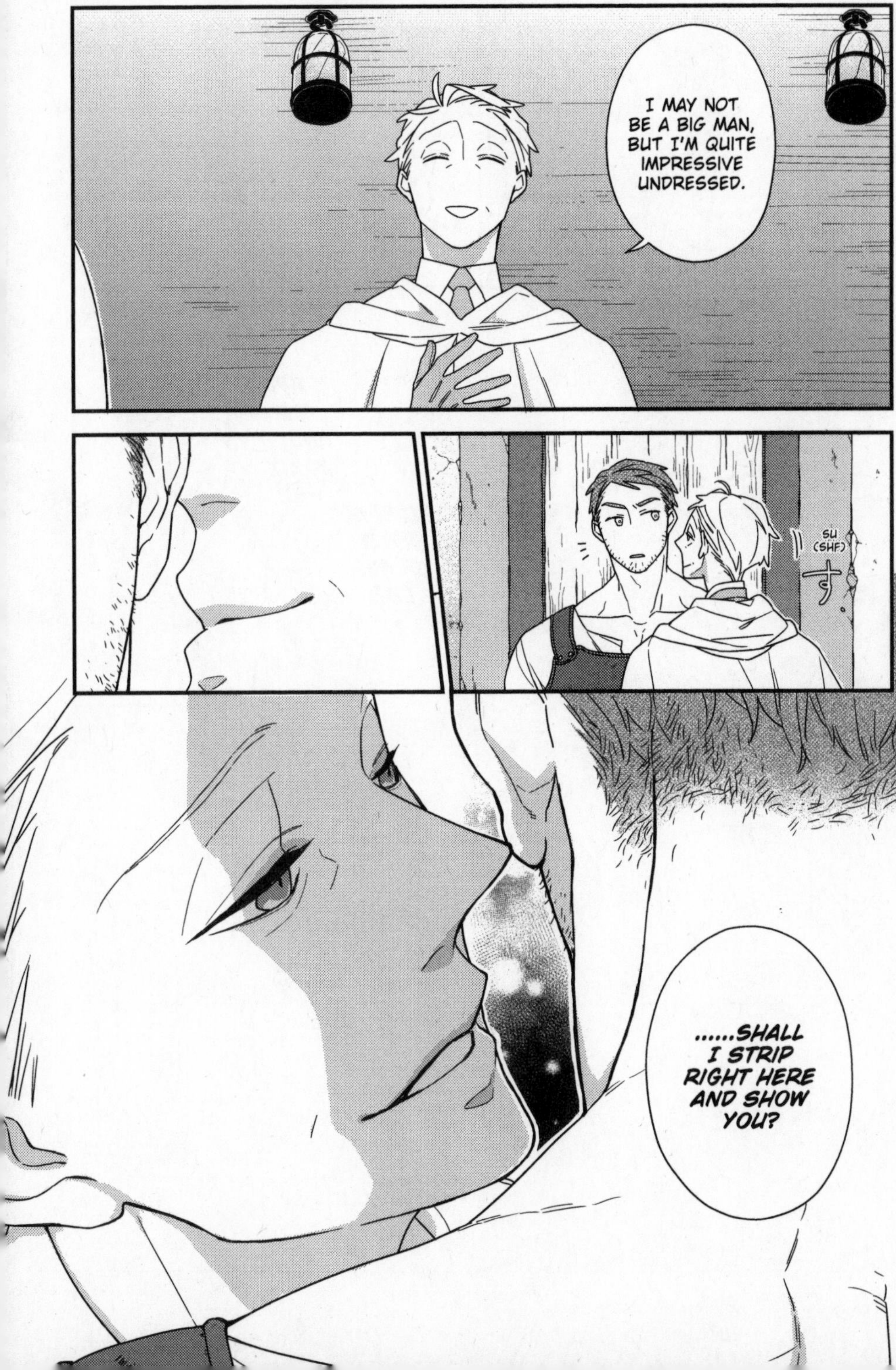
I MAY NOT BE A BIG MAN, BUT I'M QUITE IMPRESSIVE UNDRESSED.
SU (SHF) す
......SHALL I STRIP RIGHT HERE AND SHOW YOU?

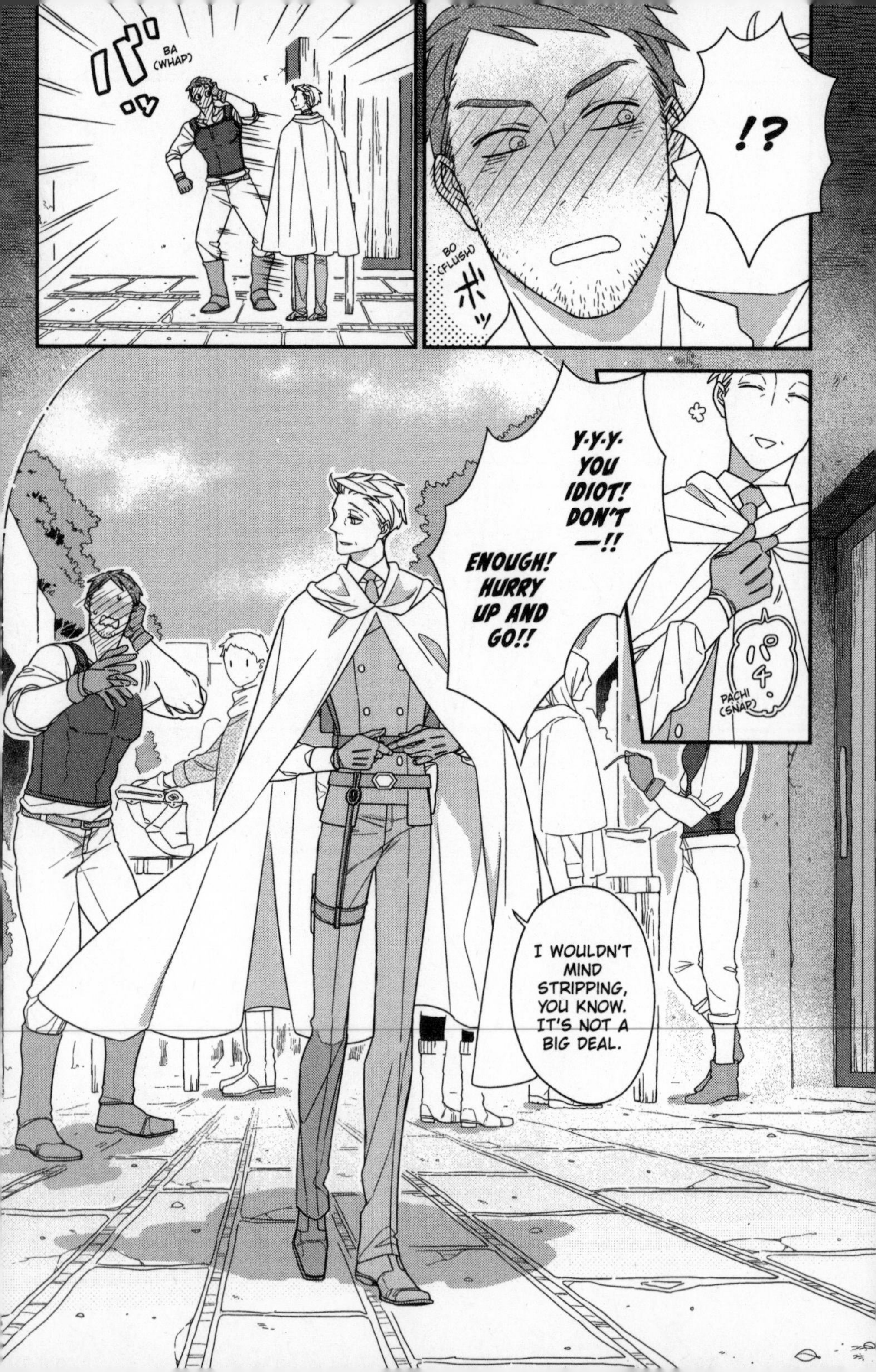
!?
ボッ
BO (FLUSH)
パッ
BA (WHAP)
パチ
PACHI (SNAP)
Y-Y-Y-YOU IDIOT! DON'T—!!
ENOUGH! HURRY UP AND GO!!
I WOULDN'T MIND STRIPPING, YOU KNOW. IT'S NOT A BIG DEAL.

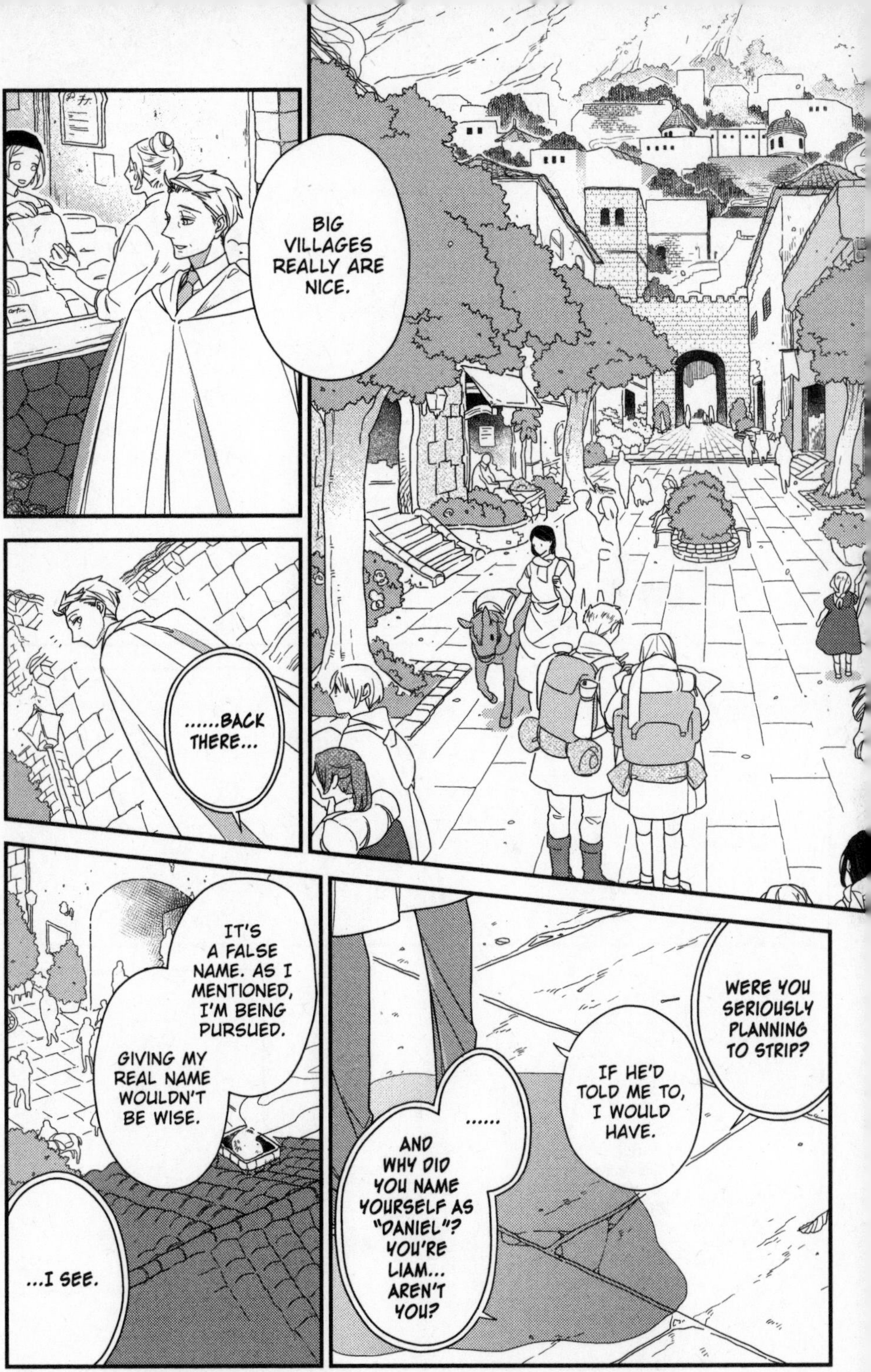
BIG VILLAGES REALLY ARE NICE.
......BACK THERE...
WERE YOU SERIOUSLY PLANNING TO STRIP?
IF HE'D TOLD ME TO, I WOULD HAVE.
......
AND WHY DID YOU NAME YOURSELF AS "DANIEL"? YOU'RE LIAM... AREN'T YOU?
IT'S A FALSE NAME. AS I MENTIONED, I'M BEING PURSUED.
GIVING MY REAL NAME WOULDN'T BE WISE.
...I SEE.

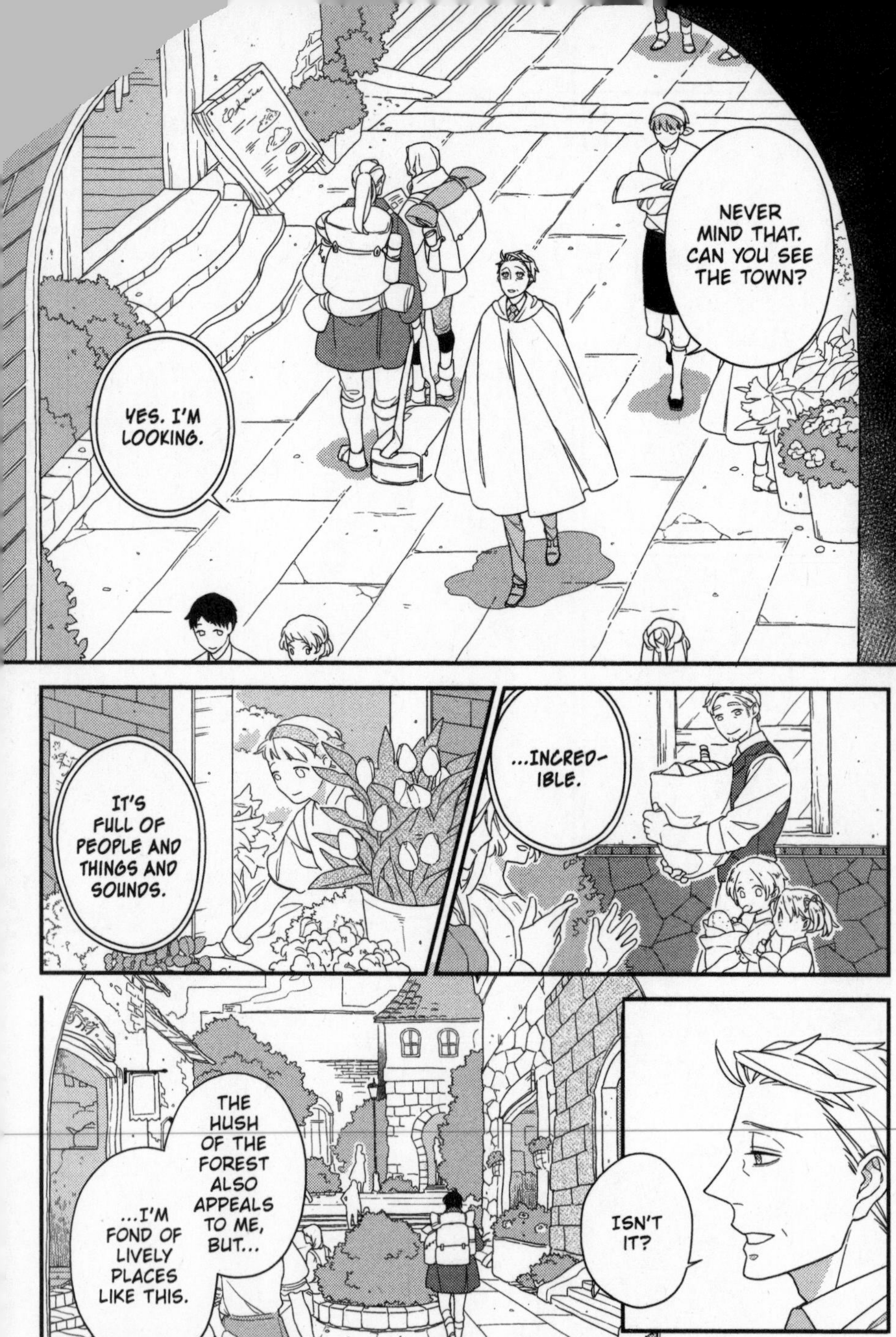
NEVER MIND THAT. CAN YOU SEE THE TOWN?
YES. I'M LOOKING.
...INCRED-IBLE.
IT'S FULL OF PEOPLE AND THINGS AND SOUNDS.
ISN'T IT?
THE HUSH OF THE FOREST ALSO APPEALS TO ME, BUT...
...I'M FOND OF LIVELY PLACES LIKE THIS.

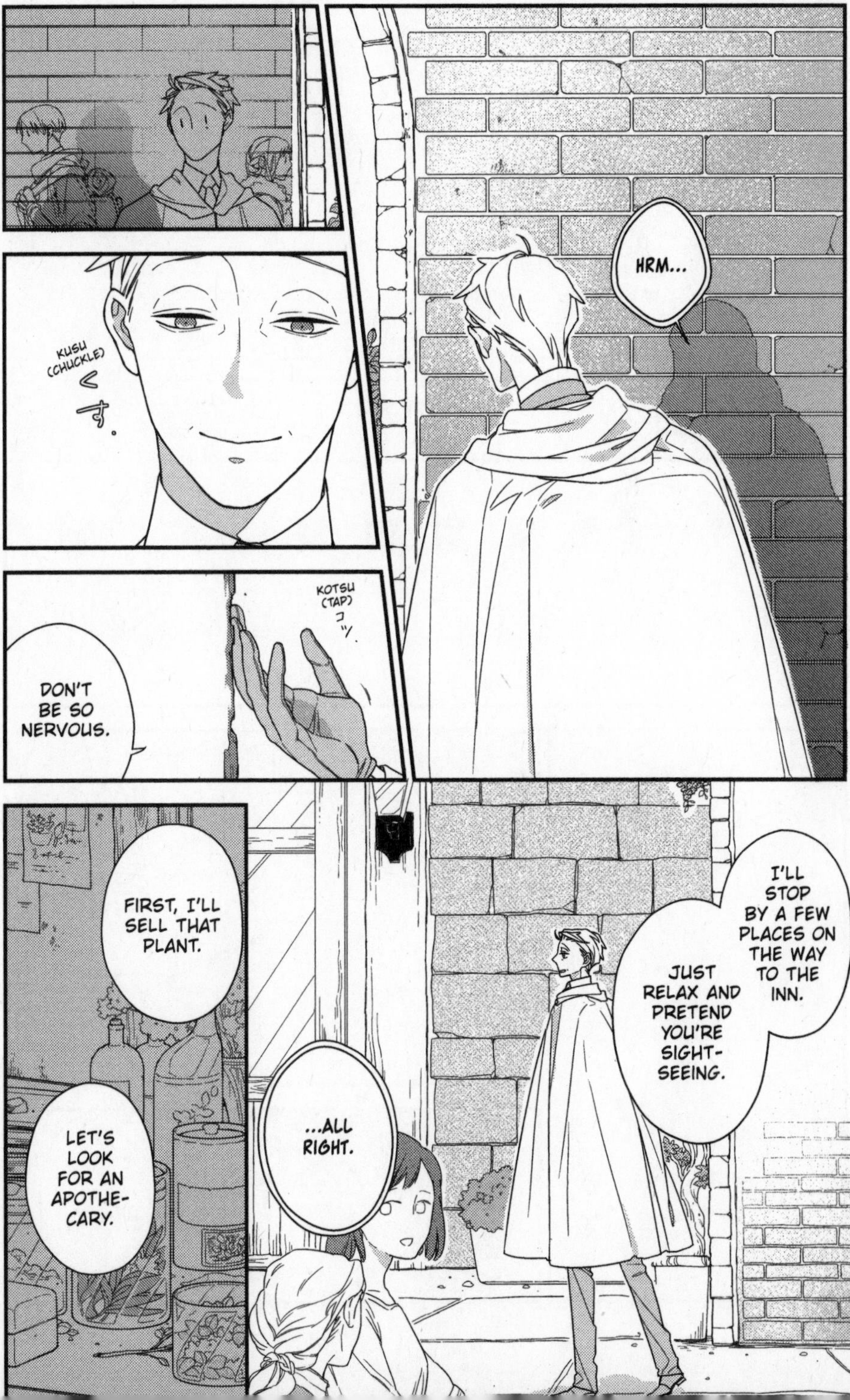
HRM...
KUSU (CHUCKLE)
くす。
KOTSU (TAP)
コツ
DON'T BE SO NERVOUS.
I'LL STOP BY A FEW PLACES ON THE WAY TO THE INN.
JUST RELAX AND PRETEND YOU'RE SIGHT-SEEING.
...ALL RIGHT.
FIRST, I'LL SELL THAT PLANT.
LET'S LOOK FOR AN APOTHE-CARY.

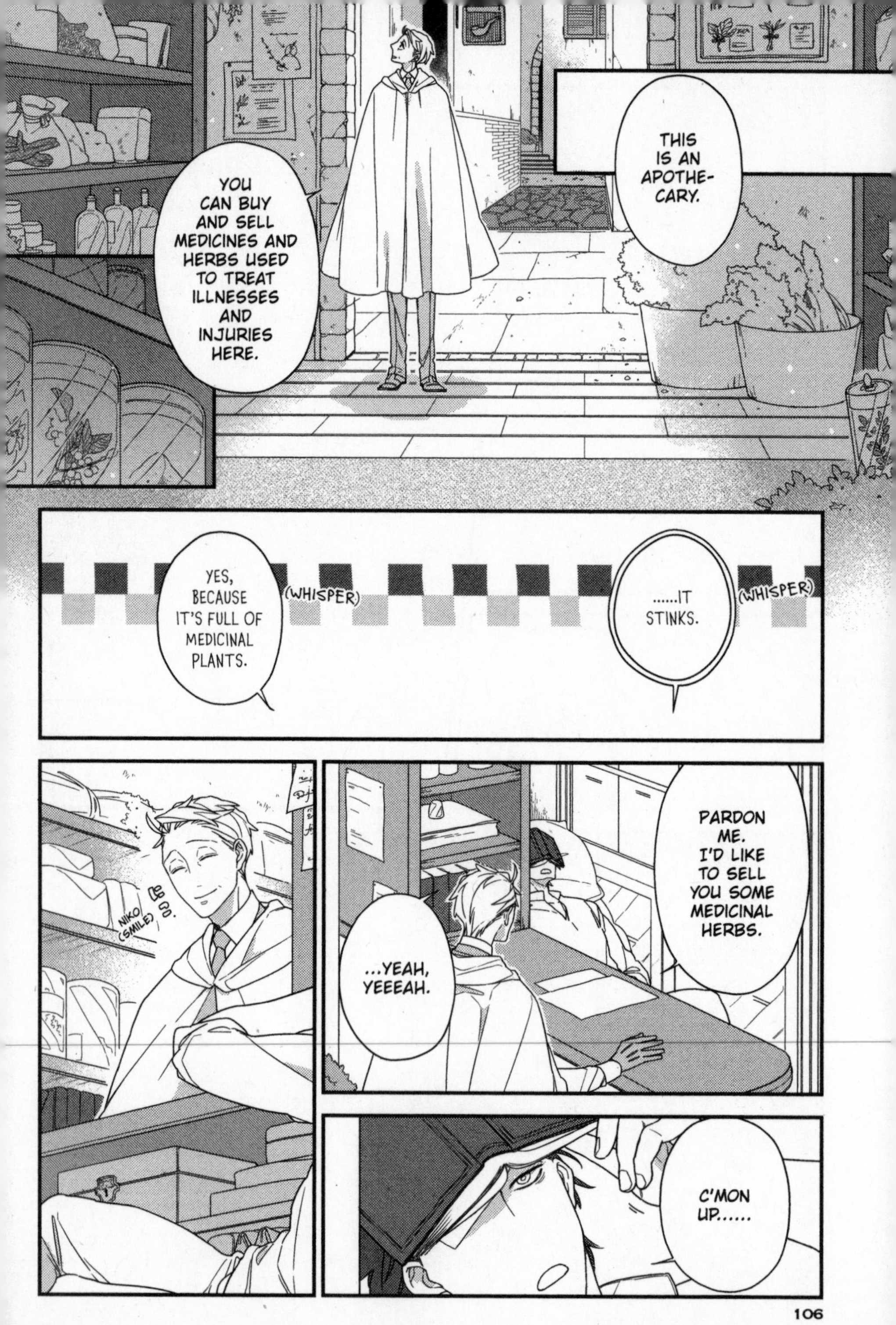
THIS IS AN APOTHECARY.
YOU CAN BUY AND SELL MEDICINES AND HERBS USED TO TREAT ILLNESSES AND INJURIES HERE.
(WHISPER)
......IT STINKS.
(WHISPER)
YES, BECAUSE IT'S FULL OF MEDICINAL PLANTS.
PARDON ME. I'D LIKE TO SELL YOU SOME MEDICINAL HERBS.
...YEAH, YEEEAH.
C'MON UP......
NIKO (SMILE)

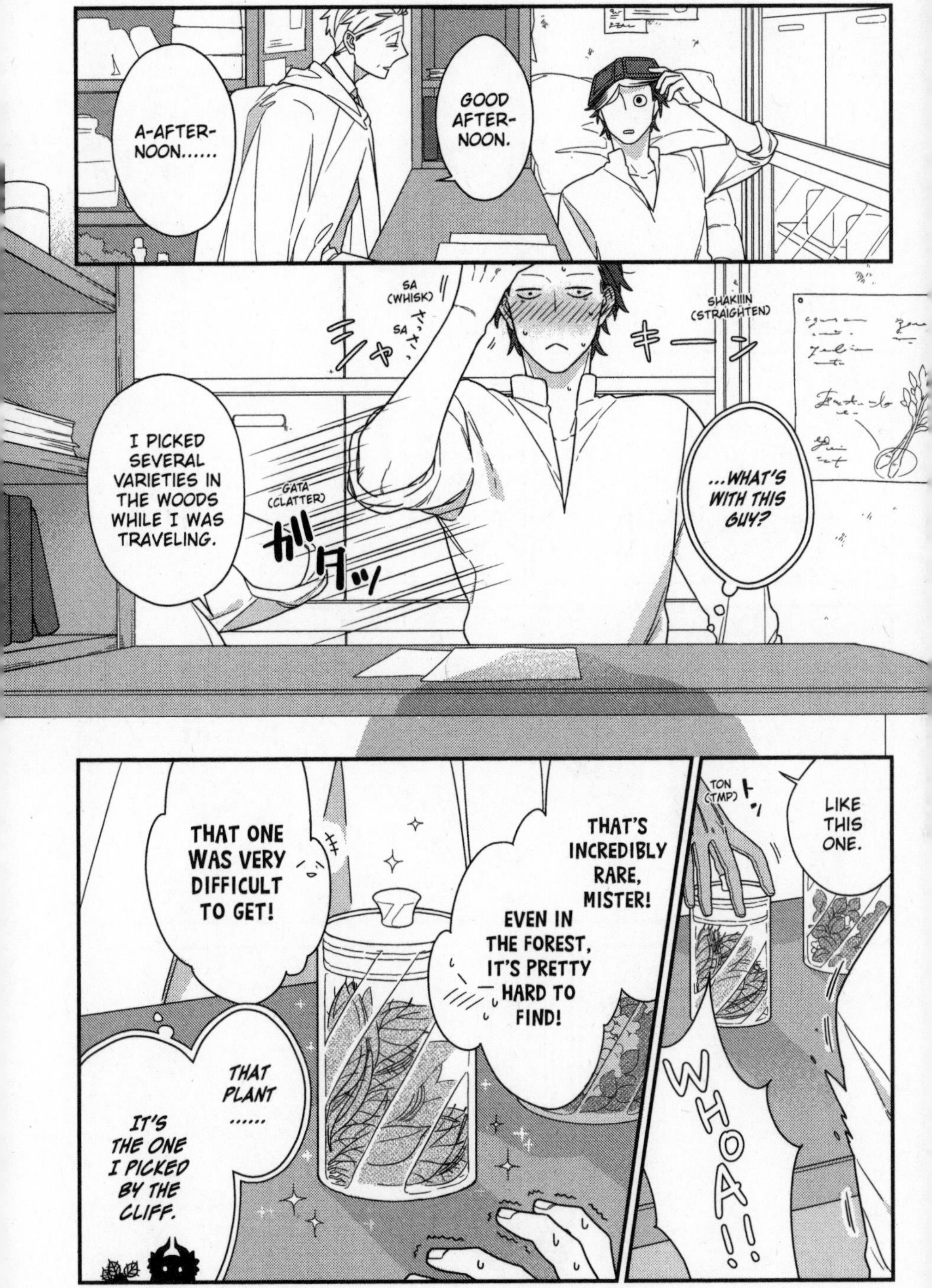
GOOD AFTER-NOON.
A-AFTER-NOON......
SHAKIIIN (STRAIGHTEN)
...WHAT'S WITH THIS GUY?
SA (WHISK) SA
GATA (CLATTER)
I PICKED SEVERAL VARIETIES IN THE WOODS WHILE I WAS TRAVELING.
LIKE THIS ONE.
TON (TMP)
WHOA!!
THAT'S INCREDIBLY RARE, MISTER!
EVEN IN THE FOREST, IT'S PRETTY HARD TO FIND!
THAT ONE WAS VERY DIFFICULT TO GET!
THAT PLANT......
IT'S THE ONE I PICKED BY THE CLIFF.

※ SEE CHAPTER 2

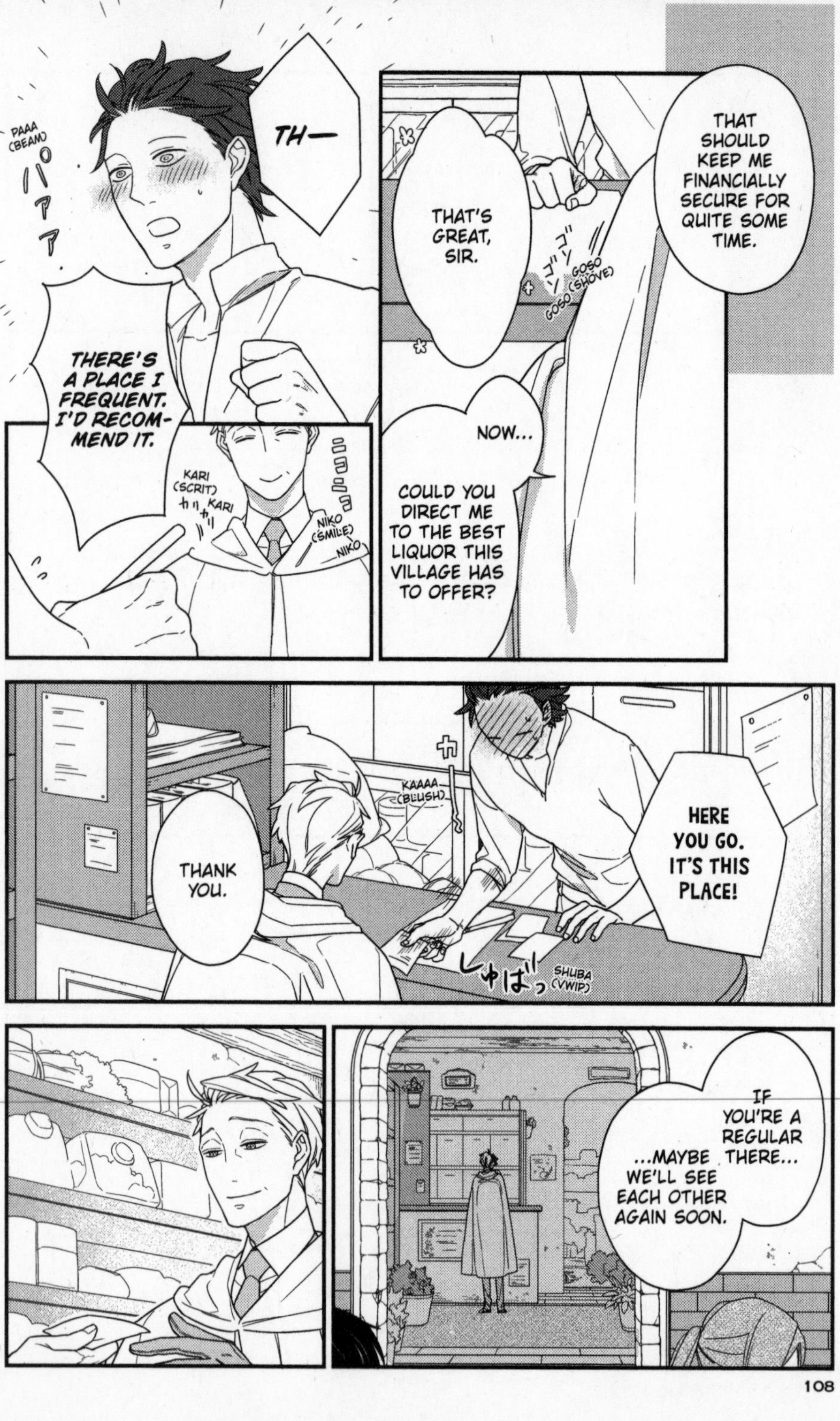
THAT SHOULD KEEP ME FINANCIALLY SECURE FOR QUITE SOME TIME.
THAT'S GREAT, SIR.
ゴソゴソ
GOSO (SHOVE) GOSO
NOW...
COULD YOU DIRECT ME TO THE BEST LIQUOR THIS VILLAGE HAS TO OFFER?
TH—
パァァ
PAAA (BEAM)
THERE'S A PLACE I FREQUENT. I'D RECOMMEND IT.
ニコニコ
NIKO (SMILE) NIKO
カリカリ
KARI (SCRIT) KARI
HERE YOU GO. IT'S THIS PLACE!
カァァ
KAAAA (BLUSH)
THANK YOU.
しゅばっ
SHUBA (VWIP)
IF YOU'RE A REGULAR THERE...
...MAYBE WE'LL SEE EACH OTHER AGAIN SOON.

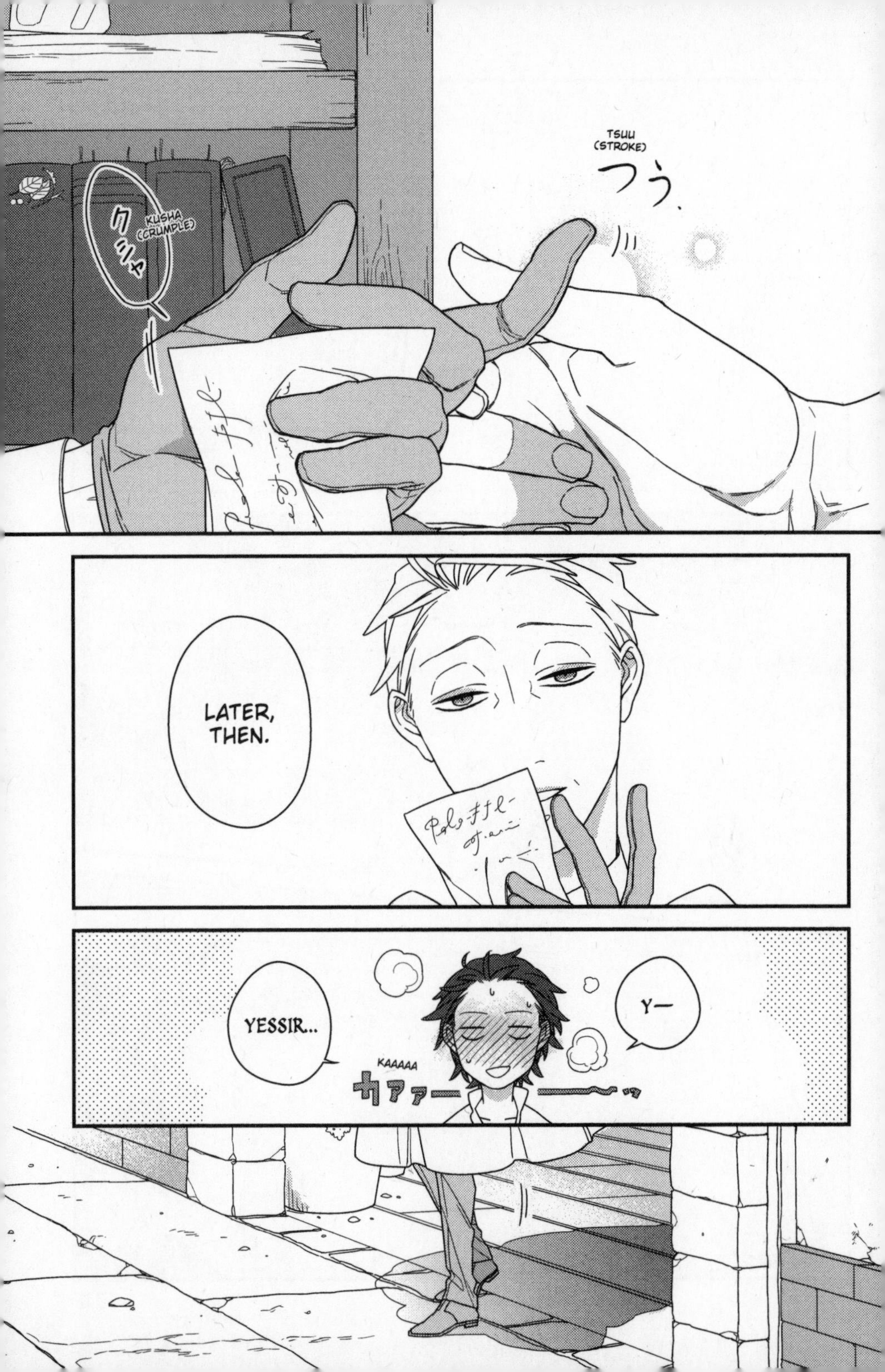
TSUU (STROKE)
つう
KUSHA (CRUMPLE)
クシャ
LATER, THEN.
Y—
YESSIR...
KAAAAA
カァァー

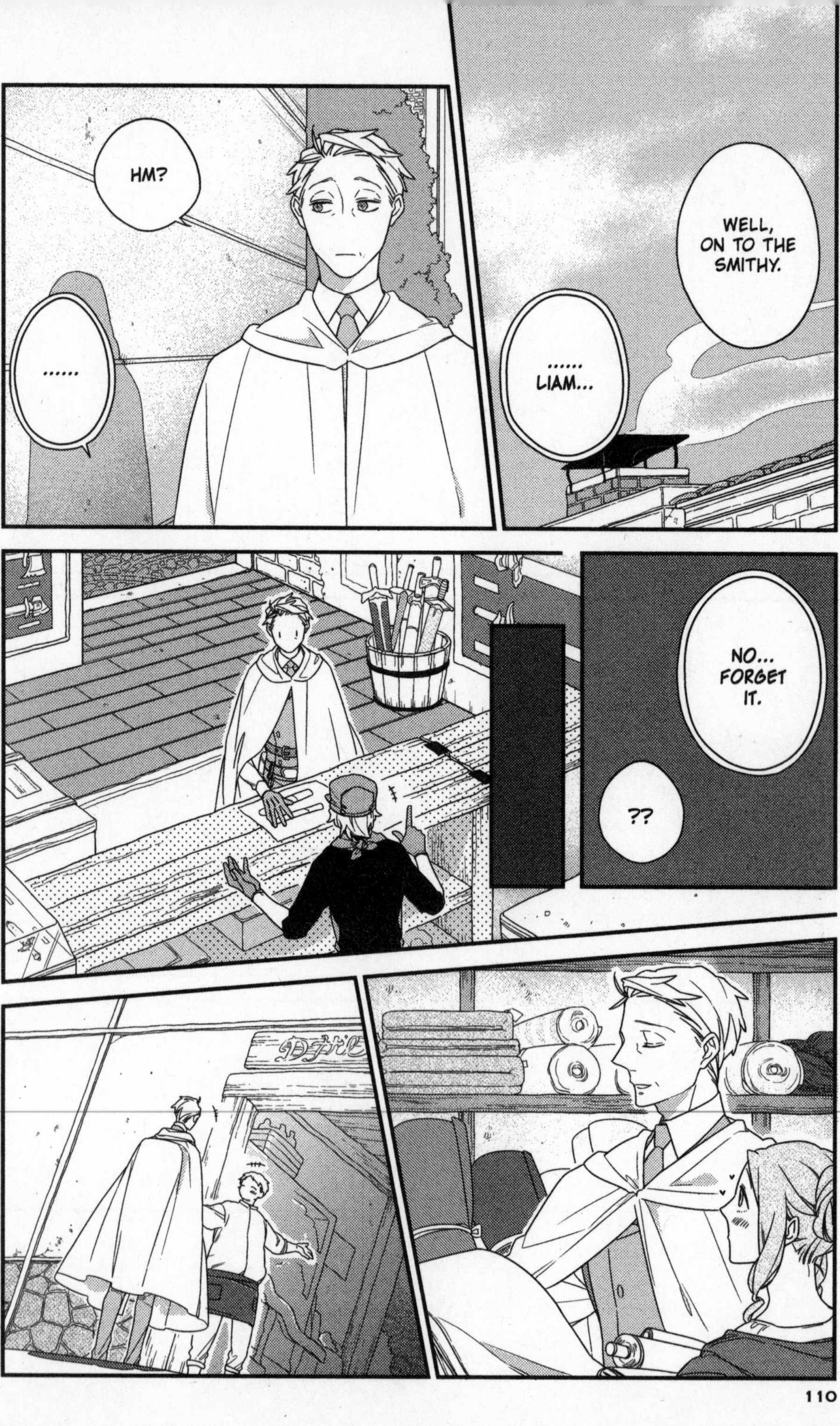
WELL, ON TO THE SMITHY.
...... LIAM...
HM?
......
NO... FORGET IT.
??

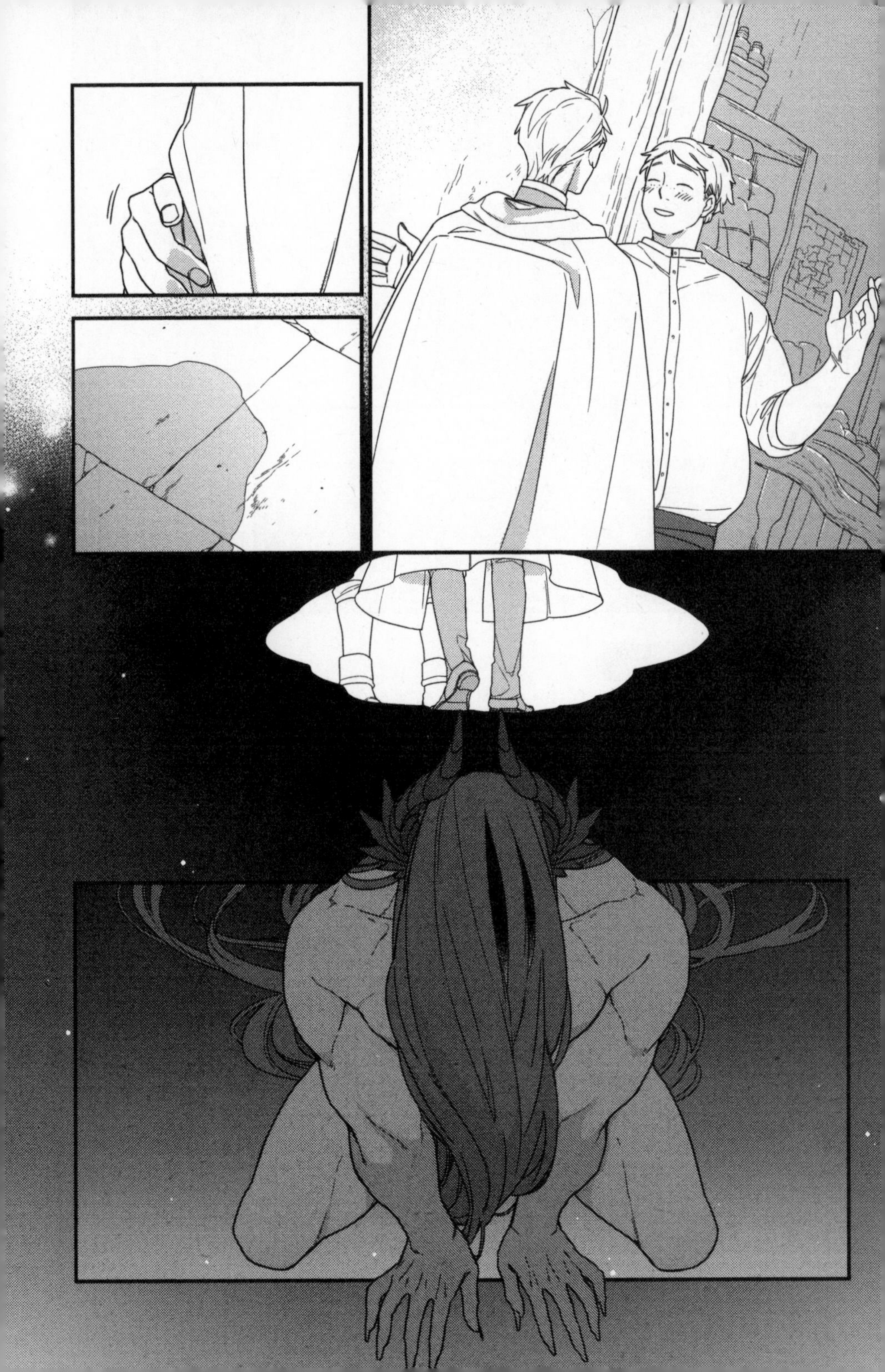

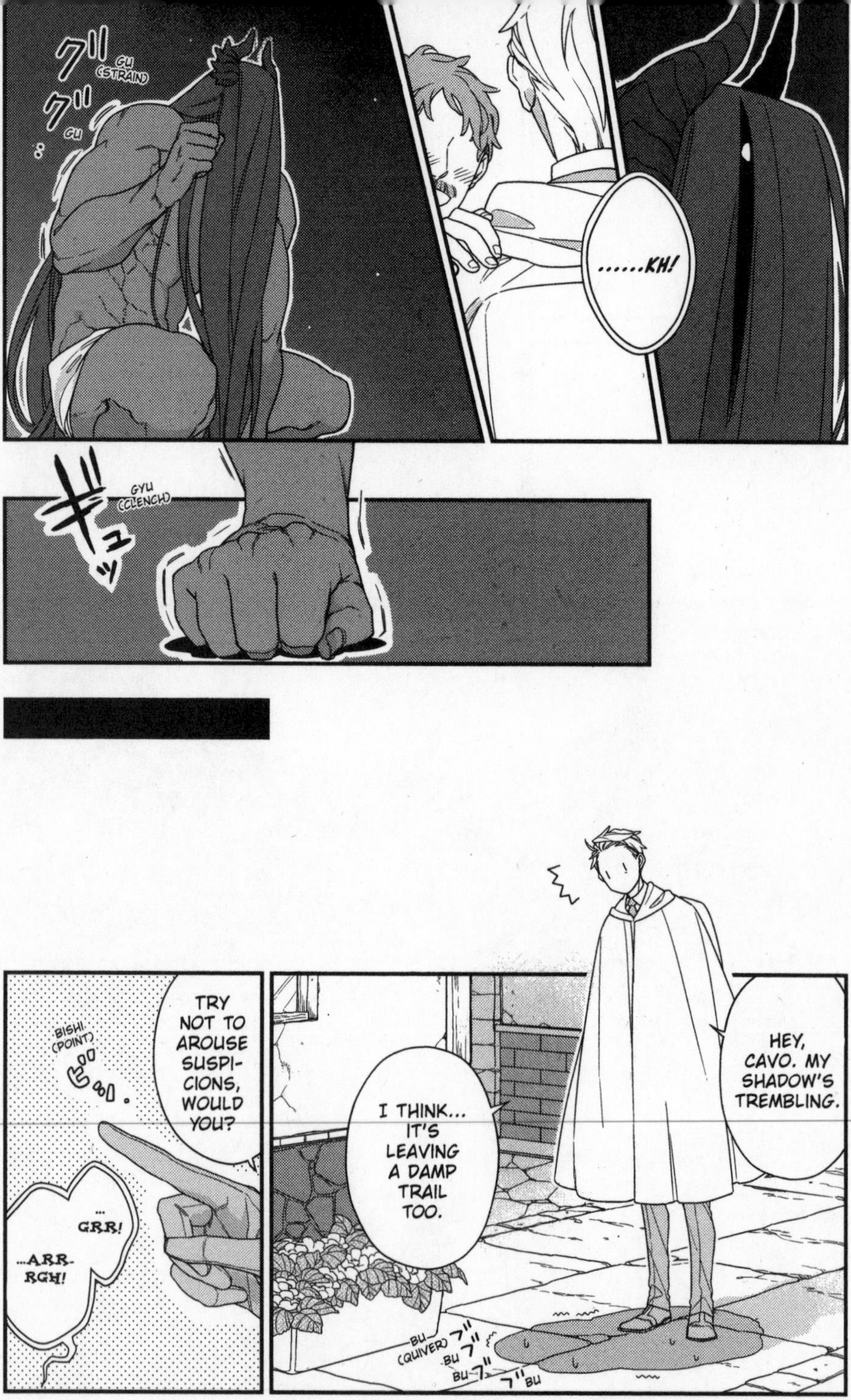
......KH!
GU (STRAIN)
GU
GYU (CLENCH)
HEY, CAVO. MY SHADOW'S TREMBLING.
I THINK... IT'S LEAVING A DAMP TRAIL TOO.
BU (QUIVER) BU BU BU
TRY NOT TO AROUSE SUSPICIONS, WOULD YOU?
BISHI (POINT)
...GRR!
...ARR-RGH!

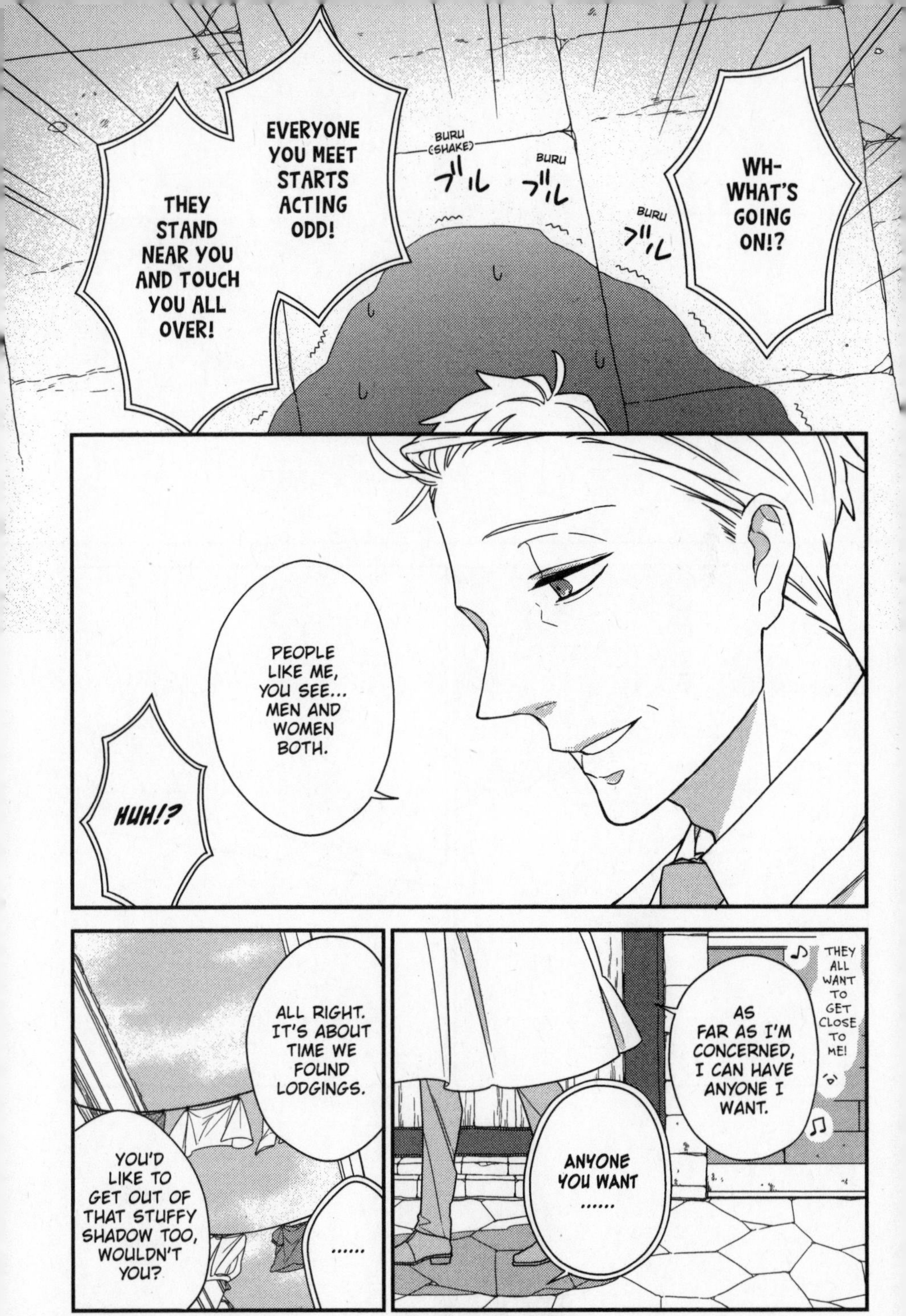
WH-WHAT'S GOING ON!?
BURU ブル
BURU ブル
BURU (SHAKE) ブル
EVERYONE YOU MEET STARTS ACTING ODD!
THEY STAND NEAR YOU AND TOUCH YOU ALL OVER!
PEOPLE LIKE ME, YOU SEE... MEN AND WOMEN BOTH.
HUH!?
THEY ALL WANT TO GET CLOSE TO ME!
AS FAR AS I'M CONCERNED, I CAN HAVE ANYONE I WANT.
ANYONE YOU WANT ......
ALL RIGHT. IT'S ABOUT TIME WE FOUND LODGINGS.
YOU'D LIKE TO GET OUT OF THAT STUFFY SHADOW TOO, WOULDN'T YOU?
......

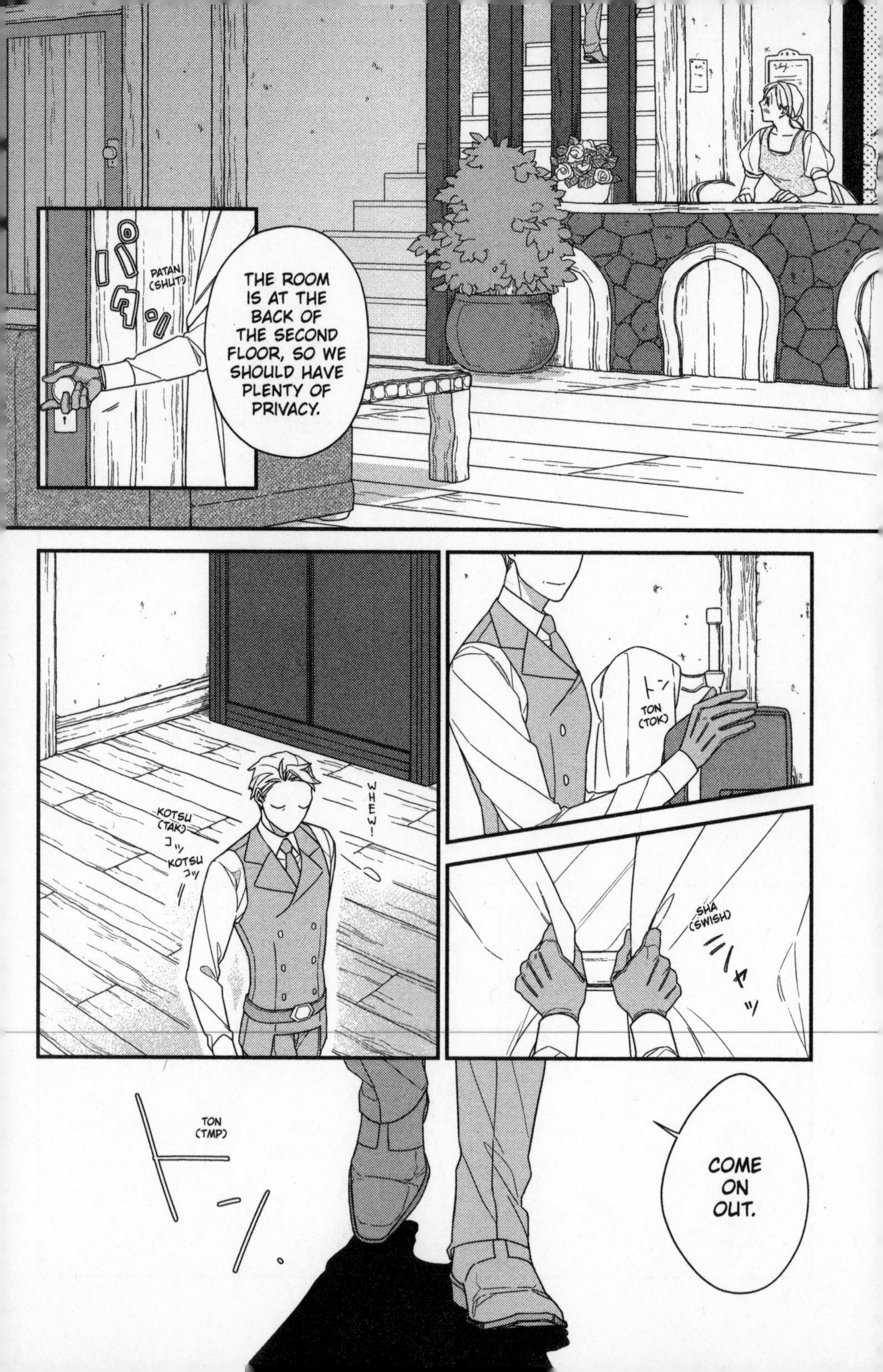
THE ROOM IS AT THE BACK OF THE SECOND FLOOR, SO WE SHOULD HAVE PLENTY OF PRIVACY.
PATAN (SHUT)
トン
TON (TOK)
SHA (SWISH)
シャッ
WHEW!
KOTSU (TAK)
コッ
KOTSU
コッ
COME ON OUT.
TON (TMP)

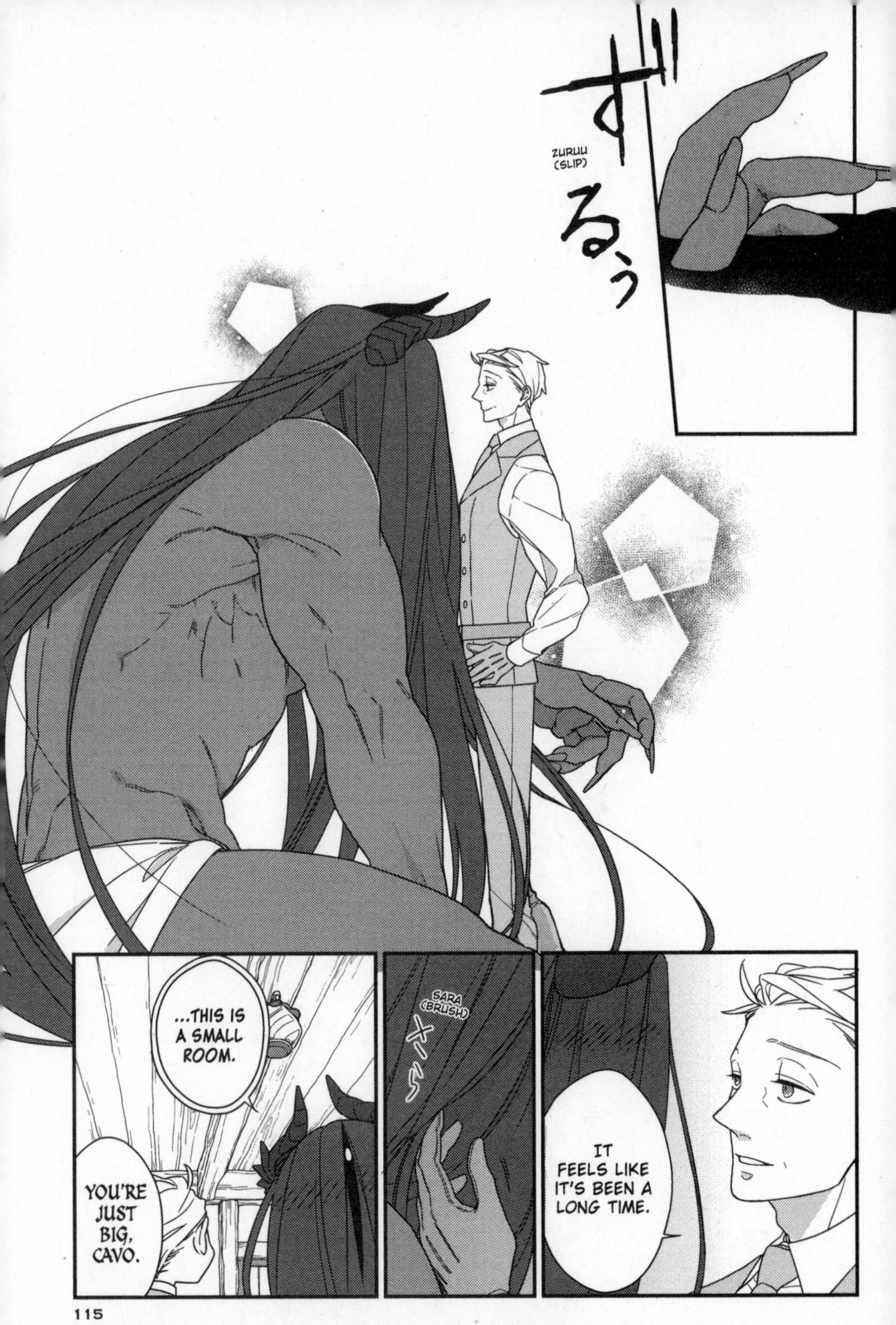
ずるぅ
ZURUU (SLIP)
IT FEELS LIKE IT'S BEEN A LONG TIME.
さら
SARA (BRUSH)
...THIS IS A SMALL ROOM.
YOU'RE JUST BIG, CAVO.

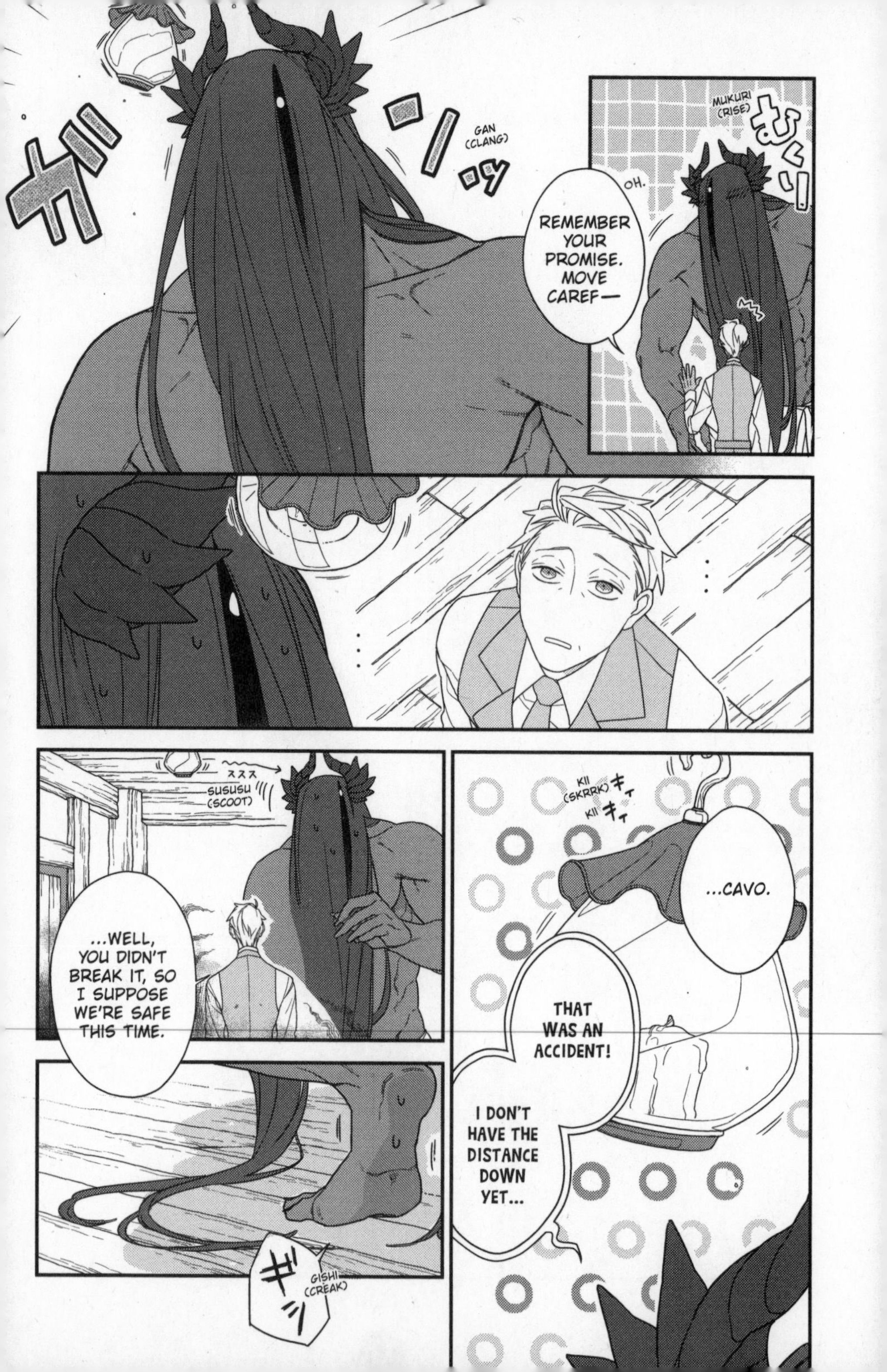
MUKURI (RISE)
むくり!
OH.
REMEMBER YOUR PROMISE. MOVE CAREF—
GAN (CLANG)
...
...
KII (SKRRK) キィ
KII キィ
...CAVO.
THAT WAS AN ACCIDENT!
I DON'T HAVE THE DISTANCE DOWN YET...
ススス
SUSUSU (SCOOT)
...WELL, YOU DIDN'T BREAK IT, SO I SUPPOSE WE'RE SAFE THIS TIME.
GISHI (CREAK)

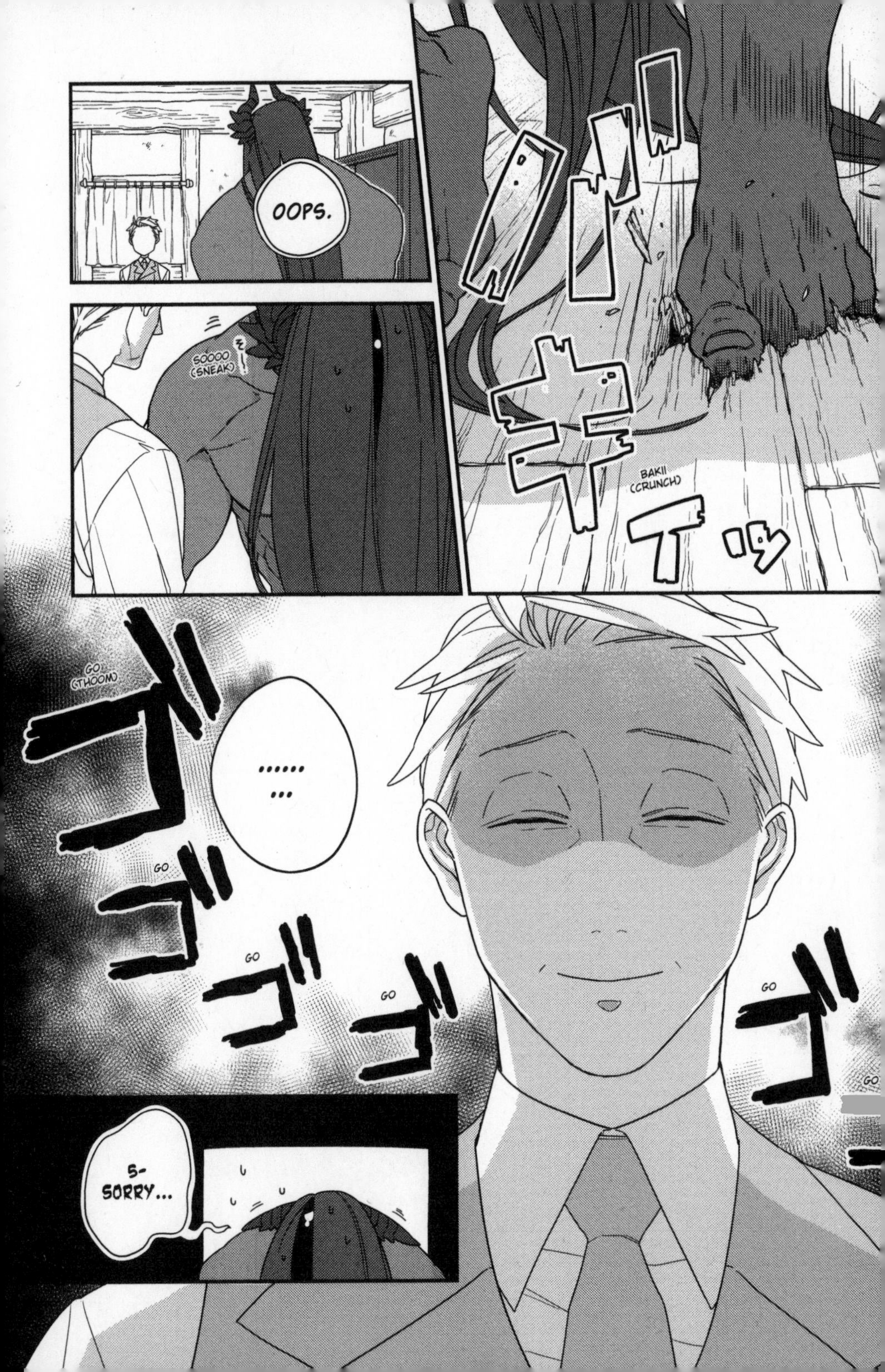

BAKII (CRUNCH)
OOPS.
SOOOO (SNEAK)
GO (THOOM)
....
GO
GO
GO
GO
GO
S-SORRY...

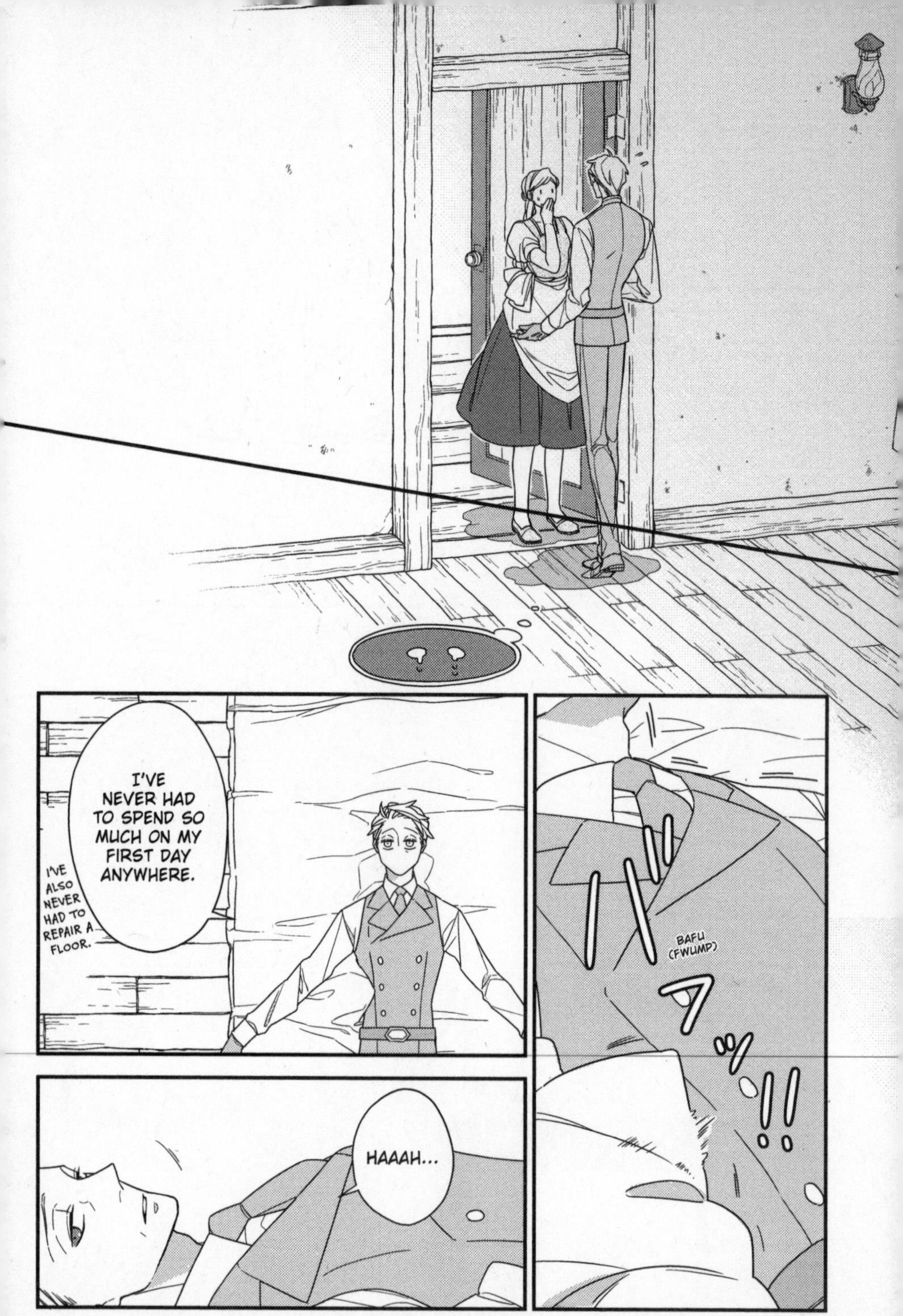
BAFU (FWUMP)
I'VE NEVER HAD TO SPEND SO MUCH ON MY FIRST DAY ANYWHERE.
I'VE ALSO NEVER HAD TO REPAIR A FLOOR.
HAAAH...

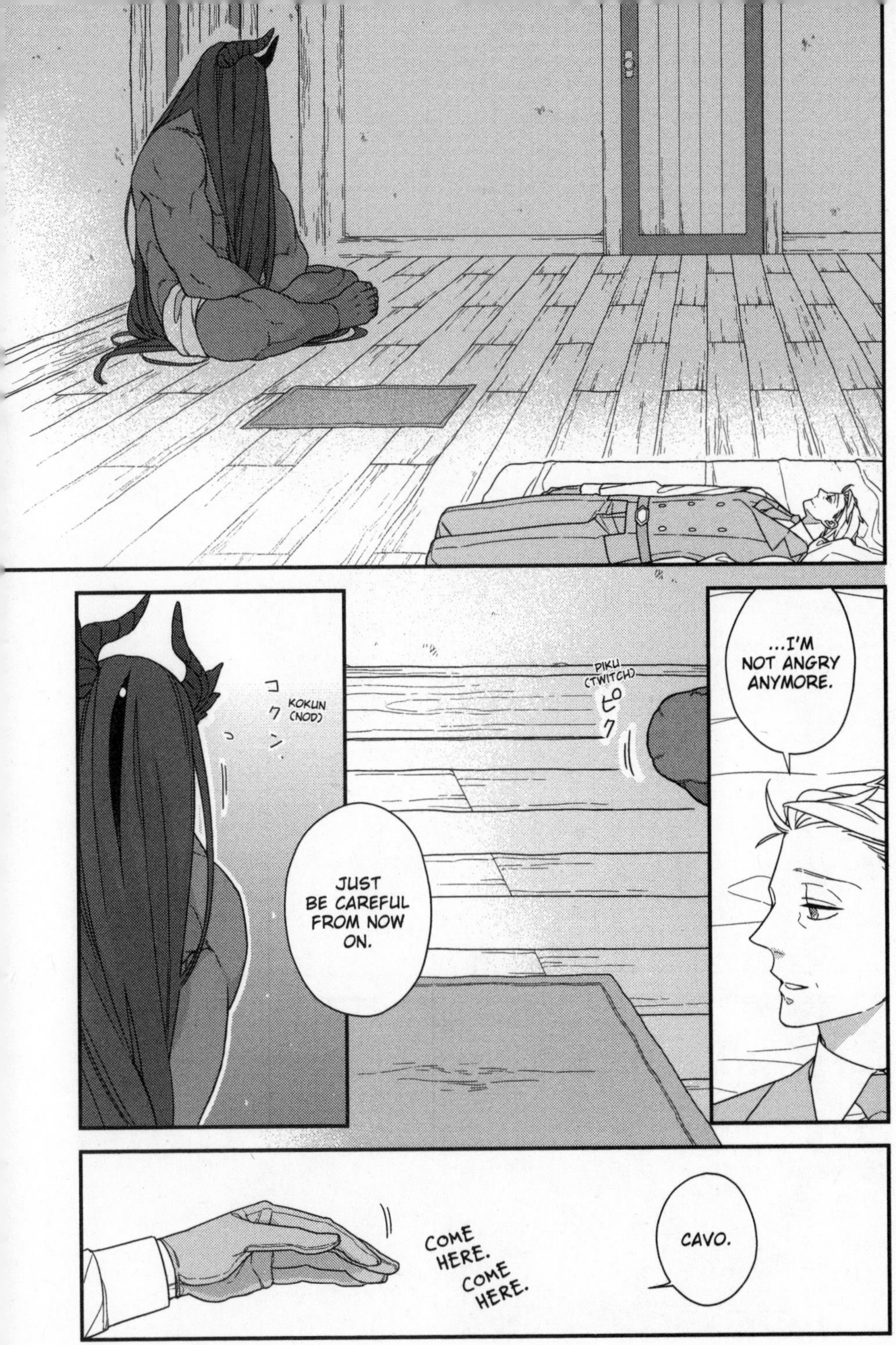
...I'M NOT ANGRY ANYMORE.
PIKU (TWITCH)
ピク
JUST BE CAREFUL FROM NOW ON.
KOKUN (NOD)
コクン
CAVO.
COME HERE. COME HERE.

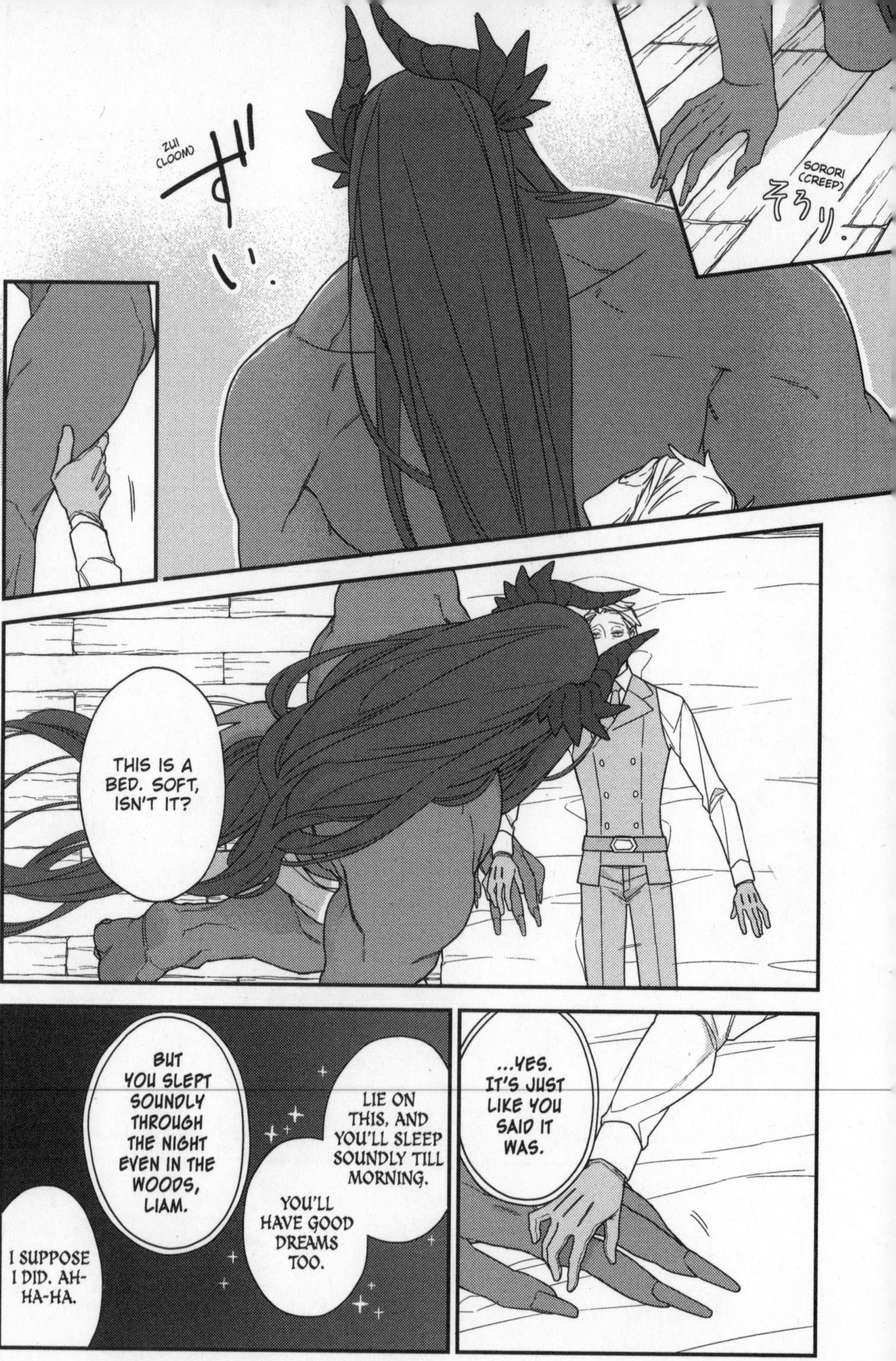
SORORI (CREEP)
そろり。
ZUI (LOOM)
ずい。
THIS IS A BED. SOFT, ISN'T IT?
...YES. IT'S JUST LIKE YOU SAID IT WAS.
LIE ON THIS, AND YOU'LL SLEEP SOUNDLY TILL MORNING.
YOU'LL HAVE GOOD DREAMS TOO.
BUT YOU SLEPT SOUNDLY THROUGH THE NIGHT EVEN IN THE WOODS, LIAM.
I SUPPOSE I DID. AH-HA-HA.

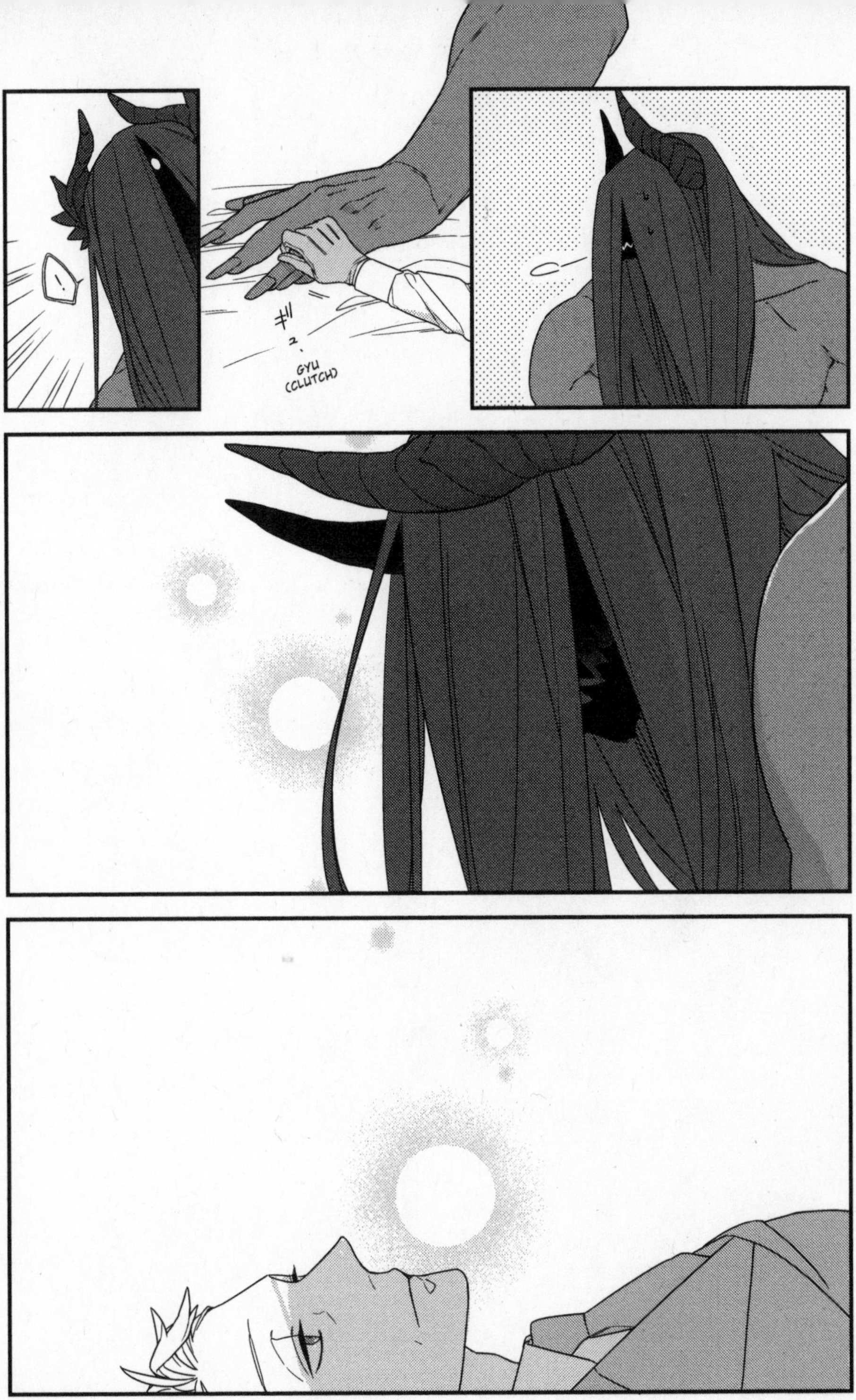
!
ギュ
GYU
(CLUTCH)

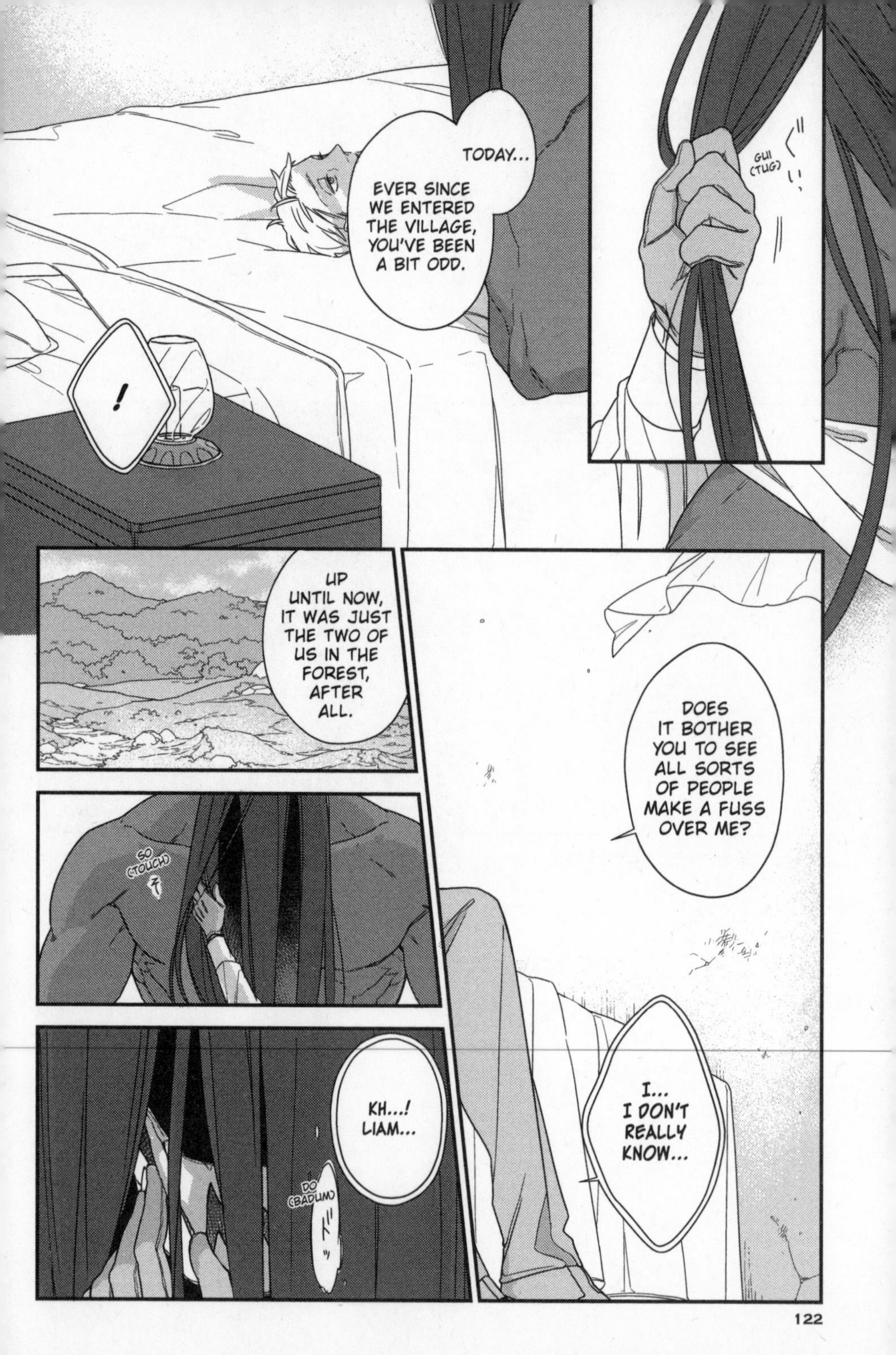
GUI (TUG)
TODAY...
EVER SINCE WE ENTERED THE VILLAGE, YOU'VE BEEN A BIT ODD.
!
DOES IT BOTHER YOU TO SEE ALL SORTS OF PEOPLE MAKE A FUSS OVER ME?
I... I DON'T REALLY KNOW...
UP UNTIL NOW, IT WAS JUST THE TWO OF US IN THE FOREST, AFTER ALL.
SO (TOUCH)
KH...! LIAM...
DO (BADUM)

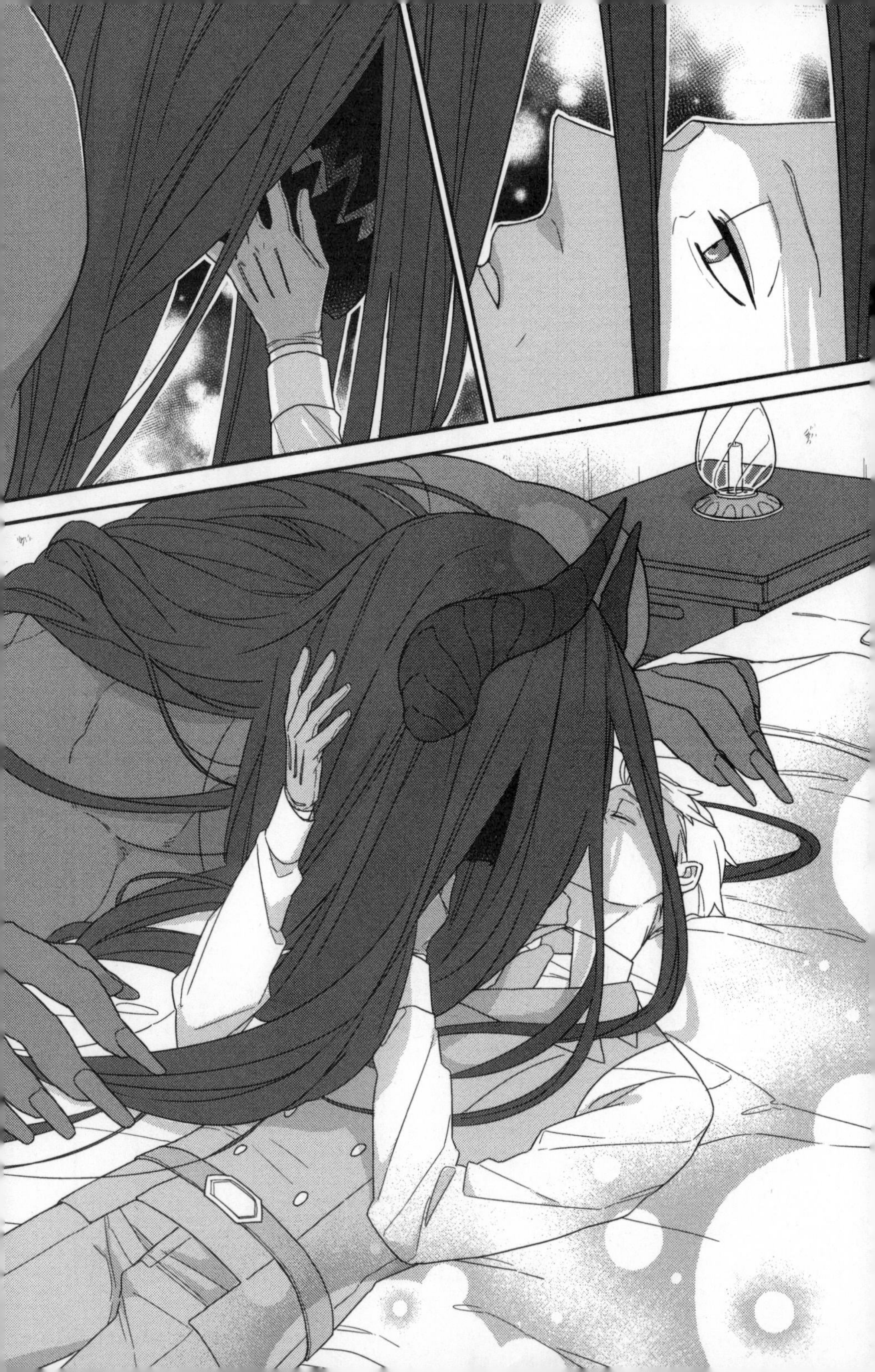

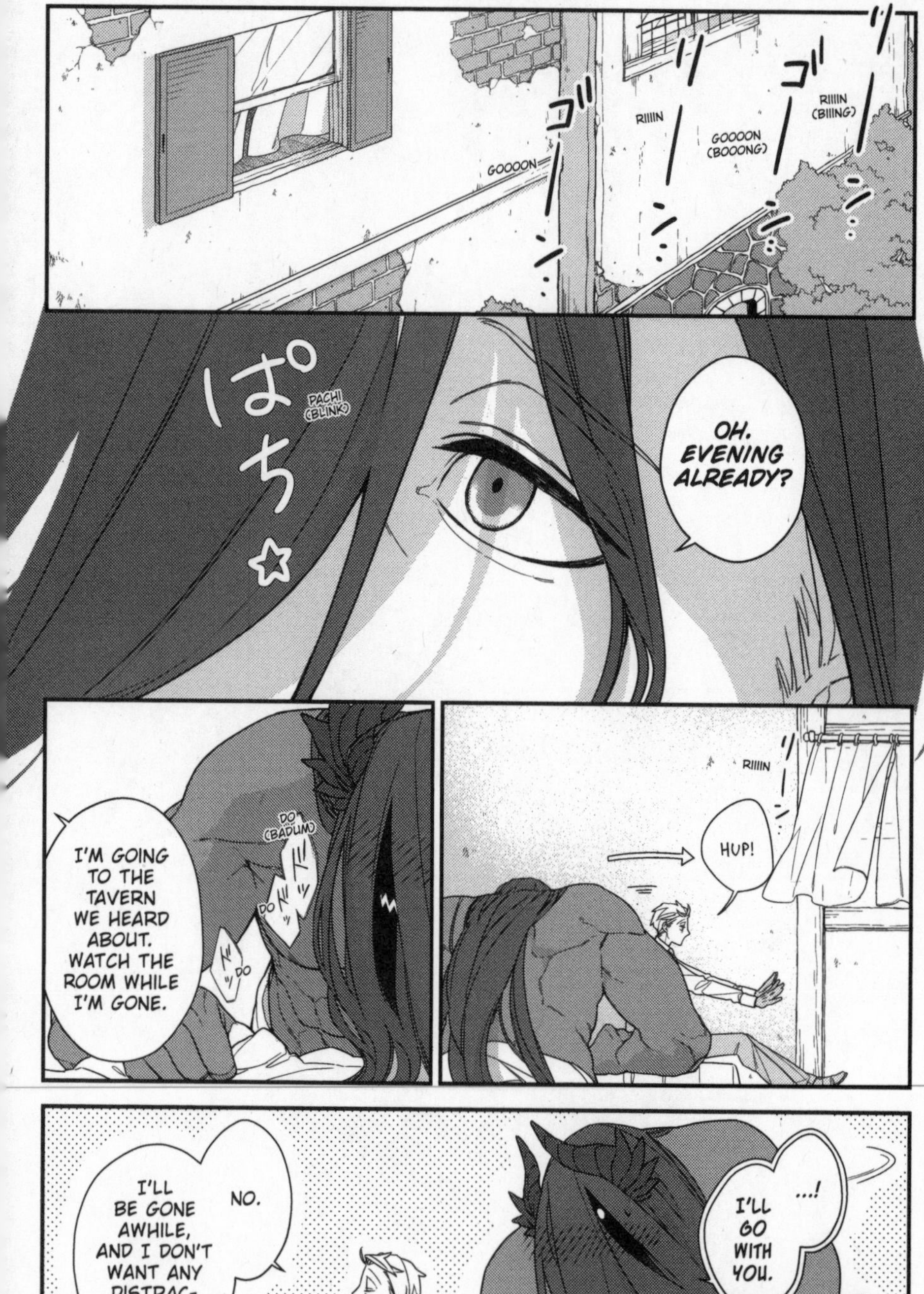
RIIIN (BIIING)
GOOOON (BOOONG)
RIIIN
GOOOON
OH. EVENING ALREADY?
ぱち☆
PACHI (BLINK)
RIIIN
HUP!
DO (BADUM)
DO
DO
I'M GOING TO THE TAVERN WE HEARD ABOUT. WATCH THE ROOM WHILE I'M GONE.
...!
I'LL GO WITH YOU.
NO.
I'LL BE GONE AWHILE, AND I DON'T WANT ANY DISTRACTIONS.

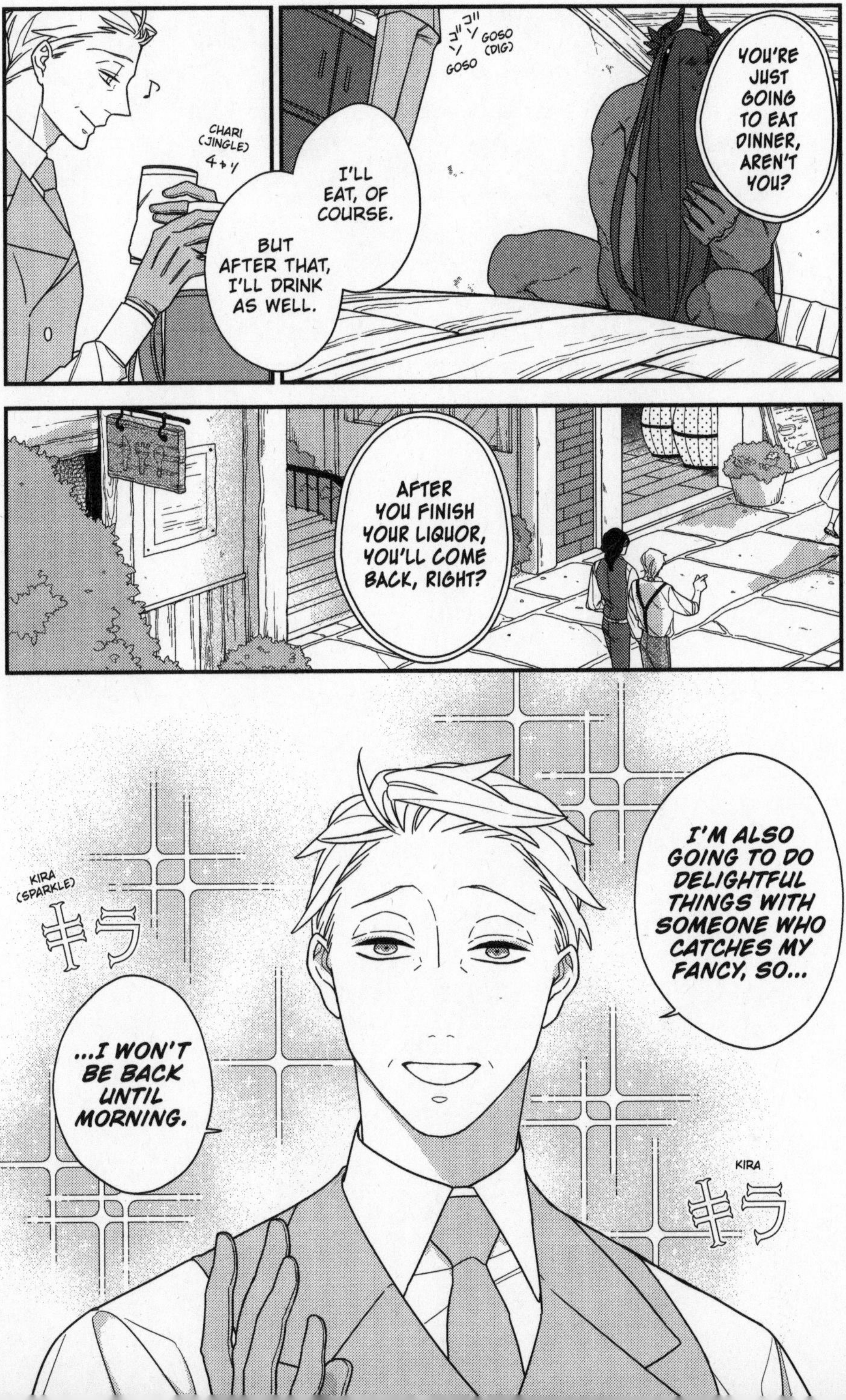
GOSO GOSO (DIG)
YOU'RE JUST GOING TO EAT DINNER, AREN'T YOU?
CHARI (JINGLE)
I'LL EAT, OF COURSE.
BUT AFTER THAT, I'LL DRINK AS WELL.
AFTER YOU FINISH YOUR LIQUOR, YOU'LL COME BACK, RIGHT?
I'M ALSO GOING TO DO DELIGHTFUL THINGS WITH SOMEONE WHO CATCHES MY FANCY, SO...
KIRA
キラ
KIRA (SPARKLE)
キラ
...I WON'T BE BACK UNTIL MORNING.

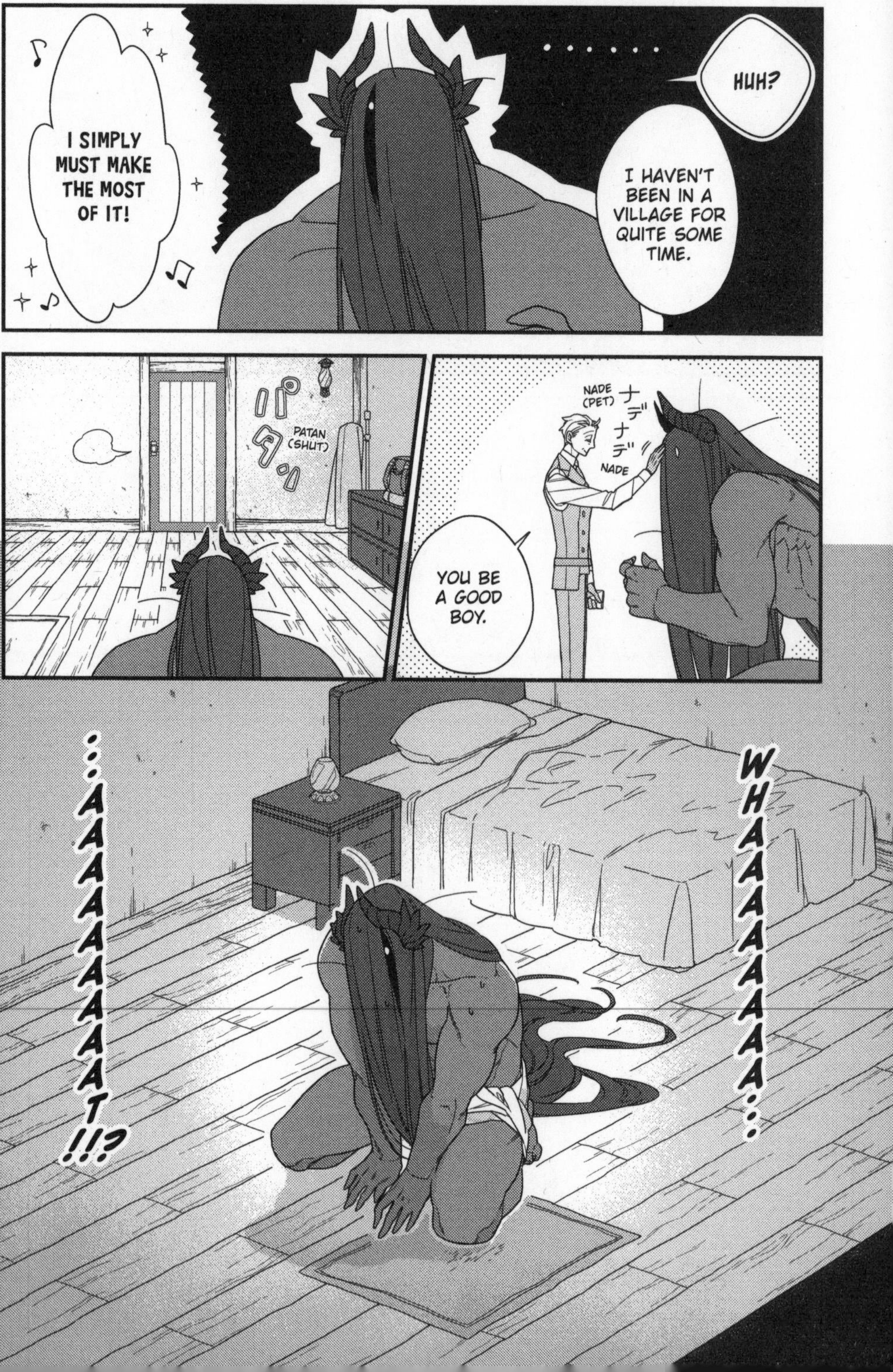
HUH?
......
I HAVEN'T BEEN IN A VILLAGE FOR QUITE SOME TIME.
I SIMPLY MUST MAKE THE MOST OF IT!
NADE (PET)
ナデ
ナデ
NADE
YOU BE A GOOD BOY.
パタン
PATAN (SHUT)
WHAAAAAAAAA..
..AAAAAAAAT!!?

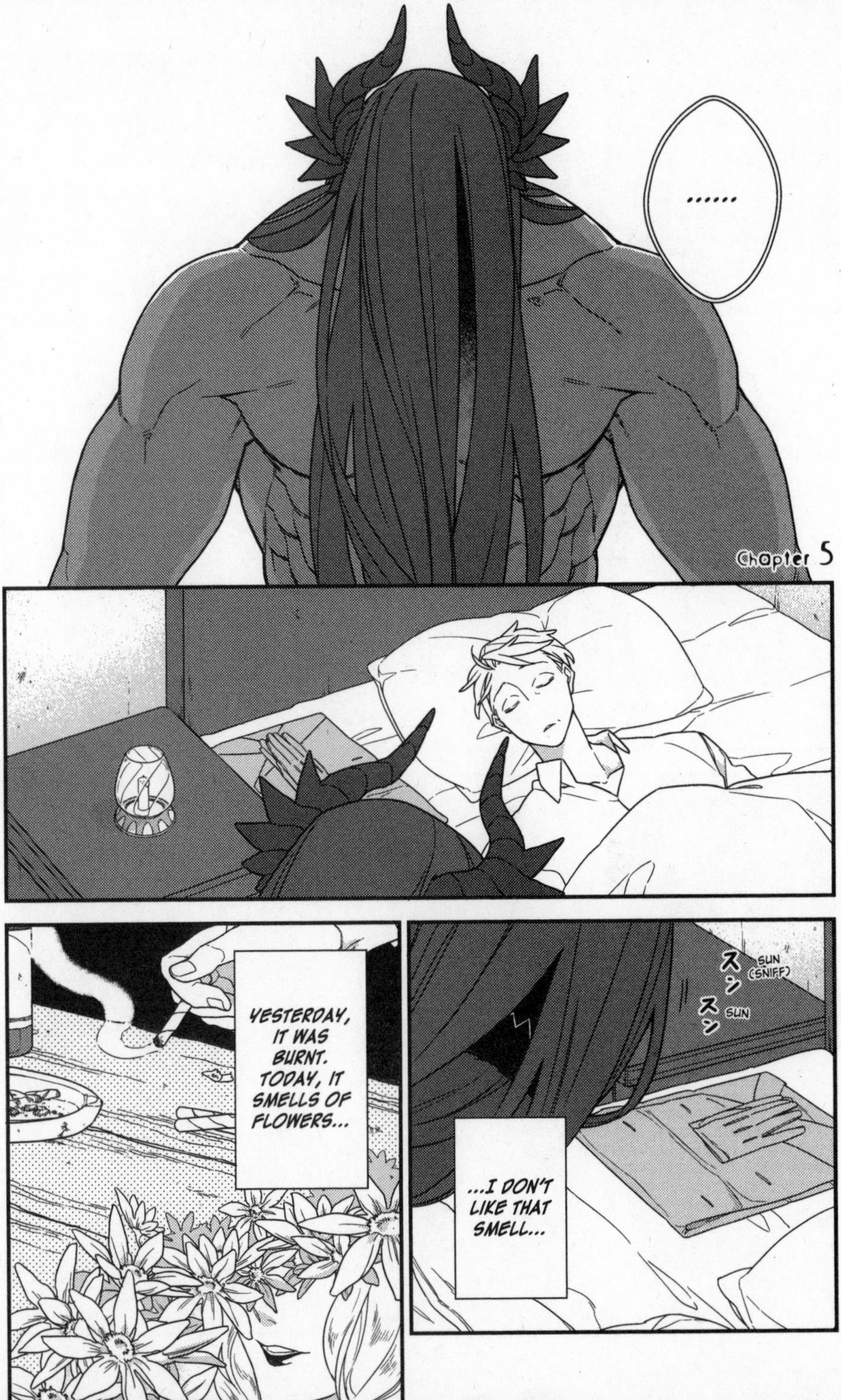
......
Chapter 5
YESTERDAY, IT WAS BURNT. TODAY, IT SMELLS OF FLOWERS...
スン SUN (SNIFF)
スン SUN
...I DON'T LIKE THAT SMELL...

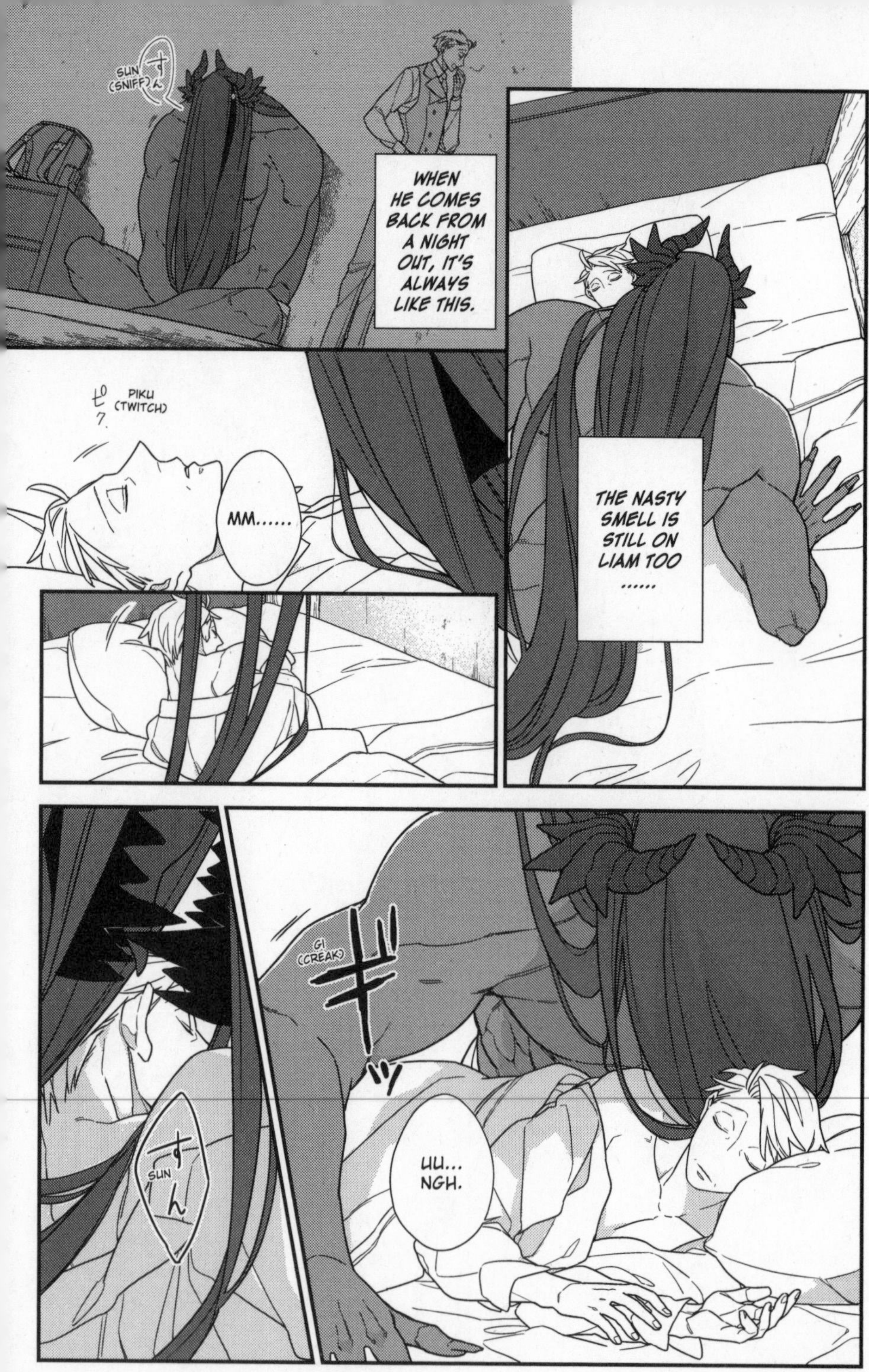

すん
SUN (SNIFF)
WHEN HE COMES BACK FROM A NIGHT OUT, IT'S ALWAYS LIKE THIS.
THE NASTY SMELL IS STILL ON LIAM TOO ......
PIKU (TWITCH)
MM......
GI (CREAK)
UU... NGH.
SUN

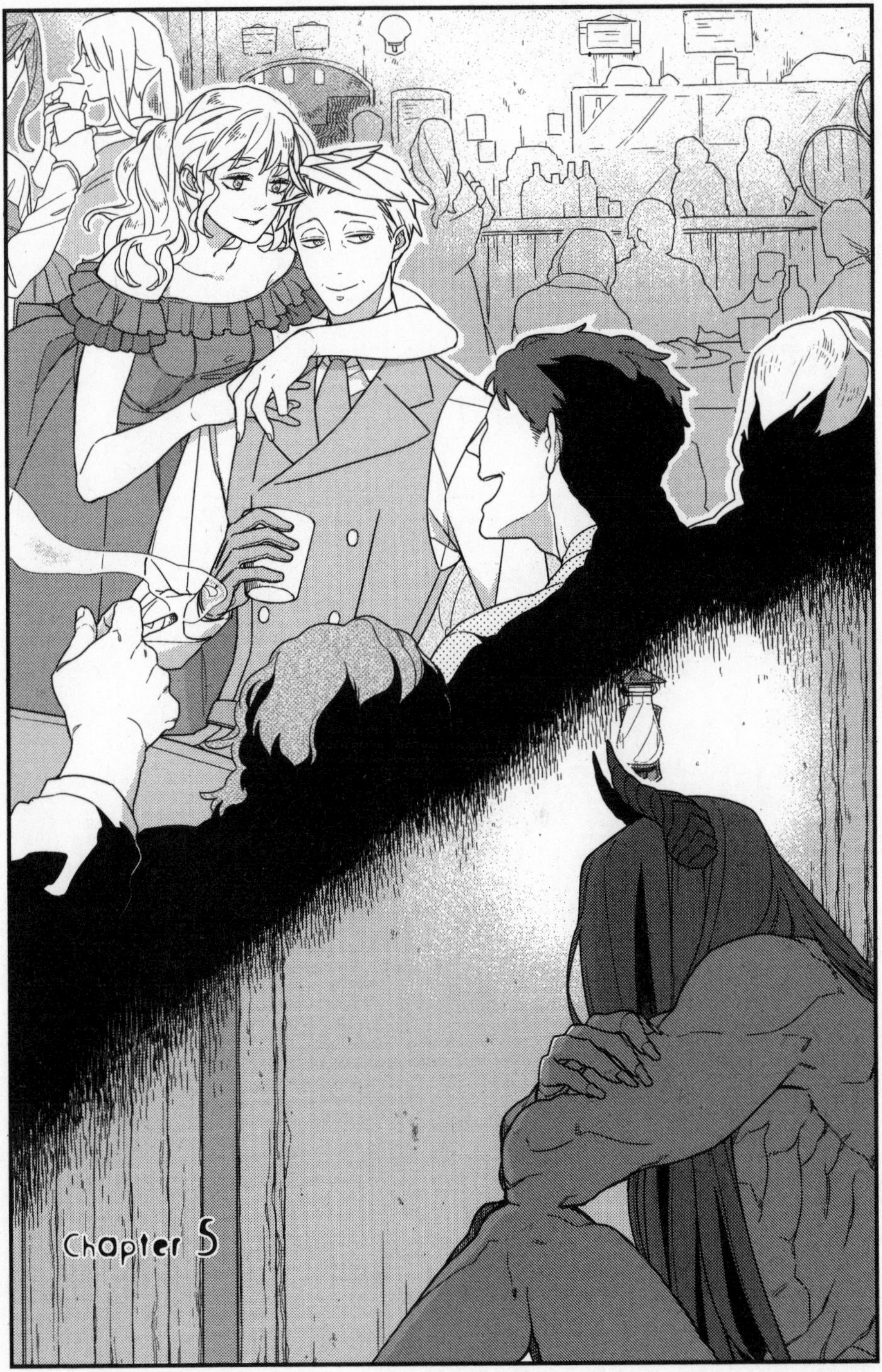
Chapter 5

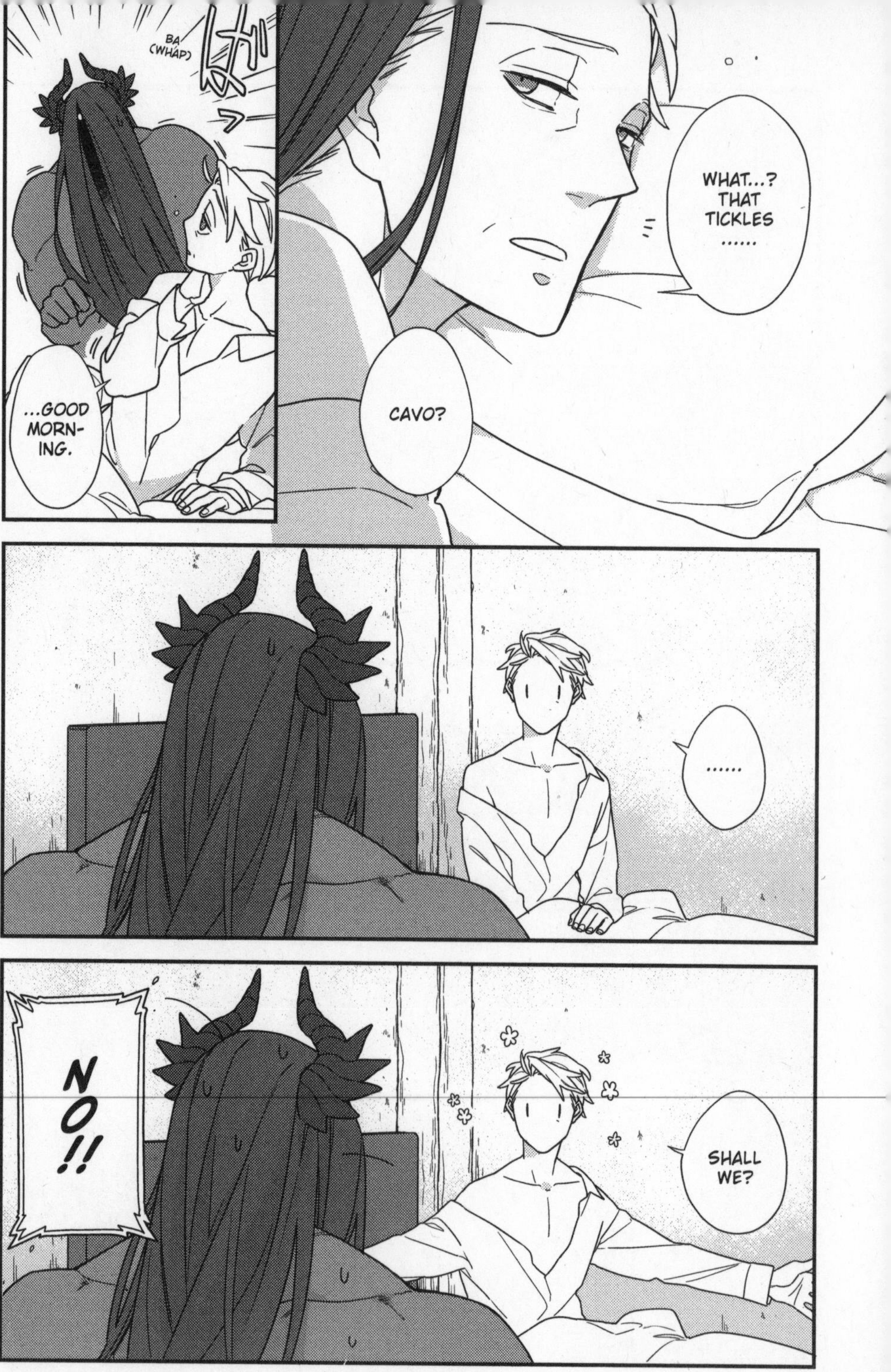
WHAT...? THAT TICKLES ......
CAVO?
BA (WHAP)
...GOOD MORN-ING.
......
SHALL WE?
NO!!

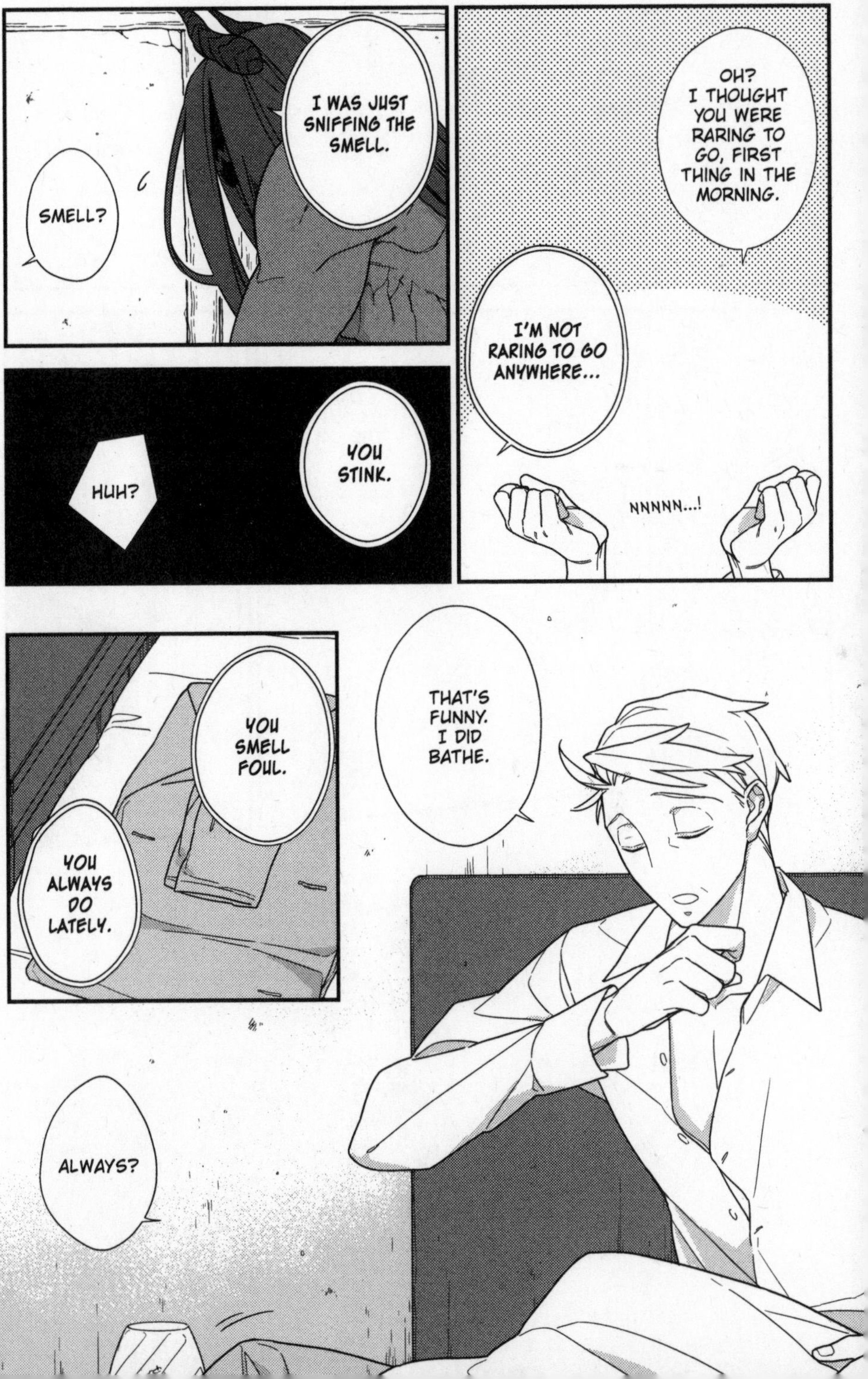
OH? I THOUGHT YOU WERE RARING TO GO, FIRST THING IN THE MORNING.
I'M NOT RARING TO GO ANYWHERE...
NNNNN...!
I WAS JUST SNIFFING THE SMELL.
SMELL?
YOU STINK.
HUH?
THAT'S FUNNY. I DID BATHE.
YOU SMELL FOUL.
YOU ALWAYS DO LATELY.
ALWAYS?

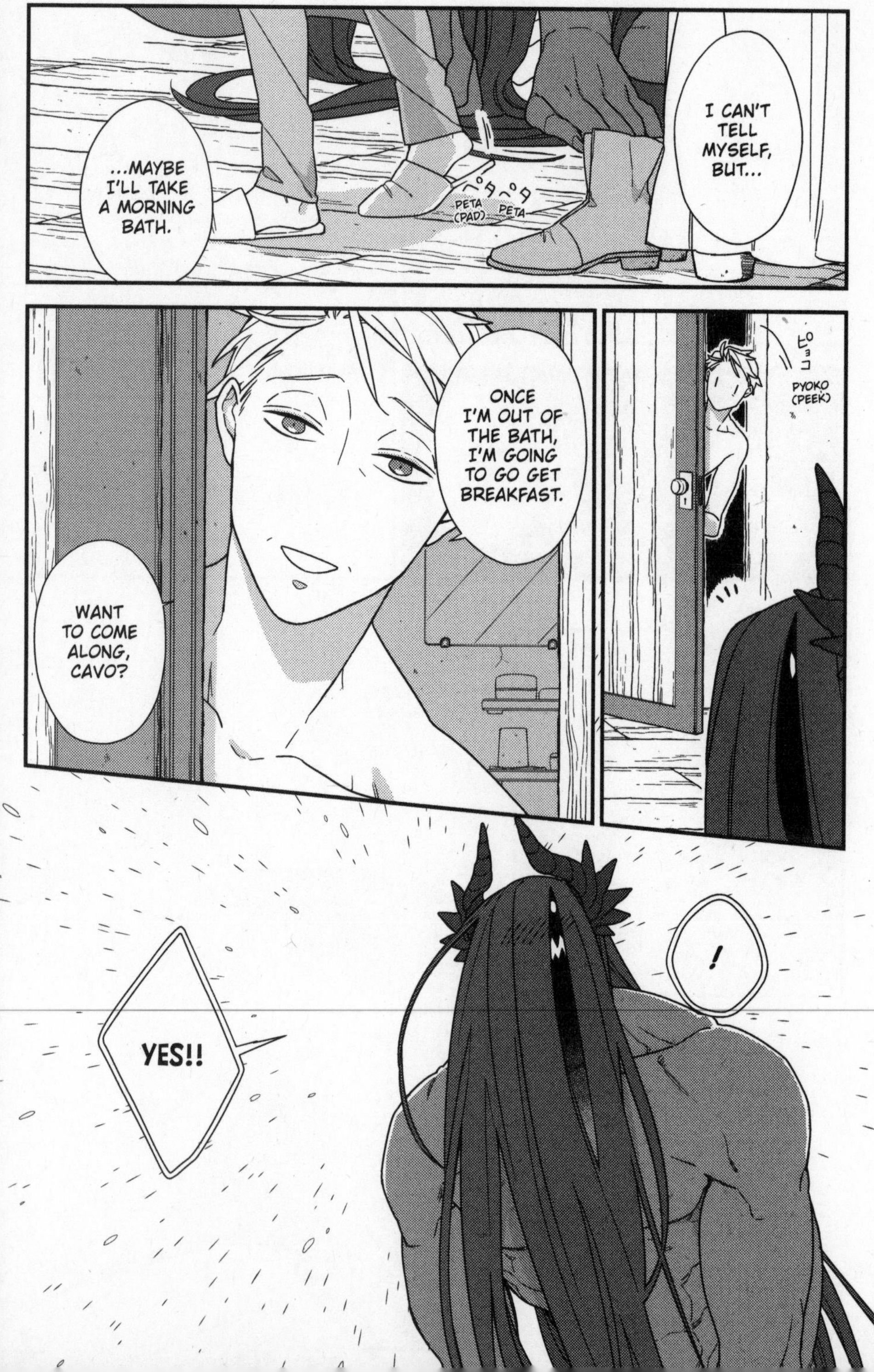
I CAN'T TELL MYSELF, BUT...
ペタペタ
PETA (PAD) PETA
...MAYBE I'LL TAKE A MORNING BATH.
ピョコ
PYOKO (PEEK)
ONCE I'M OUT OF THE BATH, I'M GOING TO GO GET BREAKFAST.
WANT TO COME ALONG, CAVO?
!
YES!!

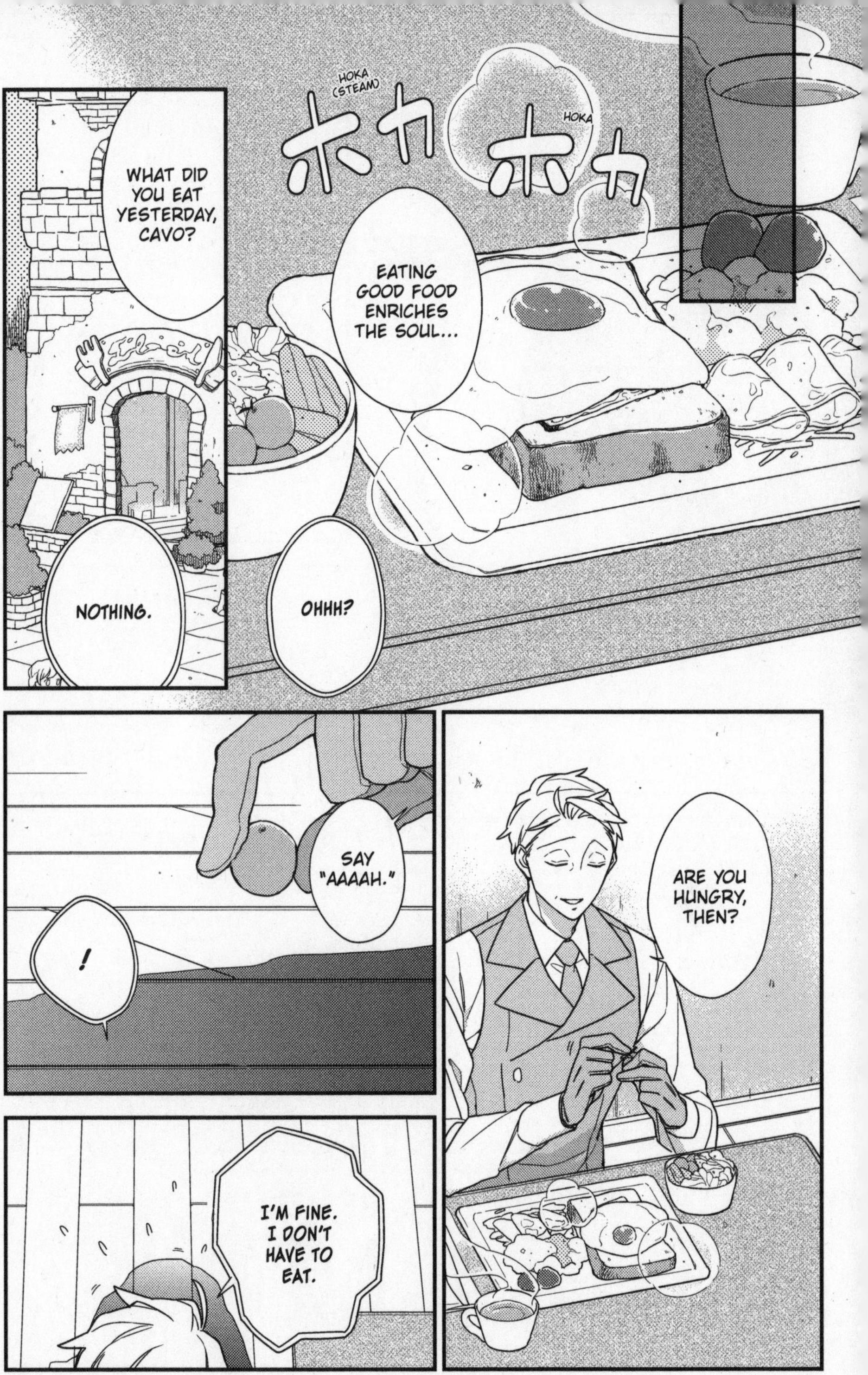
HOKA (STEAM)
ホカ
HOKA
ホカ
EATING GOOD FOOD ENRICHES THE SOUL...
OHHH?
WHAT DID YOU EAT YESTERDAY, CAVO?
NOTHING.
ARE YOU HUNGRY, THEN?
SAY "AAAAH."
!
I'M FINE. I DON'T HAVE TO EAT.

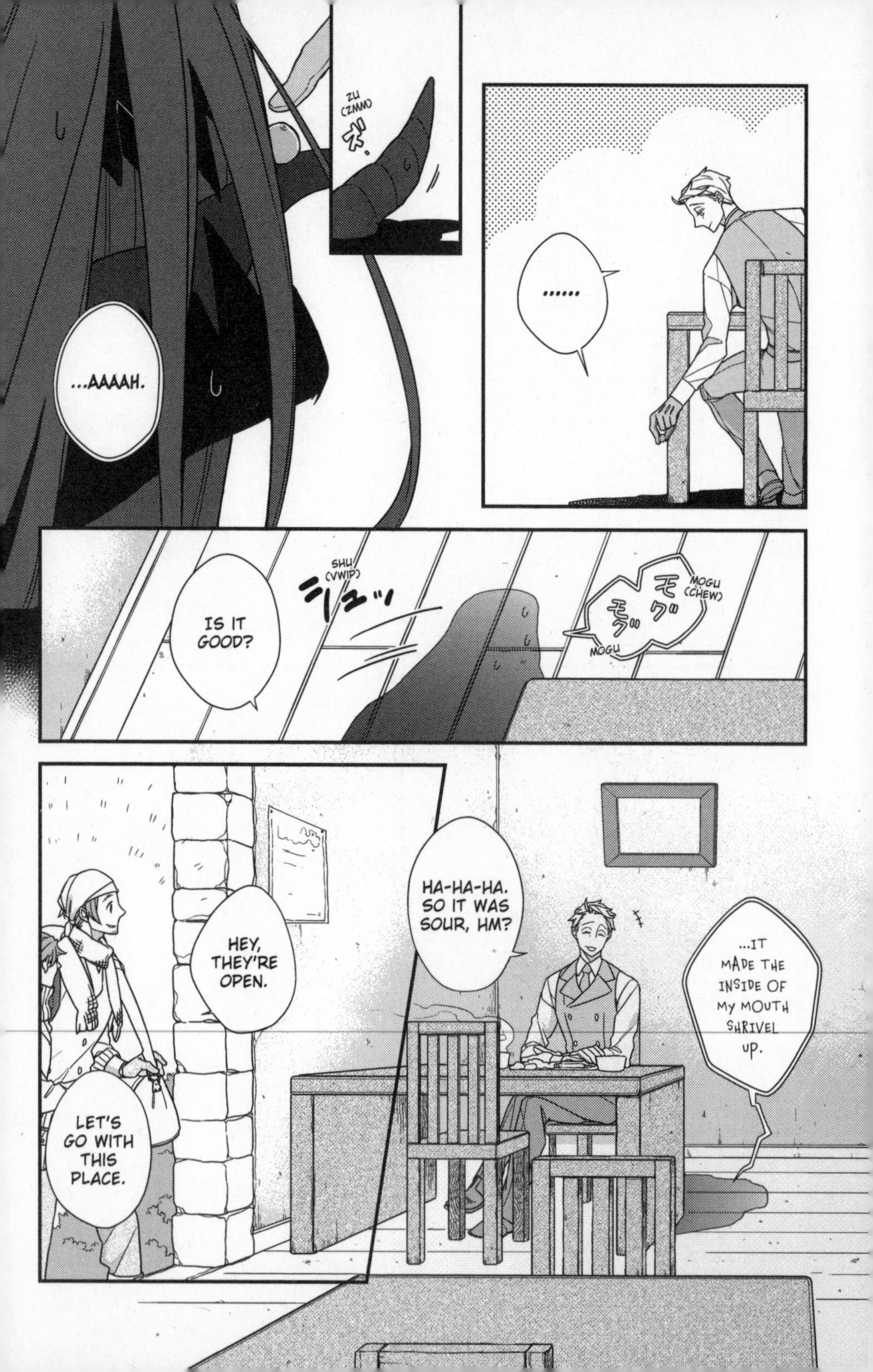
......
ZU (ZMM)
ズ。
...AAAAH.
MOGU (CHEW)
モグモグ
MOGU
SHU (VWIP)
シュッ
IS IT GOOD?
...IT MADE THE INSIDE OF MY MOUTH SHRIVEL UP.
HA-HA-HA. SO IT WAS SOUR, HM?
HEY, THEY'RE OPEN.
LET'S GO WITH THIS PLACE.

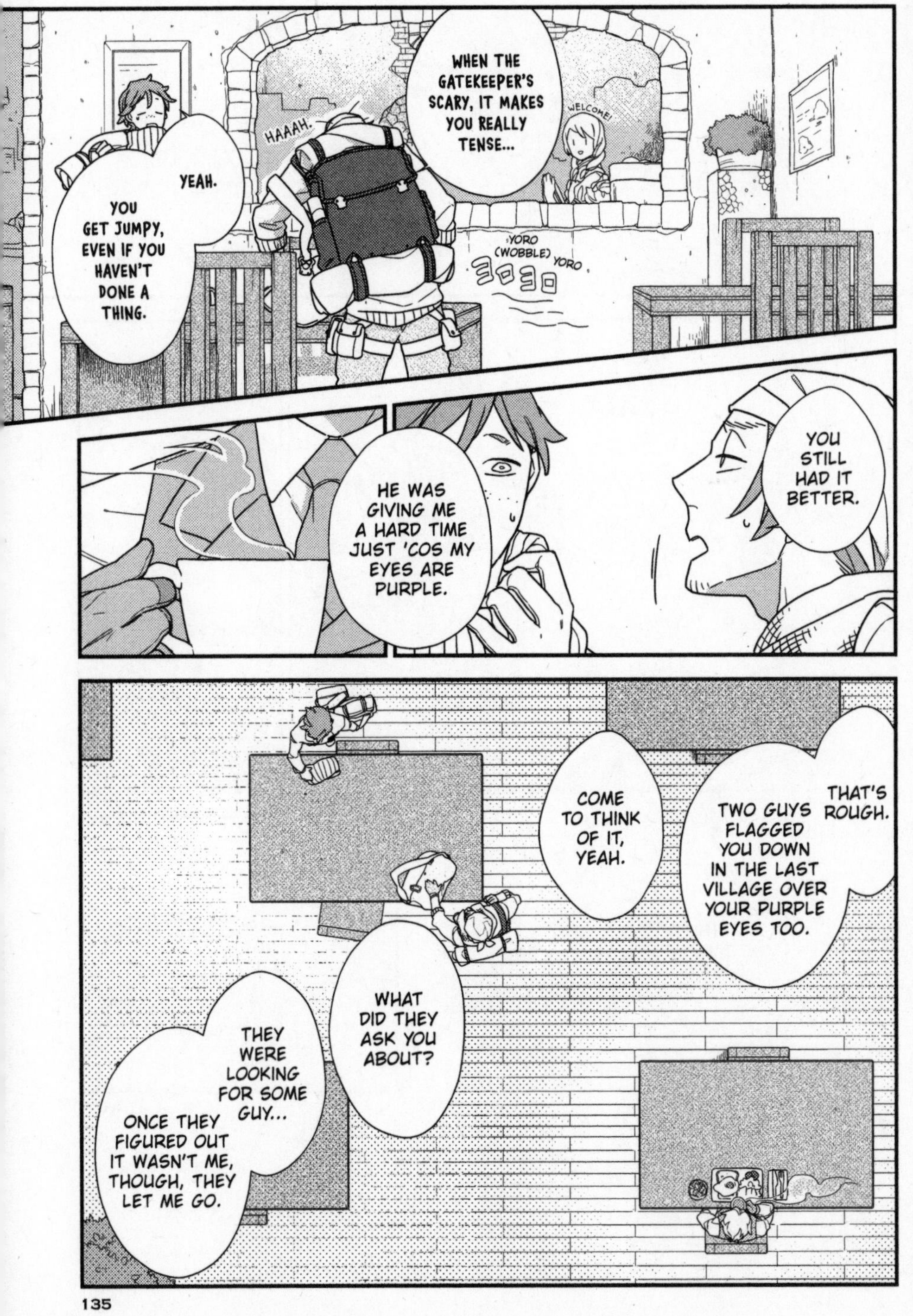
WELCOME!
WHEN THE GATEKEEPER'S SCARY, IT MAKES YOU REALLY TENSE...
HAAAH.
YEAH.
YOU GET JUMPY, EVEN IF YOU HAVEN'T DONE A THING.
YORO (WOBBLE) YORO
YOU STILL HAD IT BETTER.
HE WAS GIVING ME A HARD TIME JUST 'COS MY EYES ARE PURPLE.
THAT'S ROUGH.
TWO GUYS FLAGGED YOU DOWN IN THE LAST VILLAGE OVER YOUR PURPLE EYES TOO.
COME TO THINK OF IT, YEAH.
WHAT DID THEY ASK YOU ABOUT?
THEY WERE LOOKING FOR SOME GUY...
ONCE THEY FIGURED OUT IT WASN'T ME, THOUGH, THEY LET ME GO.

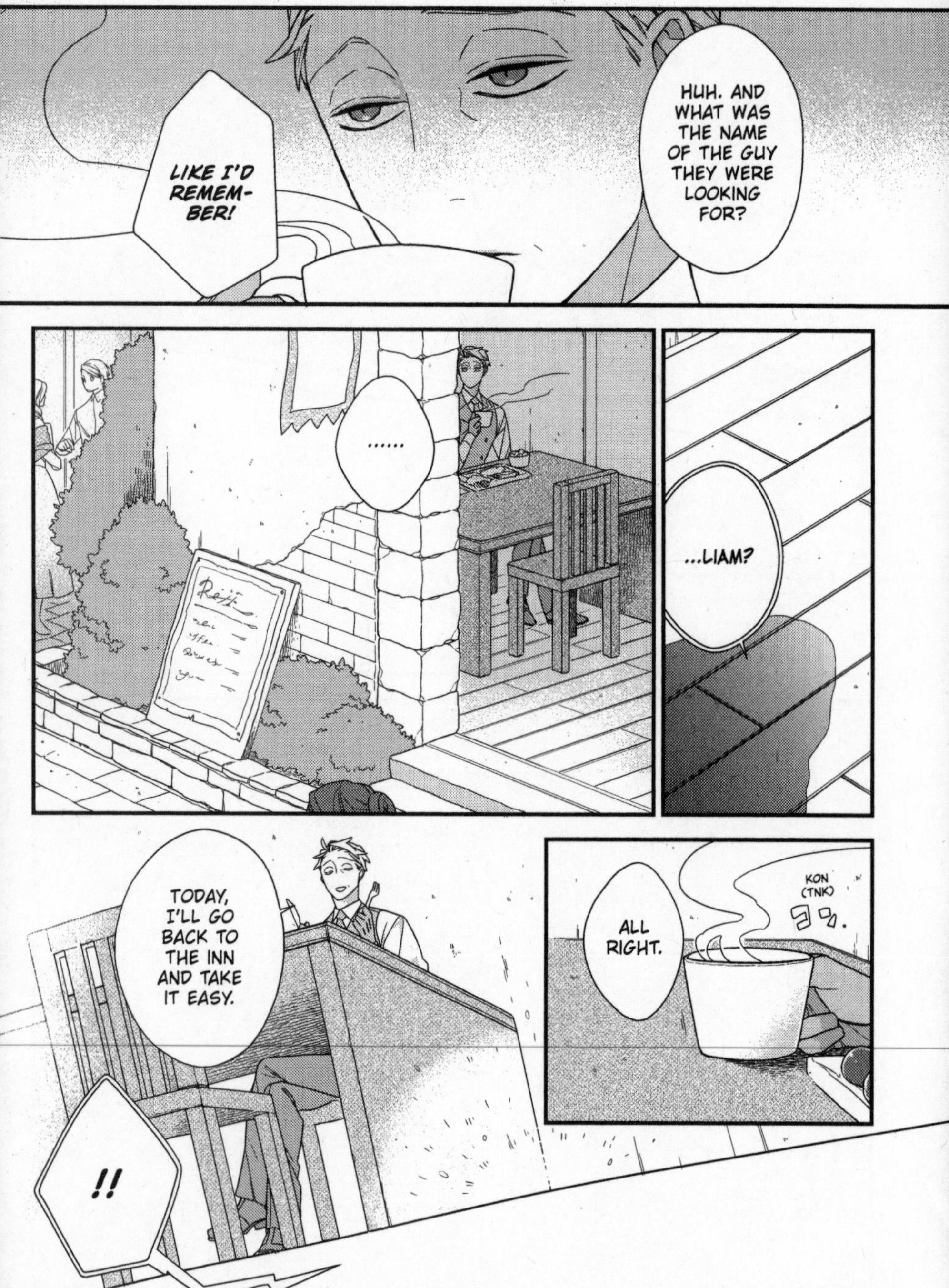
HUH. AND WHAT WAS THE NAME OF THE GUY THEY WERE LOOKING FOR?
LIKE I'D REMEMBER!
...LIAM?
......
KON (TNK)
ALL RIGHT.
TODAY, I'LL GO BACK TO THE INN AND TAKE IT EASY.
!!

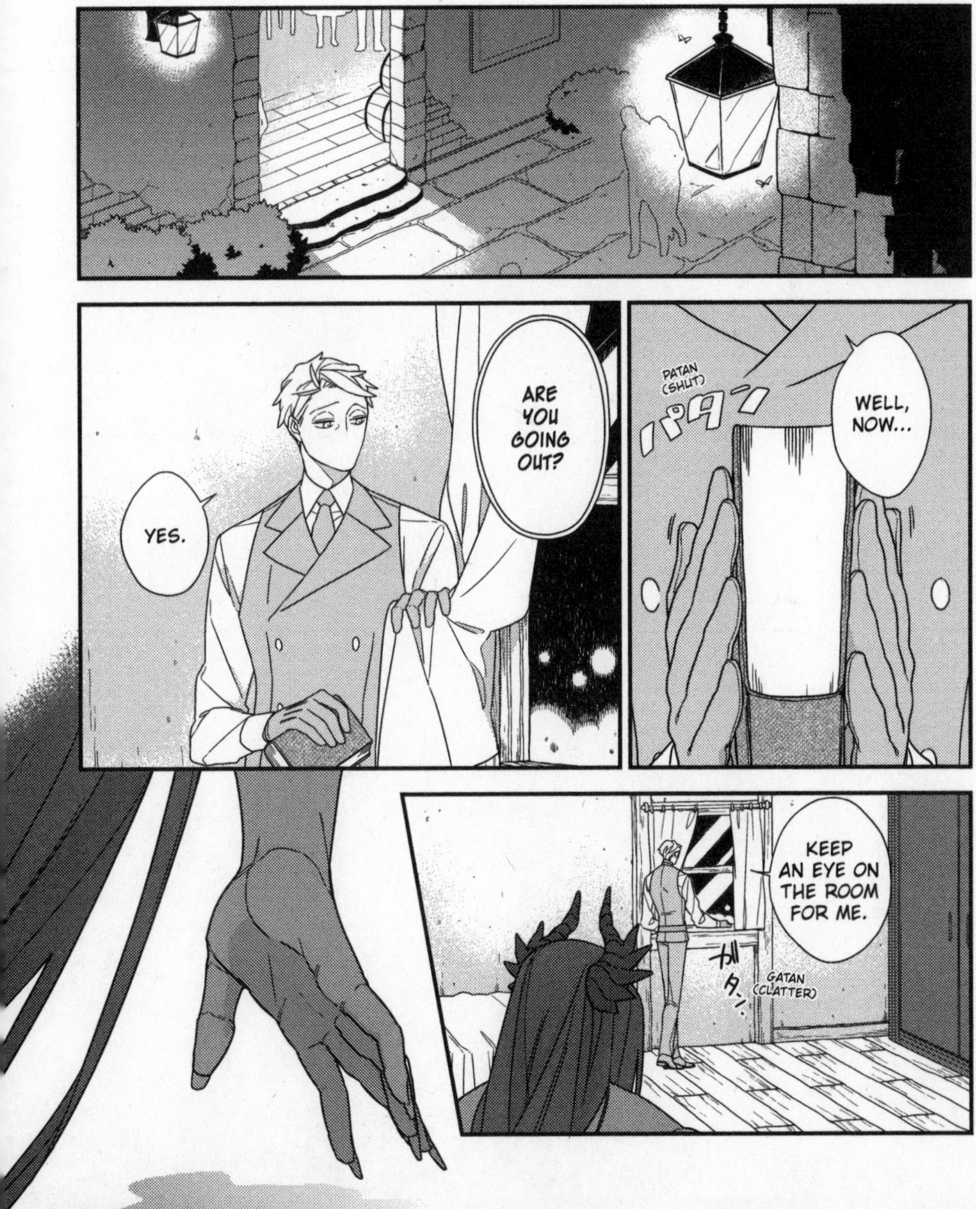
PATAN (SHUT)
パタン
WELL, NOW...
ARE YOU GOING OUT?
YES.
KEEP AN EYE ON THE ROOM FOR ME.
GATAN (CLATTER)

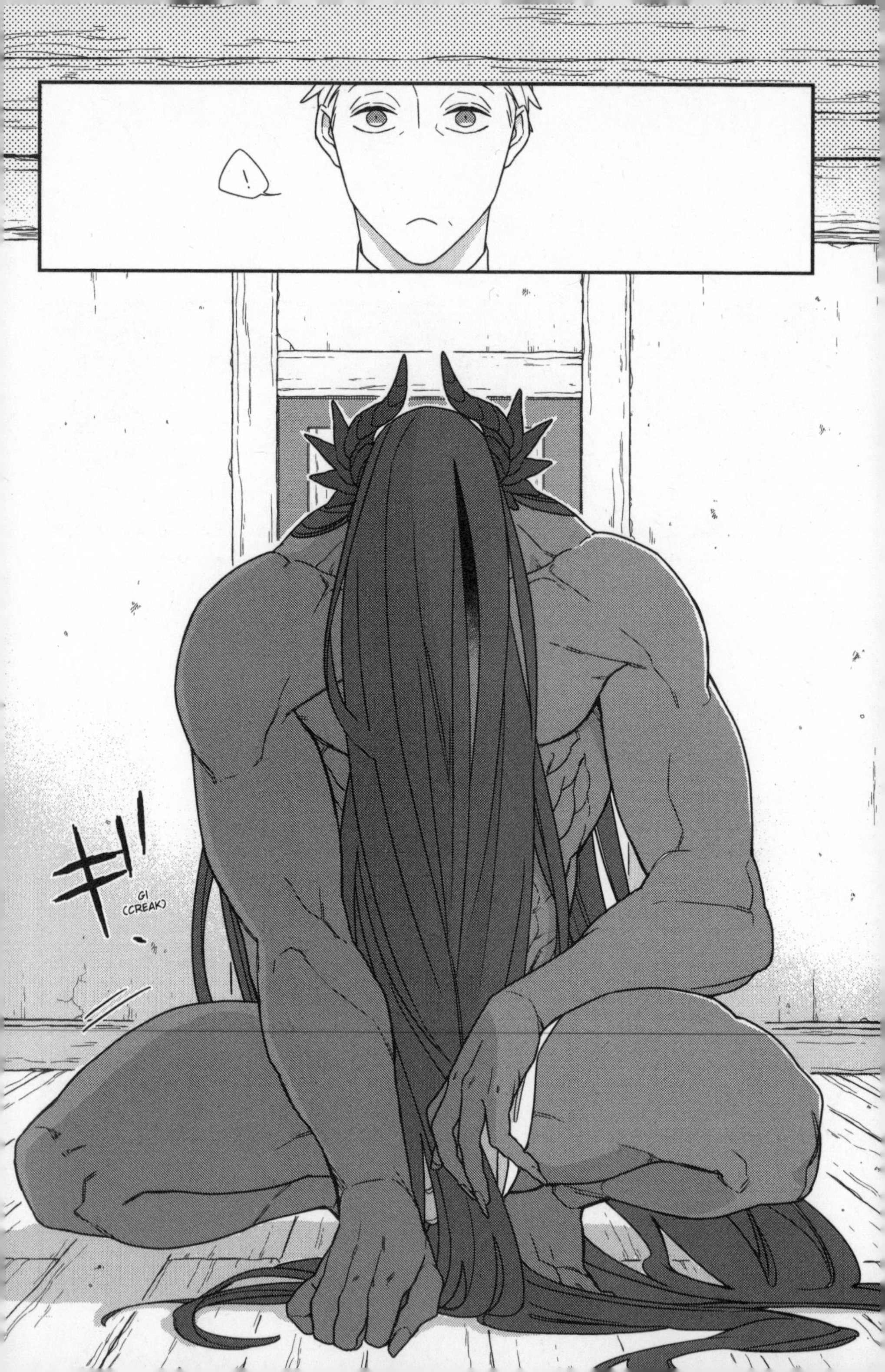
!
GI (CREAK)

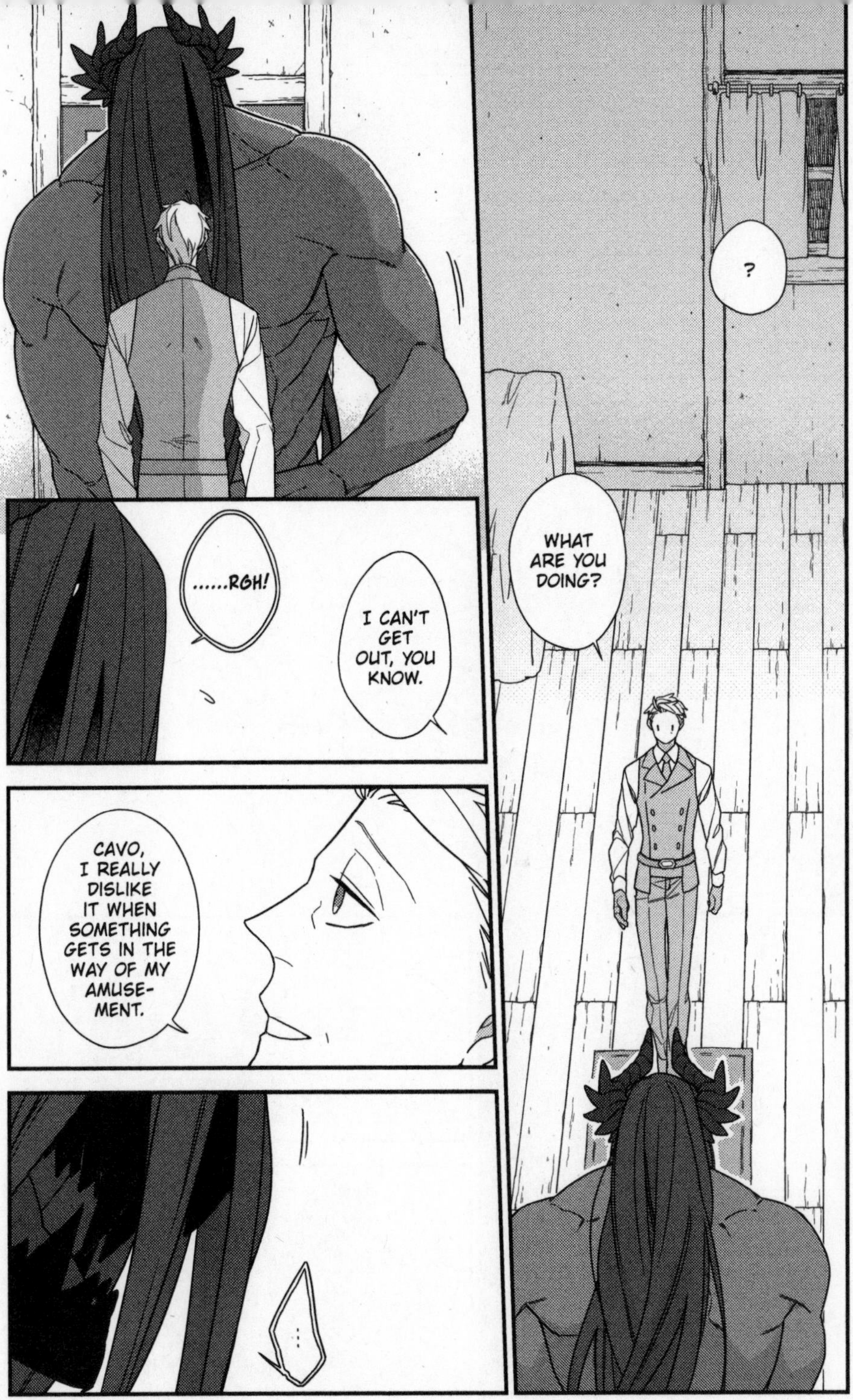
?
WHAT ARE YOU DOING?
I CAN'T GET OUT, YOU KNOW.
......RGH!
CAVO, I REALLY DISLIKE IT WHEN SOMETHING GETS IN THE WAY OF MY AMUSEMENT.
...

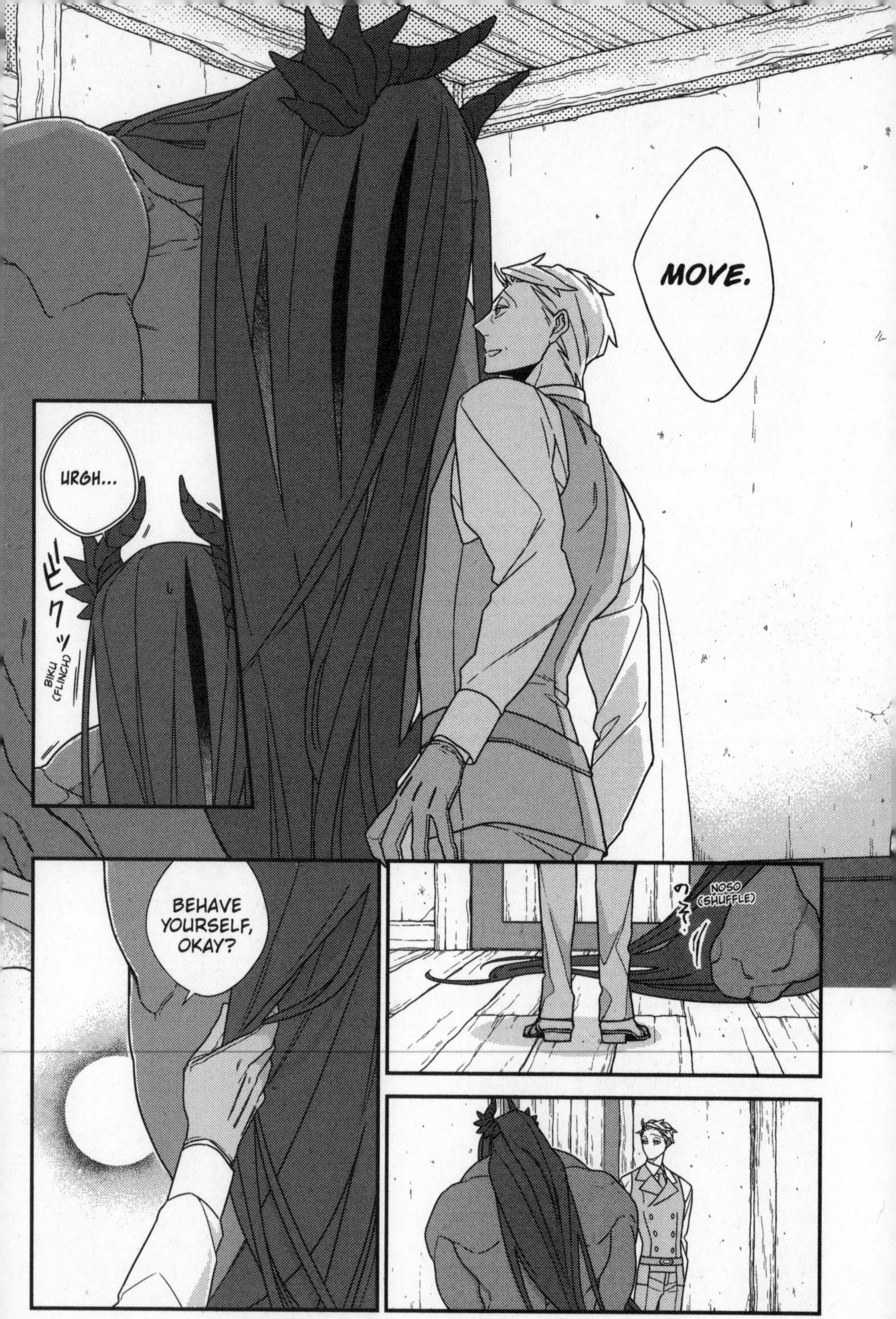
MOVE.
URGH...
ビクッ
BIKU (FLINCH)
NOSO (SHUFFLE)
BEHAVE YOURSELF, OKAY?

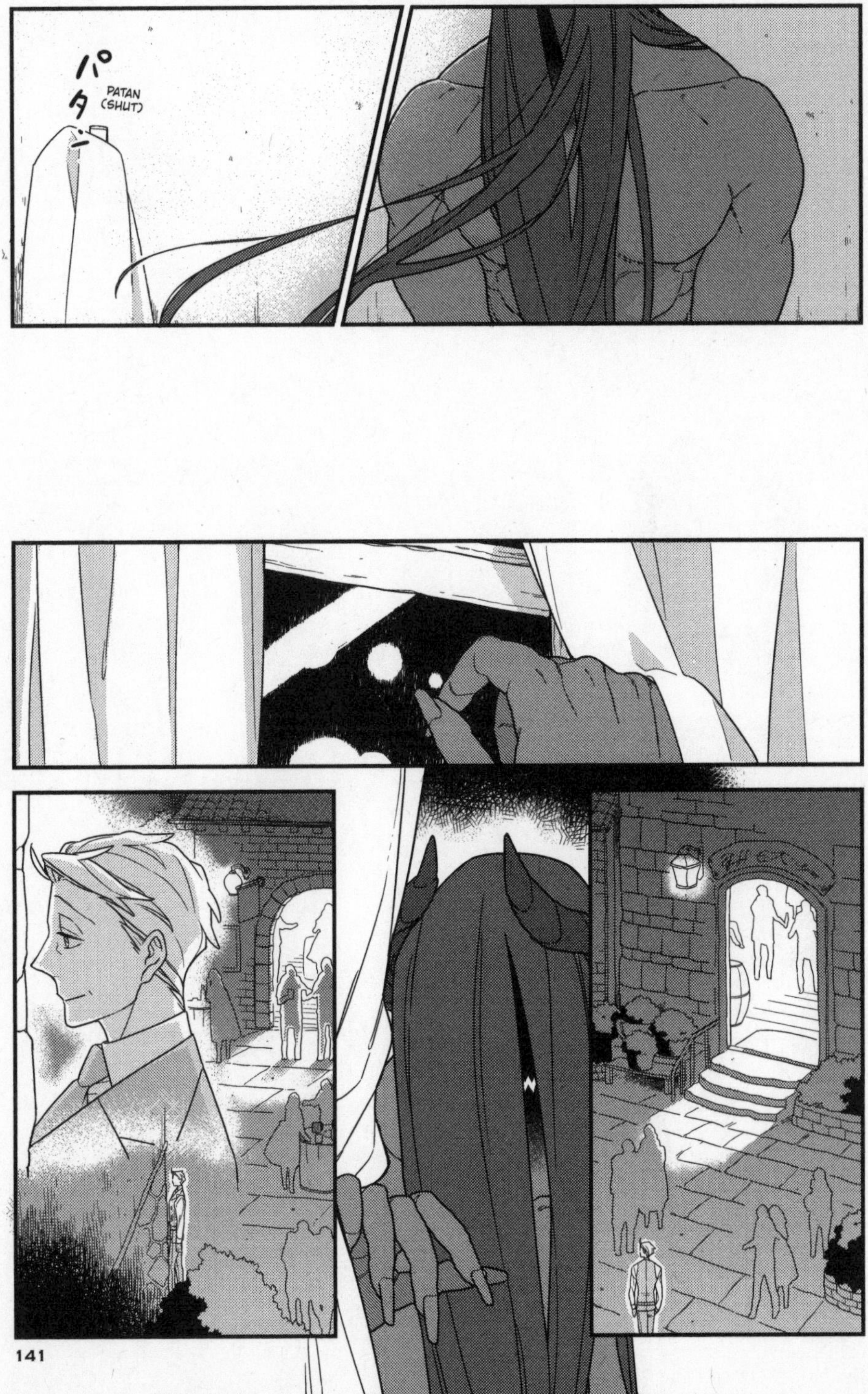
パタン
PATAN (SHUT)

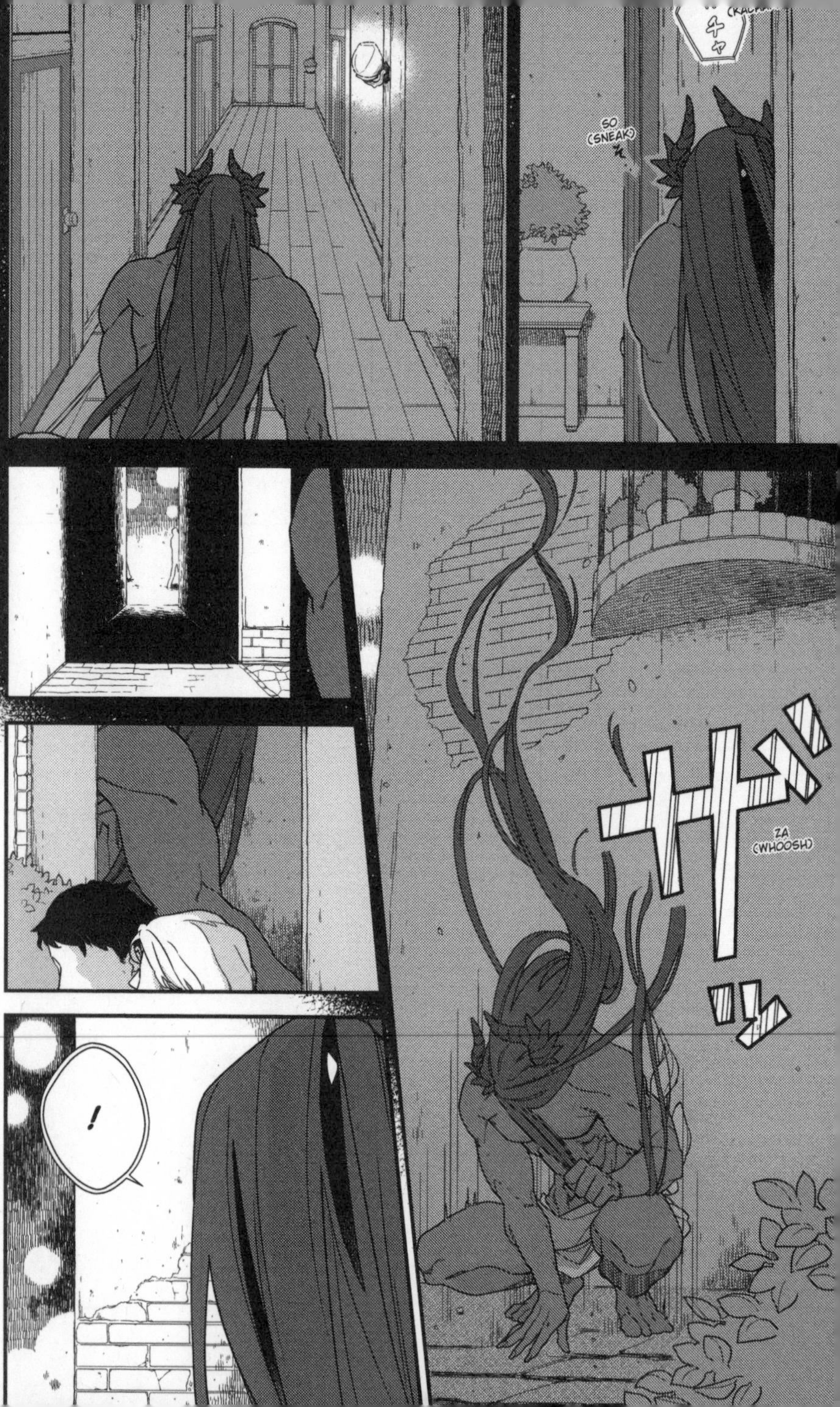
SO
(SNEAK)
ZA
(WHOOSH)
!

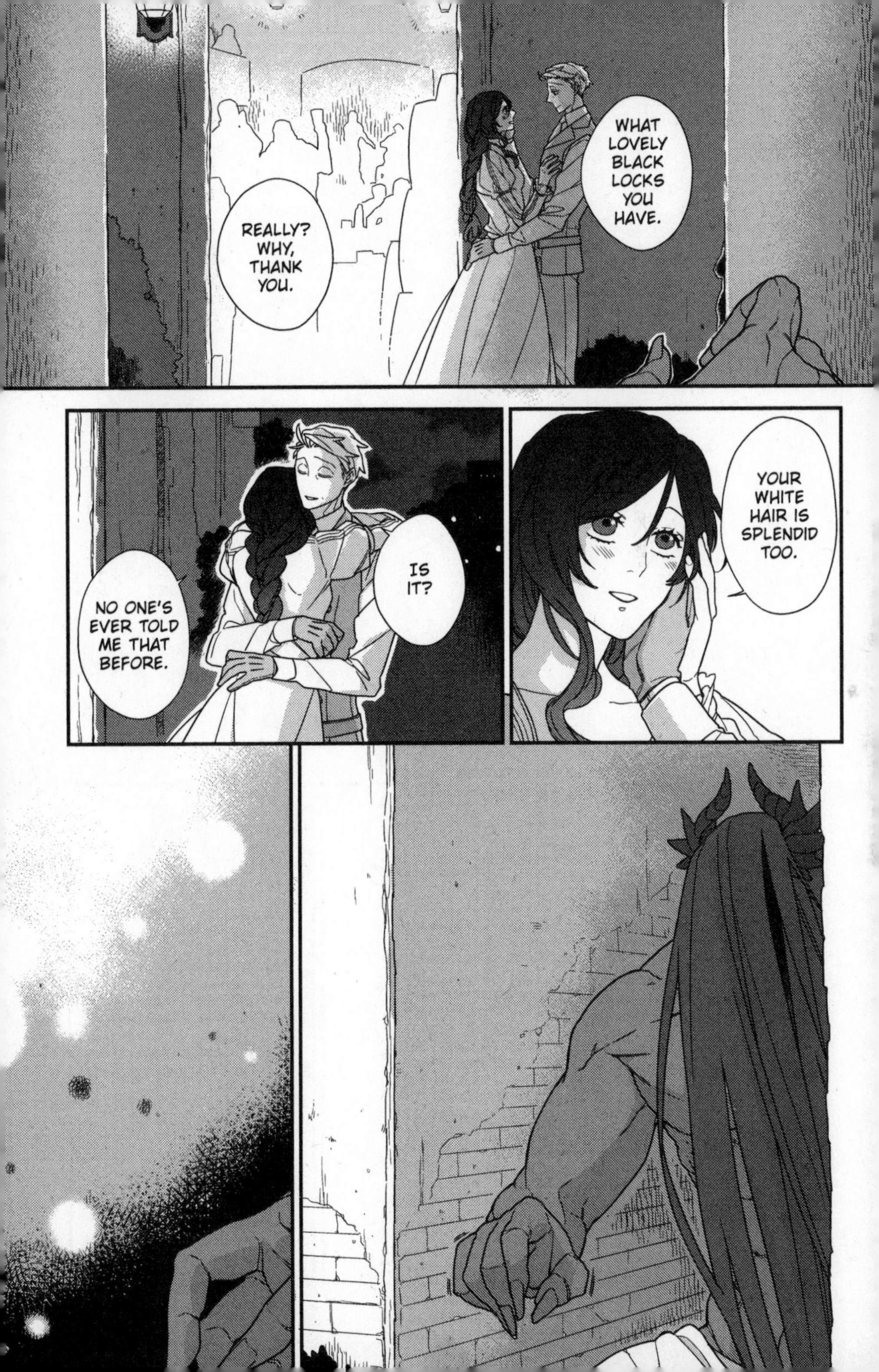
WHAT LOVELY BLACK LOCKS YOU HAVE.
REALLY? WHY, THANK YOU.
YOUR WHITE HAIR IS SPLENDID TOO.
IS IT?
NO ONE'S EVER TOLD ME THAT BEFORE.

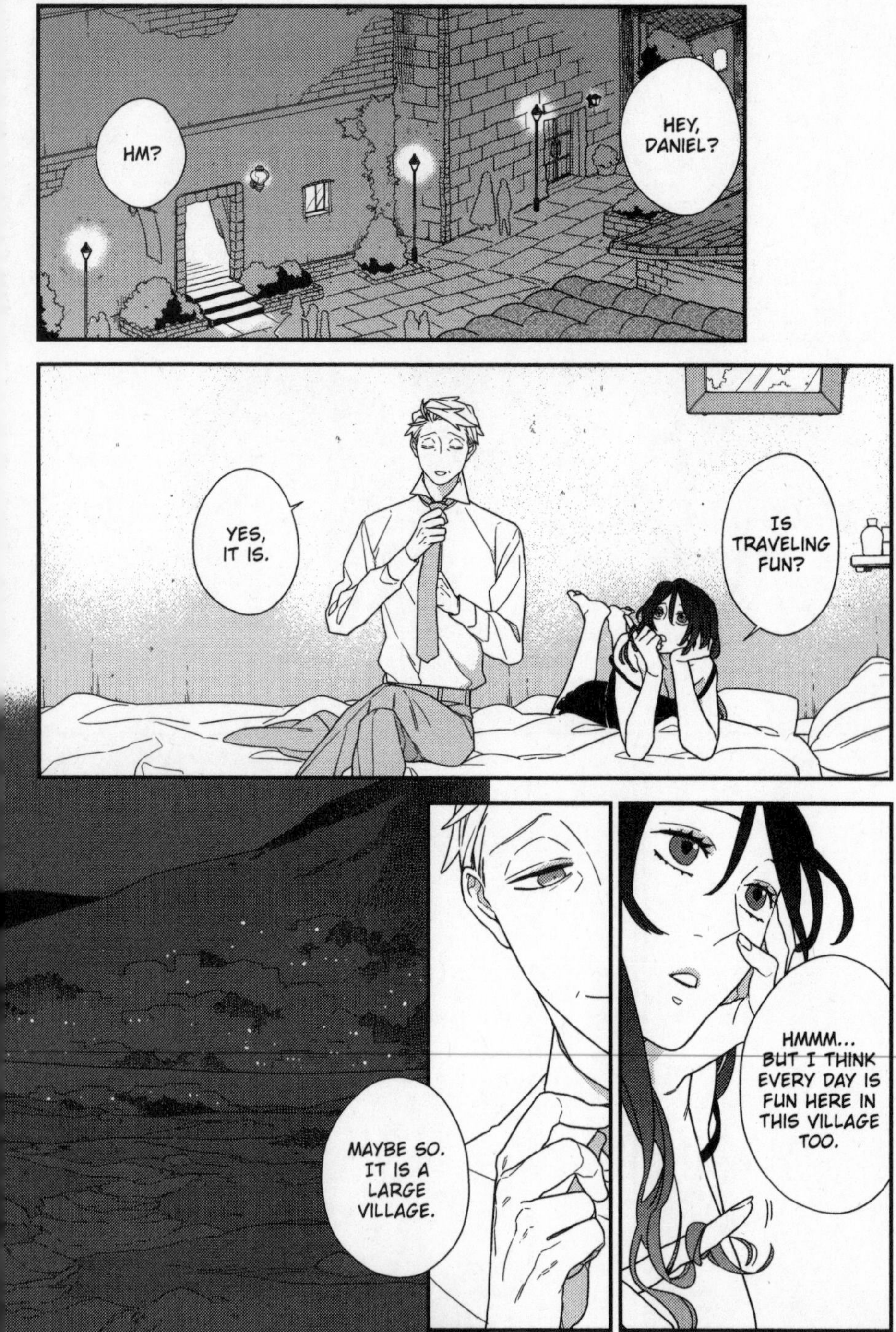
HEY, DANIEL?
HM?
IS TRAVELING FUN?
YES, IT IS.
HMMM... BUT I THINK EVERY DAY IS FUN HERE IN THIS VILLAGE TOO.
MAYBE SO. IT IS A LARGE VILLAGE.

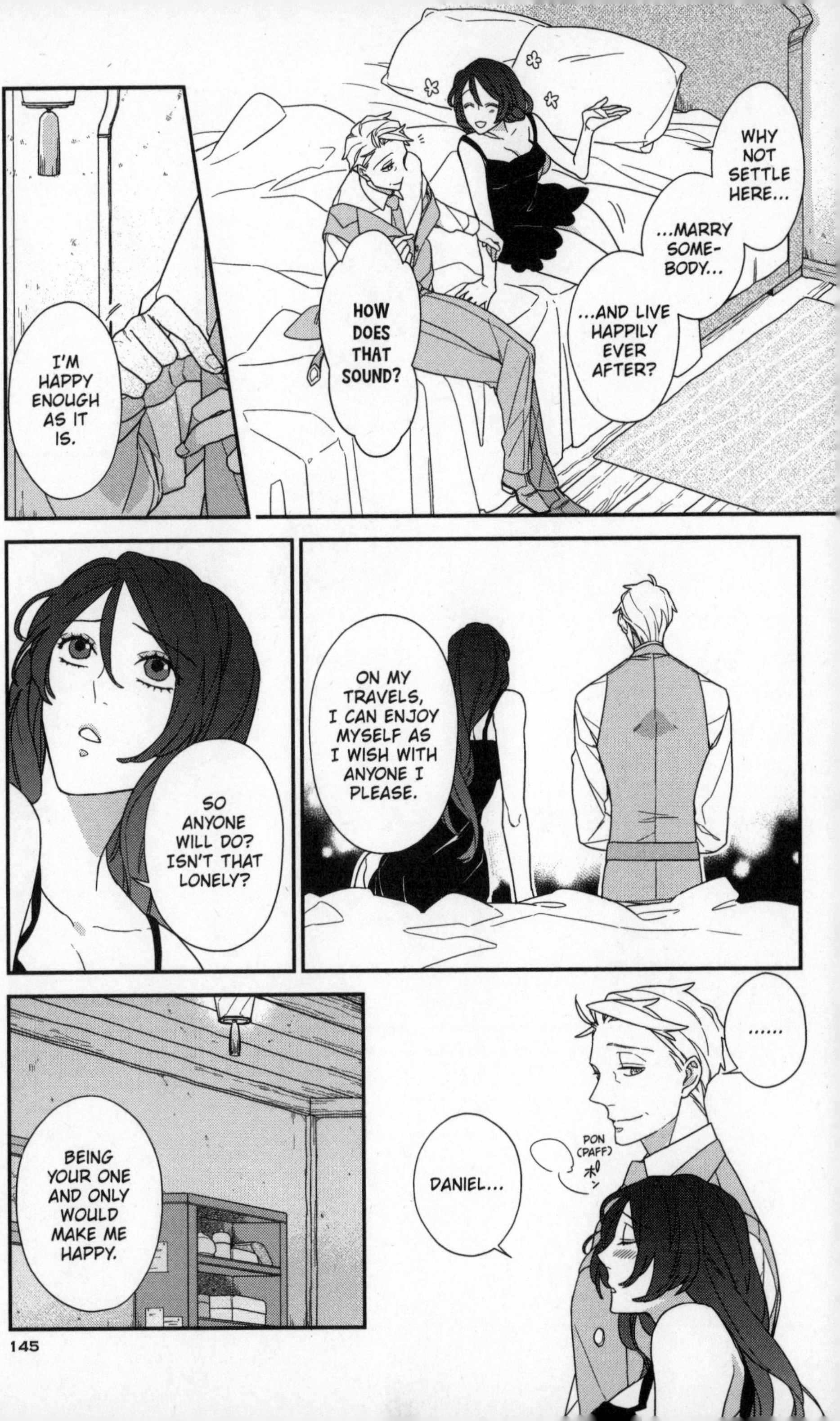
WHY NOT SETTLE HERE...
...MARRY SOMEBODY...
...AND LIVE HAPPILY EVER AFTER?
HOW DOES THAT SOUND?
I'M HAPPY ENOUGH AS IT IS.
ON MY TRAVELS, I CAN ENJOY MYSELF AS I WISH WITH ANYONE I PLEASE.
SO ANYONE WILL DO? ISN'T THAT LONELY?
......
PON (PAFF)
ポン
DANIEL...
BEING YOUR ONE AND ONLY WOULD MAKE ME HAPPY.

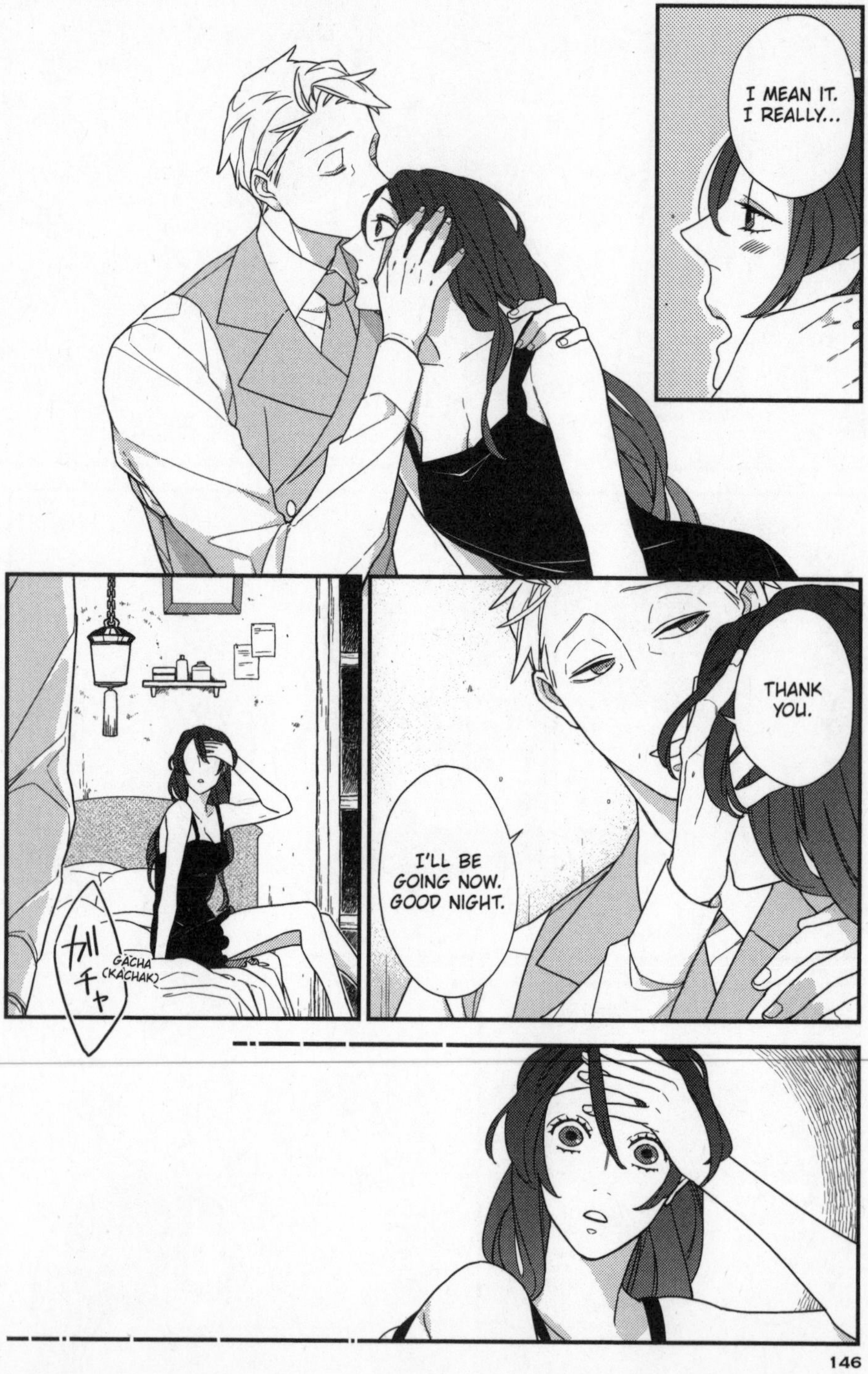
I MEAN IT. I REALLY...
THANK YOU.
I'LL BE GOING NOW. GOOD NIGHT.
ガチャ
GACHA (KACHAK)

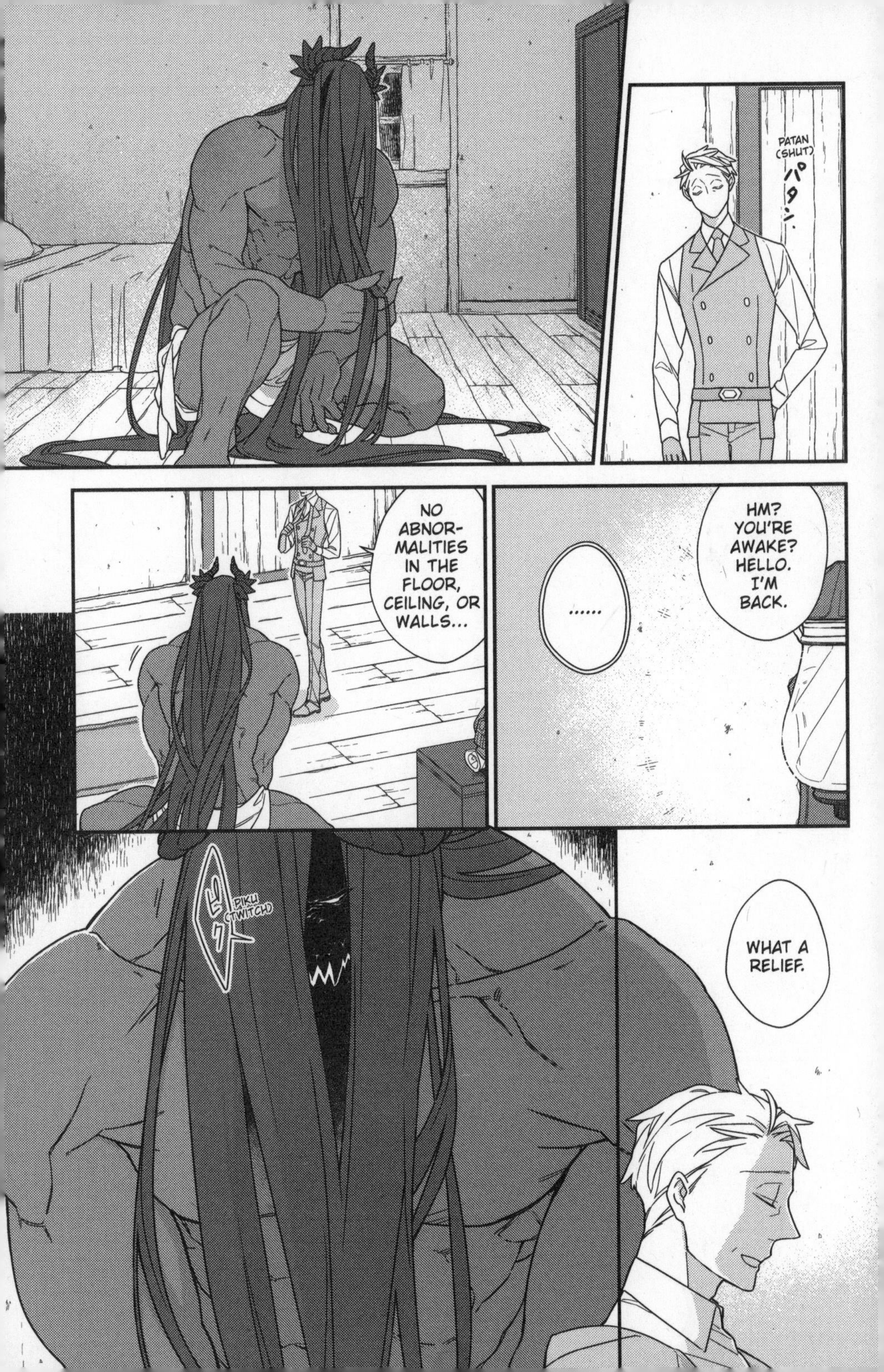
PATAN (SHUT)
パタン
HM? YOU'RE AWAKE? HELLO. I'M BACK.
......
NO ABNORMALITIES IN THE FLOOR, CEILING, OR WALLS...
WHAT A RELIEF.
PIKU (TWITCH)
ピク

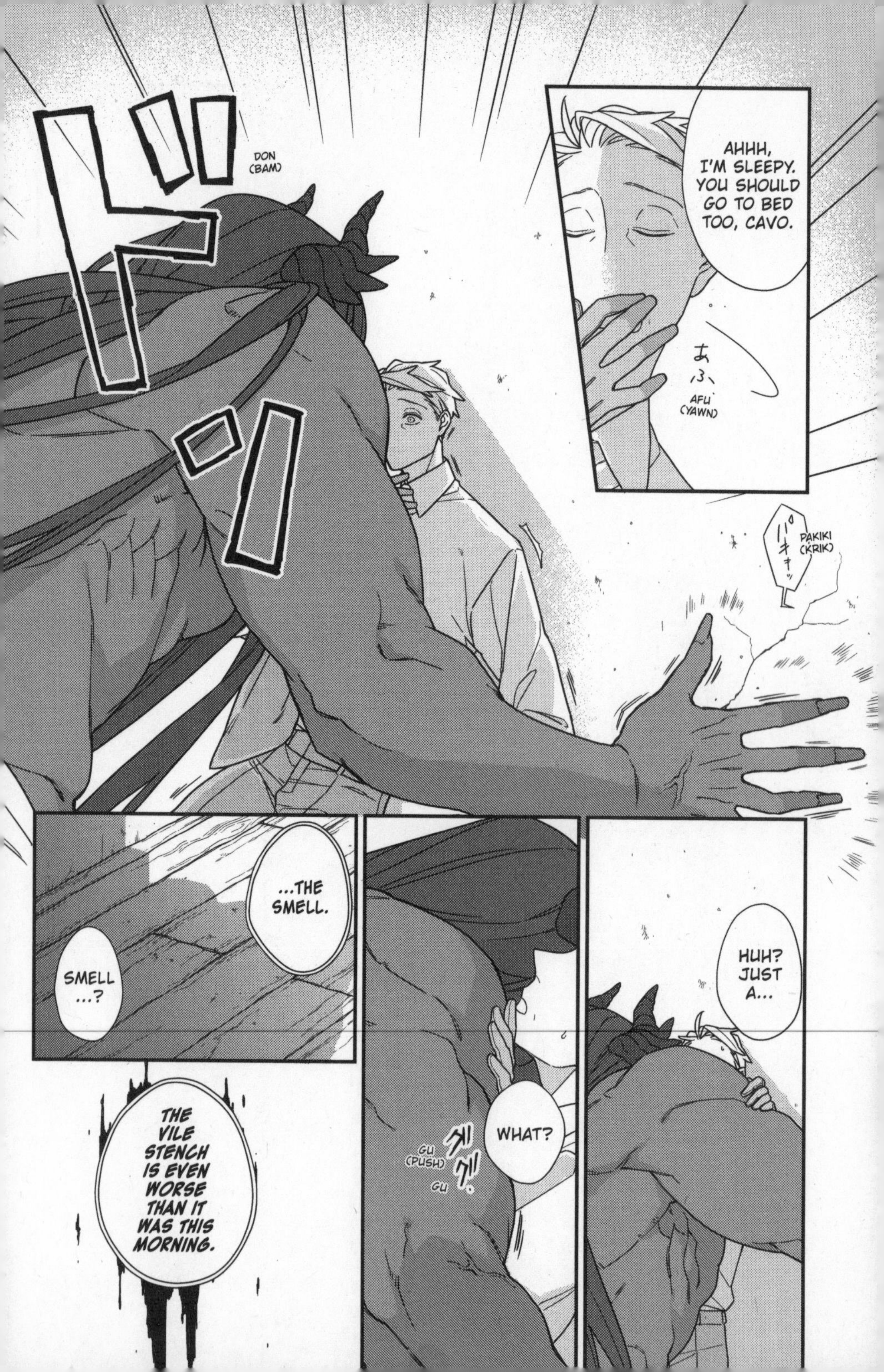
AHHH, I'M SLEEPY. YOU SHOULD GO TO BED TOO, CAVO.
あふ
AFU (YAWN)
DON (BAM)
パキキッ
PAKIKI (KRIK)
HUH? JUST A...
WHAT?
グッ
GU (PUSH)
グ
GU
...THE SMELL.
SMELL ...?
THE VILE STENCH IS EVEN WORSE THAN IT WAS THIS MORNING.

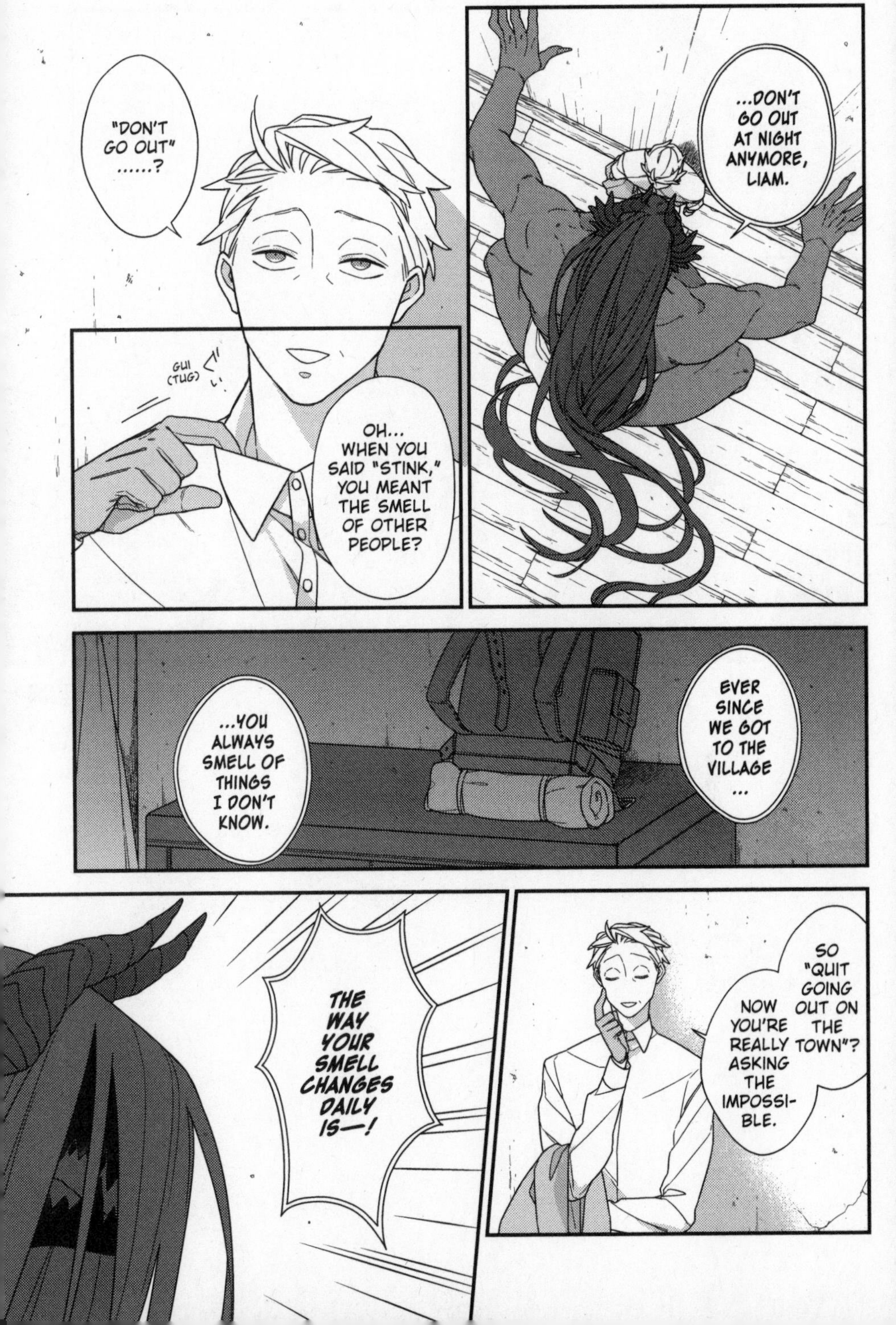
...DON'T GO OUT AT NIGHT ANYMORE, LIAM.
"DON'T GO OUT" ......?
GUI (TUG)
OH... WHEN YOU SAID "STINK," YOU MEANT THE SMELL OF OTHER PEOPLE?
EVER SINCE WE GOT TO THE VILLAGE ...
...YOU ALWAYS SMELL OF THINGS I DON'T KNOW.
SO "QUIT GOING OUT ON THE TOWN"?
NOW YOU'RE REALLY ASKING THE IMPOSSI-BLE.
THE WAY YOUR SMELL CHANGES DAILY IS—!

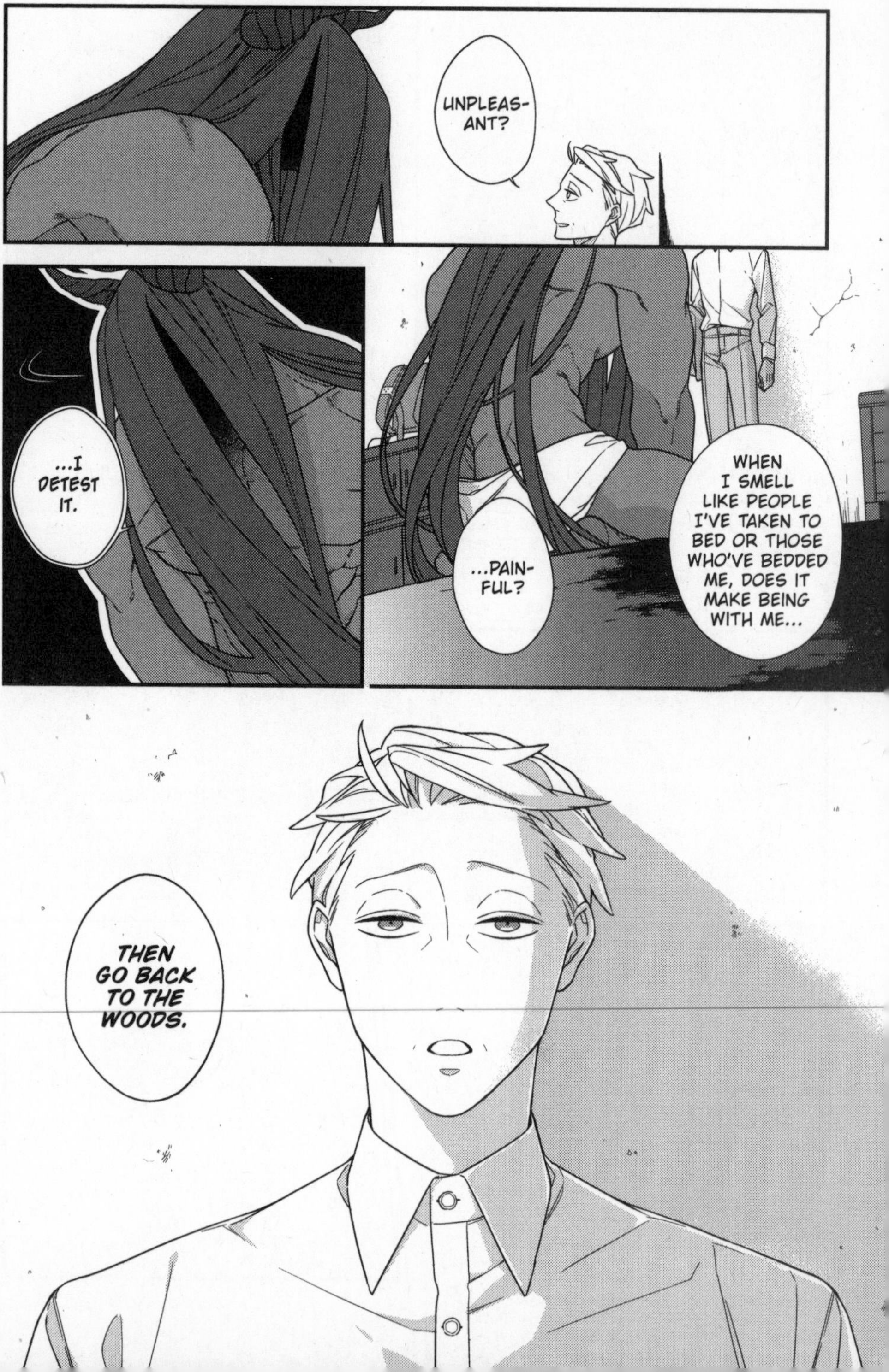
UNPLEAS-ANT?
WHEN I SMELL LIKE PEOPLE I'VE TAKEN TO BED OR THOSE WHO'VE BEDDED ME, DOES IT MAKE BEING WITH ME...
...PAIN-FUL?
...I DETEST IT.
THEN GO BACK TO THE WOODS.

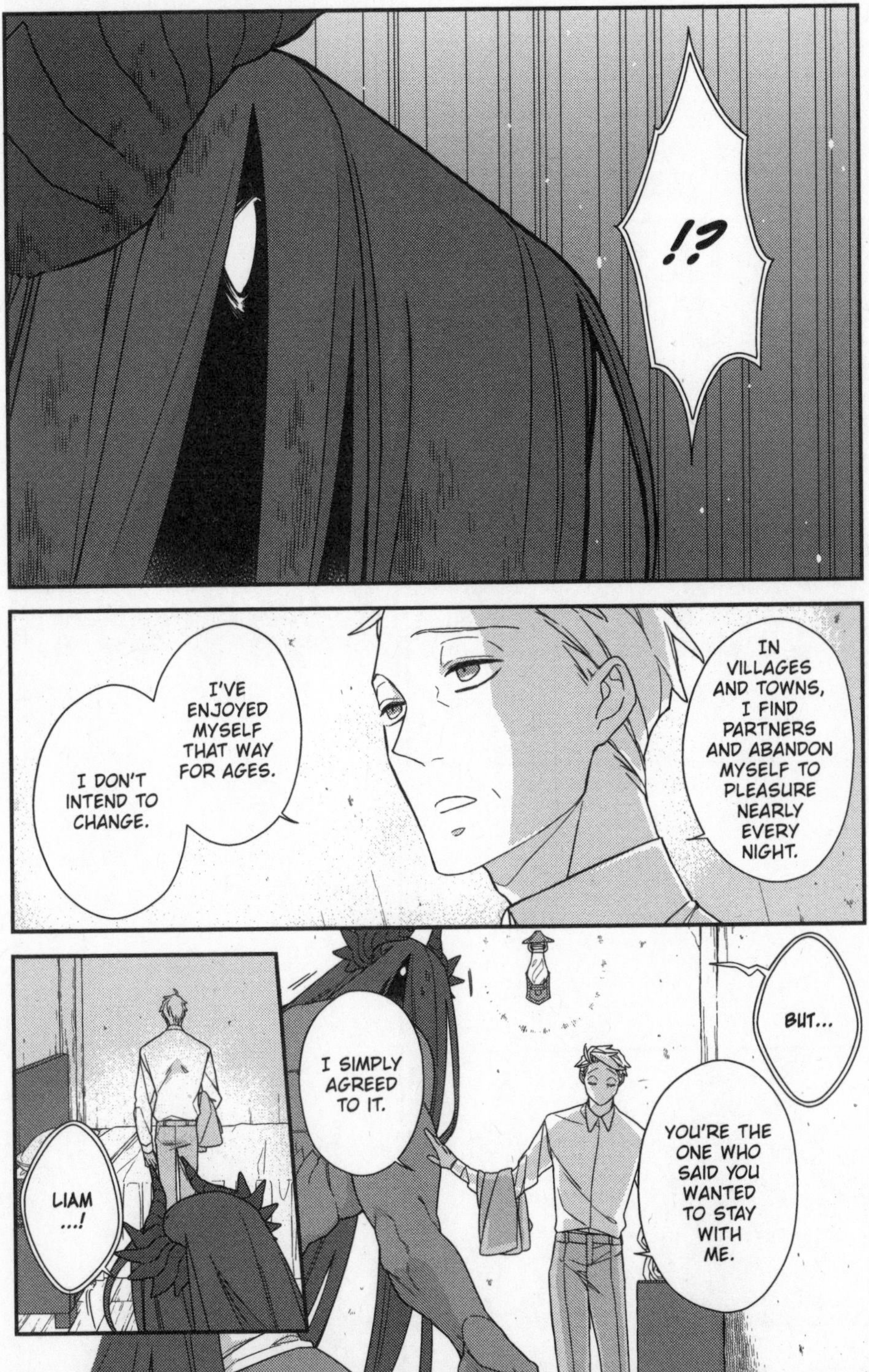
!?
IN VILLAGES AND TOWNS, I FIND PARTNERS AND ABANDON MYSELF TO PLEASURE NEARLY EVERY NIGHT.
I'VE ENJOYED MYSELF THAT WAY FOR AGES.
I DON'T INTEND TO CHANGE.
BUT...
YOU'RE THE ONE WHO SAID YOU WANTED TO STAY WITH ME.
I SIMPLY AGREED TO IT.
LIAM ...!

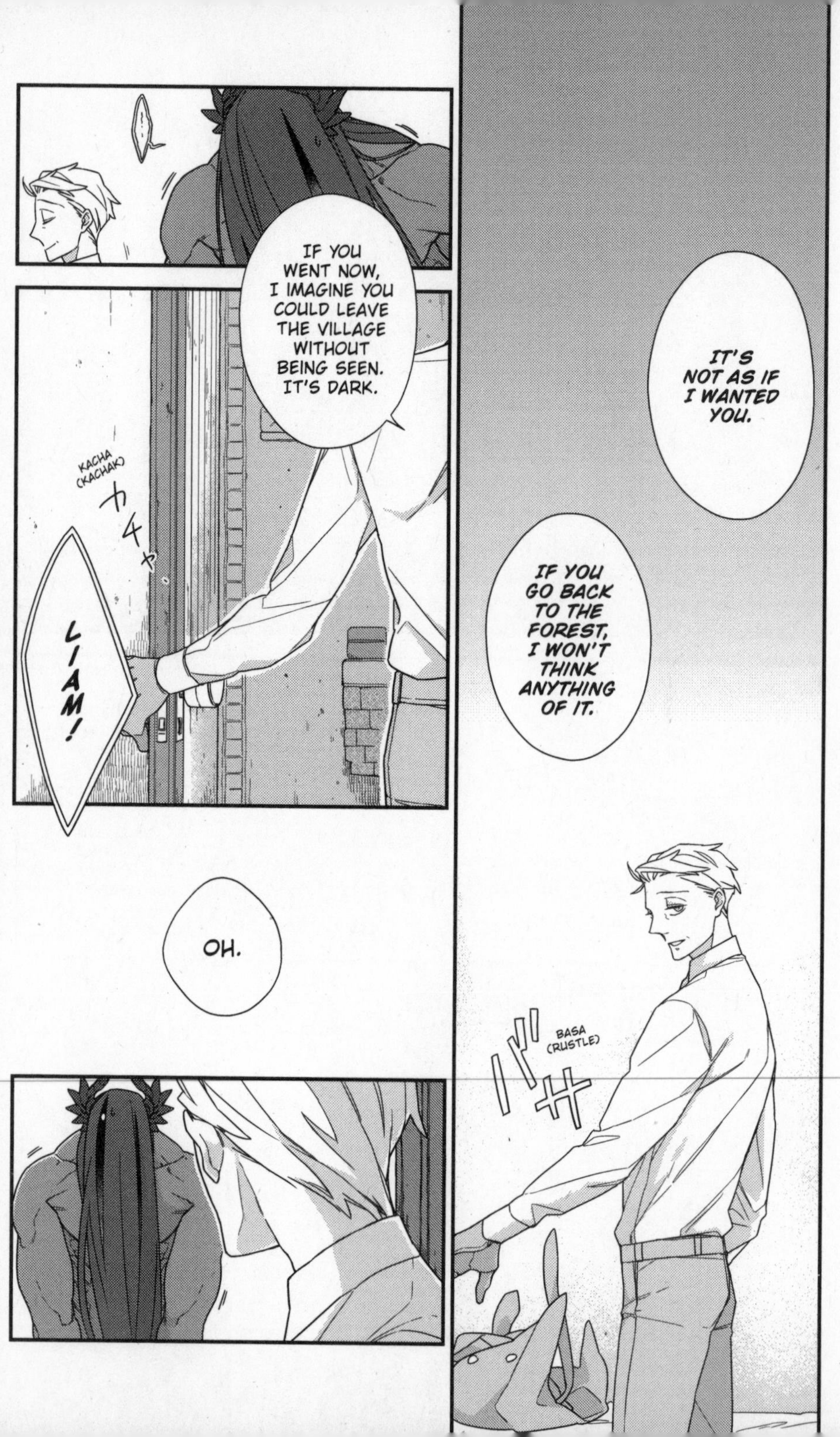
IT'S NOT AS IF I WANTED YOU.
IF YOU GO BACK TO THE FOREST, I WON'T THINK ANYTHING OF IT.
BASA (RUSTLE)
...
IF YOU WENT NOW, I IMAGINE YOU COULD LEAVE THE VILLAGE WITHOUT BEING SEEN. IT'S DARK.
KACHA (KACHAK)
LIAM!
OH.

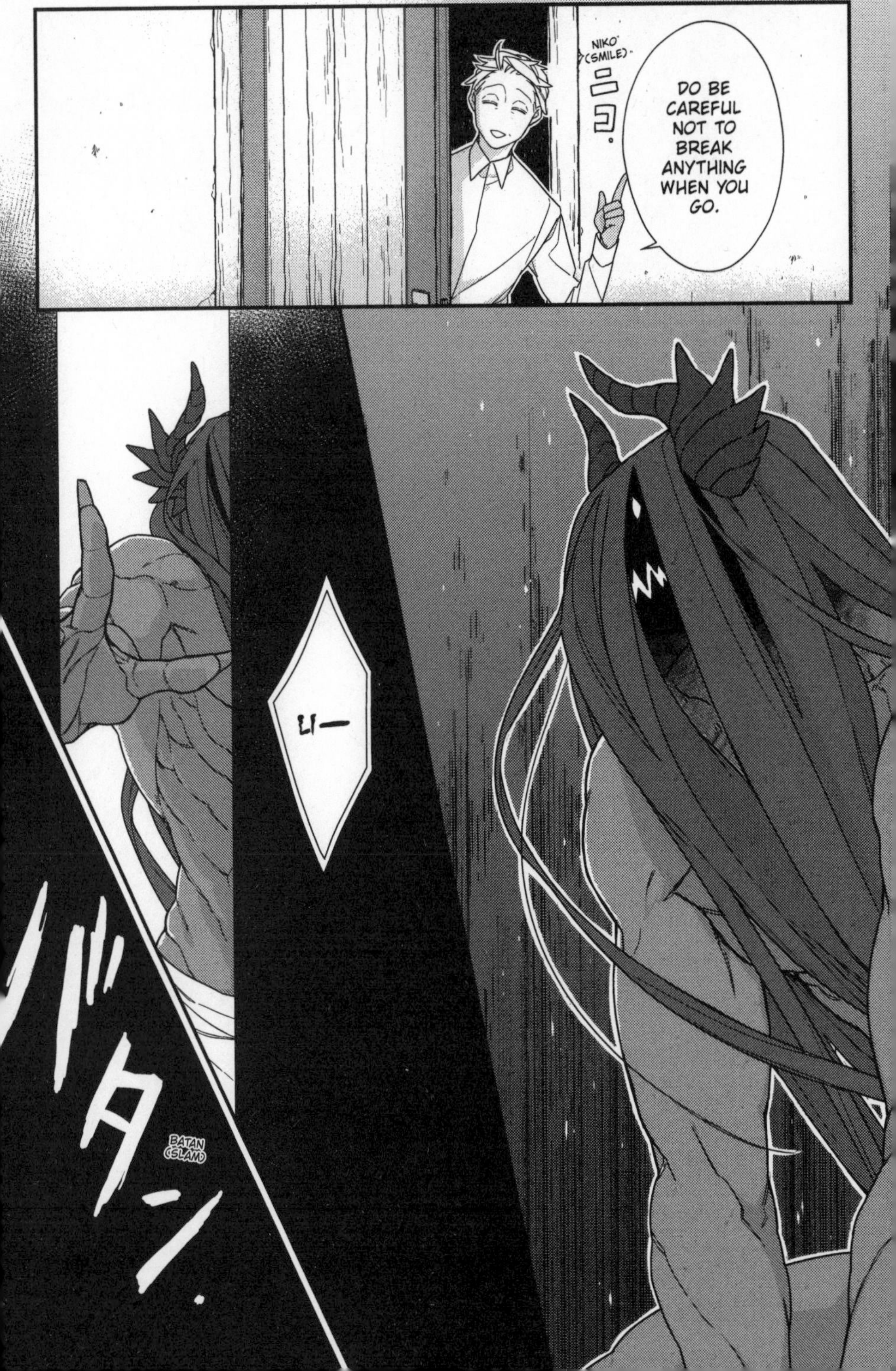
DO BE CAREFUL NOT TO BREAK ANYTHING WHEN YOU GO.
ニコ
NIKO (SMILE)
バタン
BATAN (SLAM)

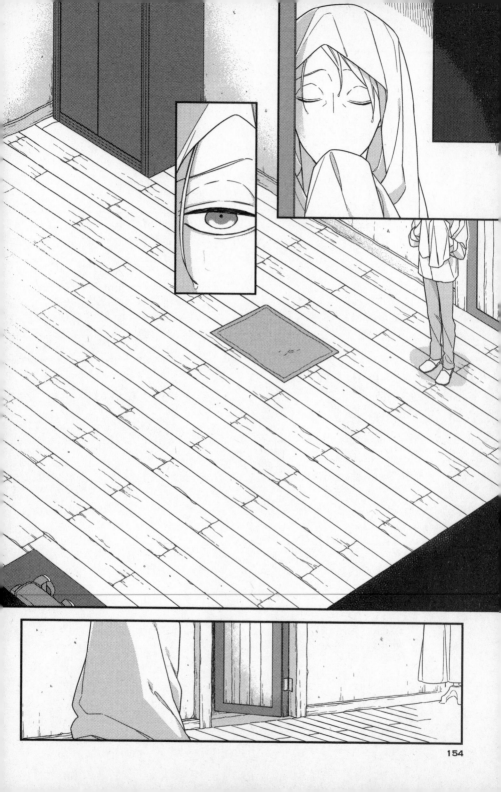

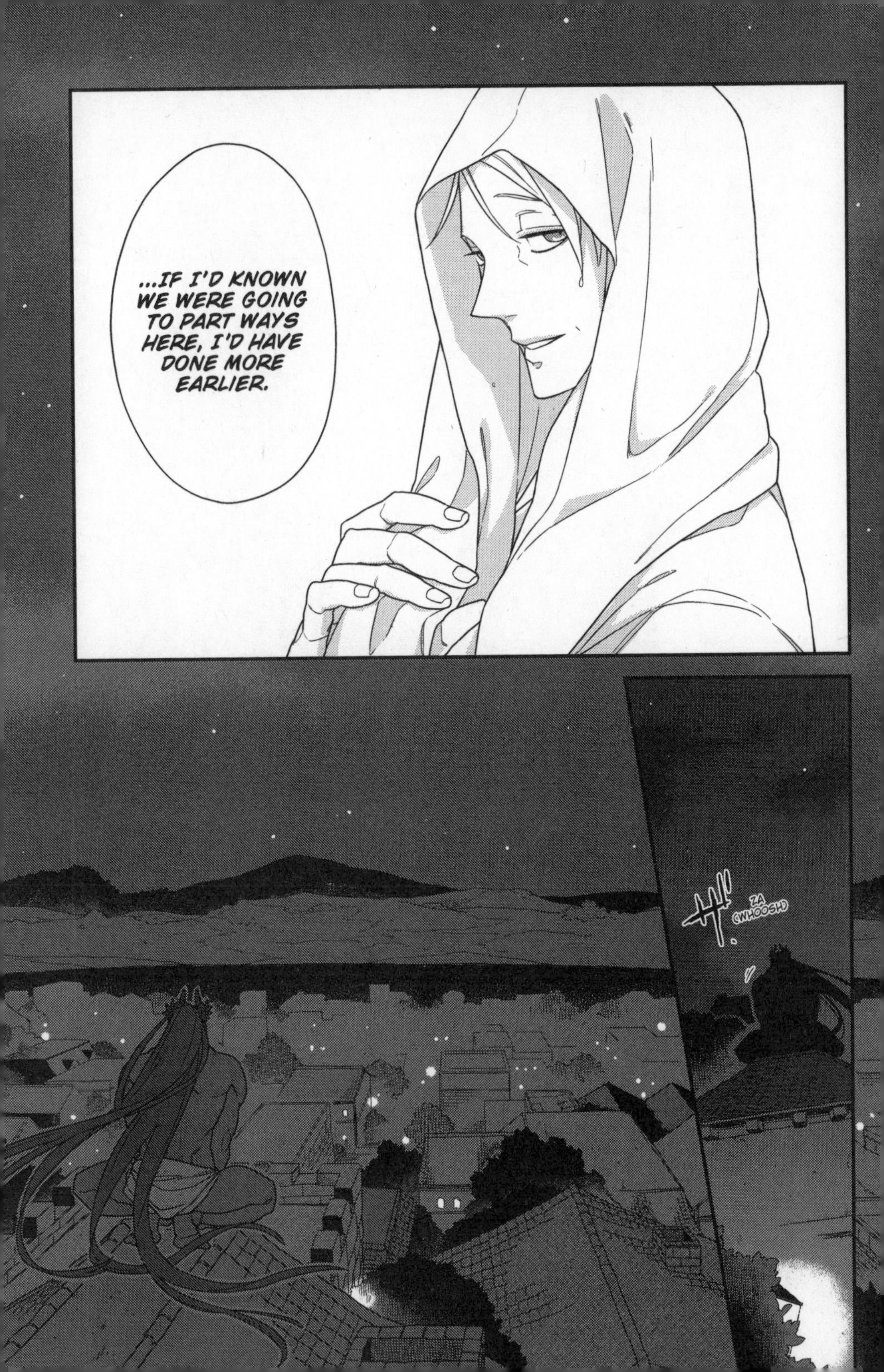
...IF I'D KNOWN WE WERE GOING TO PART WAYS HERE, I'D HAVE DONE MORE EARLIER.
ZA (WHOOSH)

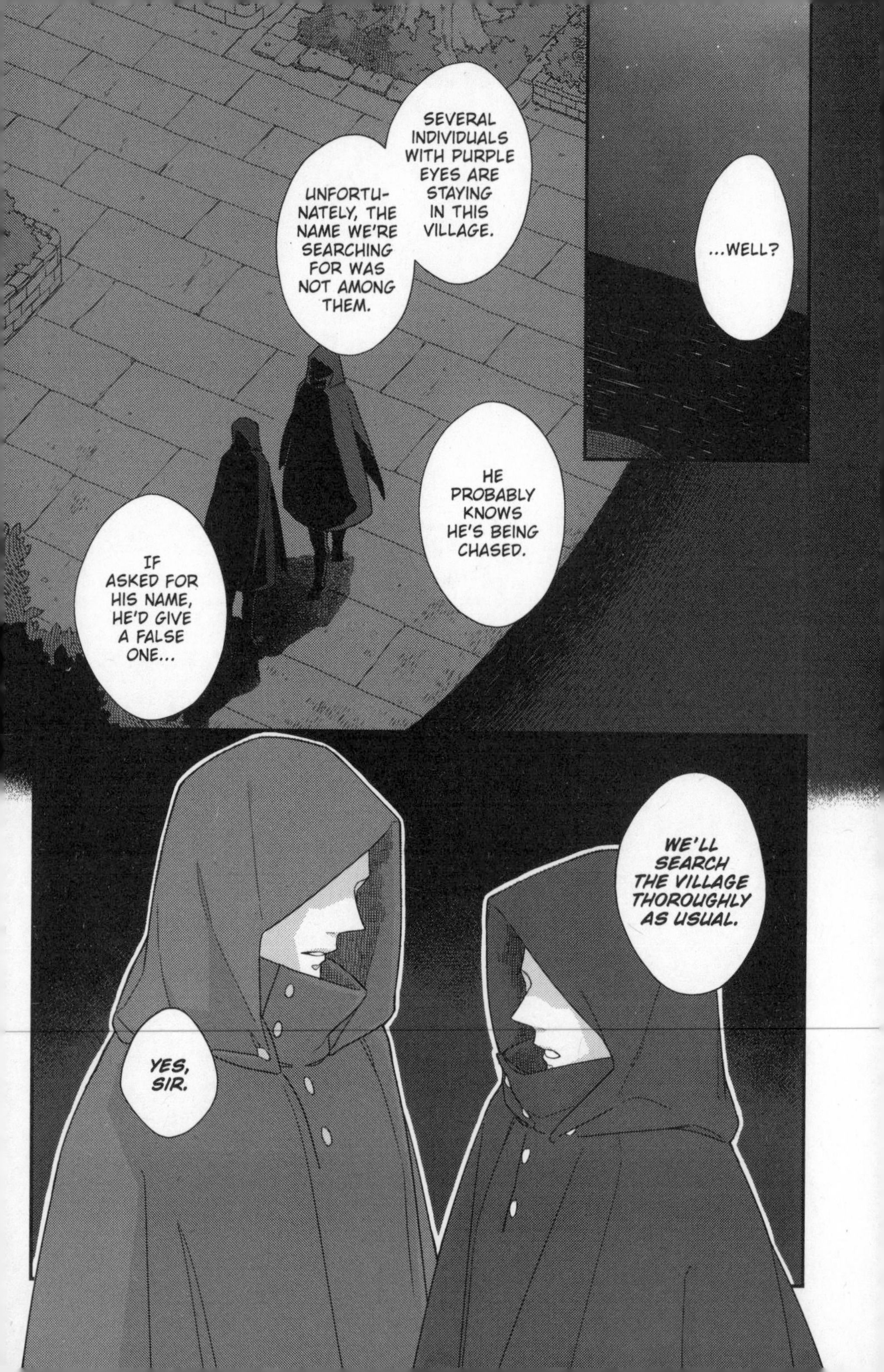
...WELL?
SEVERAL INDIVIDUALS WITH PURPLE EYES ARE STAYING IN THIS VILLAGE.
UNFORTU-NATELY, THE NAME WE'RE SEARCHING FOR WAS NOT AMONG THEM.
HE PROBABLY KNOWS HE'S BEING CHASED.
IF ASKED FOR HIS NAME, HE'D GIVE A FALSE ONE...
WE'LL SEARCH THE VILLAGE THOROUGHLY AS USUAL.
YES, SIR.

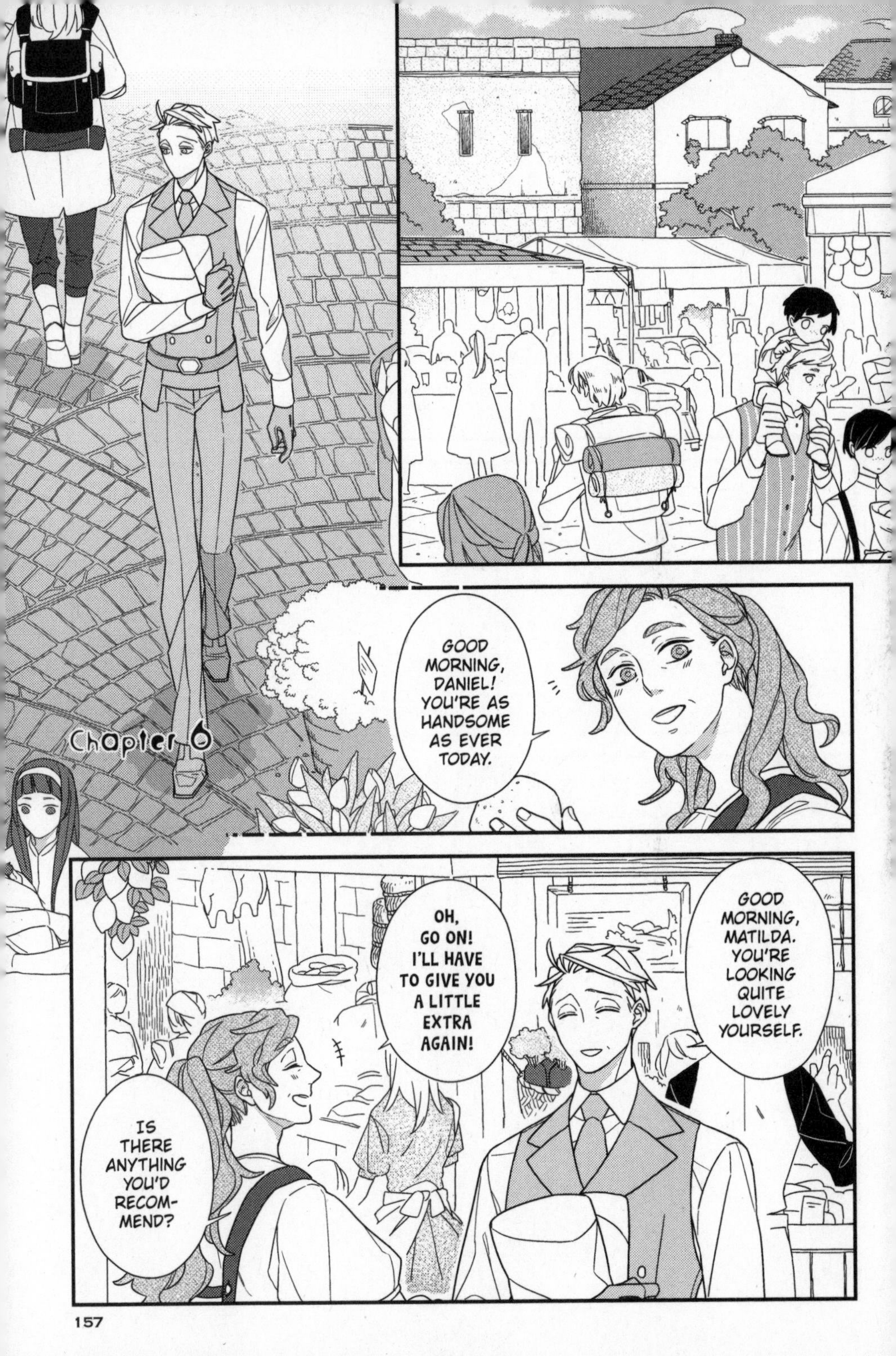
GOOD MORNING, DANIEL! YOU'RE AS HANDSOME AS EVER TODAY.
Chapter 6
GOOD MORNING, MATILDA. YOU'RE LOOKING QUITE LOVELY YOURSELF.
OH, GO ON! I'LL HAVE TO GIVE YOU A LITTLE EXTRA AGAIN!
IS THERE ANYTHING YOU'D RECOMMEND?

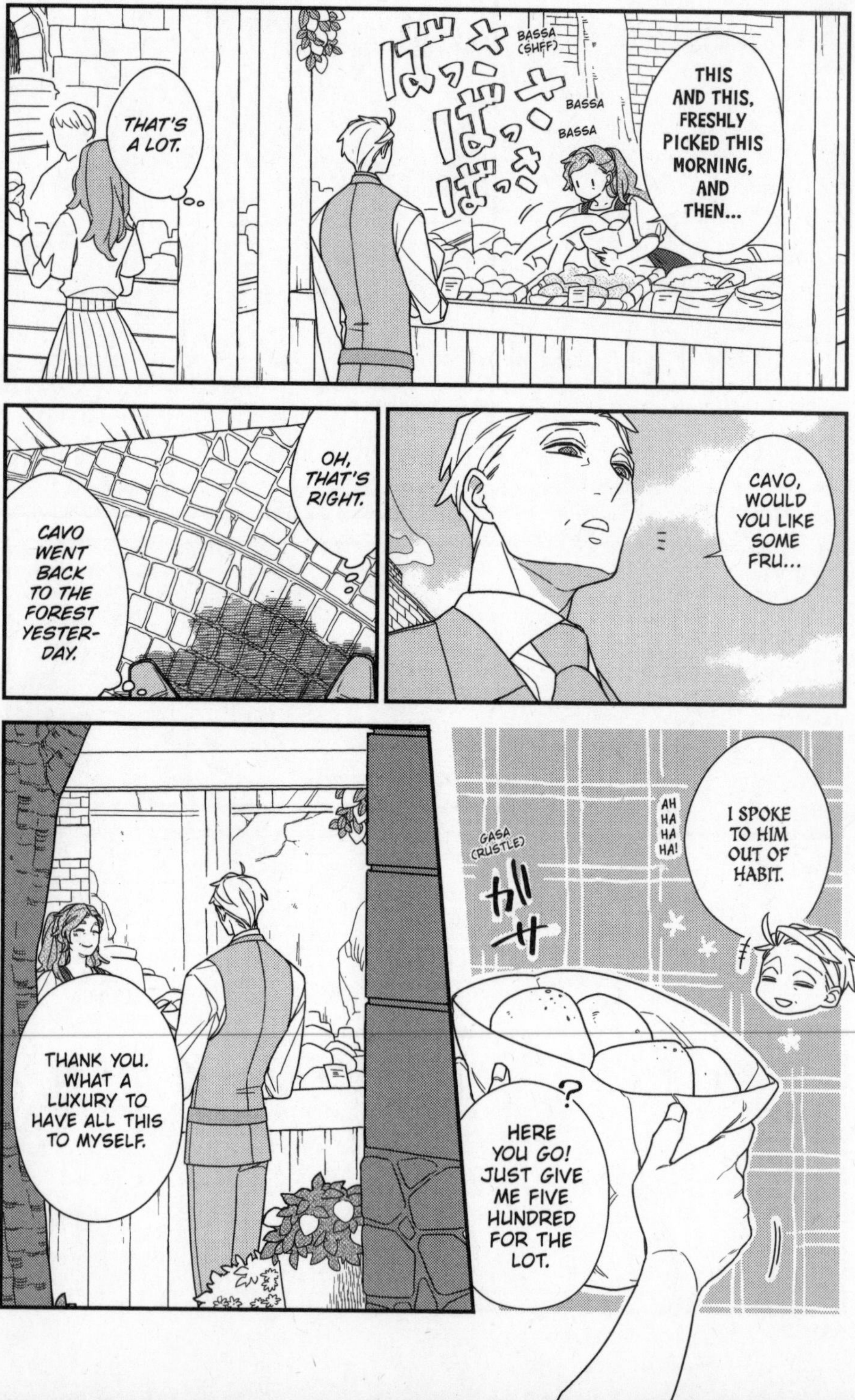
THIS AND THIS, FRESHLY PICKED THIS MORNING, AND THEN...
ばっさ
BASSA (SHFF)
ばっさ
BASSA
ばっさ
BASSA
THAT'S A LOT.
CAVO, WOULD YOU LIKE SOME FRU...
OH, THAT'S RIGHT.
CAVO WENT BACK TO THE FOREST YESTER-DAY.
I SPOKE TO HIM OUT OF HABIT.
AH HA HA HA!
ガサ
GASA (RUSTLE)
?
HERE YOU GO! JUST GIVE ME FIVE HUNDRED FOR THE LOT.
THANK YOU. WHAT A LUXURY TO HAVE ALL THIS TO MYSELF.

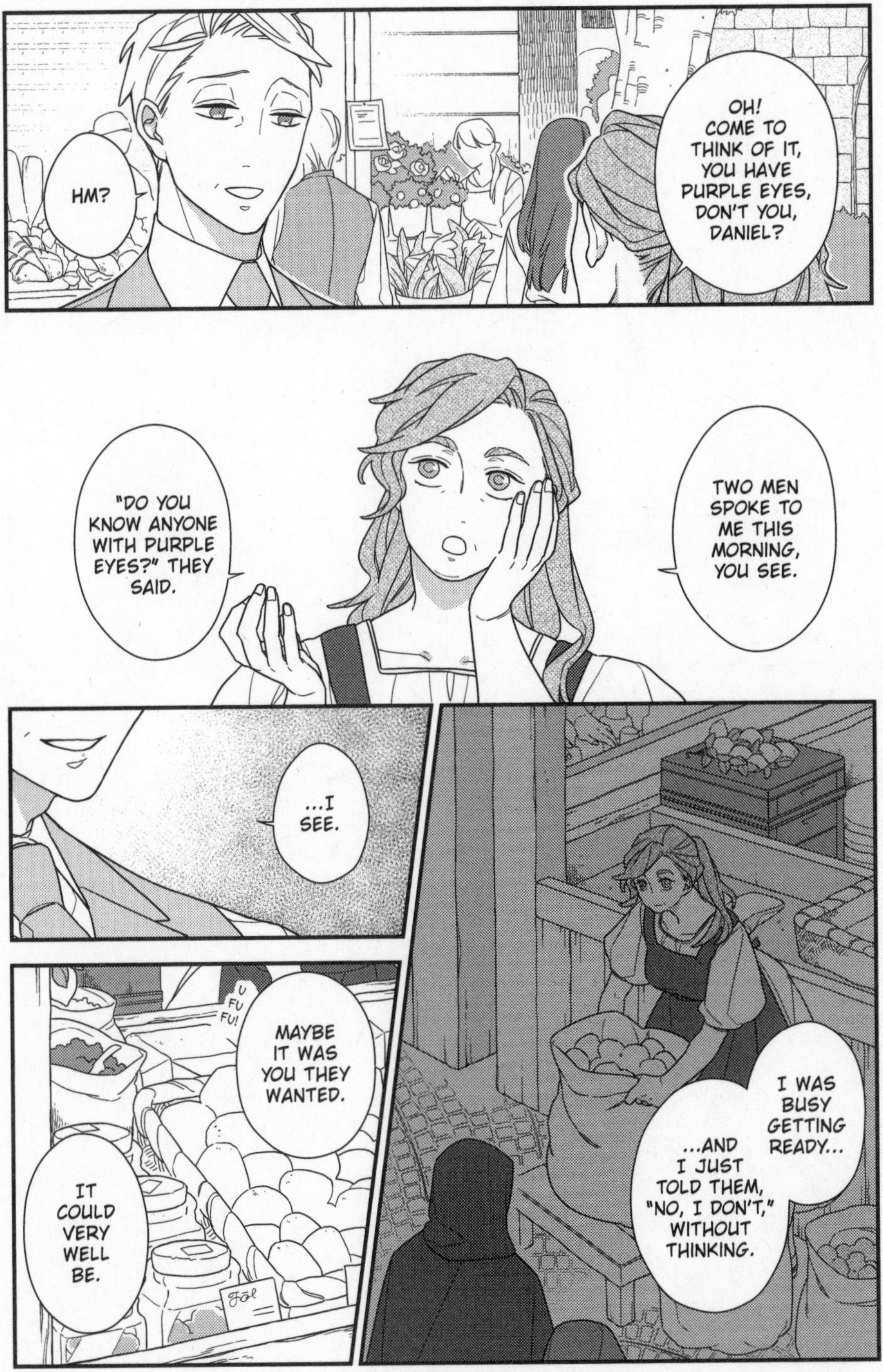
OH! COME TO THINK OF IT, YOU HAVE PURPLE EYES, DON'T YOU, DANIEL?
HM?
TWO MEN SPOKE TO ME THIS MORNING, YOU SEE.
"DO YOU KNOW ANYONE WITH PURPLE EYES?" THEY SAID.
I WAS BUSY GETTING READY...
...AND I JUST TOLD THEM, "NO, I DON'T," WITHOUT THINKING.
...I SEE.
U FU FU!
MAYBE IT WAS YOU THEY WANTED.
IT COULD VERY WELL BE.

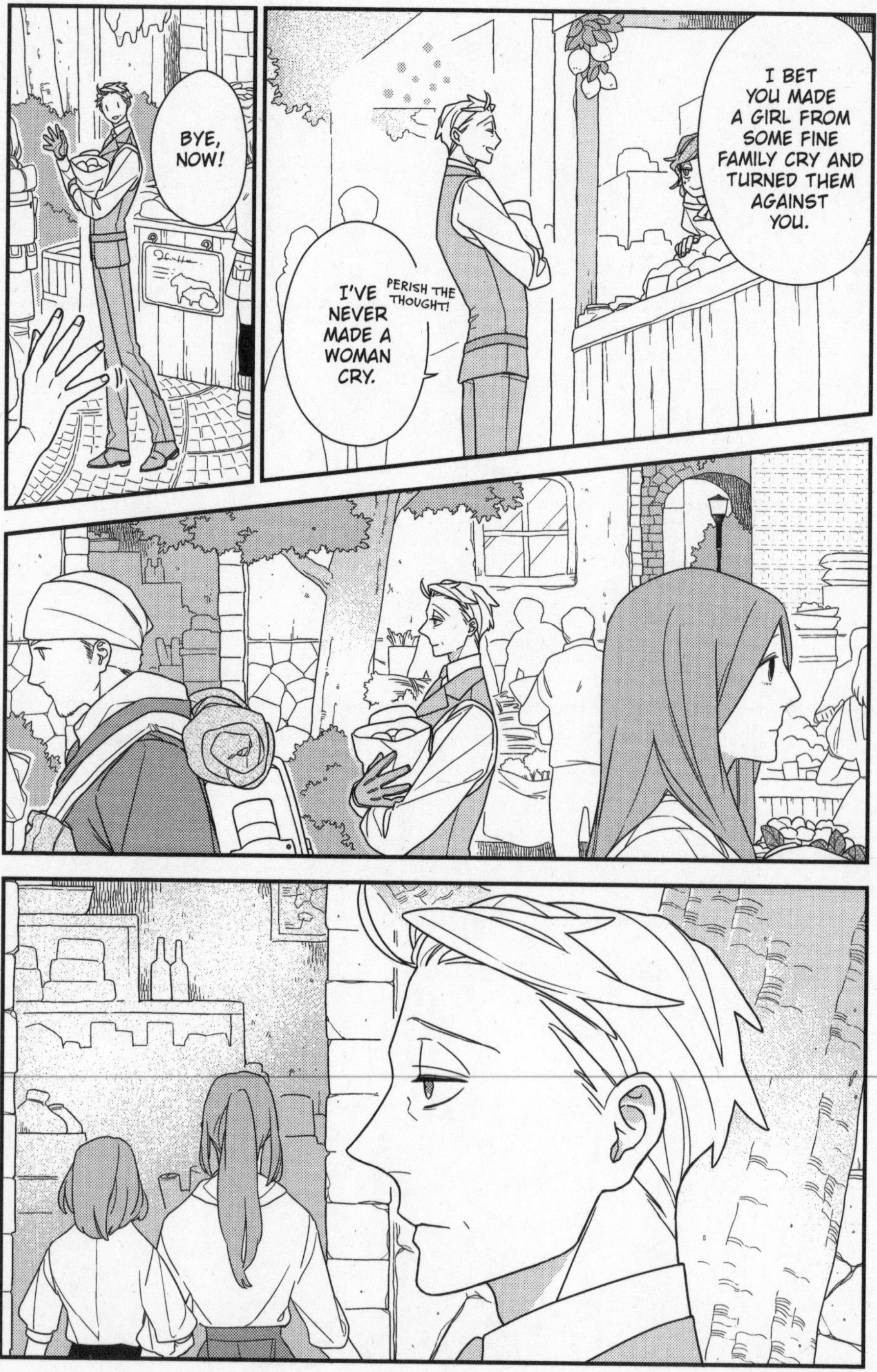
I BET YOU MADE A GIRL FROM SOME FINE FAMILY CRY AND TURNED THEM AGAINST YOU.
PERISH THE THOUGHT!
I'VE NEVER MADE A WOMAN CRY.
BYE, NOW!

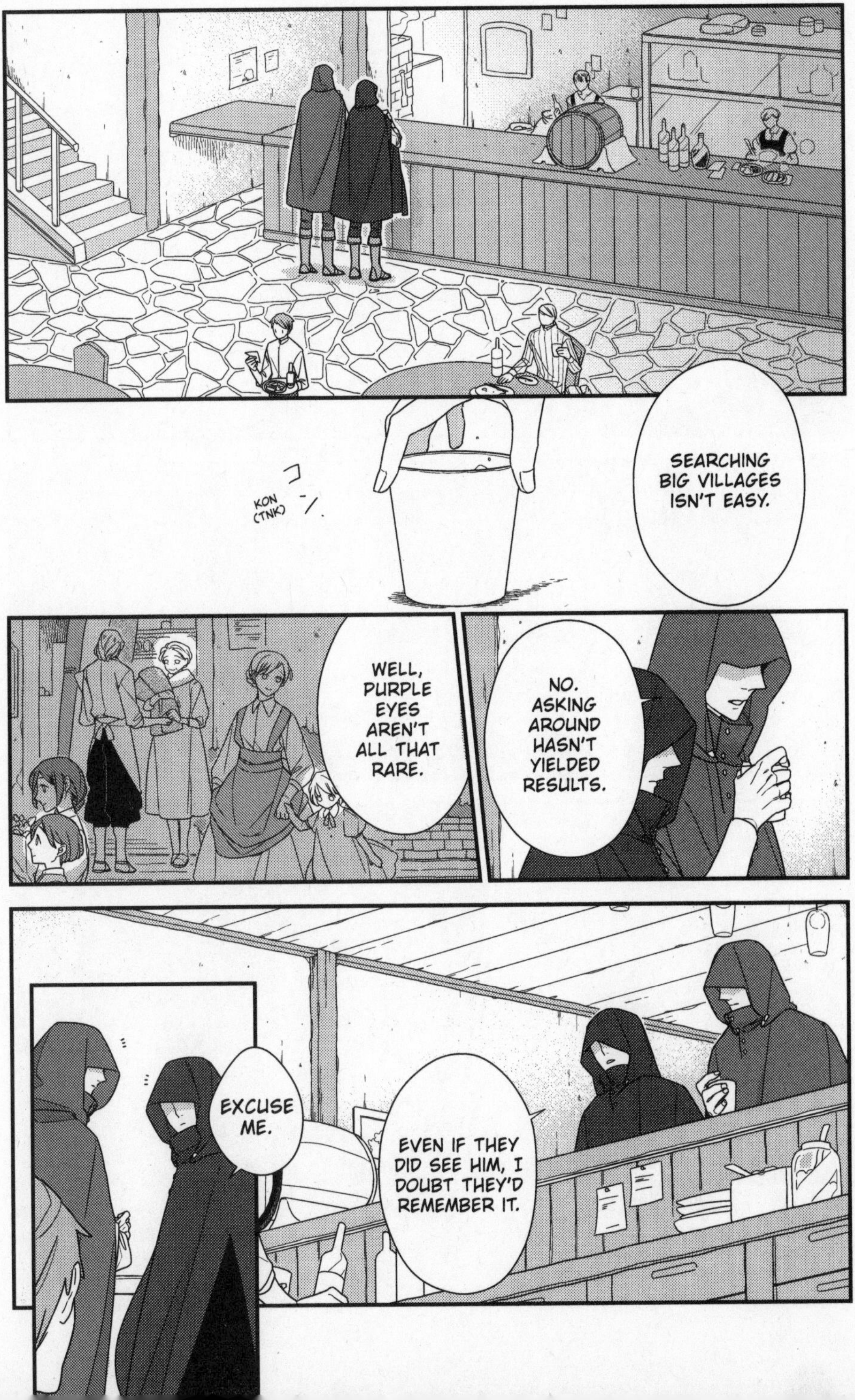
SEARCHING BIG VILLAGES ISN'T EASY.
KON (TNK)
NO. ASKING AROUND HASN'T YIELDED RESULTS.
WELL, PURPLE EYES AREN'T ALL THAT RARE.
EVEN IF THEY DID SEE HIM, I DOUBT THEY'D REMEMBER IT.
EXCUSE ME.

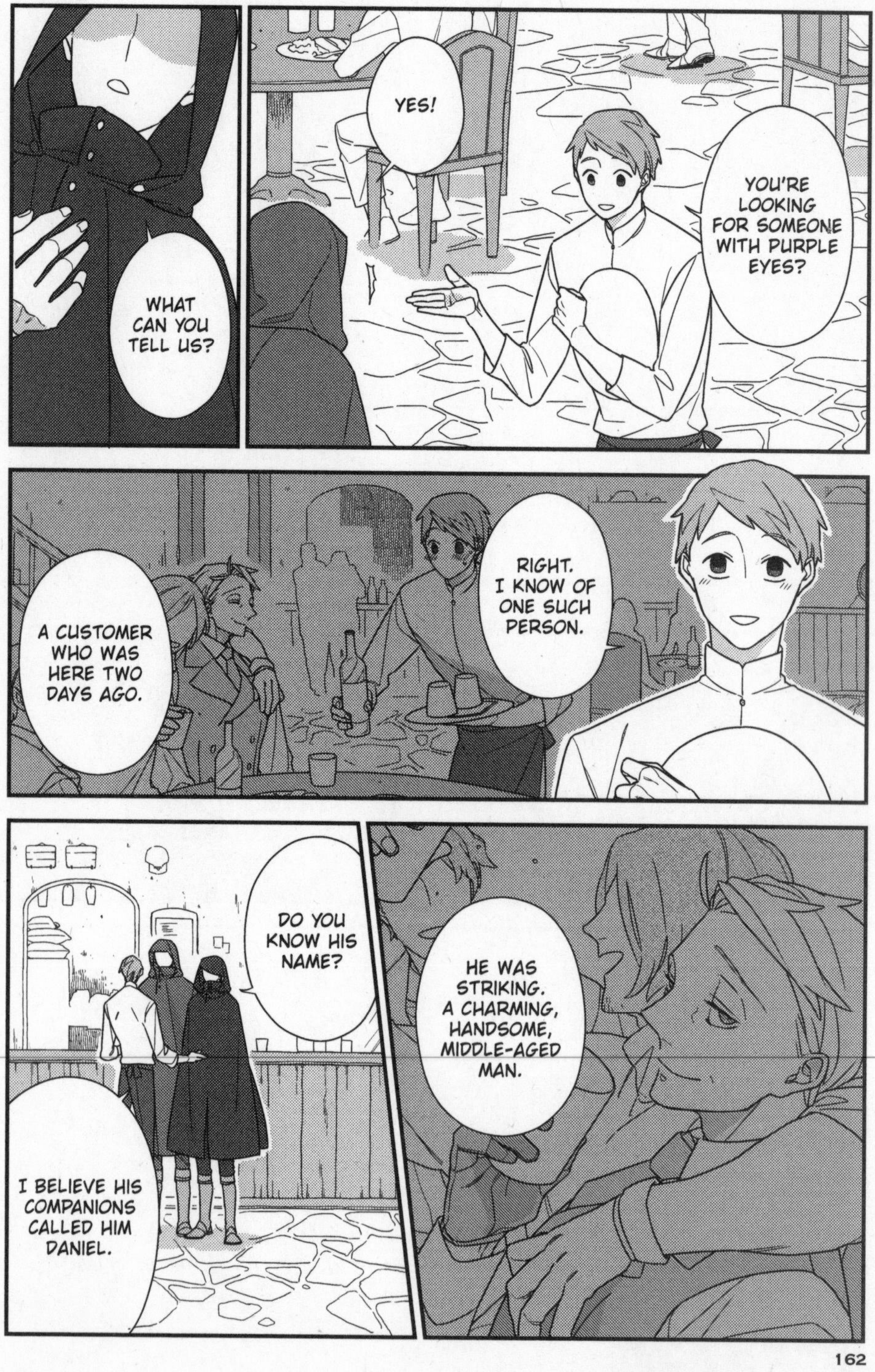
YOU'RE LOOKING FOR SOMEONE WITH PURPLE EYES?
YES!
WHAT CAN YOU TELL US?
RIGHT. I KNOW OF ONE SUCH PERSON.
A CUSTOMER WHO WAS HERE TWO DAYS AGO.
HE WAS STRIKING. A CHARMING, HANDSOME, MIDDLE-AGED MAN.
DO YOU KNOW HIS NAME?
I BELIEVE HIS COMPANIONS CALLED HIM DANIEL.

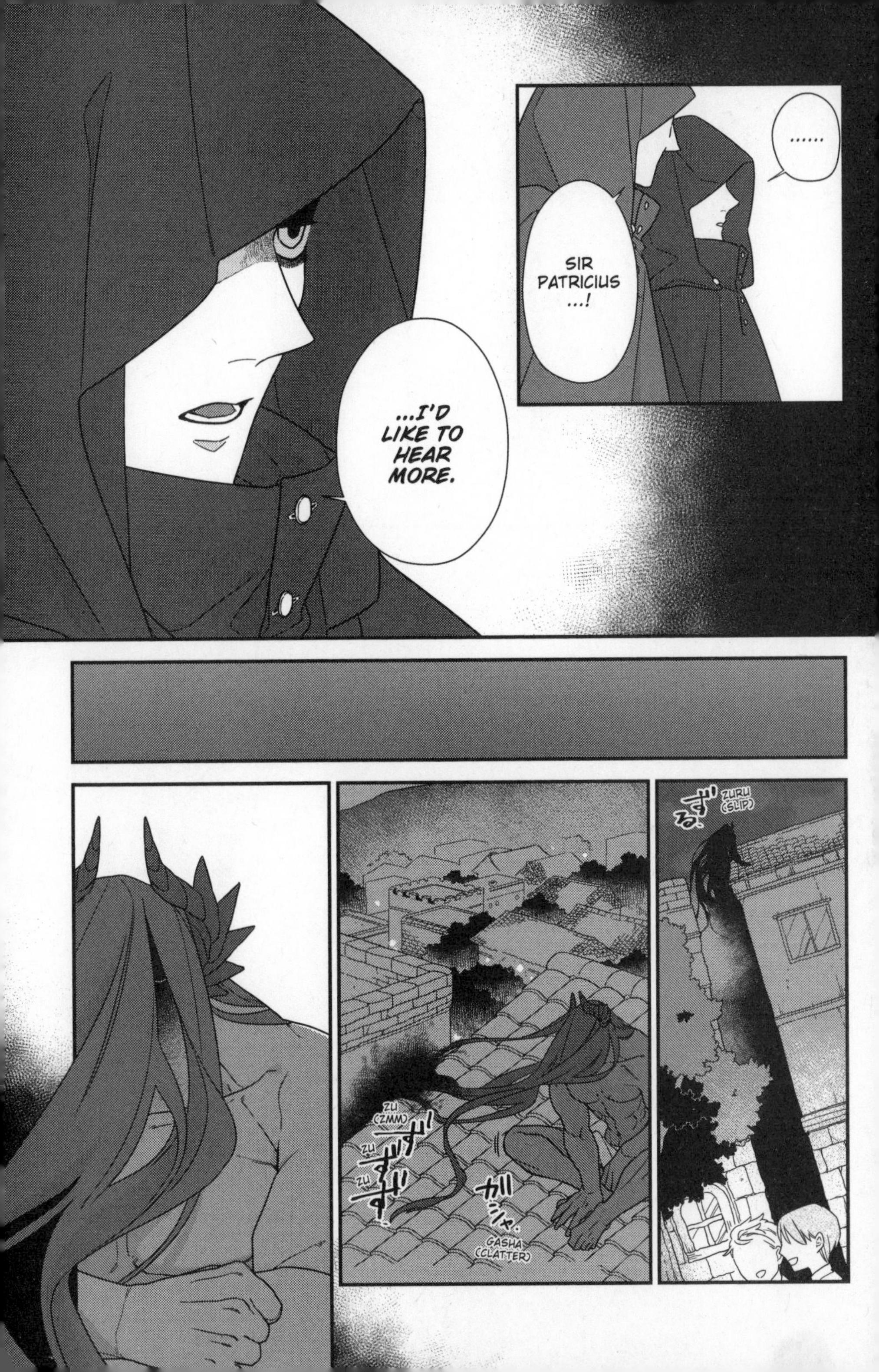
......
SIR PATRICIUS ...!
...I'D LIKE TO HEAR MORE.
ずる
ZURU (SLIP)
ずずず
ZU (ZMM) ZU ZU
ガシャ
GASHA (CLATTER)

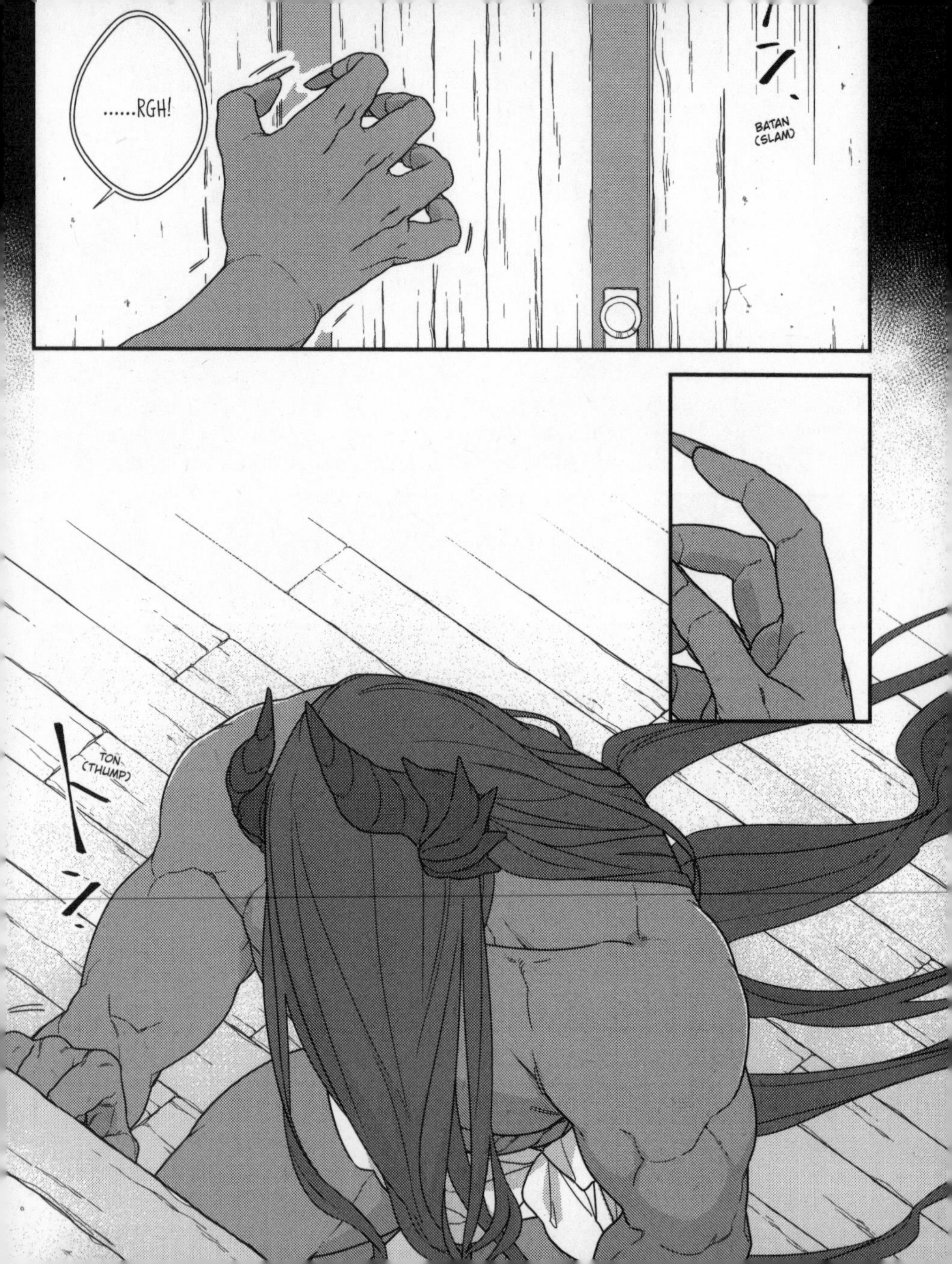
BATAN (SLAM)
......RGH!
TON (THUMP)

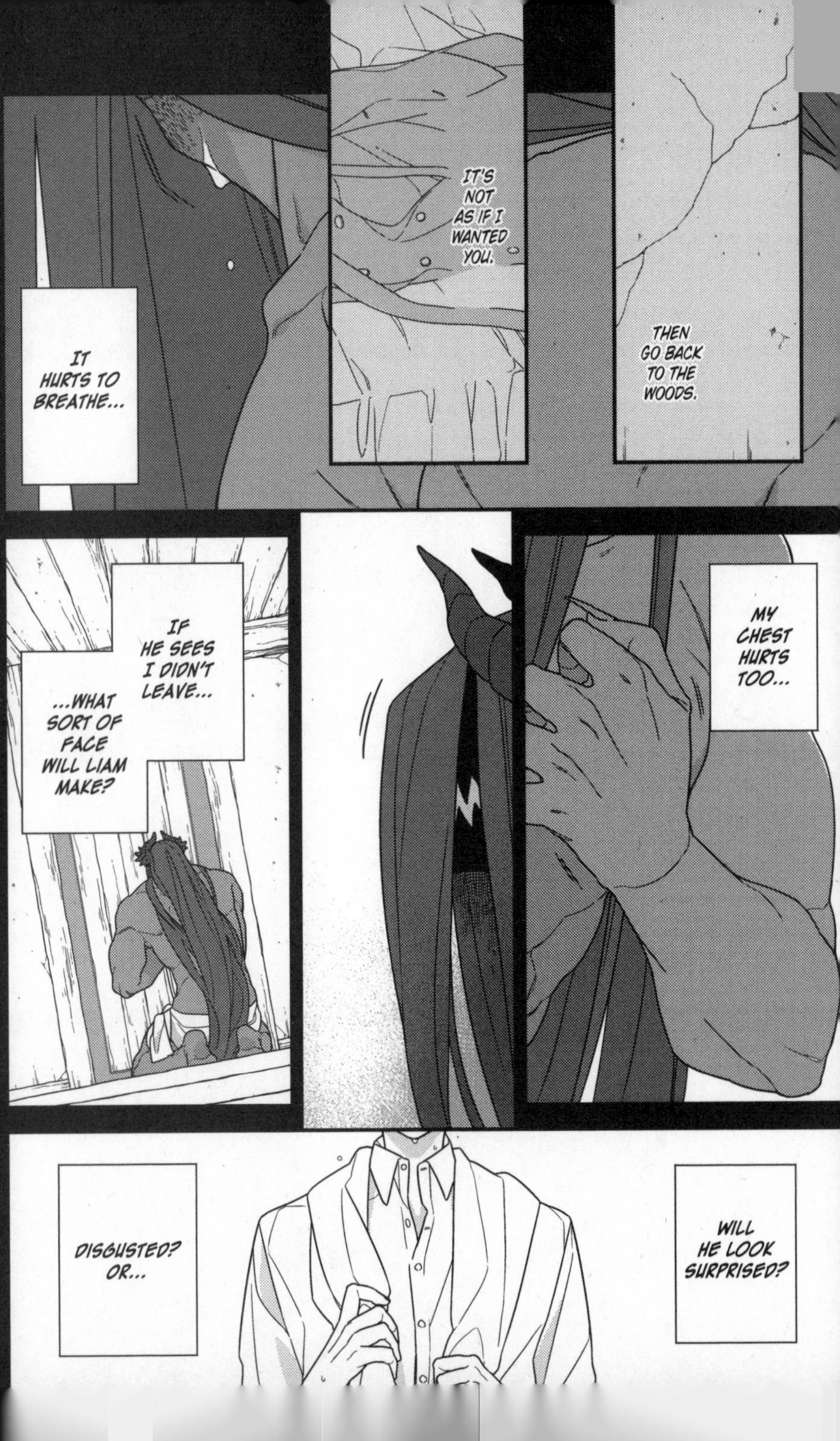
THEN GO BACK TO THE WOODS.
IT'S NOT AS IF I WANTED YOU.
IT HURTS TO BREATHE...
MY CHEST HURTS TOO...
IF HE SEES I DIDN'T LEAVE...
...WHAT SORT OF FACE WILL LIAM MAKE?
WILL HE LOOK SURPRISED?
DISGUSTED? OR...

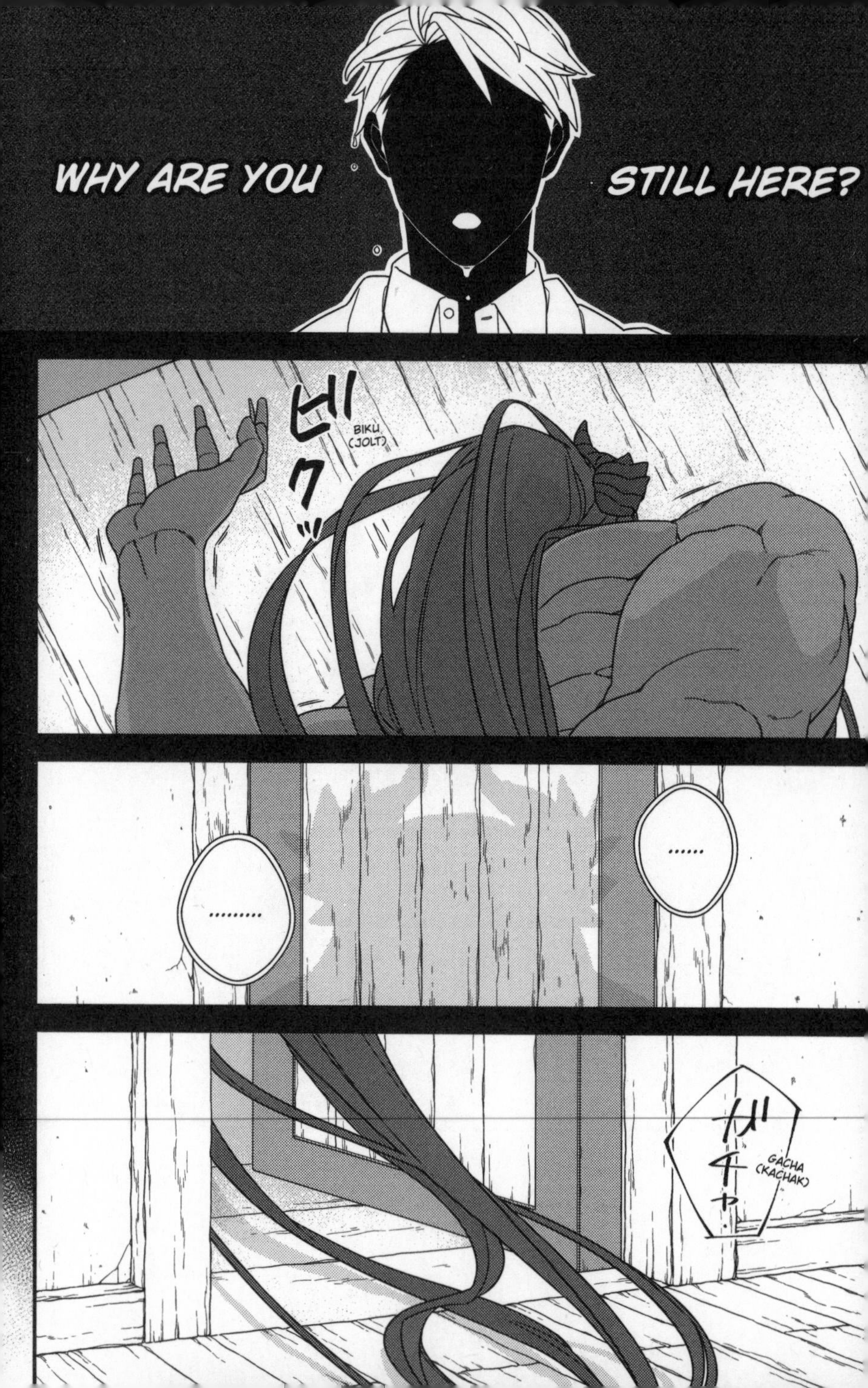
WHY ARE YOU
STILL HERE?
ビクッ
BIKU (JOLT)
......
....
ガチャ
GACHA (KACHAK)

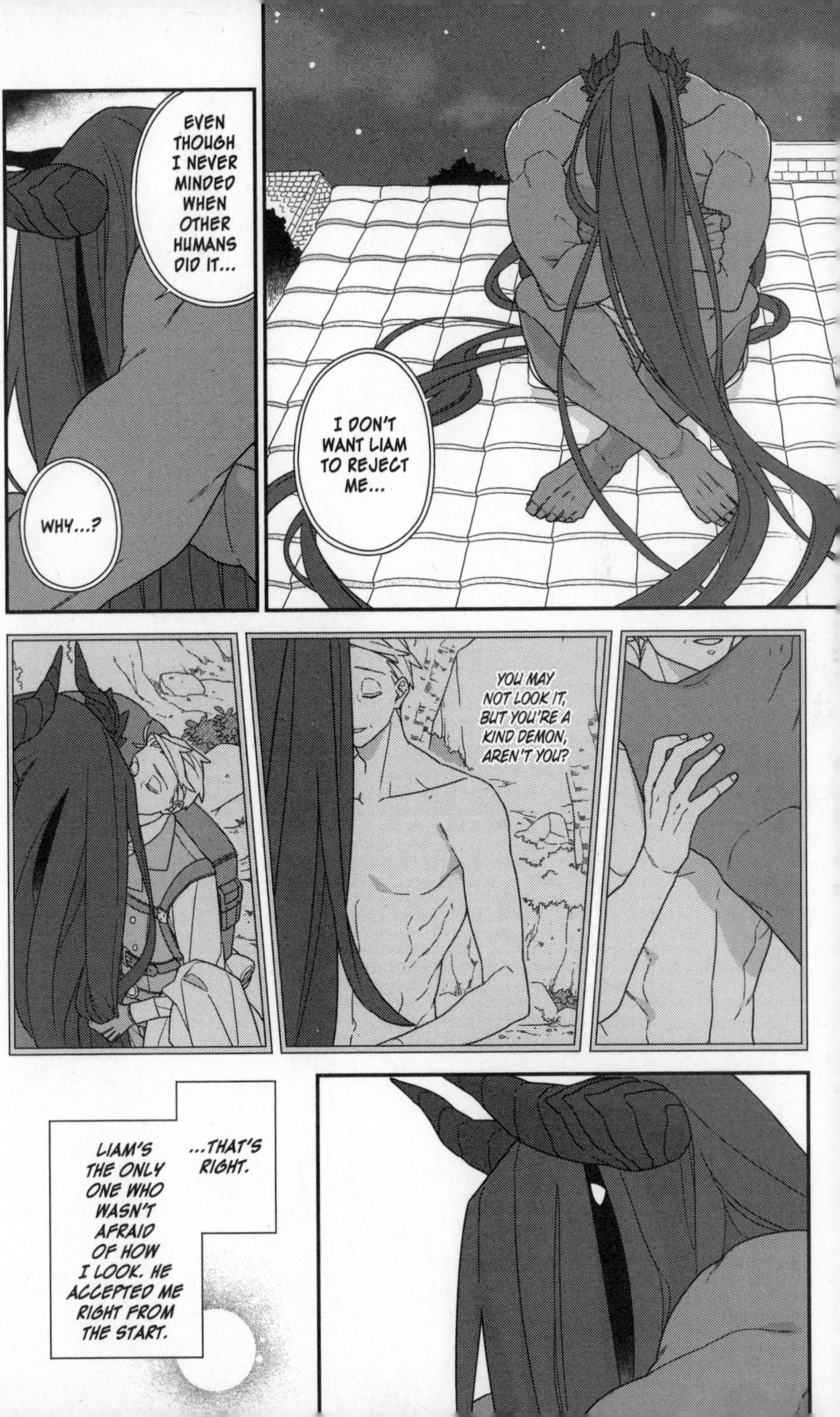
I DON'T WANT LIAM TO REJECT ME...
EVEN THOUGH I NEVER MINDED WHEN OTHER HUMANS DID IT...
WHY...?
YOU MAY NOT LOOK IT, BUT YOU'RE A KIND DEMON, AREN'T YOU?
...THAT'S RIGHT.
LIAM'S THE ONLY ONE WHO WASN'T AFRAID OF HOW I LOOK. HE ACCEPTED ME RIGHT FROM THE START.

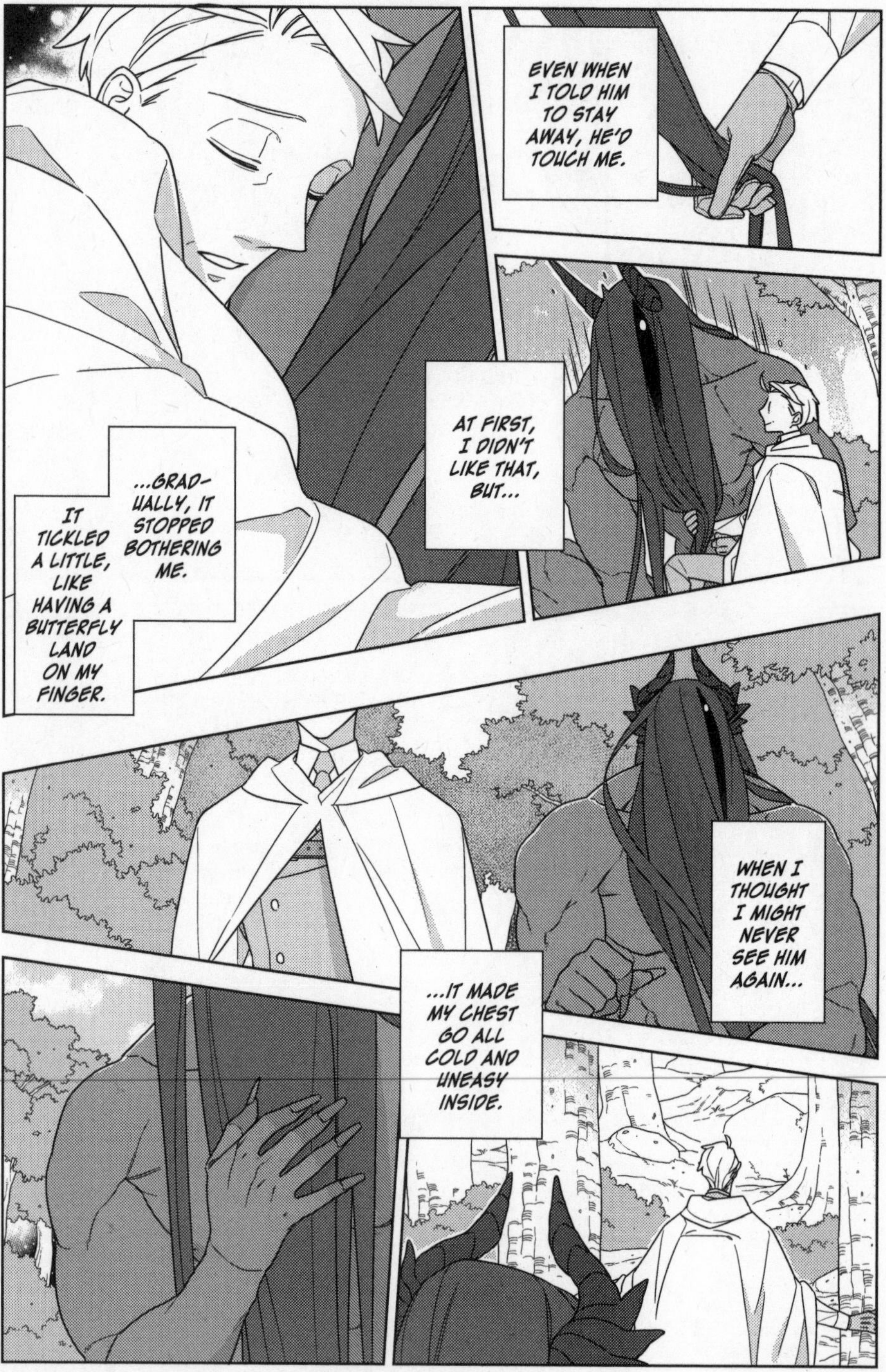
EVEN WHEN I TOLD HIM TO STAY AWAY, HE'D TOUCH ME.
AT FIRST, I DIDN'T LIKE THAT, BUT...
...GRAD-UALLY, IT STOPPED BOTHERING ME.
IT TICKLED A LITTLE, LIKE HAVING A BUTTERFLY LAND ON MY FINGER.
WHEN I THOUGHT I MIGHT NEVER SEE HIM AGAIN...
...IT MADE MY CHEST GO ALL COLD AND UNEASY INSIDE.

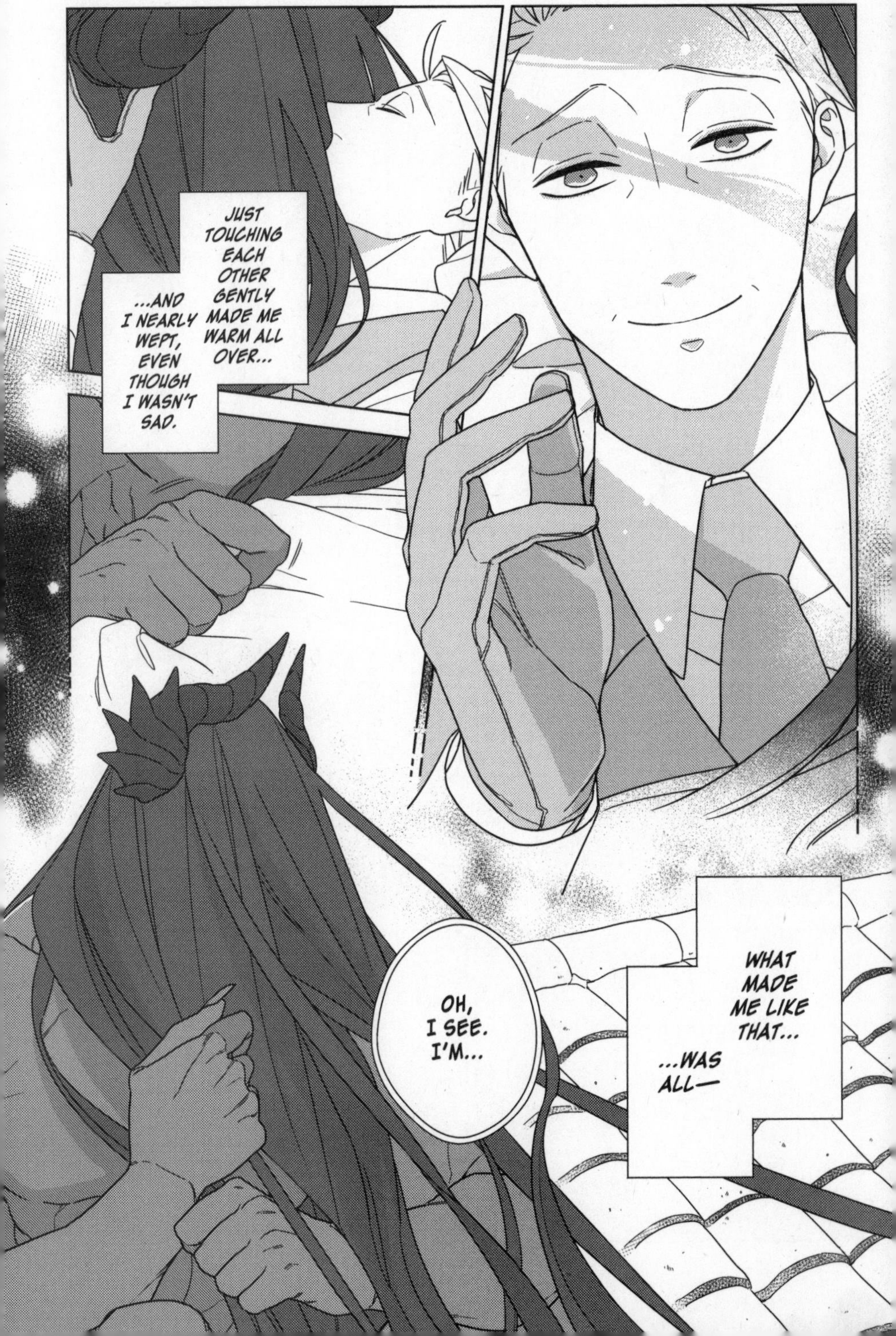
JUST TOUCHING EACH OTHER GENTLY MADE ME WARM ALL OVER...
...AND I NEARLY WEPT, EVEN THOUGH I WASN'T SAD.
WHAT MADE ME LIKE THAT...
...WAS ALL—
OH, I SEE. I'M...

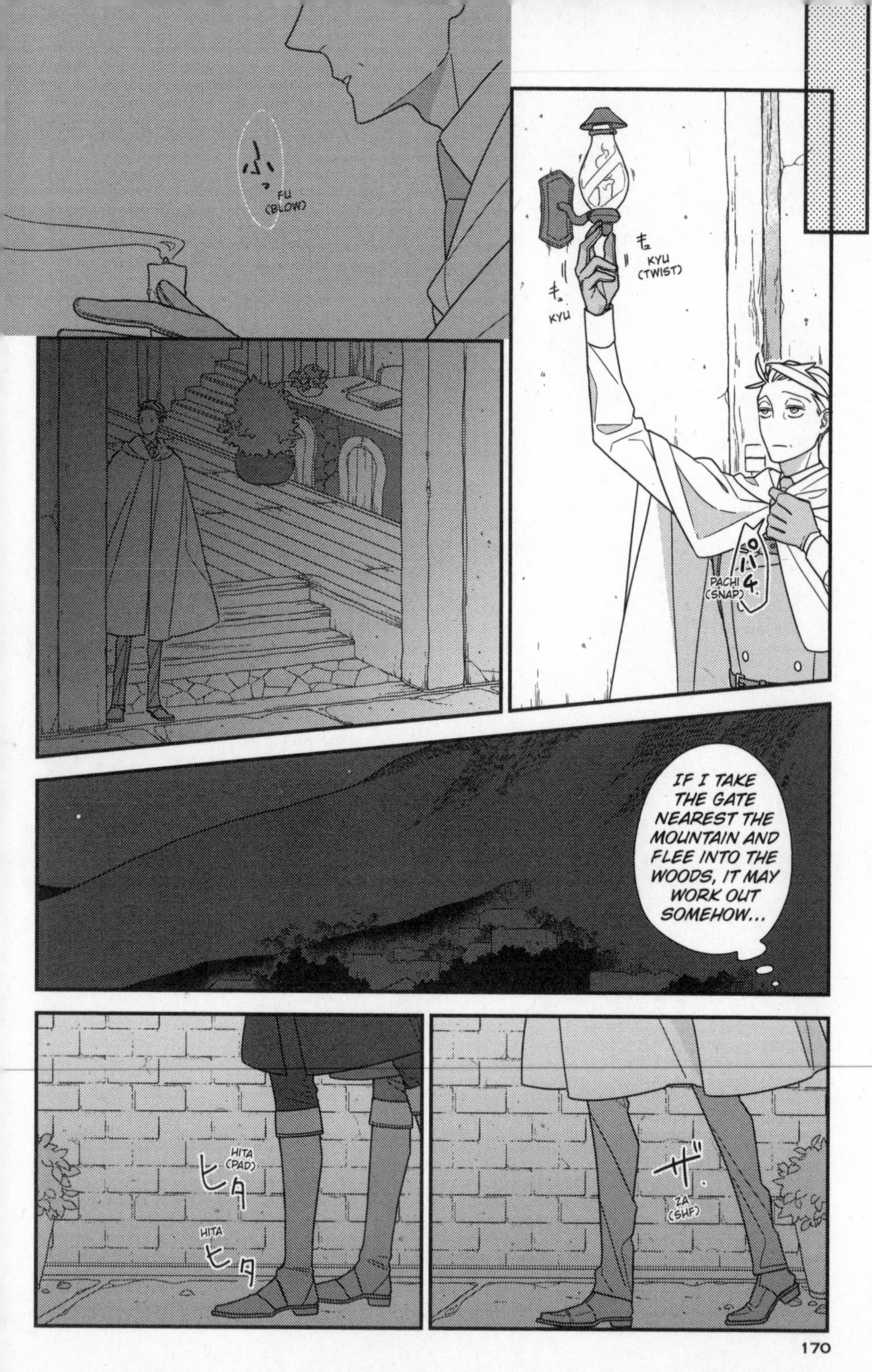
キュ
KYU (TWIST)
キュ
KYU
パチッ
PACHI (SNAP)
ふっ
FU (BLOW)
IF I TAKE THE GATE NEAREST THE MOUNTAIN AND FLEE INTO THE WOODS, IT MAY WORK OUT SOMEHOW...
ザ
ZA (SHF)
HITA (PAD)
ヒタ
HITA
ヒタ

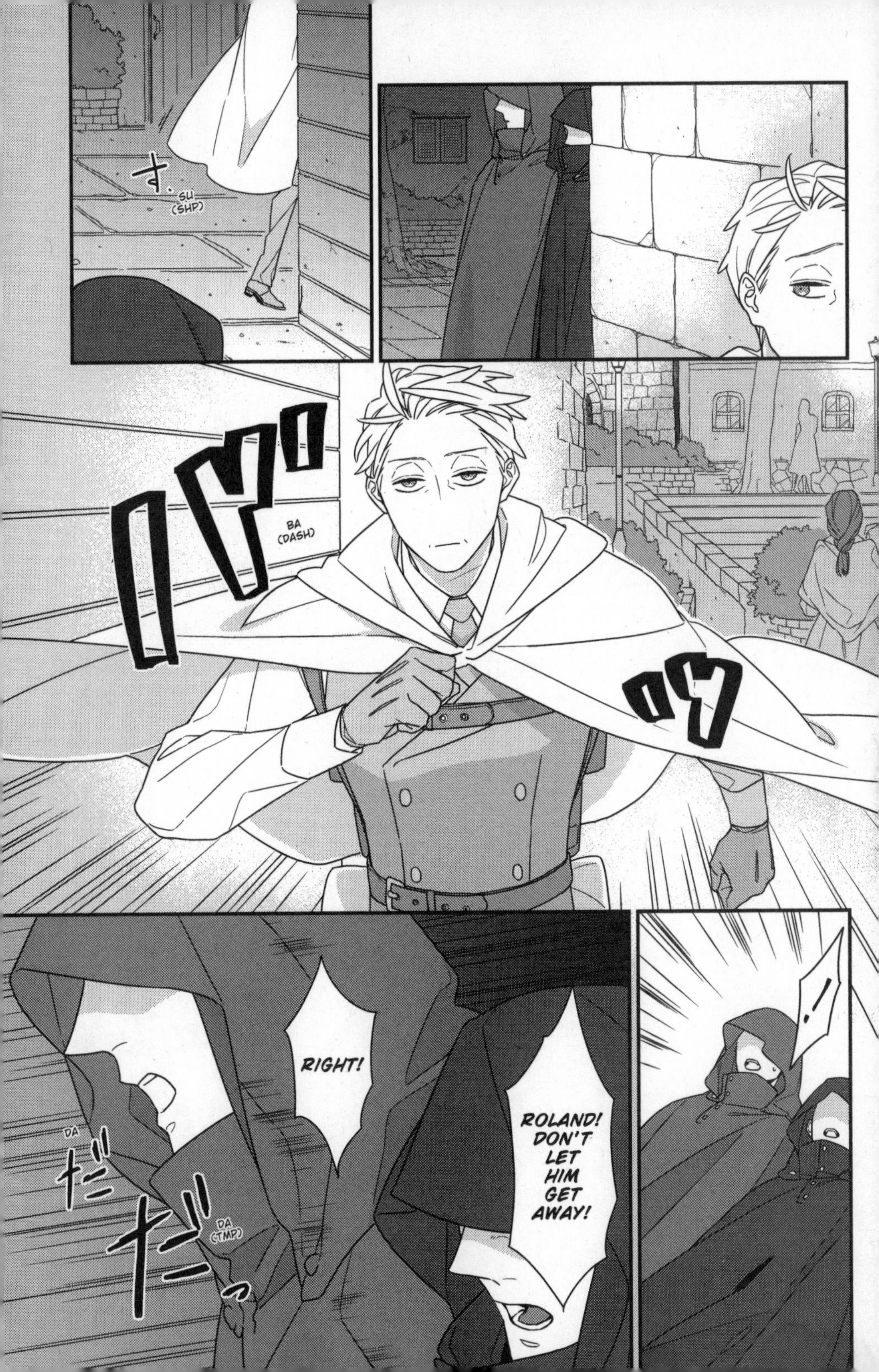
す
SU (SHP)
BA (DASH)
...!
ROLAND! DON'T LET HIM GET AWAY!
RIGHT!
DA
DA (TMP)

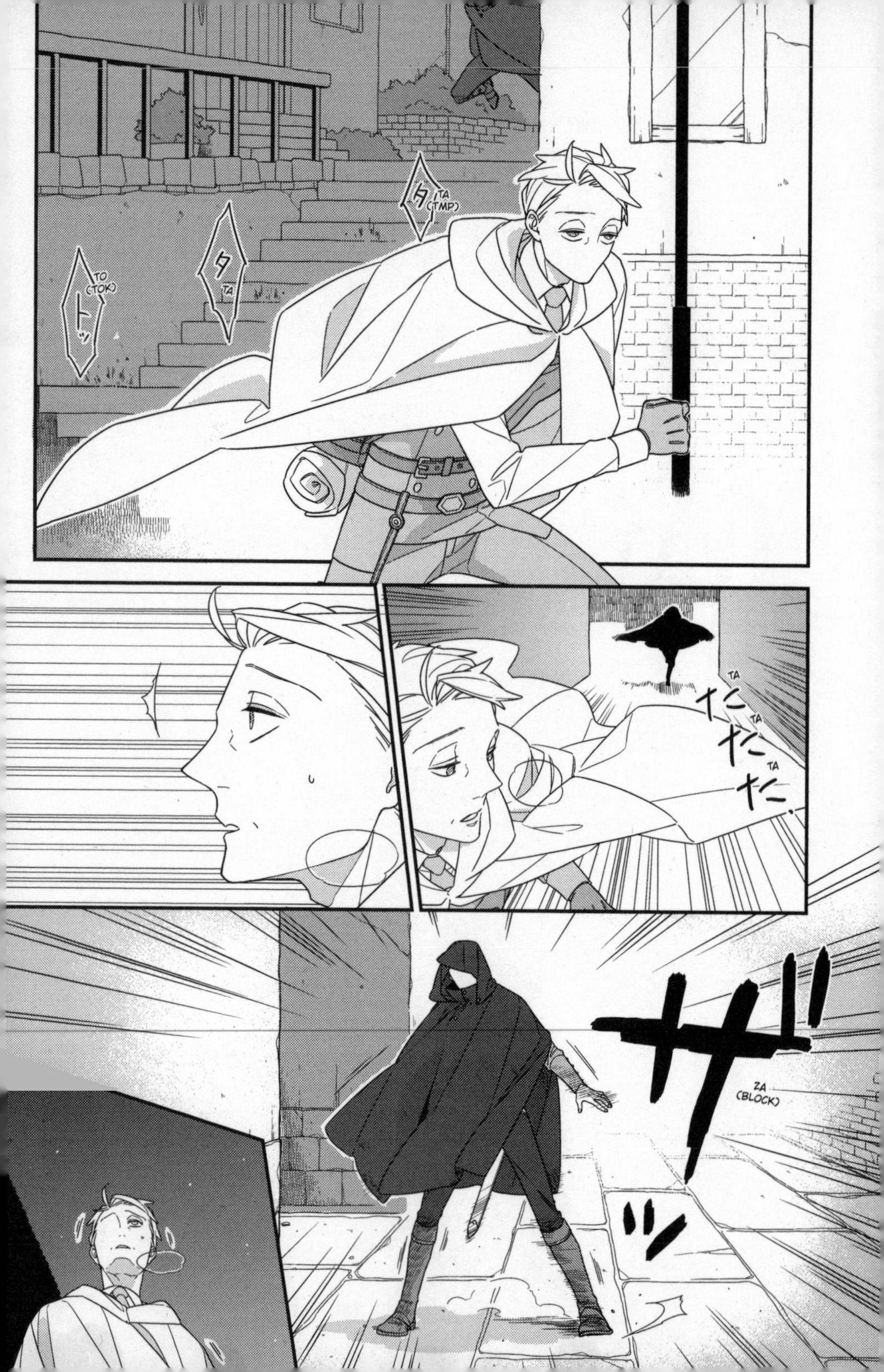
タ
TA (TMP)
タ
TA
トッ
TO (TOK)
たたた
TA TA TA
ザッ
ZA (BLOCK)

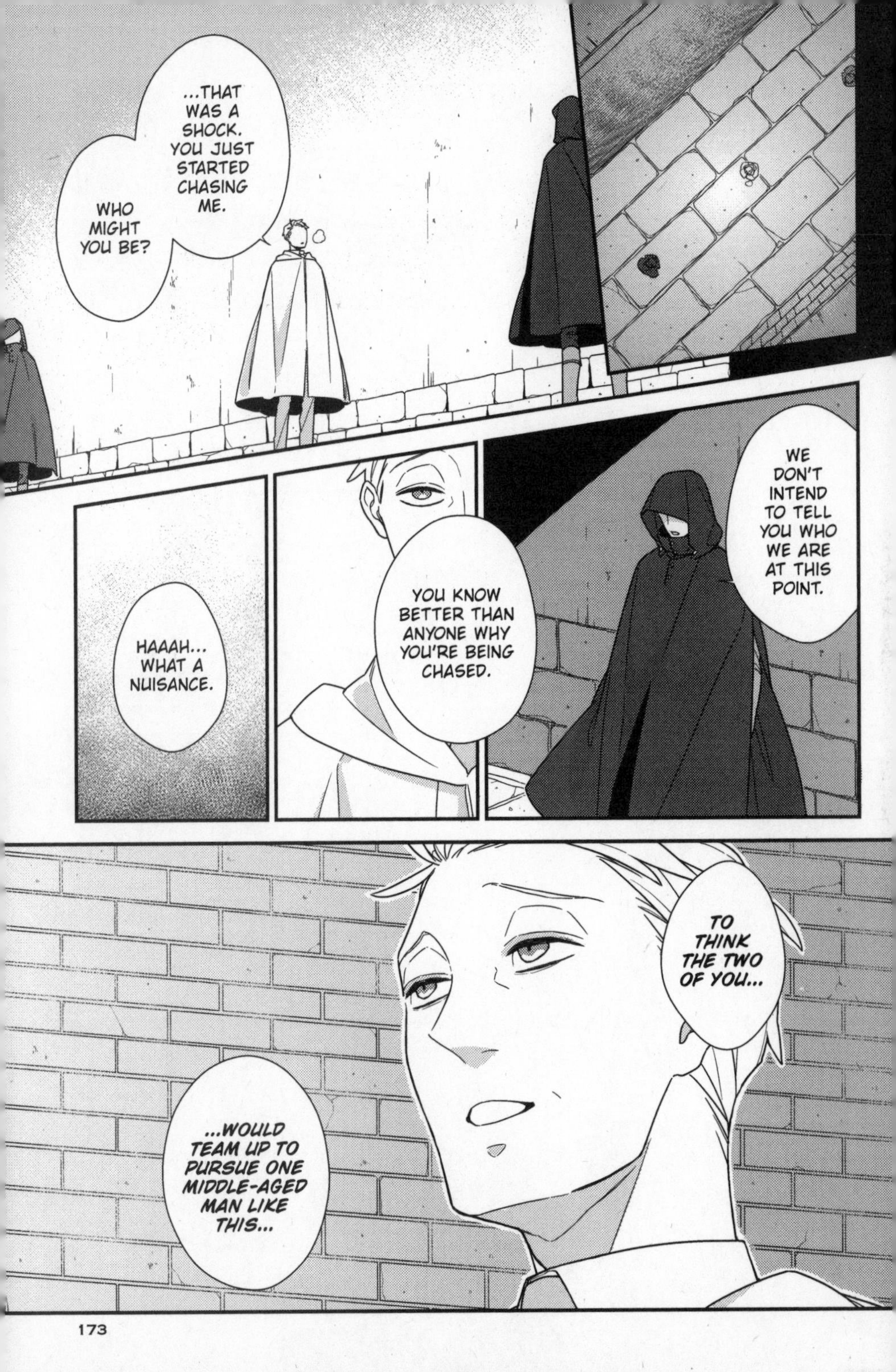
...THAT WAS A SHOCK. YOU JUST STARTED CHASING ME.
WHO MIGHT YOU BE?
WE DON'T INTEND TO TELL YOU WHO WE ARE AT THIS POINT.
YOU KNOW BETTER THAN ANYONE WHY YOU'RE BEING CHASED.
HAAAH... WHAT A NUISANCE.
TO THINK THE TWO OF YOU...
...WOULD TEAM UP TO PURSUE ONE MIDDLE-AGED MAN LIKE THIS...

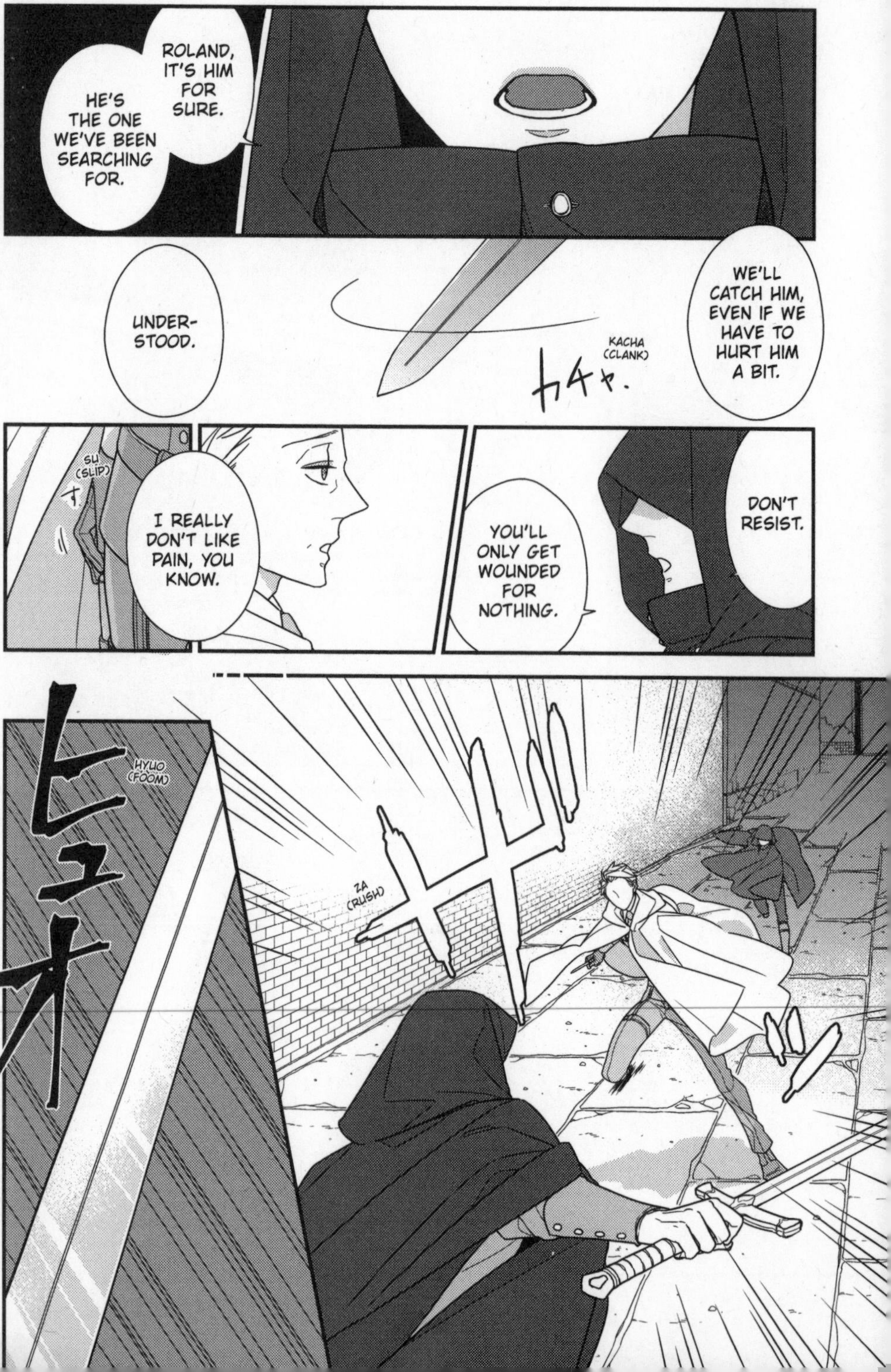
ROLAND, IT'S HIM FOR SURE.
HE'S THE ONE WE'VE BEEN SEARCHING FOR.
WE'LL CATCH HIM, EVEN IF WE HAVE TO HURT HIM A BIT.
KACHA (CLANK)
カチャ.
UNDER-STOOD.
DON'T RESIST.
YOU'LL ONLY GET WOUNDED FOR NOTHING.
I REALLY DON'T LIKE PAIN, YOU KNOW.
SU (SLIP)
す
ZA (RUSH)
ザッ
HYUO (FOOM)
ヒュオ

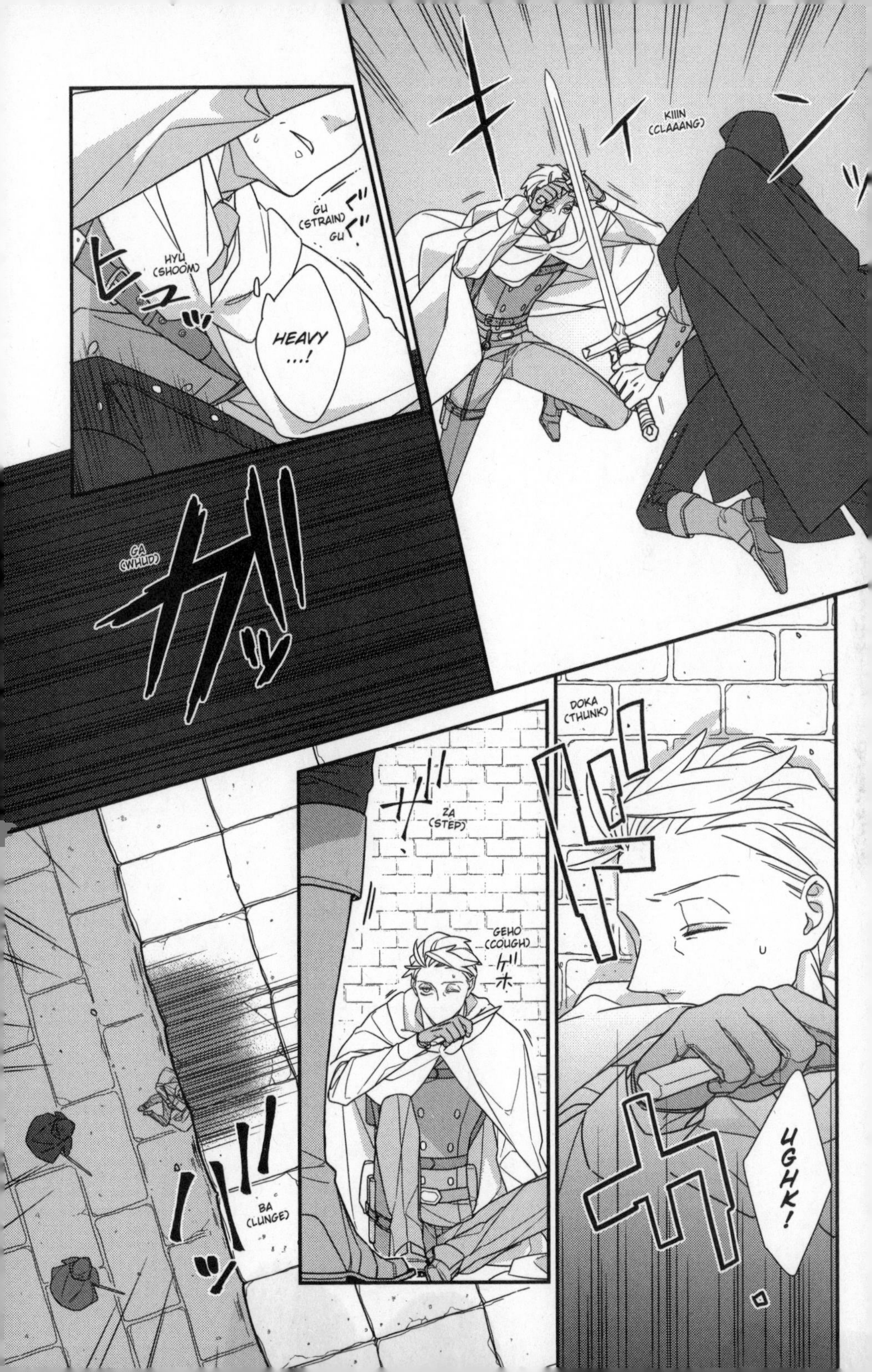
KIIN (CLAAANG)
GU (STRAIN) GU
HYU (SHOOM)
HEAVY ...!
GA (WHUD)
DOKA (THUNK)
UGHK!
ZA (STEP)
GEHO (COUGH)
BA (LUNGE)

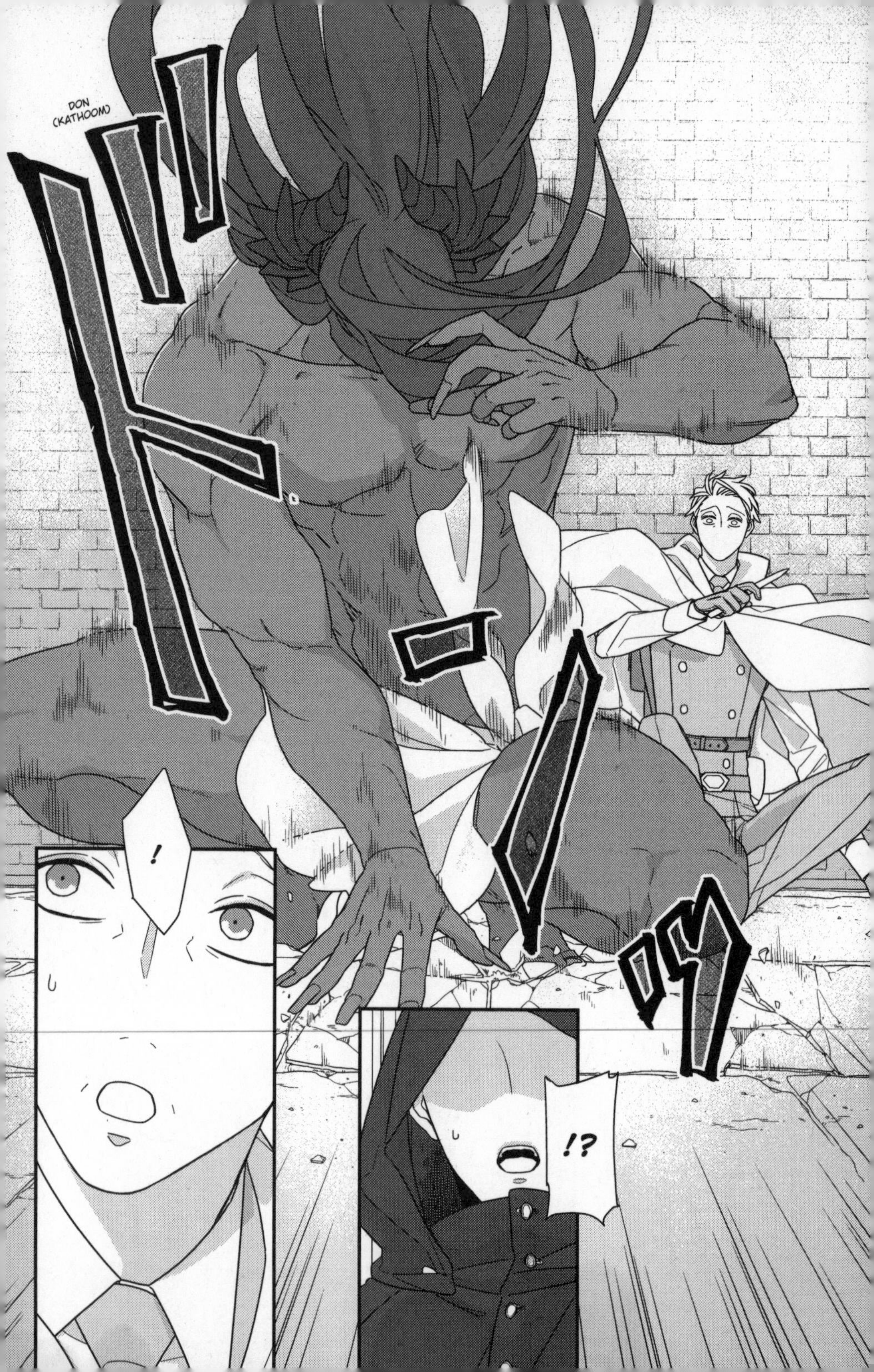
DON (KATHOOM)
!
!?

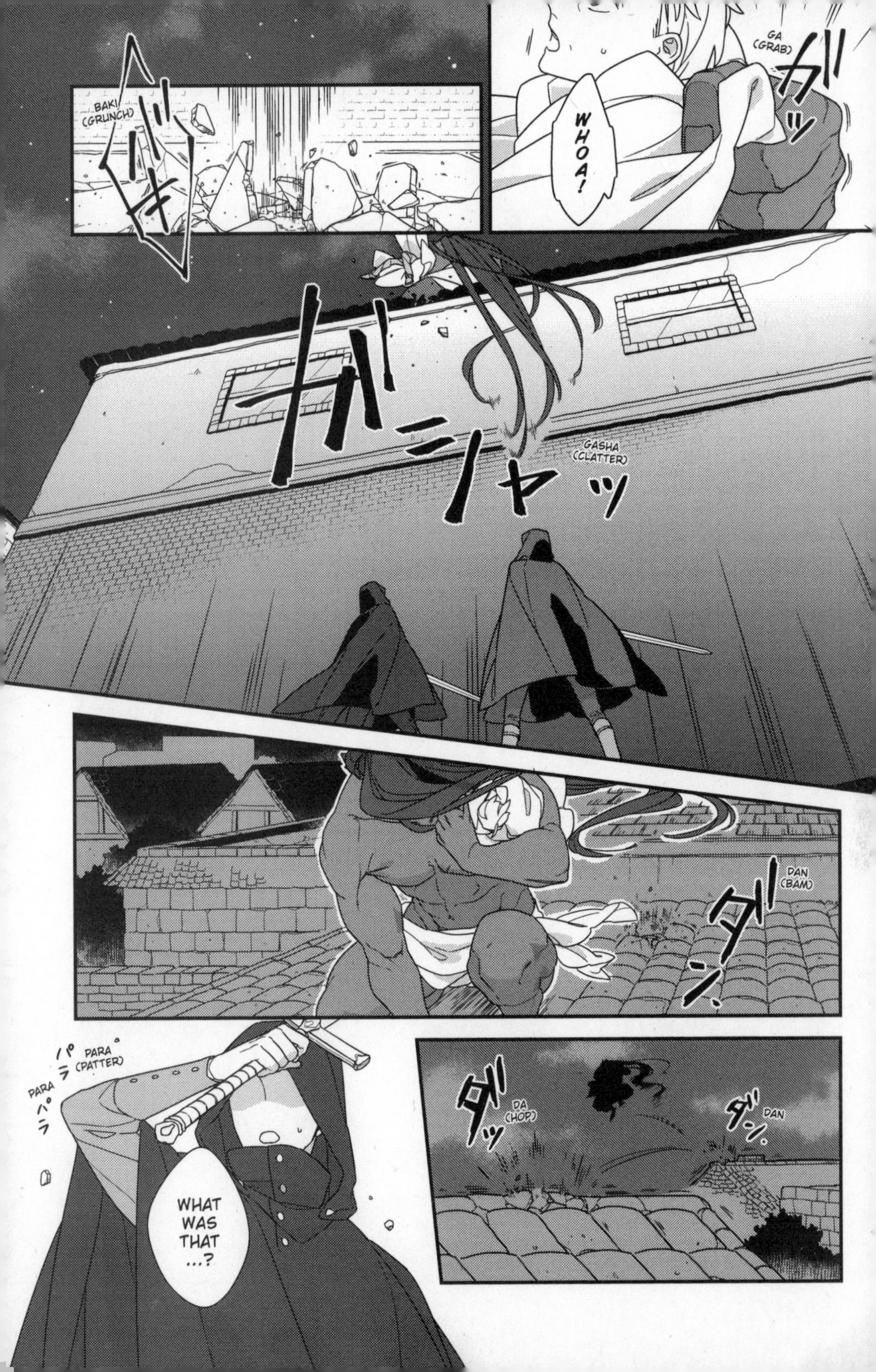
GA (GRAB)
WHOA!
BAKI (GRUNCH)
GASHA (CLATTER)
DAN (BAM)
DA (HOP)
DAN
PARA PARA (PATTER)
WHAT WAS THAT ...?

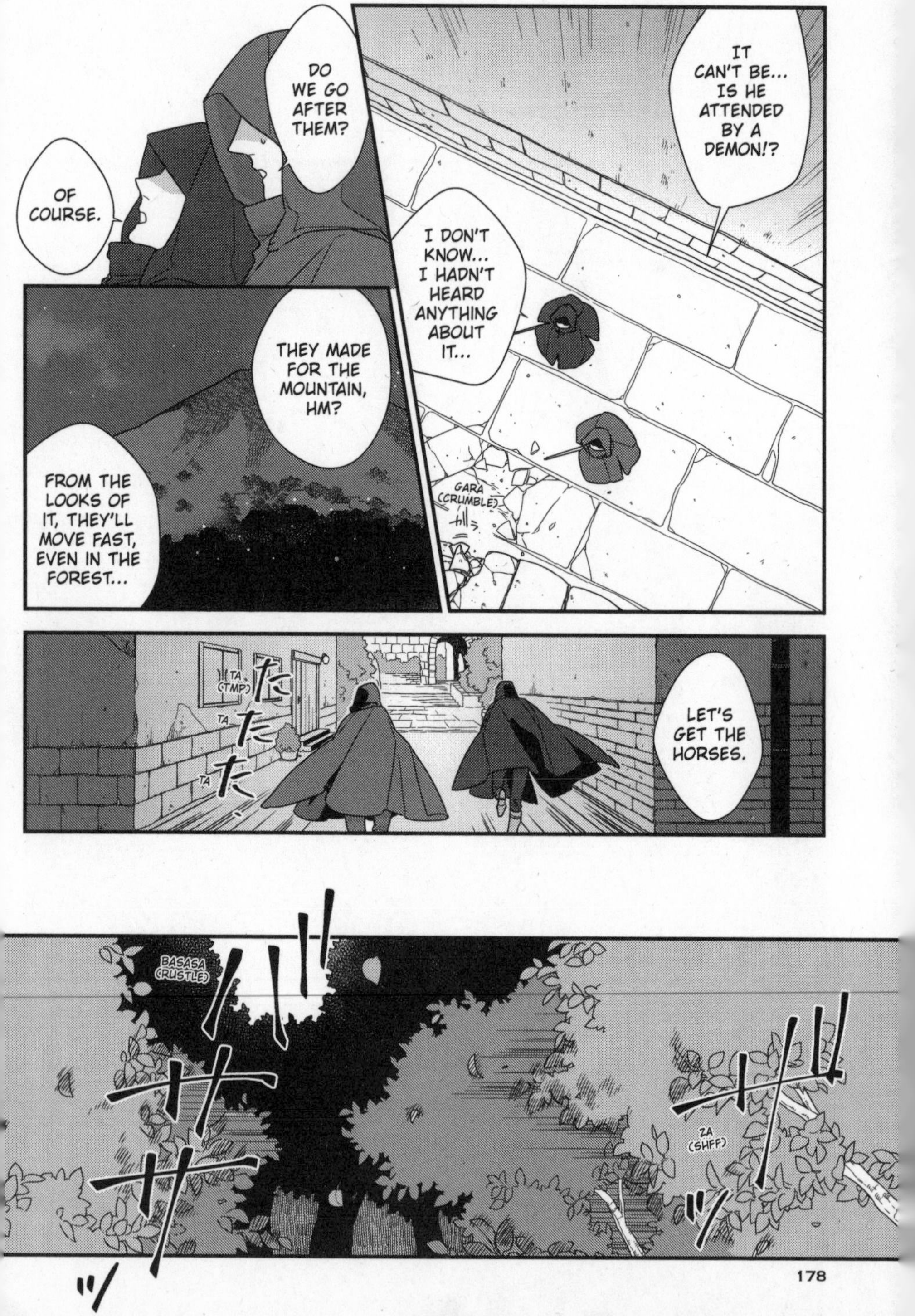
IT CAN'T BE... IS HE ATTENDED BY A DEMON!?
I DON'T KNOW... I HADN'T HEARD ANYTHING ABOUT IT...
GARA (CRUMBLE)
DO WE GO AFTER THEM?
OF COURSE.
THEY MADE FOR THE MOUNTAIN, HM?
FROM THE LOOKS OF IT, THEY'LL MOVE FAST, EVEN IN THE FOREST...
LET'S GET THE HORSES.
TA (TMP)
TA
TA
ZA (SHFF)
BASASA (RUSTLE)

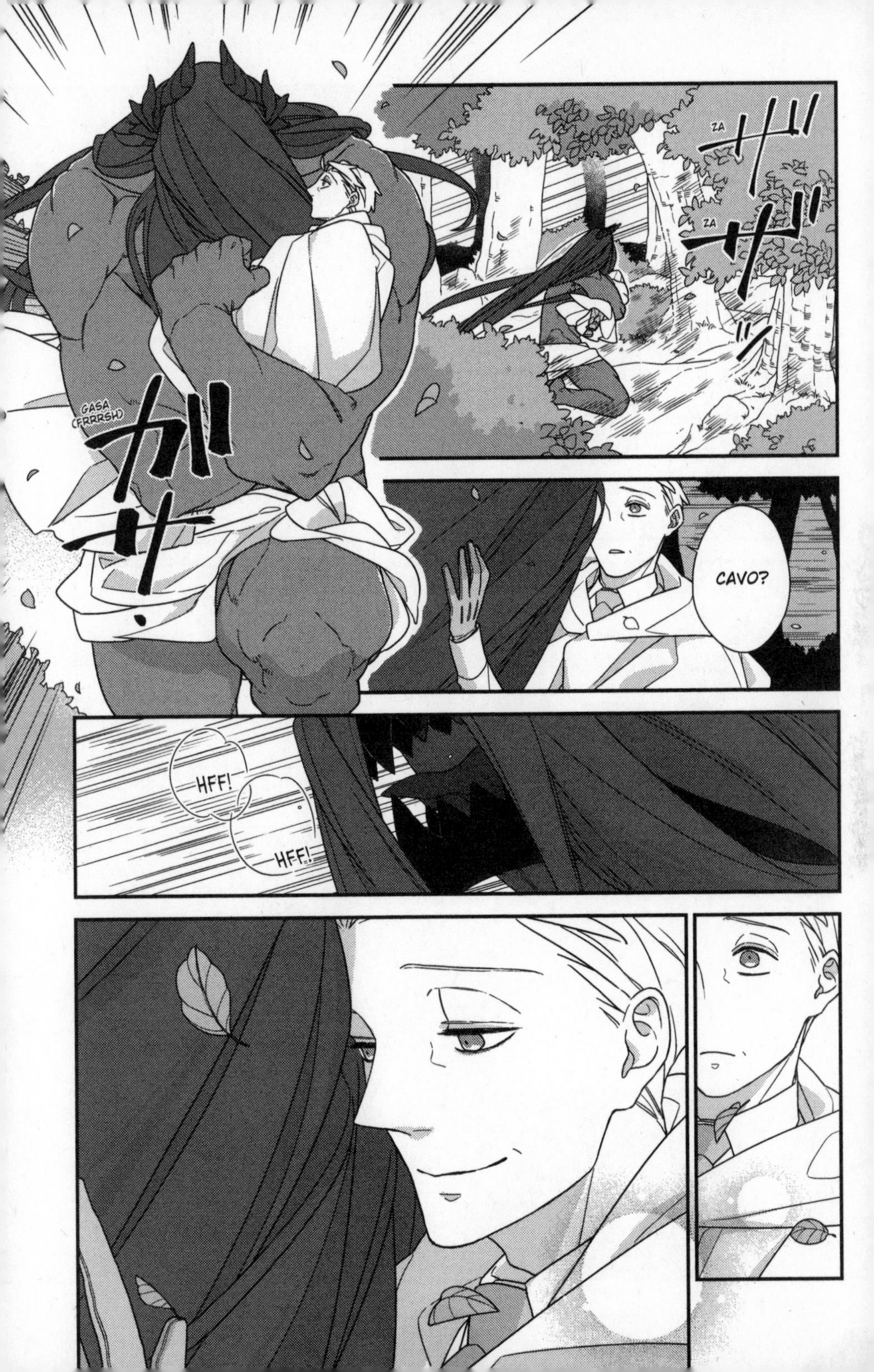
ZA
ZA
CAVO?
GASA (FRRRSH)
HFF!
HFF!

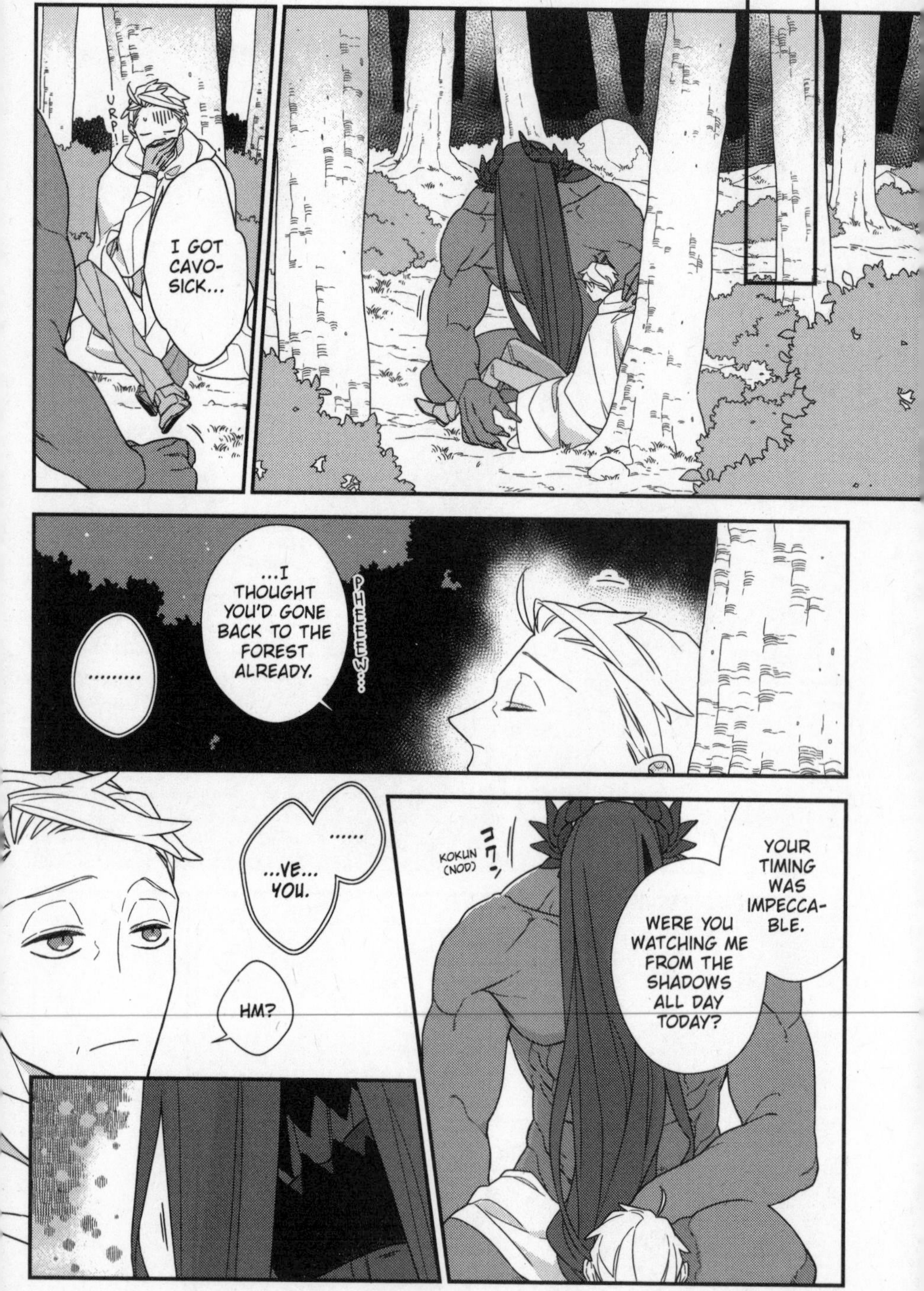
URP!
I GOT CAVO-SICK...
PHEEEEW...
...I THOUGHT YOU'D GONE BACK TO THE FOREST ALREADY.
....
YOUR TIMING WAS IMPECCA-BLE.
WERE YOU WATCHING ME FROM THE SHADOWS ALL DAY TODAY?
KOKUN (NOD)
......
...VE... YOU.
HM?

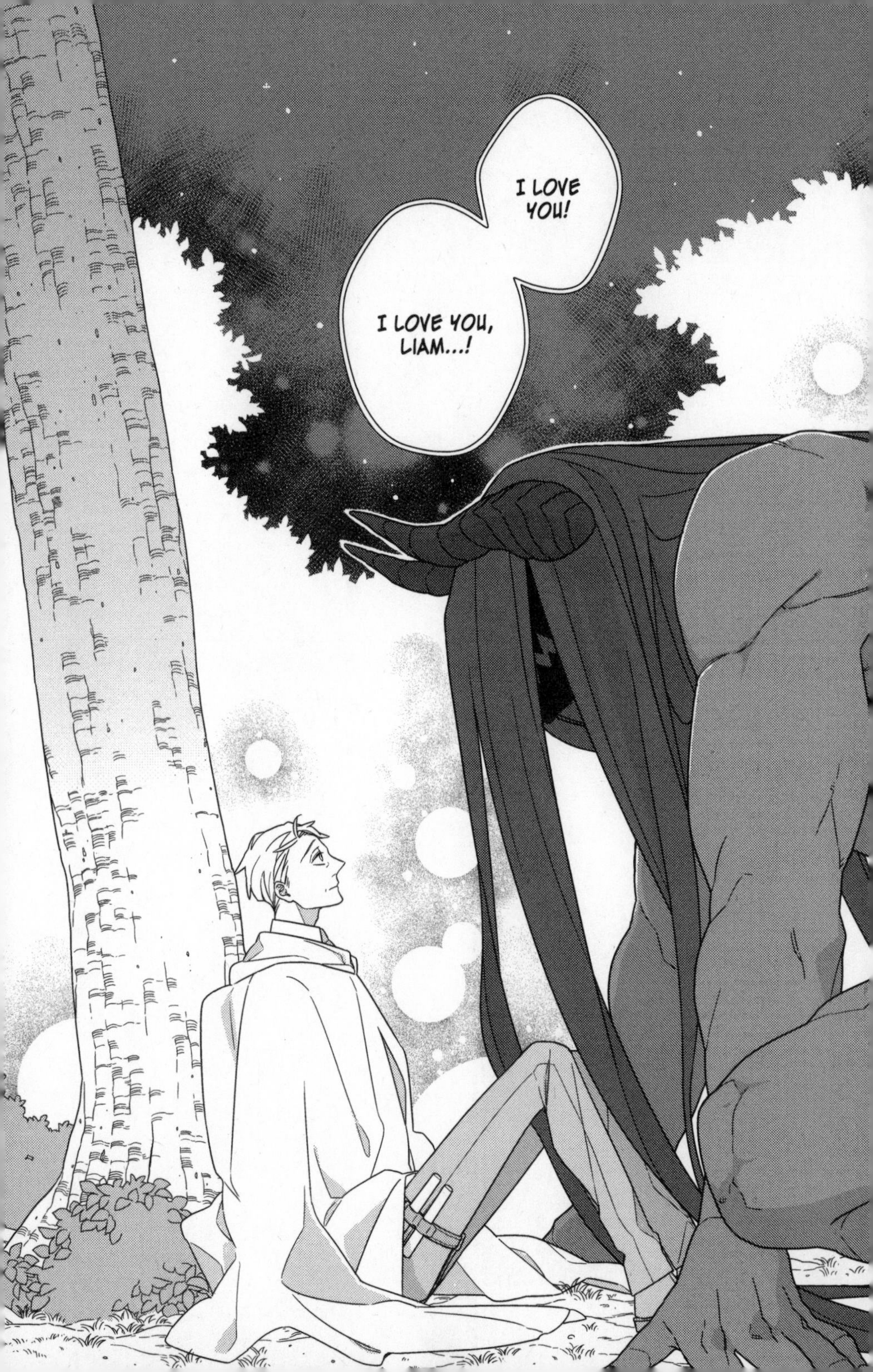
I LOVE YOU!
I LOVE YOU, LIAM...!

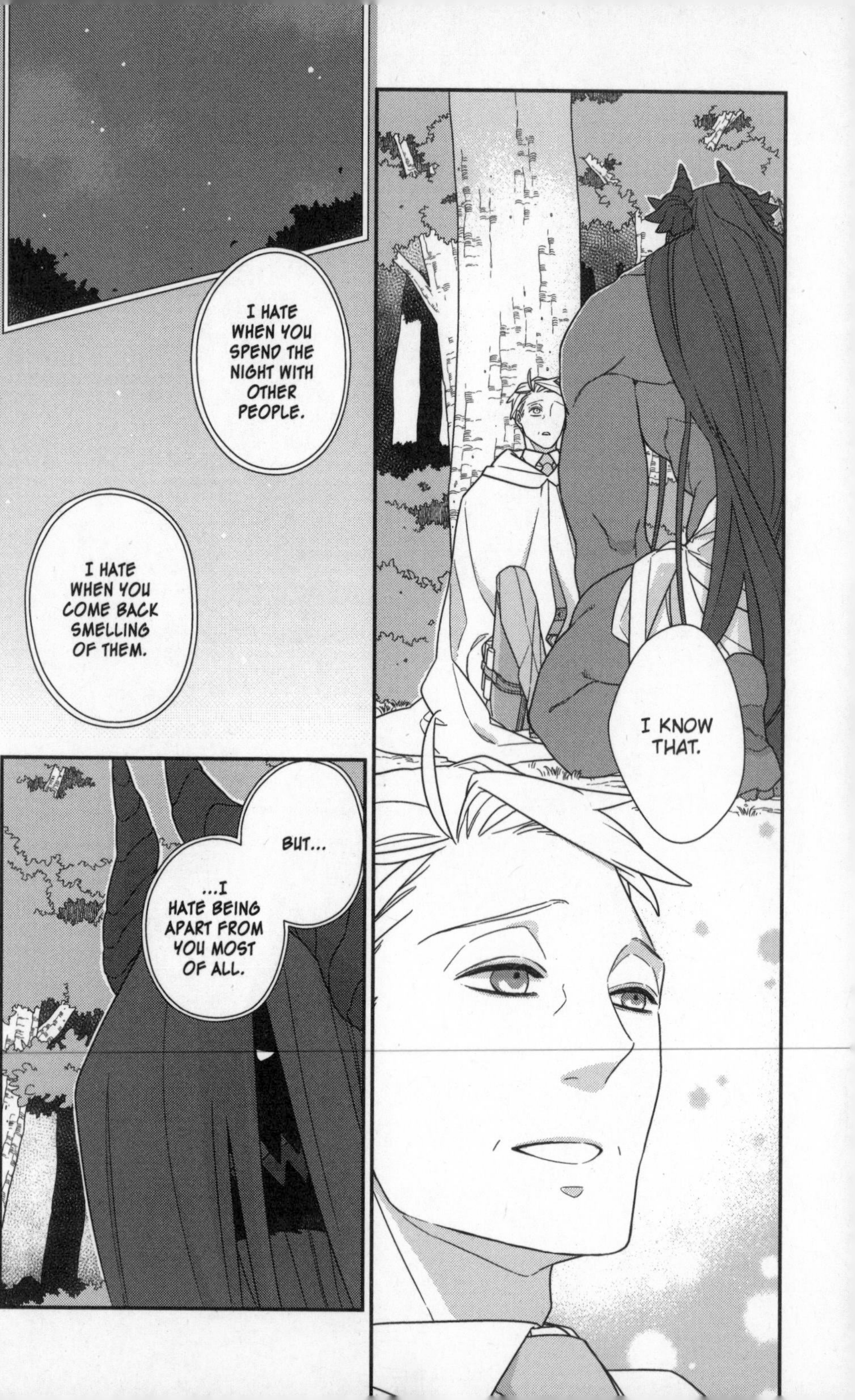

I HATE WHEN YOU SPEND THE NIGHT WITH OTHER PEOPLE.
I HATE WHEN YOU COME BACK SMELLING OF THEM.
I KNOW THAT.
BUT...
...I HATE BEING APART FROM YOU MOST OF ALL.

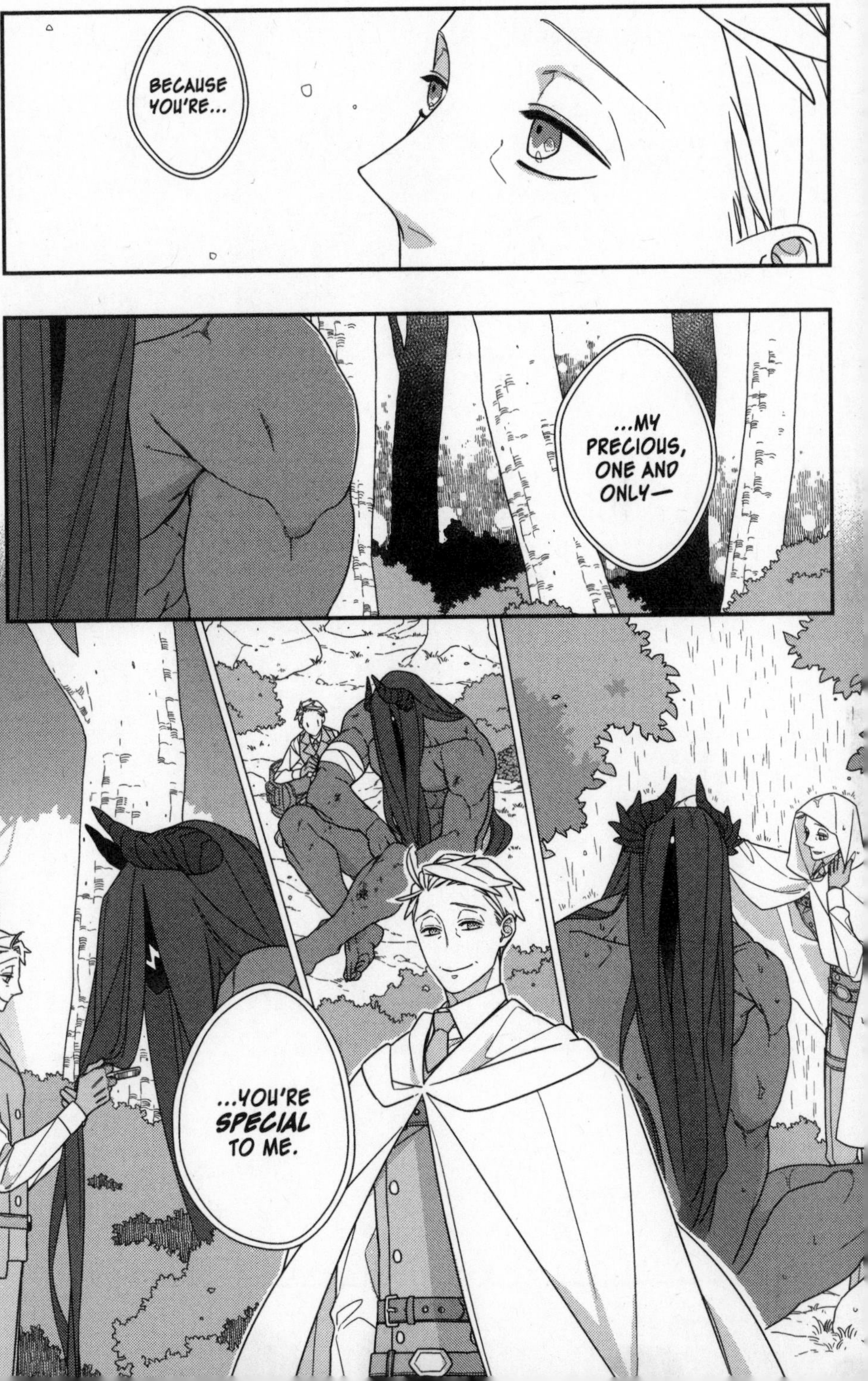
BECAUSE YOU'RE...
...MY PRECIOUS, ONE AND ONLY—
...YOU'RE SPECIAL TO ME.

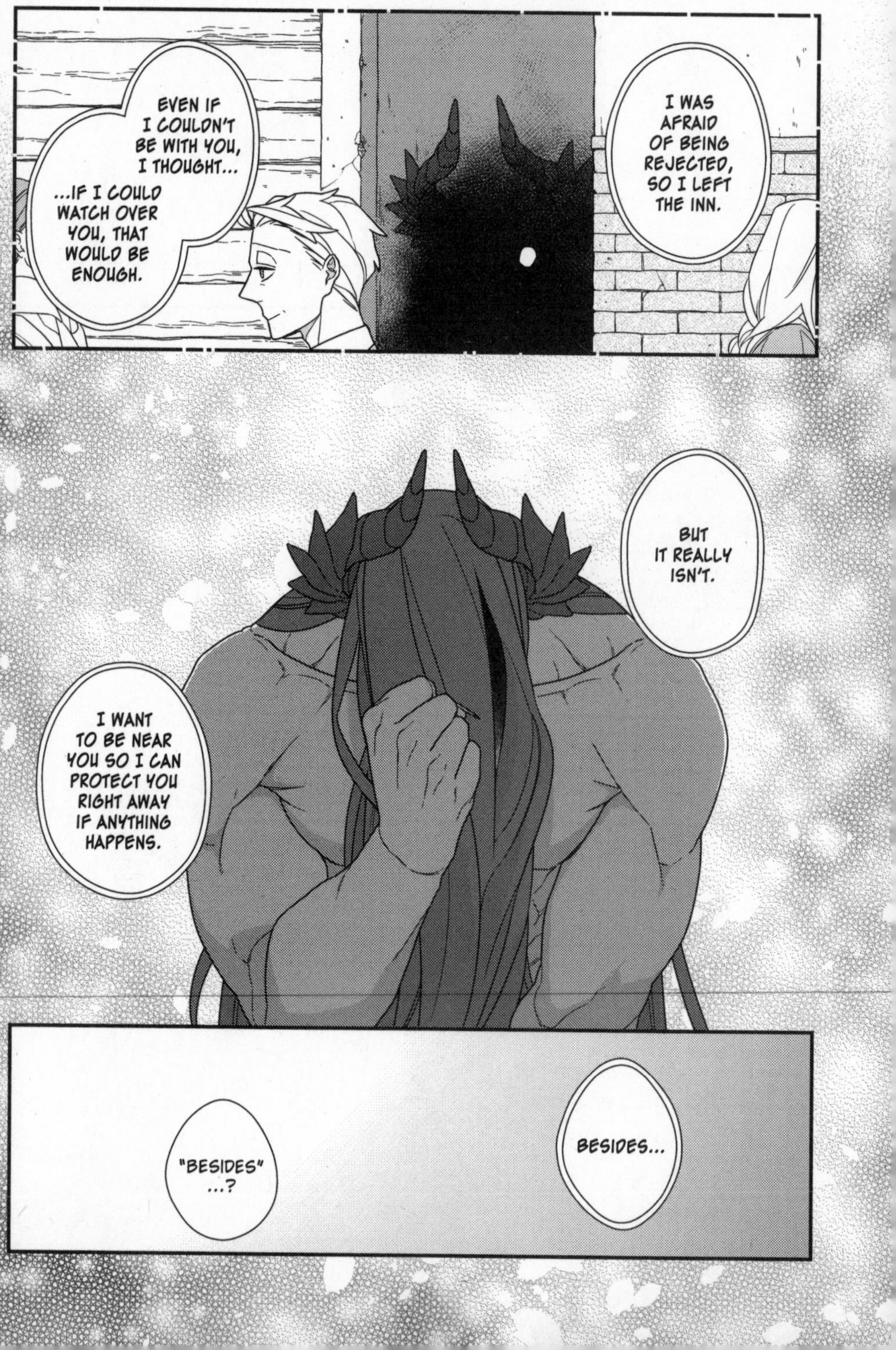
I WAS AFRAID OF BEING REJECTED, SO I LEFT THE INN.
EVEN IF I COULDN'T BE WITH YOU, I THOUGHT...
...IF I COULD WATCH OVER YOU, THAT WOULD BE ENOUGH.
BUT IT REALLY ISN'T.
I WANT TO BE NEAR YOU SO I CAN PROTECT YOU RIGHT AWAY IF ANYTHING HAPPENS.
BESIDES...
"BESIDES" ...?

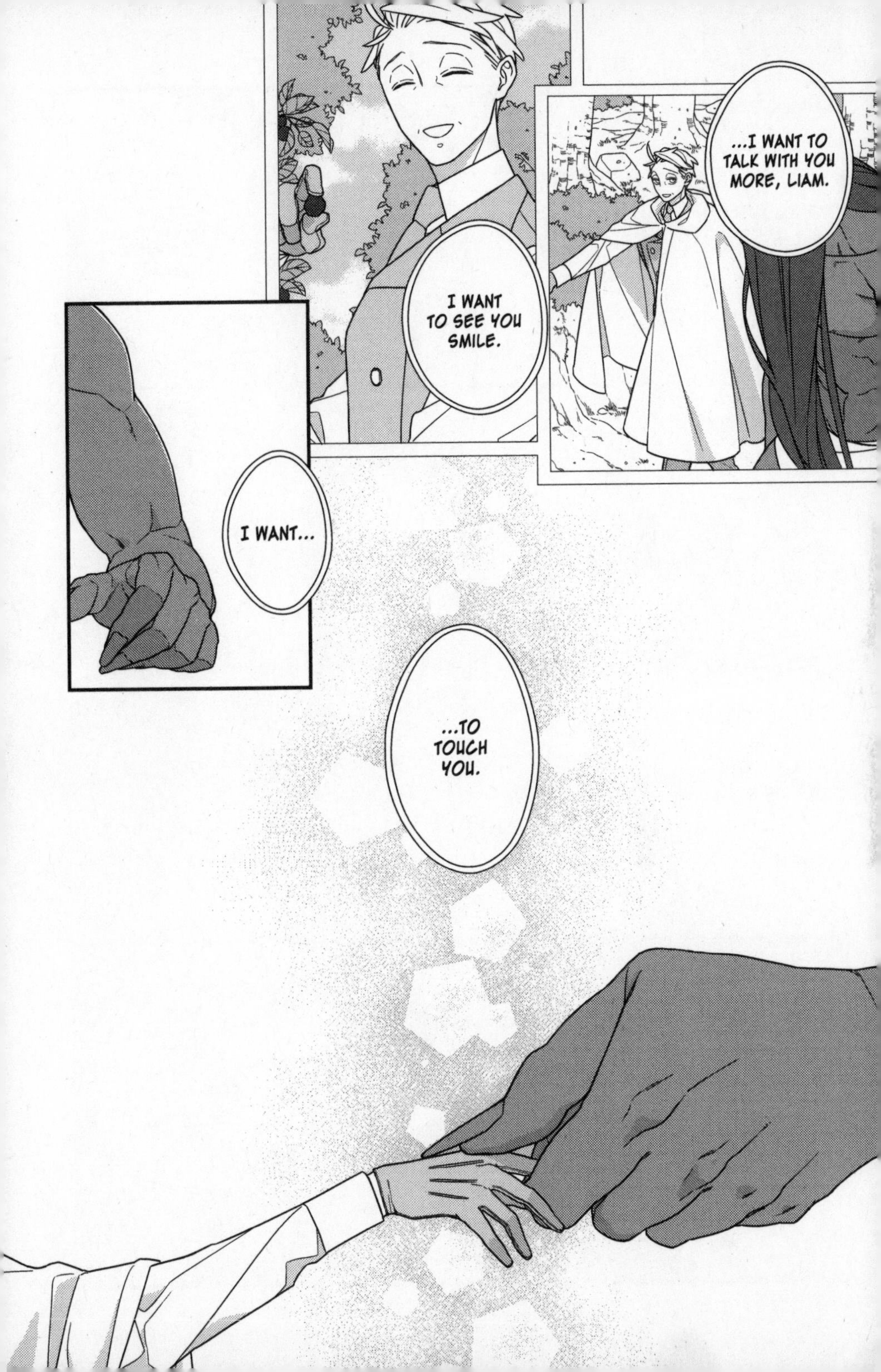
...I WANT TO TALK WITH YOU MORE, LIAM.
I WANT TO SEE YOU SMILE.
I WANT...
...TO TOUCH YOU.

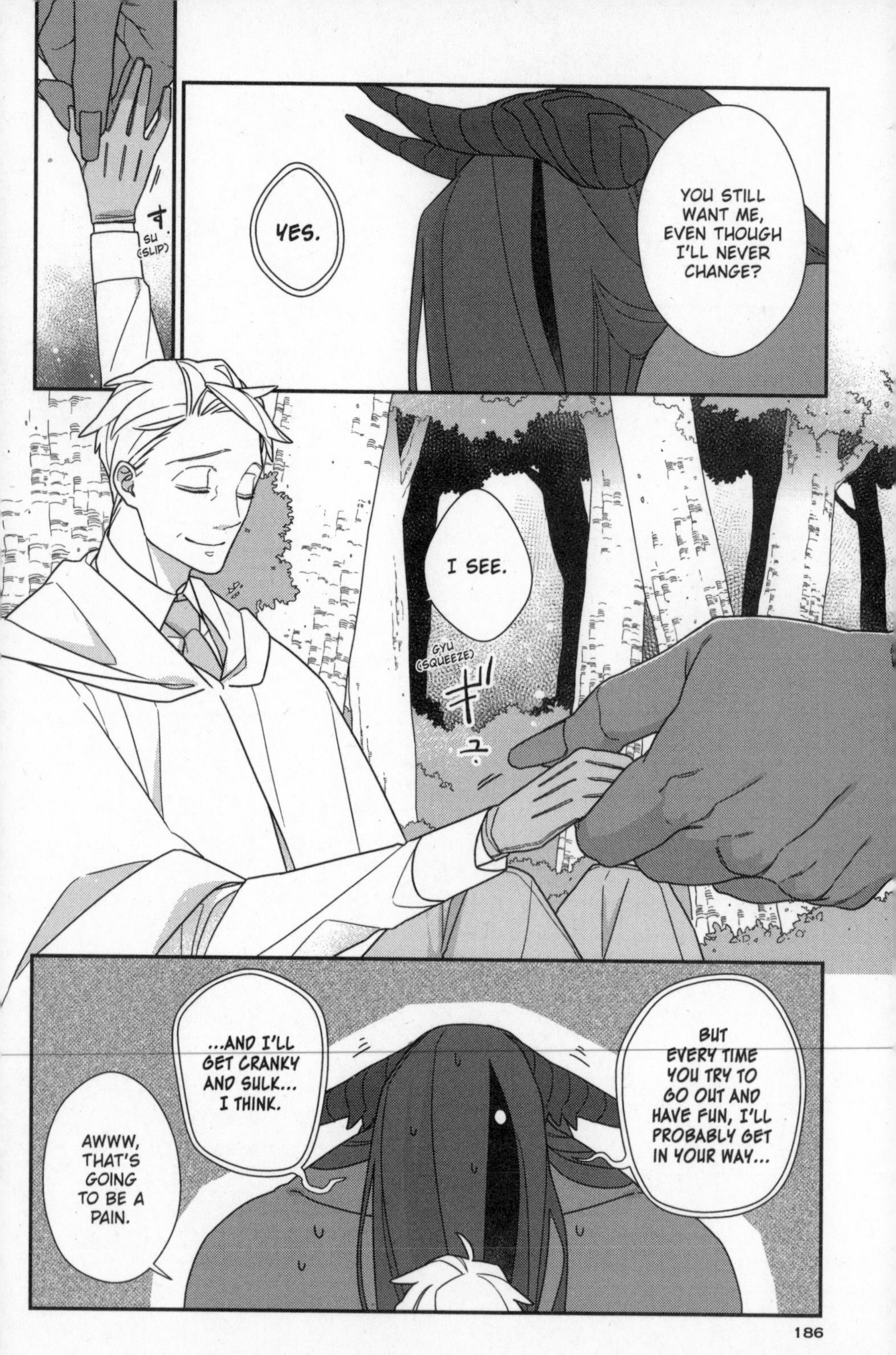
YOU STILL WANT ME, EVEN THOUGH I'LL NEVER CHANGE?
YES.
す
SU (SLIP)
I SEE.
ギュ
GYU (SQUEEZE)
BUT EVERY TIME YOU TRY TO GO OUT AND HAVE FUN, I'LL PROBABLY GET IN YOUR WAY...
...AND I'LL GET CRANKY AND SULK... I THINK.
AWWW, THAT'S GOING TO BE A PAIN.

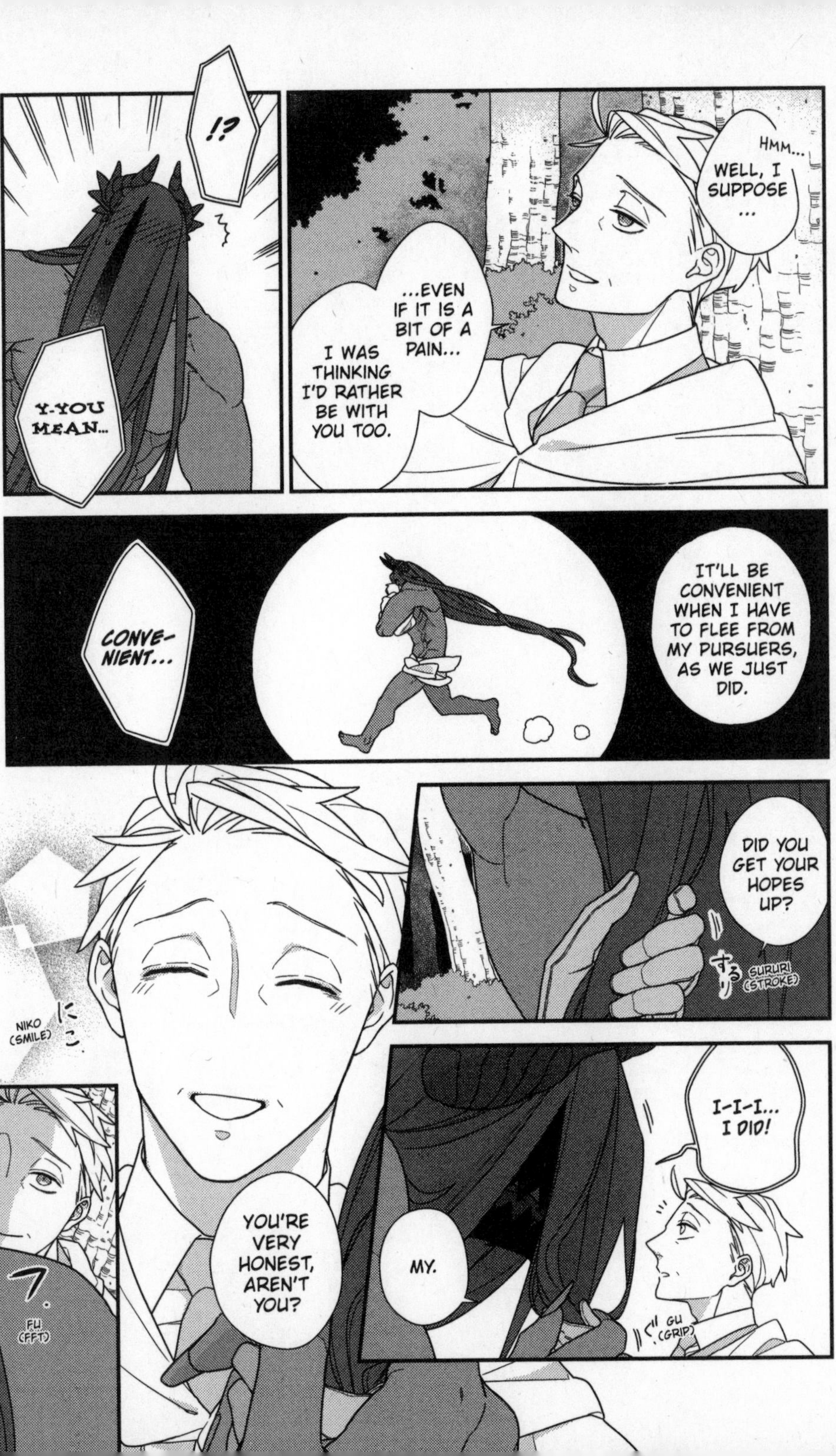
HMM... WELL, I SUPPOSE ...
...EVEN IF IT IS A BIT OF A PAIN...
I WAS THINKING I'D RATHER BE WITH YOU TOO.
!?
Y-YOU MEAN...
IT'LL BE CONVENIENT WHEN I HAVE TO FLEE FROM MY PURSUERS, AS WE JUST DID.
CONVE-NIENT...
DID YOU GET YOUR HOPES UP?
SURURI (STROKE)
NIKO (SMILE)
I-I-I... I DID!
GU (GRIP)
MY.
YOU'RE VERY HONEST, AREN'T YOU?
FU (FFT)

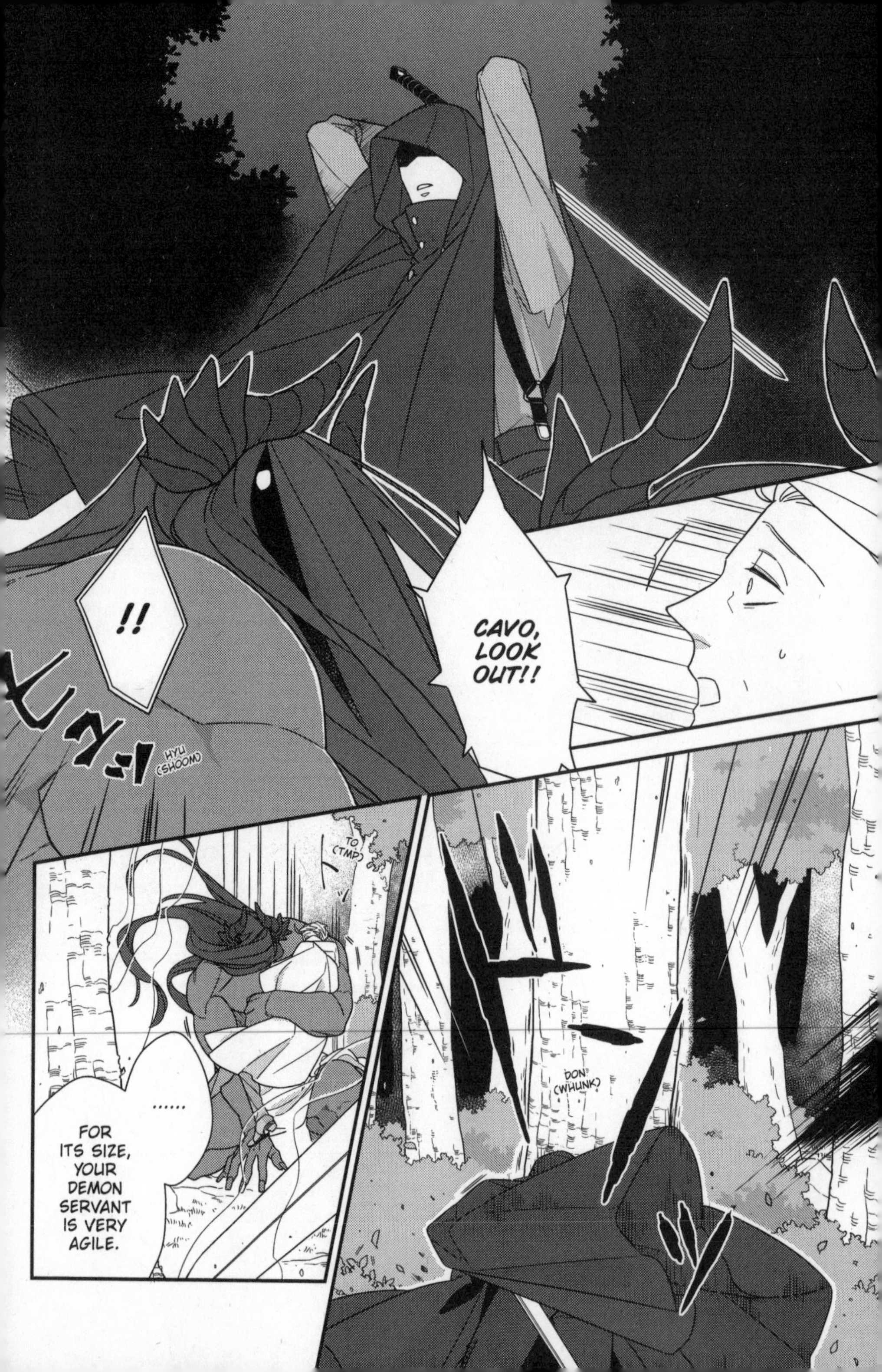
CAVO, LOOK OUT!!
!!
ヒュッ
HYU (SHOOM)
DON (WHUNK)
TO (TMP)
......
FOR ITS SIZE, YOUR DEMON SERVANT IS VERY AGILE.

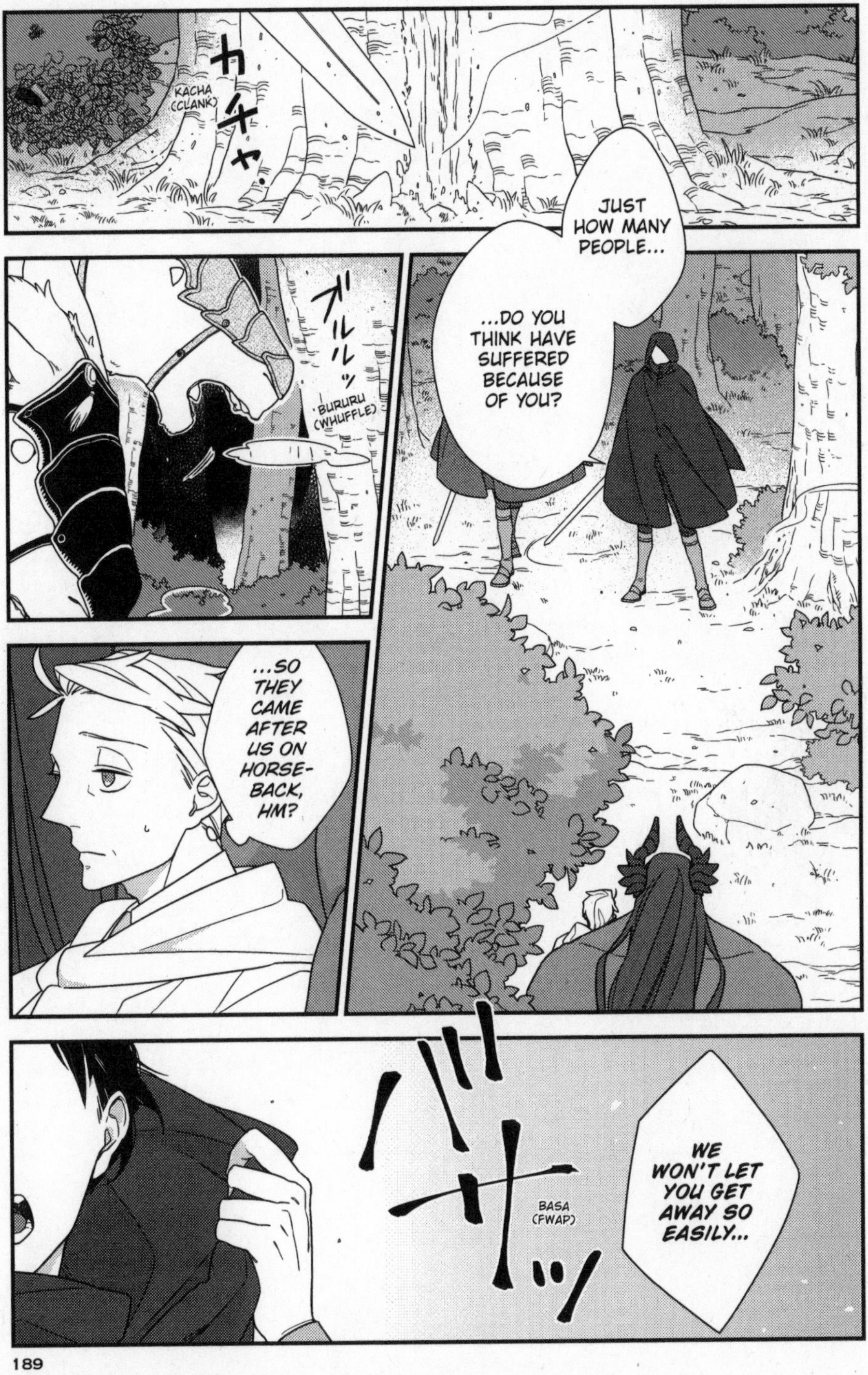
カチャ
KACHA (CLANK)
JUST HOW MANY PEOPLE...
...DO YOU THINK HAVE SUFFERED BECAUSE OF YOU?
ブルルッ
BURURU (WHUFFLE)
...SO THEY CAME AFTER US ON HORSE-BACK, HM?
WE WON'T LET YOU GET AWAY SO EASILY...
バサッ
BASA (FWAP)

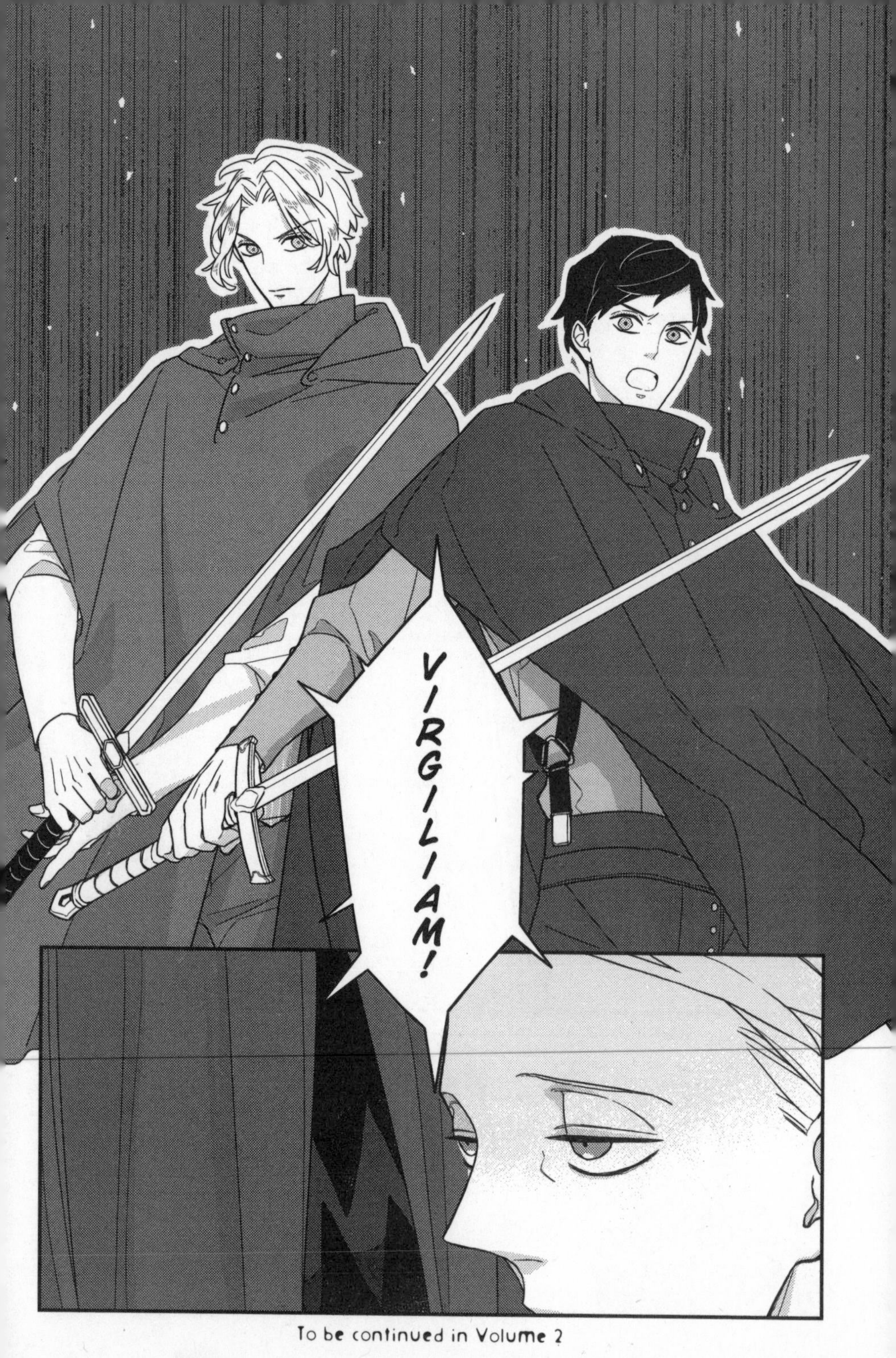
VIRGILIAM!

To be continued in Volume 2

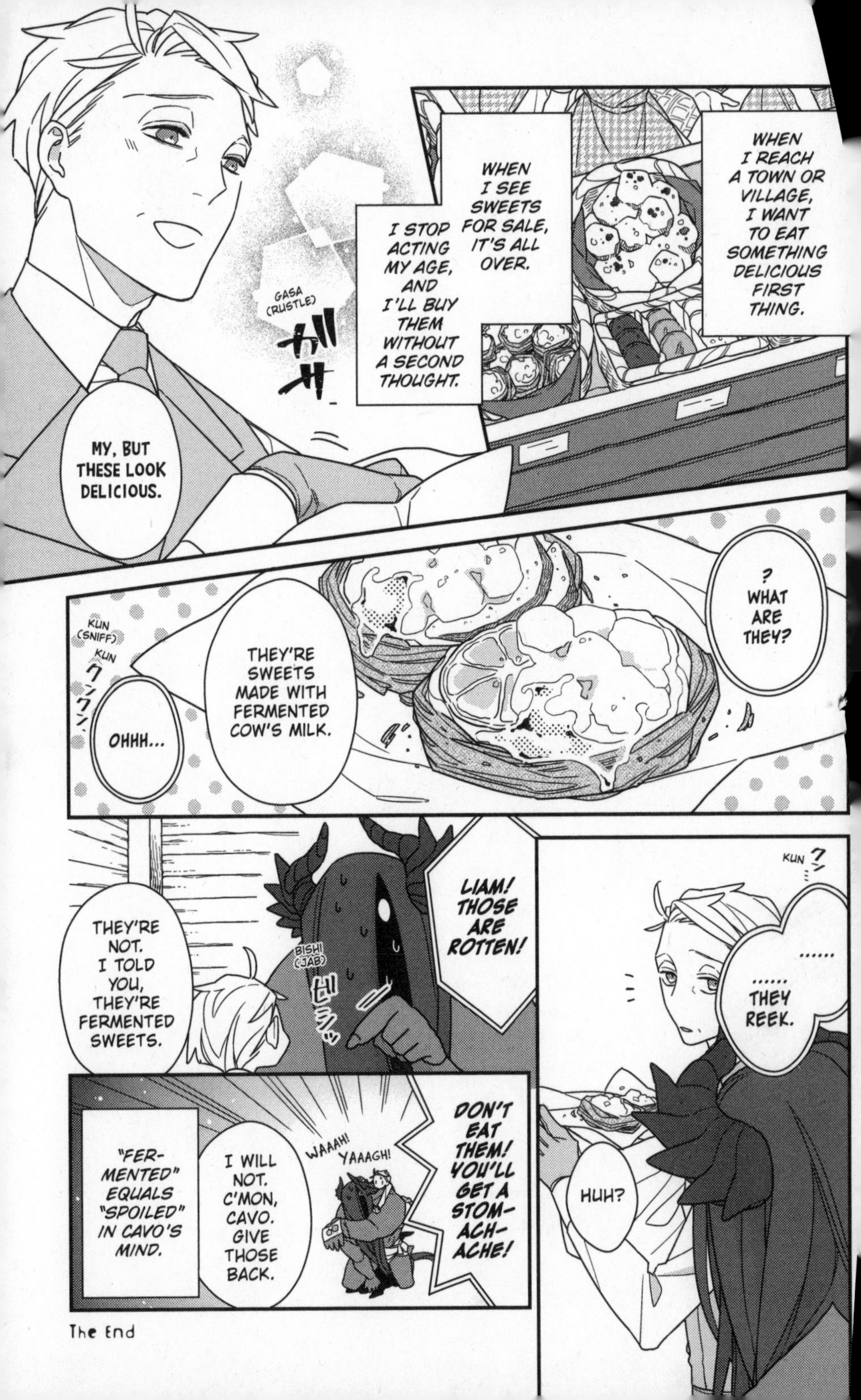

WHEN I REACH A TOWN OR VILLAGE, I WANT TO EAT SOMETHING DELICIOUS FIRST THING.
WHEN I SEE SWEETS FOR SALE, IT'S ALL OVER.
I STOP ACTING MY AGE, AND I'LL BUY THEM WITHOUT A SECOND THOUGHT.
GASA (RUSTLE)
MY, BUT THESE LOOK DELICIOUS.
? WHAT ARE THEY?
THEY'RE SWEETS MADE WITH FERMENTED COW'S MILK.
KUN (SNIFF) KUN
OHHH...
KUN
.... THEY REEK.
HUH?
LIAM! THOSE ARE ROTTEN!
BISHI (JAB)
THEY'RE NOT. I TOLD YOU, THEY'RE FERMENTED SWEETS.
DON'T EAT THEM! YOU'LL GET A STOM-ACH-ACHE!
WAAAH! YAAAGH!
I WILL NOT. C'MON, CAVO. GIVE THOSE BACK.
"FER-MENTED" EQUALS "SPOILED" IN CAVO'S MIND.

The End

Monster and the Beast

Renji

1

Translation: Taylor Engel ◆━━━━━◆━━━━━◆ Lettering: GOMAINU

BAKEMONO TO KEDAMONO Volume I
©Renji 2018
First published in Japan in 2018 by KADOKAWA CORPORATION, Tokyo. English translation rights arranged with KADOKAWA CORPORATION, Tokyo through TUTTLE-MORI AGENCY, INC., Tokyo.

English translation © 2019 by Yen Press, LLC

Yen Press
1290 Avenue of the Americas
New York, NY 10104

Visit us at yenpress.com * facebook.com/yenpress * twitter.com/yenpress * yenpress.tumblr.com * instagram.com/yenpress

First Yen Press Edition: June 2019

Yen Press is an imprint of Yen Press, LLC.
The Yen Press name and logo are trademarks of Yen Press, LLC.

Library of Congress Control Number: 2019935207

ISBNs: 978-1-9753-5721-4 (paperback)
978-1-9753-5722-1 (ebook)

10 9 8 7 6 5 4

WOR

Printed in the United States of America

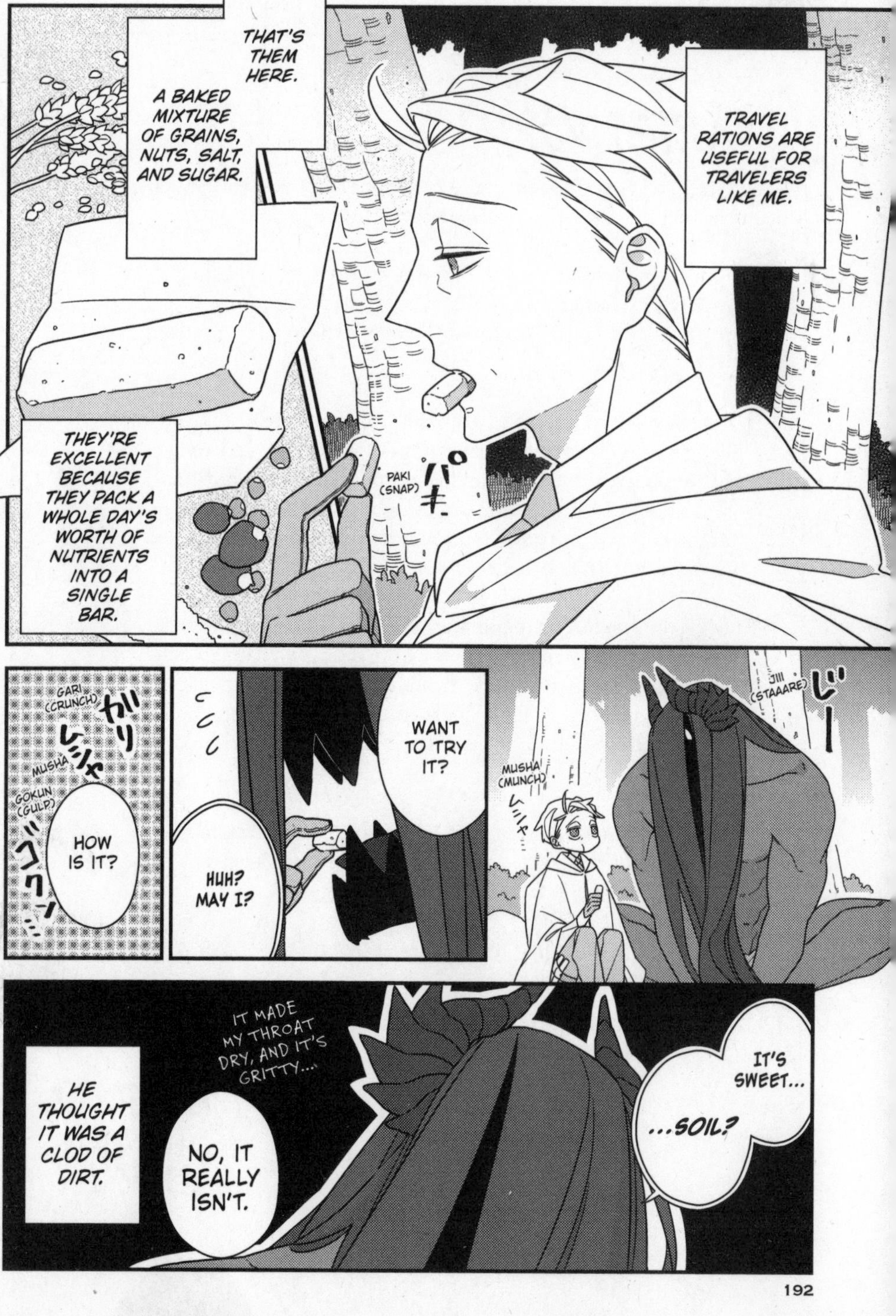
TRAVEL RATIONS ARE USEFUL FOR TRAVELERS LIKE ME.
THAT'S THEM HERE.
A BAKED MIXTURE OF GRAINS, NUTS, SALT, AND SUGAR.
THEY'RE EXCELLENT BECAUSE THEY PACK A WHOLE DAY'S WORTH OF NUTRIENTS INTO A SINGLE BAR.
PAKI (SNAP)
JIII (STAARE)
MUSHA (MUNCH)
WANT TO TRY IT?
HUH? MAY I?
GARI (CRUNCH)
MUSHA
GOKUN (GULP)
HOW IS IT?
IT'S SWEET...
...SOIL?
IT MADE MY THROAT DRY, AND IT'S GRITTY...
NO, IT REALLY ISN'T.
HE THOUGHT IT WAS A CLOD OF DIRT.

AFTERWORD

Hello, it's great to meet you. I'm Renji. Thank you very much for picking up *Monster and the Beast*, Volume 1.

This is the first manga I've ever drawn, my first series, and my first collected graphic novel...I've always liked drawing pictures, but I never dreamed I'd get to experience something like this.

One day, out of nowhere, I thought, "I want to read a Boys' Love fantasy manga featuring a middle-aged guy and an inhuman creature...!" I searched all over the place, online and off, but I couldn't find anything like it. I decided that if it didn't exist, I'd just have to make it myself, and what I started drawing was *Monster and the Beast*.

I'd never drawn a proper manga before, and I knew nothing about the dedicated software. I was practically an amateur who didn't even know right from left. However, thanks to my esteemed editor, my readers, and many other people, that manga has made it all the way to being collected in book form. Seriously, thank you all so much.

There's still a lot I'm not used to, and I'm continuing to learn as I work, but I'll keep drawing the story as best I can, so please continue to support it!

Volume 2 is scheduled to be released around the end of 2018 or early 2019 (in Japan)!

RENJI